THE ART AND SCIENCE OF
ENTREPRENEURSHIP

THE ART AND SCIENCE OF ENTREPRENEURSHIP

Inderjit Singh Dhaliwal

Serial Entrepreneur and Former Policymaker
Adjunct Professor, Nanyang Technological University, Singapore

World Scientific

NEW JERSEY · LONDON · SINGAPORE · BEIJING · SHANGHAI · HONG KONG · TAIPEI · CHENNAI · TOKYO

Published by

World Scientific Publishing Co. Pte. Ltd.

5 Toh Tuck Link, Singapore 596224

USA office: 27 Warren Street, Suite 401-402, Hackensack, NJ 07601

UK office: 57 Shelton Street, Covent Garden, London WC2H 9HE

National Library Board, Singapore Cataloguing in Publication Data
Name(s): Inderjit Singh, 1960–
Title: The art and science of entrepreneurship / Inderjit Singh Dhaliwal.
Description: Singapore : World Scientific Publishing Co. Pte. Ltd., [2022]
Identifier(s): ISBN 978-981-12-3842-0 (hardback) | 978-981-12-3932-8 (paperback) |
    978-981-12-3843-7 (ebook for institutions) | 978-981-12-3844-4 (ebook for individuals)
Subject(s): LCSH: Entrepreneurship. | New business entreprises.
Classification: DDC 658.421--dc23

British Library Cataloguing-in-Publication Data
A catalogue record for this book is available from the British Library.

For any available supplementary material, please visit
https://www.worldscientific.com/worldscibooks/10.1142/12319#t=suppl

Desk Editor: Jiang Yulin

Typeset by Diacritech Technologies Pvt. Ltd.
Chennai - 600106, India

Printed in Singapore

DEDICATION

In start-up investments entrepreneurs look for the three "Fs".
Life too is dictated by "Fs" – Family, Friends and Fortuity.

Friends and Family are critical in helping enrich our journey and give it meaning.

Without a doubt, I owe my success to my family and friends who believed in me
and supported me throughout my life journey. My family has been my bedrock
of support – my parents, my siblings, my wife Manjit and my three children.

When I started my entrepreneurship journey and politics at almost the same time,
I was away from my family and my extended family helped me tremendously to
take care of my three lovely children. I wish I had spent more time with them.

I thank my parents for giving us the foundations of great values and positive mindsets.
My siblings and I grew up close knit and we, including the younger generation,
continue to remain close. For all the risks I took, I knew my family would be my
support whenever I needed it. This gave me the confidence to move ahead each time.

My close friends remain close to me; some journeyed with me in my
entrepreneurship ventures. Having trustworthy friends is important and
I was fortunate to have many whom I continue to count on as my friends.

Fortuity led me to take the paths I took as an entrepreneur and as a politician. I had the
good fortune to do many things in life and I am grateful to God for the opportunities.

A message to my family and friends – while the road in life will be full of
potholes, remember that all obstacles can be overcome. Be driven by
your passion, engaged with your head and guided by your heart.
I hope my life journey will inspire all of you to reach for the Stars.

CONTENTS

INTRODUCTION

I began writing the first edition of this book in 2002. Back then, I did not have any plans to write a book. But by 2001, my success in starting a unicorn in United Test and Assembly Centre (UTAC) – a company my team and I created from scratch – had grown into one of the best companies in the world within a short span of three years. As I championed the cause for entrepreneurship in Parliament, many organisations in the private and public sectors started calling on me to give speeches on entrepreneurship. Initially I hesitated but subsequently I felt that it would be good to spread the message on entrepreneurship. I believed that Singapore needed to adopt the entrepreneurship path to create a successful economy for the future.

As I started giving talks, I realised that I needed to structure my thoughts. Hence, I started writing speeches. Different occasions required different angles and different takes on the topics, for example, it could be about the mindset, about fund raising, or about environmental factors. So, for each talk that I gave I wrote a different speech that captured my thoughts on entrepreneurship and my experiences as I went about my entrepreneurial journey. I had very little time to put my thoughts into writing but fortunately, since I had to travel regularly to the United States on business trips, the long flights presented the ideal time to write.

With little else to do onboard my thoughts flowed for hours on end, and these were captured in writing. After my first year of writing, I realised that each speech contained valuable lessons I had learnt including an account of my mindset as an entrepreneur. If I could capture all this in words, the resulting article could be something I could share with others, to help them understand what entrepreneurship is about. Furthermore, it could become a reference for those wishing to embark on an entrepreneurial journey. It was then that I decided to compile my thoughts into a book. So, from then on, I started structuring what I know to fit a book format. For the next two years, preparing the book became easier as the process became more structured.

By end 2004, I finished about 95 per cent of the book. However, I hesitated to publish it as I felt I needed to accomplish more. But I soon realised that an entrepreneur's journey never ends. What would possibly be the best time to publish the book? At the same time, I felt it would be a waste not to share my thoughts with anyone else, especially after having captured my life experiences in such a comprehensive manner. So, I decided the book needed to be published. But 2005 was a very tough year for me. My company was going through turbulent times, so I had little time to complete the book, and neither was I in the right frame of mind to do so. Fortunately, it was all well and good from 2005 till early 2006. I managed to add two more chapters on two important issues which were not captured earlier.

In this second edition of the book, I share many more experiences as I started more companies, experienced many more challenges as an entrepreneur, and invested in and mentored many more budding entrepreneurs. Also, after spending almost 20 years as a policymaker focusing on trying to create a more entrepreneurial economy for Singapore and being involved in entrepreneurship promotion at the global level, I have updated the content with many of my observations on entrepreneurship around the world. I have also added some theories on entrepreneurship that I now teach at the Nanyang Technological University, Singapore (NTU), and updated most of the information with my latest experiences including a chapter on "Surviving the Great Disruption (The Covid-19 Economic Impact)".

It is always good to learn from other people's mistakes and experiences and this book is to provide exactly that – the lessons I learnt and the experiences I have encountered throughout my life. As I started teaching entrepreneurship at NTU, Singapore as an adjunct professor, I researched more about theories of entrepreneurship and learned from the experiences of other successful entrepreneurs. These ideas and stories have been added to give the reader a wider appreciation of entrepreneurship.

There are many books on entrepreneurship and I have read many of them. I realised that most are academic in nature and thus fail to capture true reality. Books written by successful entrepreneurs usually capture their life story, so one has to distil the essence of entrepreneurship. I wanted to present my book differently. Instead of capturing my life journey I decided to distil key concepts and translate what goes on within an entrepreneur's mind into structured processes that I could easily impart to others.

Anyone who reads this book should be able to pick up the concepts, understand the thought processes, and relate easily on how one can go about becoming an entrepreneur or thinking like one. This book is an attempt to bridge theory with reality. I used many real-life examples throughout the book, enabling readers to have an easier time understanding what ordinarily looks abstract. I hope this book will become a useful reference guide for all who want to understand entrepreneurship, especially for would-be entrepreneurs who want to embark on a journey.

This book is structured into three sections.

Section A is basically the abstract part, one that deals with the mindset, concepts of entrepreneurship, and the thinking process of entrepreneurs. This is the most difficult part to capture in writing. I have attempted to capture my mindset and thinking, and also used examples to facilitate the reader's understanding.

Section B is the more technical part. This section captures the processes that have been widely written about how to go about starting a company. Here, I talk about the business plan, fund raising, and things to look out for when starting a new company.

In the final section, I capture the lessons learnt and things that are not so obvious. This section helps the reader understand the subtleties to look out for to better appreciate entrepreneurship. I have also described some environmental factors which help shape entrepreneurship.

The reader can read any chapter in any order. As I mentioned, I wrote the book first as a series of speeches before modifying them into a number of chapters. Hence, there is no definite link from one chapter to another.

As I intended to make this book a reference and a guide for anyone who wants to understand entrepreneurship, anyone can pick up this book and read any chapter to understand the entrepreneur's mindset. This book is a helpful step-by-step guide for those travelling along the journey of entrepreneurship.

You will probably notice a number of items being repeated in different chapters. This is intentional as the same issue can be seen in a different context and be looked at from a different angle depending on who is looking at it and the problem being addressed. Also, I expect you – the reader – to skip from chapter to chapter as you use this book as a reference so there is no need for you to read everything from front to back. In a book like mine, the repeats are intended to be helpful.

I also hope this book will become an inspiration for those who read it, especially aspiring entrepreneurs. As you read the book, I hope it gives you comfort that what you might be going through is something not everyone can manage, and despite the difficulties you face, you know that everyone who takes the same path goes through similar difficulties. I hope some of the thoughts and concepts this book provides will inspire you to overcome all your obstacles and reach greater heights. That is after all what entrepreneurs are good at. The book should give you a good feel of what it is like, and perhaps through arming yourself with the knowledge within, you are able to lessen the pain you encounter in your journey as an entrepreneur.

I have to thank many people for having supported me throughout my journey as an entrepreneur. First and foremost, my immediate family (my wife, Manjit and three children, Trishpal, Rashvin and Gurshant), my siblings and my parents. My parents have been an inspiration. They started with almost nothing in Singapore and worked hard to provide for the family, including educating all of us to our maximum potential. My mother was an entrepreneur and I must have picked up entrepreneurial skills from her. She supplemented my father's two sources of income and this gave us a more comfortable life as we progressed along. My siblings are close knit and we have supported each other throughout. Knowing you have support makes your life a little more comfortable. As I embarked on my entrepreneurship journey and life in politics, I had the support of my family, allowing me to focus on my career and political work. For this second edition of the book, I would like to thank Rosa Kang for spending considerable amount of time to help edit the book.

Throughout my career, I have worked with many excellent people, starting at Texas Instruments. In subsequent years, a big team of more than 20 people followed me to help me start UTAC and make it a tremendous success. When I had to leave UTAC, some of my colleagues from Texas Instruments and UTAC became my co-founders of Infiniti Solutions. Despite the odds and all sorts of criticism we believed in ourselves and took the chances that made Infiniti Solutions a reality. I would like to think that very few people could have survived what we went through at UTAC and Infiniti Solutions, but we not only survived but did well.

In politics, in helping improve the business environment in Singapore through the Action Community for Entrepreneurs, in teaching entrepreneurship and commercialisation of technology at NTU, Singapore, where I was a member of the Board of Trustees, I received help from several individuals which allowed me to achieve what I had set out to do. Unfortunately, naming everyone would make this message too lengthy.

I am blessed for being given many opportunities in life. I wanted to do well in the private sector, and Texas Instruments allowed me to rise to the highest level possible. I wanted to create my own multinational, world-class company, and I got the support to make UTAC possible. When I needed to create another company and turn it into a success, we created Infiniti Solutions and worked very hard to keep it going. When I needed a home base should things go terribly wrong, my brothers and my family created Tri Star Electronics, our family business, which has been a stable business for us. Finally, when I wanted to influence public policy, the People's Action Party gave me the opportunity to serve the country as a Member of Parliament. I have tried my best to create a better entrepreneurship landscape for Singapore and help shape policies with the support of the Singapore's national leaders. I have enjoyed the best of both worlds, of being from the private sector and of being a political leader. I would not have wanted it any other way. Above all, my spiritual beliefs have kept me strong despite the many failures I have faced throughout my journey. Sikhism has taught me the spirit of winning and my belief in God and the teachings of Guru Nanak have kept me strong and allowed me to survive and thrive.

Lastly, if there is one thing you should remember it is this – nothing is impossible and there is no problem that cannot be solved. If you can believe in this, you will be able to seize the opportunities and turn them into something valuable, whether in your business or in your life.

Thank you for journeying with me and enjoy the book!

INDERJIT SINGH DHALIWAL

Understanding the Entrepreneur's Mind – Converting Practice to Theory

What kind of mindset do entrepreneurs have? What governs their actions and what makes them tick? This has been discussed in many ways in academic publications or the life stories of entrepreneurs. Often, it all looks very abstract and difficult to understand.

In this section, which I call "The Art of Entrepreneurship", I will attempt to describe this concept of mindset to make sense of the abstractness of things. And better still, I will convert all the practice into theory that we can use to teach future entrepreneurs. (We are already familiar with converting theory to practice. I have attempted to do the reverse so that it becomes easier to teach entrepreneurship to others.) Basically, I have distilled the mindset of entrepreneurs into simple concepts that can be called as "Theory of an Entrepreneur's Mindset". This way we can learn the "Art" of entrepreneurship as a subject too.

This section starts with a very general discussion of entrepreneurship in Chapter 1. While I have brought in some academic content, the discussion in this chapter is mainly from a practitioner's point of view – my view of things based on experience and based on my observations of entrepreneurs. The discussion in Chapter 1 is all encompassing as I attempt to give an overall picture of what entrepreneurship is all about and share many traits of entrepreneurs. This chapter lays the foundation for the rest of Section A of my book where in other chapters I go into details to discuss the mindsets, philosophies, and practice of entrepreneurs.

In the next few chapters of this section, I have attempted to distil the complex mindset and thought processes of entrepreneurs, to create some structure out of the unstructured nature of entrepreneurship. By understanding how the mind of an entrepreneur works and why entrepreneurs behave the way they do, while knowing their beliefs and how they make decisions, we will gain a better insight of how they became successful.

This will give the reader a very good feel of what it takes to become an entrepreneur, and to think like one. This hopefully will give aspiring entrepreneurs a sense of how they should be behaving and doing things to increase their chances of success. The concepts I have shared are based on many years of understanding the mind of an entrepreneur and if the reader can imbibe some of these, they too can start doing things differently to live an inspiring entrepreneurial life.

THE ART OF ENTREPRENEURSHIP

CHAPTER 1

THE ENTREPRENEURIAL JOURNEY

What is Entrepreneurship?

There are many definitions and explanations of entrepreneurship. Here is the Oxford Dictionary definition:

Oxford Advanced Learner's Dictionary

entrepreneurship noun
the activity of making money by starting or running businesses, especially when this involves taking financial risks;

Many books and articles have been written about entrepreneurship, some academic in nature, others experiential, some about business, others about how to change the world. Here are a few ways to look at what entrepreneurship entails:

- important economic activity
- value creation
- a subject taught in business school
- creativity
- innovation
- mindset or a way of thinking

One of the most important messages I want to leave with readers is that entrepreneurship is more than creating companies. It is a mindset, a different way of thinking that solves problems – whether business problems, societal problems, national problems, or personal problems – any problem! An entrepreneurial mindset can help us solve any problem we face in our life, and I mean any!

While most books on entrepreneurship discuss business entrepreneurship, I have structured this book to theorise the mindset definition of entrepreneurship. And once we can understand the Theory of Mindset and the Way of Thinking like an entrepreneur, we will realise that any one of us can become one. It is my firm belief that anyone can think, behave and work like an entrepreneur. If we feel we are not ready, then I believe, by sharpening our skills, broadening our knowledge, changing our behaviour, and by understanding the "Entrepreneurial Way", we can all become entrepreneurs no matter what we do in life.

As you progress through this book, the question of whether it is Nature or Nurture that determines if you are an entrepreneur will become clearer. The answer is that entrepreneurs can be made and are not necessarily born to become entrepreneurs! And to understand this better we need to know what an entrepreneurial mindset is.

The Entrepreneurial Mindset

To understand an entrepreneur, and how entrepreneurs think, we must ask the following questions:

- What traits do entrepreneurs have?
- How do entrepreneurs behave?
- What comprises their mindsets?
- Why do they do what they do?

You will hear me repeating this many times in this book – that you can be an entrepreneur no matter where you are and what you do. It is all a matter of mindset. The key trait of entrepreneurs involves challenging the conventional, thinking of new ways of doing things, and being daring enough to either make the changes, or if one is an employee, to propose the changes to the decision-makers. It is therefore possible for anyone to be an entrepreneur or to behave and think as an entrepreneur, no matter what you do or where you work. This same principle applies to any cause or initiative that we believe in, be it economically, socially or personally driven.

Entrepreneurship does not simply mean you have to go out and start a company. The formation of a company is therefore not a necessary measure of whether or not a person has an entrepreneurial mindset. Entrepreneurship activity can occur anywhere as long as the environment and the circumstances are conducive enough to encourage people to be innovative.

When I was in Texas Instruments working as an engineering manager, the company was suffering losses over a period of time. While most managers were focused on better yields, greater efficiencies and better quality, I thought of how I could help the company generate additional revenues. Thinking "out of the box", differently from most of my colleagues, I came up with an idea on how we can add to the topline (increase revenues) and not just reduce the bottom-line (reduce cost). With this mindset, I then decided to see if we could make money out of the many Dynamic Random Access Memory (DRAM) chips that we were scrapping each day.

The Silicon Salvage Story (Intrapreneurship)

I have always worked with an entrepreneurial mindset since the day I started working at Texas Instruments (TI), solving several problems that many could not solve. The clearest example of my entrepreneurial experience was when I helped TI create a new business out of scrap or rejects.

As an engineer and later as a Product Engineering Manager, I noticed a lot of precious silicon went to waste for failing TI's stringent testing and quality requirements (I wrote many of these test programs in my days as an engineer). I had in-depth knowledge about what passed and what failed and about the quality and reliability of the DRAMs we were passing and failing. In TI, we had standardised test programs that tested to very stringent requirements where every DRAM we produced must meet military, automotive and in some cases, space applications. And the ones that passed were used in all applications, including in personal computers.

I drew inspiration from the *karang guni* (rag and bone) man (these people used to drive big cars and wear Rolex watches) who could create wealth out of old or discarded items. I wanted to see how I could create value from the DRAMs we were throwing away. A few ideas came to my mind. First, we know we don't use the same PC for 20 years and change our PCs every three to five years. So at TI, the DRAMs going into PCs didn't really have to last the 15 to 20 years that we were testing for. So, if we could loosen the testing parameters and retest the rejects, we could create a new range of DRAMs (and label them differently as a different product range), for the PC and less critical applications.

Second, even if one bit (bits are memory storage space within an IC) in a 64 Meg DRAM failed, we used to throw the DRAM away. If one DRAM failed on the first 32 Meg part and another DRAM failed at the second part, I could take the two halves (32 Megs each) and combine both by putting them onto a PCB and create a 64 Meg DRAM again! A third example, if even a few thousand of the bits failed, we could use that DRAM as a recording device (instead of the recording tapes being used in answering machines in the past). Even with a few thousand bits failing, the ear will hear just a little noise without losing the full message recorded. I wanted to salvage as much silicon as possible to not just save cost for the company, but also to turn that into cash for the company as TI was at that time struggling with losses and needed new revenue streams.

I took the initiative to compile my ideas on "silicon salvage" in a report and presented them to TI's global management team. The report showed that the company could generate US$100m of revenues at an 80 per cent profit margin (the margins could be high because the cost of the scrap was zero, and the cost of reprocessing the scrap was negligible compared to the value of the product created). When I made that presentation, three-quarters of the room laughed at me! Luckily, a Japanese who was a very senior executive in TI supported me.

Given the green light, to try and justify my position, I spent three weeks visiting all of TI's sites around the world to see how much scrap was being discarded. With that information, I was more convinced I had a great new idea that will help TI tremendously. In the first year, TI made US$69m of revenue from scrap. By the third year, that number increased to US$230m in revenue with a 90 per cent profit margin!

I had created a business out of nothing by thinking like an entrepreneur. I called this project, SS – Silicon Salvage – and nicknamed it "Secondary Silicon" to sound better. Till today, I proudly display the plaque I got from TI for this effort.

I was fortunate that I had someone in the company who was willing to listen to a crazy idea from a "maverick" and gave me an opportunity to do something different. I had the last laugh, received a good bonus and a plaque from a senior executive of my division to mark my achievement. My advice to everyone is this – never fear even if people think your idea is crazy. The mavericks are the ones who end up winners. Look out for the supporters in your company and don't be deterred by the detractors.

I am convinced you can become an entrepreneur anywhere, and it is not just about starting brand new companies. Even in large companies, as long as the environment is conducive for experimentation and innovation, any employee can operate as if he is an entrepreneur. In such a scenario, the person is considered an intrapreneur.

Although, it is quite difficult to do things differently in big and established companies, because of set procedures and set structures, I believe there will always be a way to make changes, and perhaps even significant changes, as a result of having an entrepreneurial mindset. I have always believed in the saying, "Where there is a will, there is a way". Hence, one should not feel that innovation and practising entrepreneurship are not possible in big corporations and organisations. Of course, in such cases, the person with entrepreneurial thinking may be taking risks in trying to change the way things are done because his bosses might not want to rock the boat and might not like it. But taking risks is what entrepreneurship entails.

Entrepreneurship is about more than just creating new companies. It is in fact about the mindset one has, about doing new things and creating something from nothing. You can have an entrepreneurial mindset as an employee, as a parent, as a teacher, as a politician, or in anything you want to do. When something is done in a manner that is innovative, pioneering, or out of the norm, whether in business or other aspects of life – that is what really constitutes entrepreneurship and having an entrepreneurial mindset.

I will go further to say that entrepreneurship does not necessarily have to occur in a profit-making or commercial organisation. It can in fact happen anywhere, including in government, welfare and social organisations, and in the civil service. If we look at the broader meaning of entrepreneurship, this is not surprising.

The best example of entrepreneurship in the most unlikely place like government can be found in Singapore. If you look at the Singapore nation-building example, there were so many politicians and bureaucrats who were entrepreneurs in their own right. The simplest examples are the likes of Mr. J. Y. Pillay, who was a career civil servant, but was instrumental in setting up and growing a world-class airline, Singapore Airlines. Of course, the economic development of Singapore was itself an entrepreneurial example, where leaders like Mr. Lee Kuan Yew and Mr. Goh Keng Swee helped create the economic miracle of Singapore. The work of the Economic Development Board (EDB) was also done by civil servants who behaved like entrepreneurs.

What was it that caused the political leaders and civil servants in Singapore to behave as entrepreneurs? It is clear their entrepreneurial behaviour allowed them to achieve an economic miracle for Singapore. In fact, it was the entrepreneurial spirit and behaviour of many political leaders around the world that resulted in the creation of nations. What was it that drove this entrepreneurial spirit? In the case of Singapore, it was the survival mentality.

Faced with great uncertainty and the possibility of failure, which could wreck the lives of so many citizens, this possibility or risk of failure brought out the best of the entrepreneurial spirit in the political leaders and those in government. Mr. Lee Kuan Yew, the founding prime minister of Singapore is the best example I can think of, for he acted as a master entrepreneur in the development of Singapore.

So how do entrepreneurs think? In an interesting article "Causation and Effectuation" (*The Academy of Management Review* 26, no. 2 [April 2001]) by Professor Saras D. Sarasvathy, she compared managerial (Causal) thinking with entrepreneurial (Effectual) thinking.[1]

Basically, the way a manager thinks, the **Causal Thinking**, is that if the future can be accurately predicted or forecasted, then you can control it. So, managers will start with a goal, analyse things before taking action – where goals will determine resource allocation – and always try to be ahead of the competition, avoiding failure at all costs (the Strategic Management process

---

[1] "Causation and Effectuation: Toward a Theoretical Shift from Economic Inevitability to Entrepreneurial Contingency", Saras D. Sarasvathy, *The Academy of Management Review*, Vol. 26, No. 2 (Apr., 2001), pp. 243–263.

that we learn in an MBA class). Causal Thinking is like a jigsaw puzzle – the goal has been defined and you have the pieces to put together.

The entrepreneur's thinking, the **Effectual Thinking**, is like this – if you can control the future, then you don't need to predict it. This thinking process starts with the means (not the end goal), processes are developed based on actions and interactions of all stakeholders (i.e. developed along the way), goals are set based on what everyone is willing to invest, control is achieved by converting current realities into new unpredicted possibilities. Failing early and failing small become a learning journey contributing to future success. Effectual Thinking is like a Lego set – you have all the pieces, no specific goal and you can end up with many possible solutions.

> **Causal:** Like Jigsaw Puzzle – the Goal Has Been Defined and You Have the Pieces to Put It Together
>
> **Effectual:** Like a Lego Set – You Have All the Pieces, No Specific Goal and Can End Up with Many Possible Solutions

We can differentiate the two types of thinking in Divergent (Effectual, Entrepreneurial) versus Convergent (Causal, Managerial) as shown in Figure 1.1.

Entrepreneurial (Effectual) thinking has the following characteristics:
1. Flexibility – observe and look out for needs you can exploit to create something new.
2. Generate options through experimentation – some may be useful now, some may be useful in future.
3. Effective use of resources – yours and those of your partners.

Managerial (Causal) thinking has the following characteristics:
1. Goal is set and not flexible.
2. You develop plans to reach the goal that has been set for you.

3. Use the resources that the organization provides to achieve the set goal.

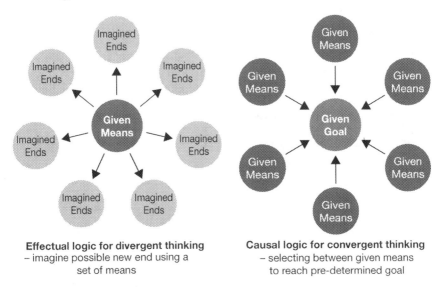

Effectual logic for divergent thinking
– imagine possible new end using a
set of means

Causal logic for convergent thinking
– selecting between given means
to reach pre-determined goal

Fig. 1.1: Effectual Logic and Causal Logic

Table 1.1: Causal versus Effectual Planning Differences

Causal Planning	Effectual Planning
Rational/Stable environment	Unpredictable outcome
Pre-existent goals set	Goals are not clear
Selection of certain ingredients and direction to meet goals	Decisions made create new possible directions to take
Someone with more resources can predict better and execute better than you	You have an equal chance to win if you are more innovative and creative and spot opportunities faster/better than others

We can summarise the characteristics of the two ways of thinking as follows:

*   **Managerial (Causal) Thinker:** Like generals out to conquer a known fertile land with a predetermined war strategy (follow SOPs).

- **Entrepreneurial (Effectual) Thinker:** Like voyagers looking for new land in unchartered territories may start with Plan A and end up with a completely different Plan X.

The Oxford Dictionary definition of an entrepreneur is:

a person who makes money by starting or running businesses, especially when this involves taking financial risks.

Based on what I have discussed above, let me suggest another definition of an entrepreneur:

An entrepreneur identifies a problem, uses innovative ways to solve the problem and creates a new opportunity using limited resources to build something valuable and meaningful to society.

Taking Risks and Beating the Odds

Entrepreneurs never fear failures, nor allow obstacles to stop them from doing what they believe in. They enjoy beating the odds and they constantly challenge everyone, including themselves. The hunger factor and the survival mentality are also very important factors that drive entrepreneurs towards success. When I left my successful career at Texas Instruments, where I was the director of operations responsible for the worldwide assembly and testing of all memory products in the company, I knew I was giving up a comfortable and very financially rewarding job to take on tremendous risks by starting a semiconductor packaging and testing company, United Test and Assembly Centre (UTAC).

The industry was already very competitive. Many similar companies existed at that time, and many were much bigger and much older with long track records and loyal customers. Nevertheless, I decided to start my company during a time when the semiconductor industry was at the bottom of a downturn. The potential competitors for my new company, many of whom had been in business for a long time, were already bleeding from excess capacity. They were trying to survive by gaining market share, which they attempted by dropping their sales prices to win business away from their competitors under the situation of a flat market. To most people, starting a company in such an environment is a very scary proposition and too risky. The odds were all stacked against me and my plan for a new start-up.

At the personal level, too, the odds were stacked against me, with many obligations and responsibilities. Mind you, my wife, who was not working, was expecting our third child, and I already had heavy financial obligations, including having put my whole house as security for another business, Tri Star Electronics, that I had started with my brothers in July 1997. Despite the severe consequences failing would entail, I was undeterred and wanted to give up all my comforts to do what I believed in. This belief was to create one of the best semiconductor packaging and testing subcontract companies in the world. This did seem like a tall order, but I believed it could be done. Everyone saw the odds against success to be very high and the risk not worth taking.

Well I beat those odds by a huge mile! Just two and a half years after I started UTAC in February 1998, the company became one of the best performing in the industry. In fact, it was on par with the best companies, and in terms of size, we became the ninth largest in the world, beating so many more that had been in business much longer than us. UTAC became a Unicorn (before the term Unicorn was first invented for successful start-ups crossing $1b valuation), valued at more than US$2b at that time. We also succeeded in obtaining approval for listing on both the NASDAQ and the Singapore Stock Exchange concurrently, within this span of two and a half years (in February 2001). The odds had been stacked against us at UTAC, and the cost of failure would have been very high for me personally, where I might even have lost my house had things gone terribly wrong.

But such thoughts of risk and failure were never foremost in my mind. The thought of creating something significant, solving the industry's problems starting from nothing was what pre-occupied my mind as I embarked on my entrepreneurial journey.

UTAC became one of the best in the industry for a long time and today, in 2020, remains a significant player in the industry because of the strong foundations my team and I laid 21 years earlier. Another record that I had set for UTAC was that I had managed to raise US$138m at just the seed stage. No other company up to 1998 and later years ever raised so much money at the first round of fund raising!

Nature versus Nurture

Many people ask: when did you discover your entrepreneurial spirit? Did you do things differently as a child? Did you know you were going to become an entrepreneur, or did someone influence you to become one? What drove you to start a company? These are all questions easily answered on hindsight. We will always try to think back and correlate what we did at different times of our lives. Typically, we can trace back to the times when we thought about things differently, the times we innovated and challenged the conventional, and the times we tried to do many different things and experiment. These are all useful guides, which if studied well can help us identify people who may become would-be entrepreneurs.

At the same time, I have come across many people who demonstrated the traits of challenging the conventional, doing things differently as a child or in a workplace – they showed the traits of entrepreneurs, but they never surfaced as successful entrepreneurs – those who never started companies. The examples of entrepreneurship in a multinational company and in government also indicate that entrepreneurs and the entrepreneurship spirit may not necessarily appear in obvious places.

Does the behaviour of "dare-to-do" necessarily define an entrepreneur? In other words, does someone who simply starts a company – even if it is a reckless move or because others have done it – qualify to be called an entrepreneur? I think not, and while on the surface we can call them entrepreneurs who mostly failed, the fact is that there are many more traits, more than the "dare-to-do" attitude that exist in people who really deserve to be called true entrepreneurs.

I call these people "copycat" entrepreneurs. Who are they? Should such people be called entrepreneurs? This issue will cloud any study about entrepreneurship. The crux of the issue is, what motivates such people may be completely different from what motivates the real entrepreneurs. It is worth studying and understanding this issue so that we can better identify the spirit of entrepreneurship, and therefore, find ways to further encourage the development of an environment conducive to breeding more of such people – the real entrepreneurs. The real question then is, what are the traits that determine the spirit of entrepreneurship? I will discuss the ten traits of successful entrepreneurs in the next section of this chapter.

To study this issue of when and where one started as an entrepreneur, it is important to look beyond the group of obvious entrepreneurs (i.e. those who ran start-ups). We can gain a much deeper insight into how entrepreneurship develops if the target study group includes more than the obvious entrepreneurs. In other words, let's also study the people in government, in companies or in any place, who demonstrated an entrepreneurial mindset, not necessarily those who started companies.

Here are some facts that I picked out from a survey done by an organisation called Inc. 500 Founders. Among successful entrepreneurs:

- 65 per cent did not start any business in their youth and did not have parents who were entrepreneurs.
- 75 per cent learned the skills that made them successful after the age of 21.
- 65 per cent developed their ideas through conversations with either potential customers or business partners.
- 70 per cent of entrepreneurs did not have a grand vision of creating a huge business. They just wanted to start something.

Case Studies

It is useful to look at a couple of case studies to reinforce these points. Two of the most famous entrepreneurs in the world are Bill Gates and Mark Zuckerberg.

Bill Gates – the conventional view is that Bill Gates had a vision that all PCs in the world will one day run on Windows and this led him to build Microsoft into one of the biggest software companies in the world.

The facts about Bill Gates and Microsoft, which are searchable online, show that this was not the case. Bill's family was wealthy and in his early years he had the privilege of attending a gifted elite school. He learned to program in high school in the 1960s, when computers were very rare, so only the privileged had such access. It seems Bill did not really drop out of Harvard but took leave of absence and could go back to school any time he wanted. Bill's mother Mary Gates was on the board of United Way of America together with IBM's CEO John Opel. Mary Gates introduced Bill's new company, Microsoft, to the IBM's CEO. As it happens, IBM was looking to develop an operating system for its first PCs. Given the connection and the introduction, the IBM CEO decided to give Microsoft a chance by adopting the MS-DOS while still allowing Microsoft to retain their IP. What a great deal it was for Bill Gates. The rest is history.

Mark Zuckerberg – the conventional view is that Mark was a visionary who saw the future of the social media network. He therefore built Facebook because of his vision and talent. He had great skills and charisma to raise huge sums of money for his company to allow Facebook to scale up rapidly.

The facts are a little different. Mark learned to write computer programs at the young age of ten and worked on many projects including one called Facemesh. Many of his early projects failed but he learned from these failures. He started Facebook with US$2,000 and built a strong core team to help him grow Facebook before securing external funding. The person who made the biggest difference in positioning the company and raising huge sums of money to grow the business was Sean Parker (known for starting Napster, a file sharing company which was highly successful but had to shut down because the concept of file sharing at that time violated many legal rights).

I hope these examples will give a sense of the reality of how successful entrepreneurs became so successful. Seldom is it a fairy tale of a visionary person of great talent and who had the greatest idea in the world. Networks, family connections, bringing in someone from outside to create greater success than what the original founders themselves could do, are important factors. Entrepreneurs are not born, they are made.

Ten Traits of Entrepreneurs

There are many books and articles written about what traits entrepreneurs possess that make them different from others. I will share in this section the ten traits I have noticed about entrepreneurs – some I possess, some I don't, but most of these traits are characteristic of the successful entrepreneurs of the world.

1. **Entrepreneurs are contrarians who challenge the conventional and are viewed as mavericks**

   Entrepreneurs always want to do things differently and are not satisfied with the status quo. They will do things to the contrary if they feel things are not right the way they are. They will challenge the norms, even societal norms, if they strongly believe in their vision or views. In fact, they thrive being contrarians – doing things differently and being unconventional. Sometimes, their plans may look unrealistic to others, including to their team members. Despite others not completely believing in their plans, entrepreneurs will still try to push for their way of doing things. This may, at times, create some discomfort among team members and other stakeholders.

Entrepreneurs are able to compete with and defeat the incumbents who may have been operating in their comfort zone adhering to conventional approaches and becoming complacent over time, while the newcomer, the entrepreneur, challenges the norms and creates a new business model and a new business. As mavericks, they are not limited by the norm – they create a new normal for the cause they believe in.

2. Entrepreneurs are courageous and have a low level of fear
Their fear level is typically very low; they are courageous, willing to test limits not fearing that they may fail. In life and at work, they are willing to test the limits and the OB (out of bound) markers, and to question people of higher authority; they may not even fear that they may be testing the limits of the law. Of course, they may never have any criminal intention or fraud in mind, except that they sometimes may make a judgement and do things without thoroughly checking the law first. Unintentionally they may then break the law. Entrepreneurs are willing to put up a good fight with any competitor that comes their way.

3. Entrepreneurs are risk takers
People equate risk taking with entrepreneurship. In fact, the conventional belief is that you cannot be an entrepreneur if you are not willing to take risks. All successful entrepreneurs will tell you this is a fact. The saying "No pain, no gain" in entrepreneurship terms is, "No risk taking, no success". Most people are risk averse, in fact societies can also be risk averse. For example, Singaporeans, for a long time have been mainly risk averse, preferring to

take the time-tested route for a career path, not willing to try unconventional routes, but focus on what has worked in the past for current situations. While Singapore has made progress, especially among the young, Singaporeans remain largely risk averse. Entrepreneurs are willing to take higher risk than the ordinary person. Entrepreneurs are able to overcome the inertia caused by risk aversion and set in motion their entrepreneurship journey.

4. **Entrepreneurs are tenacious, determined and stubborn**

   Because entrepreneurs have a clearer vision than most, they see an opportunity when others don't. By taking risks doing what they do, many people think they are crazy. While others may not believe in the plan, many do not believe in the cause and may not believe in the venture – they may see entrepreneurs as being stubborn pursuing a lost cause. While others see a possibility of failure, entrepreneurs are determined in the cause and their plan. They pursue their plans tenaciously because they can see things differently from others. They don't give up easily, remain determined, are tenacious and keep going. While entrepreneurs don't declare success or victory so easily, they also don't succumb to failure so easily. They look "stubborn" to others. People do not like mavericks, because mavericks can be stubborn when they believe in something.

5. **Entrepreneurs do things first, and assess later – they don't over-analyse before doing**

   Entrepreneurs will do what they need to do first, and only afterwards will they check whether what they did was right or wrong. Even if they are not sure, they will go ahead rather than spend too much time trying to figure out whether they should get started. They will just do it and then prepare to fight the battle later when they discover something is wrong. (For example, drawing up a business plan and talking to people to raise money while still working for a company can be considered unethical, but entrepreneurs who believe in what they are doing will take the risk of their employer finding out about their actions, and dealing with it when and if it happens – guess what: I did this for two years before I started UTAC – working on the plan at night in my office when everyone had gone home). In this respect, they also don't waste time over-analysing and trying to cover every base before venturing out. They **Just Do It**.

6. **Entrepreneurs are mistaken as dreamers – they envision the future, they are visionary**

Entrepreneurs dream of and envision the outcome of their venture. They envision a better future – many cannot see the way the entrepreneurs can. As they are able to envision their journey which is never static, it is more difficult for others to understand why entrepreneurs are taking such steps. Sparks of inspiration come to them from time to time about how they should take their next steps. People sometimes think entrepreneurs are not thinking right. Very few people believe the entrepreneurs can succeed as their plan may not look realistic to others. But the entrepreneurs can envision what most cannot. When I decided to start UTAC, I was called a dreamer and reckless for starting a semiconductor company when every other company was losing money and bleeding heavily. Well, my dream came true – UTAC is still standing after more than 20 years. So, we can say entrepreneurs are visionary and many set the future trends that may look impossible today. We have to overcome "small minded" thinking, think boldly, or think big and not think small. I am inspired by a quote by Stewart Brand "This present moment used to be the unimaginable future" in his book *The Clock of the Long Now.*

7. **Entrepreneurs are energetic, impatient, never satisfied and become bored easily**

   Entrepreneurs are mostly impatient and wish they could do everything quickly instead of at other people's pace. Their energy levels are typically very high, and this enables them to move fast and think fast, often a few steps ahead of others. Many find it difficult to keep up with their pace. Some say entrepreneurs cannot be easily satisfied and are always challenging to do even better. Having reached a goal, they want to aim higher. Entrepreneurs keep themselves busy because they are easily bored. They need to keep doing things. With a high level of energy, they tend to bulldoze through their ideas and plans, sometimes making enemies along the way.

8. **Entrepreneurs are competitive even when challenging giants**

   How did disruptors emerge from nowhere and beat incumbents? It is because entrepreneurs have a competitive spirit in them and are willing to challenge anyone, no matter how big or small the competition may be. They are like David challenging Goliath and winning the battle. Entrepreneurs will use all they have to challenge and compete even with big companies. The competitive spirit in them keeps them going, even if it means they have to compete with the giants. This is how Netflix challenged and killed Blockbuster, the first video rental company that became a giant that is now bankrupt.

9. **Entrepreneurs are adaptable and flexible and do not mind starting small**

   Entrepreneurs have a rough idea of where they want to head. However, as the path ahead is never straight, they do not really see all the obstacles ahead of them when they start out. They are therefore adaptable and flexible and willing to adjust plans as they proceed on their journey. Rigidity will never work.

To them, size does not matter. It is acceptable for them to be in a small organisation or a big company. They don't mind starting very small because they are prepared to go the whole mile, from ground zero before moving upwards, thinking they will become big one day (and the definition of big can be very different for different people). Entrepreneurs don't mind getting their hands dirty and will roll up their sleeves to do any task needed to achieve success.

They seldom would have expected what they had started to become so big. Many successful entrepreneurs around the world did plan to grow their companies from a small start-up into a big company, but most never expected their companies to become as big as they eventually turned out to be. Very few would actually have thought about the ultimate size of the company they had started. Bill Gates and Mark Zuckerberg both did not expect Microsoft or Facebook to become the giants they are today. There was someone who helped both of them go beyond what the founder envisioned.

The brothers who started McDonalds did not grow it into the giant it is today. The brothers were passionate simply to grow their eatery into a family restaurant in San Bernardino, California. They did not envision nor have the passion to make McDonalds the giant franchise engine it is today. Becoming big was someone else's passion.

Did Microsoft and Intel create their futures out of a vision?

1. When Bill Gates started Microsoft and developed the DOS for IBM PCs, he had no idea of what the world will look like today.

---

2. Founders of Intel, Andy Grove, Robert Noyce and Gordon Moore, too did not know how their future looked.
3. They started and kept changing to adapt to new realities and project future direction.
4. What they did and also were fortunate enough not to also do (luck?), resulted in the today we know of.
5. All of them will tell you they did not create the future, but they made the right decisions for their business at each crossroad.

10. **Entrepreneurs love what they do and do what they love – with passion**

I have a whole chapter to talk about passion (see Chapter 6). First, entrepreneurs love what they do. The whole entrepreneurial journey is so tough that unless the entrepreneur loves what he or she is doing, it will be very difficult to achieve success. The love and passion will keep the drive and allow the entrepreneur to see beyond the obstacles and hardship along the way before success. Second, the lucky ones became entrepreneurs by doing what they love. They created companies out of what they loved to do.

Let's look at Bill Gates as an example. He loved computers and was an amateur programmer. He was so passionate that in school at his eighth grade, he got approval from his teachers to skip his math class to give him time to design things like early video games. He converted what he loved to do into a business – Microsoft. Walt Disney is another example. From a young age, he enjoyed drawing and painting and even managed to sell a painting of his neighbours' horse at a young age. After several failures in starting a few animation companies, he created Mickey Mouse in 1928, resulting in the great success of Disney.

A Serial ("Cyclic") Entrepreneurial Spirit

There are entrepreneurs who started companies just once in their lifetime and there are others who keep doing it. I have done a few in my life, not because I planned to do so but because either circumstances forced me to start again or because I saw opportunities that I could tap to create success.

There are many who may have started the next company because they thought they could do it again. However, all the necessary ingredients for success may not necessarily be present to succeed, or they no longer have the same spirit or ability to create the next success.

So, when we talk about serial entrepreneurs, we have to be very careful in separating the true ones (true serial entrepreneurs) from those who think they can create another successful company just because they created one before.

I believe it is not so easy to be a serial entrepreneur because the circumstances and the environment do not remain static to bring out the same entrepreneurial traits in people all the time. Sometimes, the once successful entrepreneurs come back and try to start another company. Each one may come back for a different reason.

Some entrepreneurs may start another venture because they believe they can still do it or want to do it differently from before. Some come back because they failed the last time, some because they had to prematurely leave their venture (for whatever reason). Others try again because they have been encouraged by others to join a start-up team.

Then there are some who want to create more wealth by starting more new companies. Some want to do it again for the "glamour" of being an entrepreneur. But we all know things are never the same. So, the reasons a serial entrepreneur starts his or her next venture are more important than the fact they started a new venture again. To be successful again, many things have to be aligned and fall into place. This alignment of factors will be the necessary ingredients for creating successful companies. And there must be a real opportunity that exists. If the reasons for starting a new venture are wrong, then they will likely fail.

Team Entrepreneurship

Can a few entrepreneurs get together to work on a company or project? This is a very difficult question to answer. One thing is for sure, without an integrated team, one that shares the same vision, the chances of success are very low. Does this mean that everyone who is part of the team is an entrepreneur? Does everyone in a team need to have entrepreneurial traits? Perhaps yes, but inevitably, there has to be one or two visionaries whom the rest of the team members believe in. However, it is very useful for the rest of the team members to have some amount of entrepreneurial spirit, as the visionaries will keep pushing the limits for the team, pushing for more challenging goals to be achieved.

In essence, an entrepreneurial team feeds on itself. The visionaries among them will provide the inspiration, and they will keep dreaming of new and bigger things while the rest of the team members see the vision and also think of ways of doing things differently (and therefore they too are being entrepreneurs). They do challenge each other from time to time, but they keep re-enforcing each other.

As the saying goes, "Every finger is unique but alone cannot do much, but when all five fingers come together, the hand becomes very powerful". Similarly, in an entrepreneurship team, it is best that each team member should have different qualities. I read an article ("Thinkers, Doers and Dreamers" by Ayush Sengupta, 7 May 2018) about what qualities in a person will ensure success. What he wrote confirms what I learnt from my journey so far: that to create successful start-ups, each team needs a Dreamer, a Thinker and a Doer. But who is more important?

Dreamer I covered this under the section of Ten Traits. A dreamer is someone who can envision an opportunity that may not even exist. He or she proposes new ideas that may not be obvious to many. What they do with these ideas determine whether they can create success.

Thinker Someone who can think deeply, innovatively and solve tough problems. The ability to join the dots in complex situations or problems is their strength.

Doer Someone who takes an idea and acts on it. Someone who can gather resources and make things happen. The ability to execute on a plan and focus on how to achieve the set goals.

Of course, the best entrepreneurs are Dreamers, Thinkers and Doers all in one (see Figure 1.2). An aspiring entrepreneur should try to develop all these attributes but it's tough. So it is best to assemble a diversified team that can work together and one that collectively has all the three attributes of a Dreamer, Thinker and Doer.

The truth is that the leaders or the visionaries also depend on the team members to respond to them, and to their "dreams" and their plans. They – the entrepreneurs – derive strength and inspiration from team members who also think in almost the same frequency. Working as a team, they strengthen themselves and their plans to create a better chance of success.

This feeding off on one another is a very important ingredient of success in a company or a start-up. While a few entrepreneurs getting together will have a good chance of success, if all of them are the visionaries, it will be difficult to create the "feeding" mechanism that is so important to reinforce

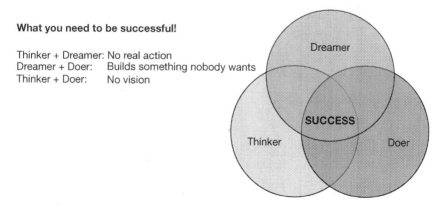

What you need to be successful!

Thinker + Dreamer: No real action
Dreamer + Doer: Builds something nobody wants
Thinker + Doer: No vision

Fig. 1.2: Team Entrepreneurship

confidence in the entrepreneur and in the team. Too many visionaries will mean there would be just too many things to "feed" on, and it will instead de-focus the team. This is like the famous saying, "Too many cooks spoil the broth".

One cannot have an army solely comprised of generals. Some have to be generals, some colonels, and others majors, leaving some to be the soldiers. Some will be advisers, while some will have to be the ones to challenge the plans. Having everyone be a general will result in the generals losing the ability to lead as they will get no response to their leadership, and will in the long run lose their direction due to a lack of feedback on what they are doing.

The Unending Entrepreneurship Journey

Successful entrepreneurs will never consider themselves as successful along their journey or declare that they have reached the final goal they aspired to. Instead, in their minds, they always feel that they are still very much on a journey looking for success. If you ask any one of them (who by any of our usual societal definitions is already successful), almost none will tell you that they consider themselves successful or have reached their ultimate goal. Most will tell you they are still on their way there. It is my belief that the day you as an entrepreneur start considering yourself as having achieved success, you will then begin the end of your journey as an entrepreneur. You will become comfortable and complacent and therefore all the values and virtues of what good entrepreneurs do will start to diminish in you.

Entrepreneurs continue to aim for new heights and continue to think of new things that will bring them even greater success. They will continue their journey no matter how long it takes, whether or not success ever comes to them. They continue to believe they will create even greater things and will have an even greater impact on their industry or business, other people's lives or even society at large. What really motivates them is that they want to continue to do things differently and to challenge the conventional by constantly innovating and creating wealth for themselves and for others.

Entrepreneurs never stop thinking this way even if they actually face real failure along the way. Seldom will entrepreneurs declare victory, while at the same time it is difficult for them to admit to failure. So even when an entrepreneur exits his or her business, he or she will continue doing other entrepreneurial things – start another venture (the serial entrepreneurs), change society, mentor other entrepreneurs, invest to facilitate the creation of new ventures. This is the sign of a good entrepreneur – one who never sees himself or herself as having achieved great success, but one who continues to do new things. Those who have retired are no longer considered as entrepreneurs.

The creation of wealth is one easy measure of conventional success, and it is a proxy that entrepreneurs use to gauge that they are indeed heading the right way.

At my personal level, somehow, after handling so many start-ups and after being involved in helping a number of other start-ups, I've always felt I haven't achieved much for myself. The innermost feeling I've had is that there are so many more people who are truly successful and compared to them I am nothing but merely trying my best to achieve my ultimate goal. Yet this ultimate goal is also not a very clear one and looks like something so distant that I still have a very long way to go before I can see the fruits of my labour.

It is quite normal for entrepreneurs to not be easily satisfied with their results or with the extent of their achievements, even if most of them feel they have accomplished much more than many others. Entrepreneurs always feel that there is much more to do and much more to achieve and this feeling continues to occupy their mind and drive them forward – it keeps them going.

I have a passion to achieve certain goals – dreams that I envisioned many times. As I pursue my dreams, I don't know whether or not I have arrived. Entrepreneurs don't know when they have arrived, as they keep on going until someone tells them they are successful. Even then, true entrepreneurs don't really believe they have arrived. The day an entrepreneur believes he is successful is the day his entrepreneurial life starts to decline.

Chapter 1 Summary

The Entrepreneurial Journey

SUCCESS

You never know that you have arrived

You are always innovating

You do things differently

I can always achieve more

I create something out of nothing

I never fear failure

START

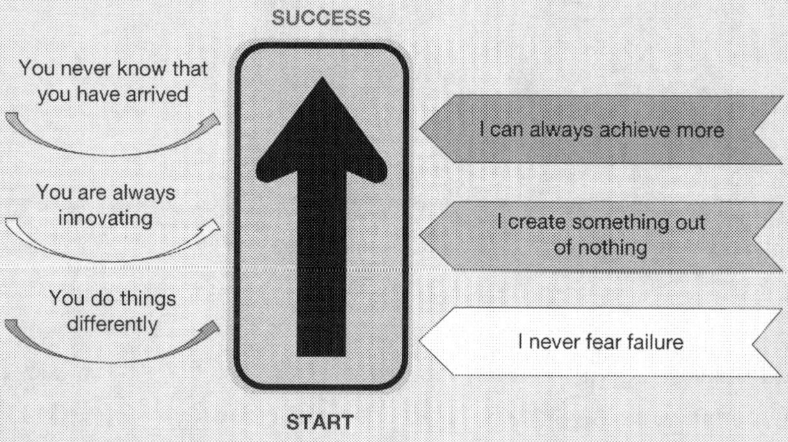

Fig. 1.3: The Entrepreneurial Journey

- Entrepreneurship is not just about starting companies, it is a matter of having an entrepreneurial mindset.

- You can act and behave like an entrepreneur no matter what you do in life and this can transform your life.

- Entrepreneurs are "effectual" thinkers – they imagine a possible outcome and work with a set of limited means or resources.

- Risk taking and beating the odds are inherent qualities of an entrepreneur.

- Entrepreneurs are not just born, they can be made or trained.

- Understanding the ten traits of entrepreneurs will help you think like one.

- An entrepreneurial team should be a diverse one – have dreamers, thinkers and doers in your team if you want to succeed.

CHAPTER 2

THE THREE MANTRAS OF ENTREPRENEURS

We often read about successful entrepreneurs and hear them at gatherings or conferences telling their stories and their journey to success. I have closely analysed what these successful entrepreneurs say and do to understand the essence of why they became successful or why they can be called true entrepreneurs. Based on the research I have done as I prepared for my lectures on Entrepreneurship (I teach a Master's of Science, Technopreneurship and Innovation Programme at the Nanyang Technological University, Singapore (NTU)) and based on my own personal experience, I have observed a few common philosophies or mindsets with which most successful entrepreneurs operate. These become very apparent in the way entrepreneurs behave and the way they go about their daily lives. While we can classify these philosophies of thinking in many ways, I have been able to distil them into three very common philosophies that entrepreneurs typically follow. I call them the "Three Mantras of Entrepreneurs".

These three mantras are quite consistent with what I have personally practised over the years, not only when I started new companies, but also how I have done things since my very early days. As I interact with the many entrepreneurs from around the world, and as I observe the way they think, I again consistently see these three mantras in their thinking process and operating philosophy. Intuitively, we know about such mindsets through the behaviours we observe in entrepreneurs, but it is more useful to understand what these mantras are in depth, what they really mean, how they help shape the mindset of the entrepreneur, and also how they guide the day-to-day thinking and workings of such people.

If you want to be an entrepreneur, I suggest you take a close look at what these mantras mean and try to follow them as you go about doing what you do. I personally have never lost sight of these important mantras, and have always used them as my guiding principles, not just in my journey as an entrepreneur, but also as a way of life.

Mantra No. 1: Have a Winning Spirit

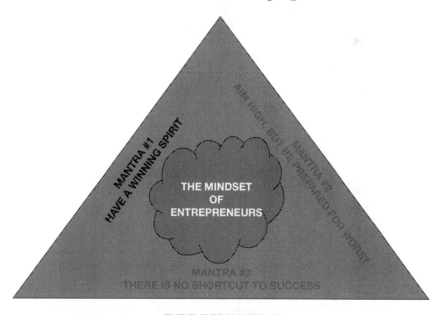

THE THREE MANTRAS

There are many variations to describe a winning spirit, here are a few:

1. "Can do" attitude
2. "Never say die" attitude
3. "There is no problem that cannot be solved" attitude.

The spirit of winning is the most important spirit all entrepreneurs and business people should possess. This is also something I have always strongly believed in, whether I worked for a multinational company or when I started and operated my own companies, or for that matter when I used to lead my hockey team in school. Among the three mantras I will discuss here, the winning spirit or the "never say die" attitude is one of the most important philosophies I have practised throughout my life.

The main mindset I embrace is the spirit of "Chadri Kala" (this Punjabi term is one of the central beliefs of Sikhs – a mental state of eternal optimism, a positive attitude and is an equivalent of a mind that never fears, never despairs, never admits defeat and refuses to be crushed by adversities). This is what we call a "can do" attitude.

I have always operated with the **spirit** that there is no problem that cannot be solved. A "never say die" attitude means you keep trying until you feel you have solved the problem or have achieved the desired outcome, which is the outcome you are satisfied with. I have always believed that any problem we face can be solved – **there is no problem that cannot be solved**. Throughout my working life, whenever someone approached me with a problem which they claim is beyond solving, I take it as a personal challenge and it further encourages me to take over the problem and work on developing the solution. The solution may not be exactly what everyone might expect, but nonetheless, there will definitely be a solution. So, I always tell people there is no problem in the world that cannot be solved; the only difference is how the problem gets solved. It then follows that there are always several alternative ways to solve the problem at hand. The outcome may vary depending on the path of solution chosen, but the problem will not remain unresolved in its original form.

I believe the winning spirit or spirit of "Chadri Kala" must exist in all entrepreneurs and is a prerequisite for anyone to emerge as a successful entrepreneur. In starting a business, when an idea is converted into a real business, there will always be countless obstacles, many of which were never even expected at the time of planning. These obstacles, if not solved or cleared properly, will result in business failure.

Every Problem Can be Solved

Whenever you face a problem, your ability to believe that you will definitely be able to solve it will make a big difference in the outcome – whether you succeed or fail in solving the problem depends on your belief in being able to solve it. This belief is what gives the entrepreneur the confidence to move forward undeterred in both good and bad times, knowing that he will successfully solve any problem. You can observe this confidence in all successful entrepreneurs. One must believe it is never the end of the road when faced with difficult problems or when faced with an obstacle, no matter how unexpected it might be. The mindset that there must always be a way to overcome the obstacle or to solve the problem makes all the difference and is the mark of a true entrepreneur. If you ask any one of the entrepreneurs who has made it, they will tell you the many war stories, show you their many war wounds, and describe how they managed to overcome each of the obstacles they faced as they went about their entrepreneurial journey. In fact, if you plan to become an entrepreneur, I believe the biggest issue you need to resolve is the one of self-censorship or self-limitation. What do I mean by this?

When we start thinking that something cannot be done or that a problem cannot be solved, we are already starting with a great handicap, because our mindset would immediately be one of self-limitation. In other words, we would have started the process by imposing restrictions on ourselves, and as a result, we will surely not be effective in trying to find ways to solve the problem. In such instances, people give up too quickly. In reality, it is this mindset of *thinking* that the problem is too difficult to solve that becomes the real obstacle. Those who can overcome all the mental barriers and have a mindset that they can solve any problem no matter what it is, are the ones who will succeed as entrepreneurs. The mind that would have otherwise been occupied with negativity would be freed to give the person more mental capacity.

I am reminded of a cartoon I used to watch. I cannot remember its title, but among the many characters in the show, one used to just say, "We are doomed, there is no hope." No matter how big or small the problem, this would be the standard phrase from this ever-pessimistic cartoon character. Without any effort, he would just give up. But fortunately, the other characters in the cartoon never let this pessimistic character deter them – they always ended up solving the problems and appeared victorious.

The Panadol at Texas Instruments

When I was at Texas Instruments, I started my career as a Product Engineer. That job entailed creating test programs to effectively test the DRAMs that we were manufacturing in our Singapore factory. But more importantly, it involved solving technical problems to improve the robustness of the product, improve yields and improve quality. Right from the beginning, I was involved in solving such technical problems and somehow, always thinking out of the box, I was able to resolve many engineering and quality problems. I started working in the 64K DRAM section and helped resolve a number of issues. Just after a few months, I was asked to move to another section, the 256K DRAM section that was facing a chronic quality problem and the engineers tried their best but could not get to the root cause and therefore could not bring the quality under control.

I was tasked to move over to that section to help them solve the engineering problem. It was a tough job, but after about a month of work, I managed to identify where the problem was in how the 256K DRAM was tested, and identified a solution to strengthen the test program. Well, we managed to bring the quality from a few thousand ppm to less than 100ppm (parts per million) failure, which was the measure of quality (the lower the number, the better the quality). It was a satisfying experience and with a few more similar problems that I solved, I earned the nickname "Panadol" (a Panadol is a paracetamol that doctors prescribe to treat various medical problems).

> What helped me solve problems more easily than other staff could, was my mindset that "There is no problem that cannot be solved."

Every problem was solved and like all cartoon shows, there is a happy ending.

Decisiveness and Problem-Solving

The way we make decisions affects the way we solve problems. In making decisions, I always believe that if you face a situation in which you are left with just a couple of alternatives that are difficult to choose from, then the solution is to just go ahead and choose any one of these alternatives. If need be, you may toss a coin to decide. Why? Am I asking you to depend on luck? Not so. In reality, since it was in the first place difficult to choose among the two or three alternatives, the final outcome will be almost the same anyway. But even if the outcomes were not the same, you would certainly get some results, which may or may not be what you expected. Nevertheless at least the new results will give you a new direction with new inputs and new data to work with to further solve the problem. What is most important for entrepreneurs in such a situation, where there are a few possible solutions to a given problem, is the ability to make a decision fast. It is in such situations that entrepreneurs excel, as not everyone can be decisive in the face of uncertainty.

Most people require much more visibility and need many more data points before they can make a decision. You can call it gut-feel – it is this gut-feel ability that sometimes helps entrepreneurs solve problems fast. Now, gut-feel is not just guesswork, as some people might believe it to be. To me, gut-feel is more of an ability to make decisions or solve problems with much less information on the problem. I have dedicated one chapter to this gut-feel aspect, which I also refer to as "thinking with the heart". You will understand this concept better when reading Chapter 7.

It is important to note that the difference between an entrepreneur and a non-entrepreneur is this: an entrepreneur is able and also willing to be decisive even when there is a certain amount of uncertainty and lack of clarity, while the non-entrepreneur will want the problem to be clearer and is unwilling to make a quick judgement without enough information or data points.

In some ways, this is related to the mindset about risk taking. By deciding with fewer data points or with much less information at hand, one can conclude that the entrepreneur is taking higher risks. As I mentioned earlier, I feel that the bigger sin is in the delay in making the decision. This delay is a bigger sin than choosing a less effective solution, because even if the decision leads to a less effective solution, with that as a new starting point, further changes, modifications, and additional solutions can help move the process of problem solving further on, and when new information later becomes available, fine-tuning can lead to an even better solution. In the worst case, having to make a U-turn later would not be too bad, if it is the right thing to do as things become clearer. In the whole process of solving the problem at hand, lessons would have been learnt, and with the new insights, you would be able to make better decisions in future. The worst thing to do (which many actually do), would be putting off making a decision in the hope that the problem will just disappear or solve by itself. Most of the time, the problem never goes away. This is definitely not the way of entrepreneurs or is definitely not in the spirit of entrepreneurship.

Self-Confidence

Related to this mantra is the tremendous self-confidence entrepreneurs demonstrate and possess. We have seen and heard of so many entrepreneurs who believe that no matter how big or small the competitor may be, or no matter how established or promising the competitor may be, the competitor can be defeated fast.

In the face of formidable competition, entrepreneurs still believe they can do better than their competitor, even if others consider that competitor is the best in the world. This is how insurgents have, in history, always been able to beat the incumbents who may have been around for a much longer time. Had entrepreneurs not believed in their ability to beat the incumbents, had they not had their "never say die" or "can do" attitude, and had they tried to impose self-censorship or self-limitations on themselves, the economic landscape of the world would be very much different from what it is today. It is so important for entrepreneurs to possess this self-confidence. They will need to have the necessary knowledge and the ability to solve problems as they occur. They also have to assemble people in their team who can collectively help solve problems more effectively.

Because of a "can do" spirit and "never say die" attitude, entrepreneurs are able to solve every problem and issue, and in the process, they create world-class companies.

In any business or in anything you do, you will always face problems; obstacles will always come your way. A fighting spirit with the will and confidence to overcome all obstacles will definitely help you create successful businesses and successes in life. This can only be done if you believe in this mantra of a **Winning Spirit**.

The UTAC Story

When I started UTAC, there were already many similar players in the industry. The environment was also very tough as all the companies in the same industry were losing money and had excess capacities but strong investors to back them. It seemed an impossible task to start a company that would compete with the many giants already present. But because I believed in our ability to become another great company, and my team also believed in our ability to create a successful company, we were undeterred and unaffected by the many negative things we heard or faced. Instead, we believed we could beat the big players in the same game by changing some rules.

We built UTAC from scratch, zero base. When we started, we operated out of a temporary office with nothing in it. Then we built our customer presentations as we also built our execution plans – the specifications, the equipment selection, the customer contacts, etc. We started looking for a building and proceeded to bid for a 400,000 square feet building that everyone said would be too expensive for us. But I thought otherwise. Because of the circumstances and the industry condition, we were confident of a creative deal for the building – and we got it! Then, without an operational factory, we went to visit a big European multinational company, where we presented our plans and asked for their business. Their initial reaction was: "You don't even have a factory and you are asking for my business?" We convinced them of our ability to execute our plans, and with the confidence they had in my team, we finally got their business. They were our first customer the moment our building was refurbished. Then, we went on to target other customers who were already doing big business with our competitors, most of whom were much more established and bigger than us. We understood the problems the customers faced with these competitors and presented how we would do things differently. We won many customers this way, including one customer in Taiwan whose CEO had past disagreements with me while I was still in Texas Instruments. Despite this CEO having problems with me in the past, I managed to convince him to switch from his local Taiwan supplier to us, and even at a slight price premium. I have many similar stories to tell, but the key point is that our "never say die" attitude led us to never consider how small we were or render us unable to compete. Instead, we challenged our competitors head on and grew our company to become a very significant player in the industry.

The most telling story is one in which we won the business of a very big US-based company, taking them away from our competitor's incumbent factory, which had been dealing with them for five years. From scratch, we became the customer's single biggest test service provider in just one year. And in the second year, when their vice-president for operations gave us a plaque for being their best supplier, he told me I should be proud of it, especially since my competitor tried for five years without getting any award from them. All this was only made possible through the mantra of a Winning Spirit.

Mantra No. 2: Aim High but be Prepared for the Worst

THE THREE MANTRAS

The sky is the limit, as the popular saying goes. This is without doubt the essence of the entrepreneur's mindset, which results in great companies being created. So, everyone should aim as high as they possibly can, to whatever their imagination can create, and they should plan without placing artificial limits or ceilings to what they can achieve. Practising self-censorship or

41

self-limitation and putting in place a premature "ceiling", especially during the planning process, can be self-defeating. So, almost all entrepreneurs live with the "can do" spirit and always aim for the sky.

Risk Taking Must Focus on Worst-Case Scenario

To be realistic, one should also never forget to be prepared for the worst. I would be lying to everyone if I say "aiming for the sky" is the only thing entrepreneurs think of. Entrepreneurs may dream about things, but they are not just dreamers *per se*. In fact, entrepreneurship is never about blind risk taking, a topic I discuss in Chapters 4 and 18.

The fact of life is that taking blind risks is irresponsible and reckless, and people who take blind risks are not only irresponsible to themselves but also to all the stakeholders involved in starting up a company. It is also reckless for one to expect that things will always continue to go up and up, and to grow and grow, and never ever come down. Such was the phenomena of the dot.com era, where most participants in the dot.com boom, whether entrepreneurs or investors, only saw the upside but never the potential downside. No one bothered to think about the unrealistic expectations everyone had. During that era, because the downside was blindsided, many forgot to plan for a rainy day and failed to put in place the contingency plans for their companies and for themselves.

Some questions every entrepreneur should ask are: Is there a course of action for the company that will be put into action should something go wrong with the execution? What should the course of action be if the business fails? Should you as the entrepreneur be prepared to lose everything you put into your company, and will your life come to an end? If, having lost everything, how will you support your family? The situation can be very scary, but there is always a real possibility that such an outcome will happen for most entrepreneurs. In fact, most ventures fail, not succeed, so why are so many people not prepared for such failure? It can be devastating for those who are unprepared.

Because entrepreneurs are very confident of themselves, they should all have thought about what they would do when and if they fail. The possibility of a failure will not stop them from doing what they want, but they know that having thought of the downsides, they are prepared for any eventuality, including failure. Without being prepared for failure, the fear of failing and the potential of wrecking their life would have resulted in the entrepreneurs not having taken the path of entrepreneurship in the first place. They take that step to becoming an entrepreneur because they are prepared.

Plan for Failure and Backup Plans

In any business planning, we should take all the necessary risks to achieve the highest possible returns, but if the risks are not calculated, it becomes a recipe for failure. Taking risks blindly is recklessness, as I have mentioned earlier. The keywords here are *being prepared* and *calculated*. At the individual level, the best state of mind for an entrepreneur is one in which he or she knows that in times of failure and in times of difficulty, there will be backup plans to minimise the setbacks and pain associated with the failure, and therefore enable one to better face and handle the failure should it occur.

For your company, when doing up your business plan, think of all the possible risks and obstacles that may jeopardise your plan. For each potential problem or obstacle that you may face, think of possible solutions to overcome, or circumvent the obstacles you are facing. Have these plans ready and set aside, to be used when the need arises. This is how entrepreneurs handle risk – they have contingency plans.

The real issue here is that of being prepared for failure. In all your plans, are you prepared to fail? Will you or your business be able to take and accept the failure? If at the beginning of your venture and adventure you had thought of the possible pitfalls, the possible problems, and the result of a possible failure, and if you have drawn up a set of actions to face failure or obstacles, then you will be more prepared when failure eventually knocks on your door. Again, are you ready with your contingency plan in case you fail to achieve some milestone goals?

Since in any business venture, the possibility of failure is much higher than the possibility of success, every entrepreneur should embrace this mantra. The question I ask you is this: Did you plan this mantra into your life? Are you prepared when the outcome is not what you expected? I am not saying we should plan to fail, but we should at least plan to handle failure when it occurs, because with the benefit of a contingency plan, the entrepreneur will be more relaxed because he or she would have visualised what needs to be done in the event of failure. With such a state of mind, the entrepreneur will be more focused in executing the business plan as opposed to having to always look behind his or her back because of the fear of failing. Such behaviour of having to always glance behind your shoulders for fear of something going wrong will inevitably slow down the entrepreneur. Looking forward all the time with peace of mind that there will be backup and survival plans in the event of a failure, will free up the entrepreneur's mind to be positive and proactive to do a good job and to help increase the chances of success. In short, plan for the best, but be prepared for the worst.

Some examples of backup plans for entrepreneurs, with respect to their personal life should they fail are: going back to work as an employee again, or starting a career at the bottom of the rung, perhaps as an engineer all over again (which is what I was prepared to do when I started my entrepreneurial journey) or starting another venture by looking for more funding to support yet another idea. The key thing is that entrepreneurs have confidence that they will be able to pick up the pieces if they fail and move on with life. They do not cry over spilt milk but start looking for another glass of milk. This does not mean that entrepreneurs are not hurt by the failures. Some are devastated by the unexpected outcome and by the failure itself, and some may even see their lives as being turned upside down.

The differentiating factor of true entrepreneurs is that they are able to handle all the downsides, the emotions, the failure, and then move on to their next step or to their backup plan, which they would have thought of before they started their venture. I have therefore always believed in this.

Yes, I am always aiming high, but I also know that at all times, I have to be prepared for the worst possible outcome. I do not necessarily plan with a scenario of the worst possible outcome, because this will defeat the first mantra by placing unnecessary ceilings in my plans, but at the back of my mind, I know that I will be prepared if things do not work out for me. This is what has allowed me to move on from one venture to another.

Survival Strategy

One lesson I have learnt throughout my life, particularly in an economic downturn, is that there are no heroes, only survivors. How do survivors survive? They are always mindful and prepared for the worst, and they plan for survival early.

An entrepreneur must know how to sense the downturn, and then plan and execute his or her survival strategy promptly. Having a plan ready when the worst-case scenario hits is useful because one can immediately execute the backup plan when failure occurs. If one tried to both plan and execute a survival plan at the same time, the chances of a successful execution are greatly diminished. In some cases, it may be too late and done in desperation. The mind, when in a desperate state, will never be capable of doing the planning and the execution simultaneously. The plans should really have been developed before the failure occurs.

So how does one behave in a downturn? The trick is to plan for survival, and to also plan for a slightly longer period of downturn than the expected duration. It is better to err on the downside than on the upside. It is okay to make less money during an upturn. However, losing more money than planned during a downturn can be detrimental for companies, and sometimes even threaten their survival especially when cash flow becomes unexpectedly tight. Thus, plan to be conservative during a downturn, even if it means you cannot be too aggressive during an upturn; it will not hurt you. Instead, it will be the difference between survival and failure. In good times, people focus on growth, profitability, winning more customers, and hiring more staff – embarking on an offensive strategy. But in bad times, or during a downturn, having a mainly ***defensive strategy*** will be more useful and important. This defensive strategy can also be called a survival strategy.

In a survival strategy, all the plans must be adjusted to be able to outlast the competition. In such an environment, the guiding principles should be positive cash flow, minimising the cash drain or the burn rate, cost control, and cost reduction. Of course, the entrepreneur who has become business savvy will also take the opportunity in such times to prepare the company to grow stronger, so that when the good times return and opportunities arise, the company should be able to quickly spring back into action and be ahead of the competition. Planning for this early and accurately will determine how successful a company will be and how much better the company will perform when there is a period of growth. Of course, all of this starts with the presumption that the entrepreneur is able to judge when the downturn is going to occur and how long it will last. Those who can make the judgement correctly will be more successful than those who cannot.

Most companies fail because they did not plan for the worst-case scenario, or did not have a downturn strategy, or did not have enough alternatives and contingency plans. In good times, when businesses are booming, the economy is growing healthily, and when sentiments are good, even weak companies may seemingly do well. I recall an analogy relating to ships. When there is a high tide at sea, all ships, big or small, structurally strong or weak, well maintained or poorly maintained, will remain afloat and can successfully navigate the seas. However, when the tides drop, and when there is a very narrow navigation space, only the best prepared and the most skillful of captains and sailors, and those who already have a plan to navigate in harsh conditions, will successfully sail the seas. The weak ones will hit the rocks below, or will collide into each other and become shipwrecked, bringing their journey to an end. Companies are like these ships. Those that survive or even grow during the bad times are the strong companies. Most of the time, they survive because they had already planned and were prepared for the worst during their journey. Never forget this mantra of aiming high and being prepared for the worst. It will help entrepreneurs move along with great peace of mind and keep them prepared when they face a failed scenario.

Plan for the Worst-Case Scenario

When I was in Texas Instruments working in the memory division, one of the most volatile sectors of the semiconductor industry, the vice-president of the division constantly reminded us of how volatile the whole industry was. One phrase he used to preach is, "When you are in heaven, be prepared that hell is coming, so do not get complacent." The semiconductor industry, being cyclical, has its peaks and troughs, like a sine curve, and the peaks were the times in heaven, while the troughs were the times in hell. Understanding this principle has been very useful in my quest to create two successful semiconductor companies.

Unfortunately, since we started Infiniti Solutions, we faced many adverse conditions, often because of things beyond our control. For example, when we started raising funds and then tried to make an acquisition of a company, September 11 got in our way, which caused delays and made things slightly worse for us. But we succeeded in raising US$36m in 2001. Then, when we made the first acquisition, we faced a long downturn, which was one of the longest in the industry, and then another sharp downturn struck before we could stabilise – this was around 2004 to 2005. The reality was that we did not have very much cash, for we had raised a limited amount and had stretched our dollars by doing more than what we had originally planned with our limited cash. So, when we faced the second downturn, which many industry analysts said would be a short downturn, we did not believe it.

Instead of working on the assumption of a short downturn, we betted on a longer than expected downturn, and therefore, immediately planned our survival strategy to stay afloat in difficult times. I say survival because we did not have the luxury of a lot of cash. Even if we did have cash, I would still have planned for a survival scenario, and our strategy was simple: what could we do to outlast our competition during this downturn?

At Infiniti Solutions, we continued to survive the tough times because we always planned early, were prepared with the right strategies, and executed the strategies when the time came. We were never caught off guard. So, despite our company being among the smaller players and the least likely to survive, we continued to operate despite many odds till the 2008/2009 Global Financial Crisis hit the world. At Infiniti, demand dropped by 60% and this was even tougher than the previous downturn we had faced in 2005. After 2009, we could no longer raise money as the industry was not as attractive as the Internet economy. So, we knew we would never be able to raise more VC money. We missed our IPO in 2004 and we knew it was not possible to do another IPO.

We went into a Survival strategy again, knowing we had to stretch our dollar and manage our cash flow. Fortunately, even during the good times, we had kept our sights on the next downturn with a view to surviving the bad times when they came back.

We did survive, the management team bought out our VCs so that we could manage without interference from them (that would have slowed us down and made us less agile). We got back into being adaptable and flexible, stabilised Infiniti Solutions by the year 2010 and as a team we decided that we had to plan an exit strategy that worked because an IPO would not work. Our exit strategy was to do a trade sale of Infiniti in parts. We sold our mass production factory in Philippines in 2011, then sold three different units in the Silicon Valley from 2012 to 2014 before we completely exited Infiniti Solutions.

Mantra No. 3: There is No Shortcut to Success

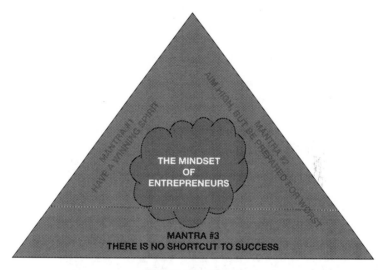

THE THREE MANTRAS

This is no magic formula to the three mantras. I am sure everyone can relate to this third mantra that there is no shortcut to success. Many entrepreneurs will tell you how they have gone through the school of hard knocks, having put their heart, soul and sweat to produce results, and how hard they have worked to make their business tick. This is one important thing many dot.com company founders forgot.

During the dot.com era, everyone was in a hurry to make money. Many thought that starting a company was an easy thing as they perceived others as having done so effortlessly. Many also thought that having an initial public offering or IPO event was the end game and the sign of a successful entrepreneur. The sooner aspiring entrepreneurs realised this mantra, the better it was for them, as the entrepreneurial journey is not easy at all. When you ask any successful entrepreneurs, two items which surely always appear in their menu of success are hard work and long hours. These (hard work and long hours) are, undoubtedly, a necessary condition to achieve success. Without the passion, the personal commitment or the time put in, very few will make it. Someone once told me, success is one per cent inspiration and 99 per cent perspiration. This I fully subscribe to. In anything we entrepreneurs do, if we do it seriously, it is really hard work and persistence that will ultimately determine our success.

Transforming Ideas into Businesses is Hard Work

I also believe that while ideas are difficult to come by, it is our ability to transform an idea into a business that is most in deciding whether a person can be called a successful entrepreneur. (I talk about transforming an idea into a business in Chapter 8.)

Transforming an idea into a working business is the part that requires tremendous amounts of effort, detailed planning, and a lot of push, persistence, personal involvement, and drive to make things happen and to make a business tick. To do this, you have no choice but to put in the hours, the very long hours, and with a very watchful eye to track the progress of your actions (which again means you have to put in the time and cannot be distracted or relaxed for too long). You have no choice but to keep an eye on many details in the early stages of the company's life cycle, and this requires your 100 per cent and unconditional attention. The whole exercise can be so intense that you will be on your feet all the time. You simply must put in the investment of your time and effort to make things happen, and there is no other way to create success or a successful business.

Commitment is Hard Work

Related to this principle of working hard for success is the issue of how committed one is to the business or the company. Many of us know this expression: "It is a bacon and egg story." What is this story about? Well, in preparing a bacon and egg breakfast, the pig is committed while the chicken is involved. What does this mean? The pig is committed to providing its meat. The pig has to be slaughtered, and it is completely committed to delivering the breakfast. However, the chicken, which provides the egg for the breakfast, is definitely involved because it provides the egg, but it did not commit itself to being slaughtered. So, the pig had no choice but to be fully committed, while the chicken was simply involved in preparing the breakfast.

An entrepreneur who seeks success has to be like the pig. You cannot be half-hearted about your involvement, and you have to face the slaughterhouse, put your neck on the line, and give yourself to the cause you are after.

During the dot.com boom days of the 1990s and to some extent in the era of the Apps economy, I noticed that the so-called and would-be entrepreneurs were half-hearted about becoming entrepreneurs and in running companies they wanted to start-up. Many of these entrepreneurs wanted to have the best of both worlds. Some wanted to have their cake and eat it too. What do I mean by these two statements? Well, I know of some who wanted to try to become "entrepreneurs", perhaps because it was a fanciful thing to do at that time, but at the same time they were not prepared to make the necessary sacrifices. They wanted to keep their comfortable jobs, and therefore spend only part of their time executing a start-up. It was like having "one leg in and one leg out". They wanted to enjoy being called entrepreneurs while still enjoying the safe haven of their jobs, which paid their salaries. While this might have worked for a while, it was not possible for too long, especially when they had to actually build the company from scratch. While some could multitask and do many things in parallel, most people cannot easily manage two full-time jobs, let alone run a start-up, which is a very intensive exercise. Of course, there are some exceptional people who can do it; it's not impossible. But the end result in most cases for those who are not fully committed to the start-up, is failure.

Unless you have the passion, and unless you spend all your time on your start-up, there will be little chance of success. Having one foot in and the other foot out the door and doing a part-time job as an entrepreneur rarely works in the real world; you have to get both feet in the door. I am not saying it is impossible, but it is rare that such an approach will yield good results. Perhaps one can do this at the very early stages of planning a start-up company, but when it comes to executing and starting the company, there is no other way but to be fully immersed into it and to become the "pig" that is fully committed to the final outcome.

Being Committed Means Doing It 24/7

Successful business owners eat, breathe, sleep, and wake to what they do as a business. Worries about the execution of the business, about cash flow, about the customers, about paying your employees' salaries, and about not breaking rules and regulations, all continue to run through the minds of entrepreneurs in a non-stop cycle. You cannot suddenly switch off when you go home from the office or when you are engaged in some other activity. Running the start-up will always be at the back of your mind.

Anything short of a twenty-four-by-seven commitment will result in insufficient time to resolve all the issues and execute all the plans necessary to create successful businesses. Of course, I am not suggesting you should be on the shop floor all the time or be continuously on the phone, or your computer. You will of course need to balance your life, family, community service, and leisure activities in addition to your work. I am also not suggesting that you put in the hours just for the sake of putting in the hours. This will result in a sheer waste of time. Particularly, in a start-up, no one watches how many hours you put in, but what they do watch are the results you produce. What I am saying is, your role as an entrepreneur is always at the back of your mind and can be activated any time, not just when you are in the office. Experience has shown that results only come if time, effort, and perspiration are invested into the business; there is no other way to do it right, especially in the early stages of starting and growing a business.

The "no shortcut to success" mantra also means you have to go through the whole mill of planning and executing your business. This includes making your business plan, looking at the risk factors, figuring out your financials and cash management, choosing and deploying a good team, researching the type of competitors you will have to contend with, being aware of the rules and regulations, amongst others. You have to be prepared to address all these matters, and guess what, you need all the 24 hours in a day to manage it.

This mantra of "no shortcut to success" is not only applicable to entrepreneurs but is also true for anything in life. Whether you want to develop a good family relationship, a successful career, or excel in sports or anything else, you have to put in the time needed to achieve success. It is no different for entrepreneurship; sometimes people tend to forget this part and think they can do it with minimal effort because others seem to achieve success so effortlessly. The issue is that the "grass always seems greener on the other side," and what I mean by this is that one always thinks others have made it good easily. Some people may not realise the effort others have put in because they don't see the difficult part of the process; they just see the successful results.

It is All About Having the Right Mindset

What I have shared in most of this chapter is having the right mindset if you want to be successful at anything in life. It is a matter of attitude and behavior both of which can be changed if we can change our mindset. I am a firm believer that we need to change our mindset embracing these three mantras if we want to be successful entrepreneurs. Let me share my experience in the military which was also a life-changing experience for me, from being a timid person to becoming an officer and a leader that has helped me throughout my life.

My Mindset Story – Officer Cadet School

I started my national service with the Singapore Armed Forces (SAF) in December 1978, immediately after completing my A levels. Those days, based on our background and also based on an interview, certain NS men were selected to go directly to the Office Cadet School (OCS). I was the hockey captain for Temasek Junior College and was physically very fit, being a long-distance track and field champion for my college. So, I got selected to go directly to OCS for a 10 months' gruelling training programme to mould us 18-year-olds into officers.

The first day I stepped into my camp, Echo Company, 9th SMC at SAF Training Institute (SAFTI), we were asked to go to our bunks to change into our uniform and come to assemble quickly. A Lieutenant who was in charge of training was shouting at all of us and I got a load of scolding, with many vulgarities that I had never heard in my life. I felt terrible and humiliated. It was a bad start and I started hating national service after that. I developed a negative attitude and my performance for about one month was terrible because I was not doing things wholeheartedly. The OCS training, one of the toughest forms of training of mental and physical stress for 10 continuous months, is not easy to survive.

Then came a terrible incident. To cut a long story short, five of us from our company Echo were charged for something that was not really our fault. When the Officer Commanding (OC) took our charges, he told us that he knew it was not really our fault, but he had been instructed to charge us and he had no choice. For the whole week, the five of us were punished terribly. When everyone was resting, we had to go down to the guardroom every hour with our "full packs" and display all our items for a check to be conducted by some corporals. These corporals ridiculed us each time and kept saying that once charged, we would never graduate as officers. This was devastating for all of us.

The turning point came for me during the weekend when everyone got to go back home except the five of us who were charged – we were confined to the camp for the whole weekend. Those who have done national service will know how important the weekend is to unwind and refresh to get ready for the next week of "torture". We continued to be punished with the hourly guardroom routine and it felt terrible. During the night, I could not sleep and must admit I cried that night. But at the same time, I reflected on what had happened the past one month. Because of the bad start on the first day, I had developed a bad attitude towards my national service.

I reflected and told myself, "I have no choice but to do this for two and a half years and I either enjoy it and learn or hate it and suffer." It was a defining moment for me and a lesson in life, too. From the next day on, due to my change of attitude, I slowly started liking my training and over the months did very well to the point that in my senior term, I became a Platoon Under Officer (PUO). A PUO is like a cadet taking on a role of a platoon commander, helping to manage the whole platoon. In a major training, I was given the role of a Company 2IC which is a role played by "Captains" in an operation. I transformed from one of the worst performers to one of the best performers in my platoon.

And how did that happen? It was all a matter of a mindset change to have a better attitude despite the very tough training (more than 50 per cent of those who started their OCS training failed to make it to become officers at the end of the 10 months). I overcame the very tough training by having a good attitude, a change of mindset from hating to liking my training and of course with a "mind over matter" approach to life.

Chapter 2 Summary

The Three Mantras of Entrepreneurs

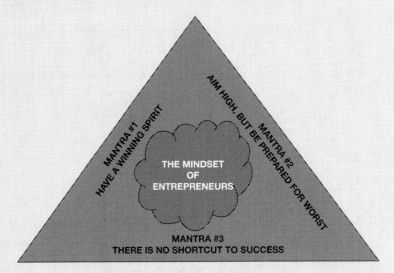

THE THREE MANTRAS

Fig. 2.1: The Three Mantras of Entrepreneurship

Successful entrepreneurs are guided by the Three Mantras of Entrepreneurs:

1. A winning spirit

2. Aim high but be prepared for the worst

3. There is no shortcut to success.

True entrepreneurs:

- possess a winning spirit and relish challenges

- recognise that there are no problems that cannot be solved

- have the ability to make decisions quickly

- have the self-confidence to embrace the spirit of winning

- live with a "can do" spirit and always aim for the sky
- never take blind risks; take calculated risks
- always have a backup plan to provide peace of mind in case of failure
- know that there are no heroes but only survivors in the journey of entrepreneurship – they have a survival mentality
- accept that there is no shortcut to success; only hard work and persistence will ultimately determine success
- are committed 24/7 to their business.

CHAPTER 3

THE THREE BELIEFS OF ENTREPRENEURS

Entrepreneurs have certain beliefs that guide them, and which they never forget. Having certain beliefs is very important for the mind. For instance, believing in religion can help guide you in how you live your life. Similarly, with certain beliefs, entrepreneurs can set certain directions for themselves. I have summarised these into three beliefs, which are:

1. I seize opportunities where others fear failure
2. I can change the world
3. I am fearless and relish challenges.

Belief No. 1: I Seize Opportunities where Others Fear Failure

This is a very important belief, and perhaps one of the most significant aspects of a mindset that differentiates entrepreneurs from others. In Chapter 1, I wrote about how many of the most successful entrepreneurs in the world became successful because of their contrarian views. When everyone else sees failure, and when everyone else sees a lack of opportunities, entrepreneurs are able to see the opportunities. The best of entrepreneurs can seek out opportunity even in very bleak conditions.

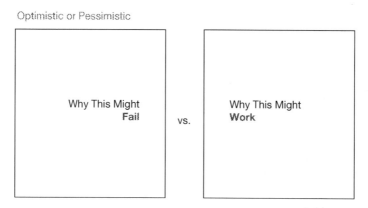

Fig. 3.1: Opportunity or Failure

Investing During Downturns

The ability to discover the right formula for success despite the worst of times makes all the difference and creates the best of entrepreneurs. For example, investing during a downturn may not necessarily be a bad thing. In fact, research has shown that some of the most resilient and good performing companies are those that started during downturns or recession years. I went back to study the start-ups that emerged in the USA during the Great Depression of 1929 and was pleased to note that many continue to be in existence almost 100 years later! In Chapter 20 titled "Surviving the Great Disruption", I focus on the Covid-19 crisis that hit the world in the year 2020 and share many examples of the resilient companies that survived and remained strong during and after the Great Depression of 1929.

My own experience has also shown me that I have been able to create very strong companies that I started during downturns. Three of the companies I founded, which are among the best performers of my portfolio of companies, were started during downturns. One, I started together with my brothers exactly when the Asian Financial Crisis hit the Asian region, in mid-1997. The impact of the Asian Financial Crisis was so severe for companies that many businesses started failing simply because of a big loss of confidence, even if the companies were still viable. The bankers pulled the plug prematurely and such companies collapsed. Many companies also defaulted on payments to creditors and banks because of the sudden devaluation of currencies, and those who borrowed in US dollars suddenly had terribly poor balance sheets. Many companies gave up and started to fold as they saw the deterioration all around.

During this period, however, my brothers and I had a great plan. My brothers had a great network of business contacts in many parts of the developing world, an area in which, until today, they continue to have expertise. Coupled with a great team that had many years of similar experience, we found immediate business opportunities.

What was lacking for us was the availability of the right level of financing. No bank was willing to finance the company even as we showed confidence in our ability to execute the plan. Everyone just saw the potential of failure, while we saw the possibility of success. Despite all the odds, and with a lot of personal sacrifice and risk, we managed to secure financing from only one bank! Now, 22 years later, we continue to grow Tri Star profitably. Tri Star later went on to survive the 2014/2015 oil crisis that crippled many countries dependent on oil to fuel their economies – particularly Angola and Nigeria, where Tri Star has the biggest business, came to a standstill. In 2021, Angola's economy is still in very bad shape, but Tri Star has survived. Companies started in a downturn are more resilient than those started during good times.

I started the second company in 1998, right in the middle of the Asian Financial Crisis too, and also at the bottom of the semiconductor cycle. So, this was a double whammy downturn. Everyone thought I was mad to start a company when there were already so many players in the same industry. Many of these companies had been around for very long periods of time and were very big players in the semiconductor industry. Very few people believed that a start-up could ever survive, and that any new entrant could ever succeed in beating the many incumbents.

As I mentioned in an earlier chapter, during the Asian Financial Crisis of 1998 many of the existing players in the industry were performing very poorly and almost all of them were bleeding badly, draining cash from their respective companies. By comparison, the company that I started in 1998, called United Test and Assembly Center (UTAC), went on to break many records and became the ninth largest in the world in a span of two and a half years, with a financial performance matching the best in industry. This company was started against many odds and at a time when many felt I would fail; many incumbents could have easily "killed" the new entrant in the industry. Today, after 21 years, although I have already exited the company, the company continues to remain fundamentally strong and I believe should be among the top five players in the world in its field. This is a company that I had created at a time which people considered the worst time possible to start a semiconductor company.

UTAC was listed on the Singapore Stock Exchange in 2004 and later purchased by some private equity firms. UTAC remains a private company at the time when this book was published. Because of the strong fundamentals that my team and I had put in place in the early years, UTAC continues to do well, having caught up with the bigger players that had existed way before I started UTAC. Again, we saw opportunities when others only saw the possibility of great disaster for any similar start-up. The opportunity we saw was the continued trend towards outsourcing by the big Integrated Device Manufacturers (IDMs). Many thought that because of the weak environment, many of these IDMs would decide to pull production back to their own factories, but what we saw was that precisely because of the weak environment, the IDMs would prepare for the next downturn by outsourcing more so that their own internal factories would be buffered from the weak industry condition as the business cycle turned southwards.

As for the third company, I started it at a time when, again, many would have considered it poor timing. This company, Infiniti Solutions, was set up after I left UTAC during the 2001 recession. When we started raising funds from venture capitalists (VCs) in July 2001, we made good progress because we had a great plan and a great team assembled. However, just before we signed on the dotted line for the VCs to commit their funds, along came September 11. All deals were off, and many VCs cancelled the deals they were considering.

My management team faced tremendous pressure in the face of great uncertainty, but we believed we could create a great company. It was in any case the worst downturn the semiconductor industry had experienced. Instead of seeing the possibility of failure, we saw many opportunities, and while others saw it as an impossible task, we were confident of executing it. What opportunity did we see at that time? We saw that in a weak environment, there would be many struggling companies, and it would be a great time to acquire some of them. Our initial strategy was to jumpstart our company by acquiring one such company that fitted in with our long-term strategy of building a global company. We made not one but two acquisitions, one in each of the first two years of our existence.

Infiniti Solutions did well too, receiving approval to list on NASDAQ in 2004. We put in great effort for the IPO process, going around the world to do a roadshow. But as luck would have it, 2004 saw another downturn for the industry and on the day of pricing our IPO, we pulled the plug and decided not to list the company. Infiniti tried to get our VC to do a follow-on investment but by that time in 2005, VCs were no longer interested in hardware and asset-based companies, focusing instead on the Apps-based start-ups. So, we at Infiniti had to continue to fund our business from our own cash as we could not find any new money.

UTAC: The Fairy Tale Start-Up

Record pace for set-up and operations:

The company commenced operations just 10 months after set-up and grew rapidly:

March 1998	Company formed
April 1998	Core management team formed
June 1998	Equipment supplier selected
July 1998	Building purchased, started renovations
August 1998	First customer secured
September 1998	Renovations completed
October 1998	First batch of equipment moved-in
November 1998	Production line qualification
December 1998	Customer qualification
January 1999	Production commenced
April 1999	Achieved profitability and cumulatively broke even
October 2000	Approved for concurrent IPO on NASDAQ and Singapore Stock Exchange

Strong revenue growth:

Revenue grew from US$4m in 1Q99 to US$23m in 4Q00, averaging between 20–30 per cent growth sequentially quarter on quarter. Starting with two customers in 1Q99, the number of customers grew to 25 by the end of the year. This included a range of top-tier customers spanning both the DRAM, Flash and Mixed-Signal/Logic communications industry; and included names like Broadcom, Marvell, Cirrus Logic, Infineon, Philips, Fujitsu, Toshiba, NEC, National Semiconductor, Lucent, M-sys, Nanya Technology, and Powerchip Semiconductor.

Very strong bottom-line performance:

The start-up was profitable from the *second month* of operations. By the second quarter of operations, the company had *cumulatively broken even since start-up*. Profit margins were one of the highest in the industry.

3Q00 performance	Revenue ($m)	Gross profit margin	Operating margin	Net margin
UTAC	21.4	34.6%	21.7%	22.0%
STATS	90.5	30.2%	14.4%	18.2%
ASE Test	120.8	40.6%	27.2%	27.2%
Amkor	648.6	27.6%	18.5%	11.2%
ASE Inc.	448.5	29.3%	19.7%	11.7%
ASAT	104.1	35.2%	25.4%	19.1%
Chip PAC	155.8	22.8%	14.8%	7.1%
SPIL	165.4	23.7%	18.7%	16.6%

We were doing quite well in Infiniti Solutions till 2008. Then came a third whammy – the Global Financial Crisis of 2008/2009. For Infiniti Solutions (and I think most companies faced the same problem) we saw business drop by around 60 per cent! We struggled to survive (I will share more on Survival Strategies in Chapters 18 and 20) and we did. We finally exited Infiniti via a trade sale in parts and did the last one in the year 2014.

For Infiniti Solutions, we survived not one but three downturns. The second and third downturns occurred just when we thought we were going to have a good upturn. Fortunately, we did not fail but managed to exit the company after a while. So, I have three companies that started during downturns – all were resilient and survived many difficult times.

Different Rules of the Game

To succeed, the entrepreneur needs to create new "rules of the game". In other words, don't just be a copycat start-up doing what other companies are already doing. You will never fully know the formulae for success of your competitors (the best chefs never share all their secret recipes). Doing the same as what others are doing will be a sure formula for failure for a new entrant in any industry. If you want to enter any industry, even if it is a crowded one, you can still win by creating new rules for that industry – new business models and differentiated strategies that can allow you to catch your competitors off-guard.

For the companies I started, despite the fact that our competitors had much stronger resources than we did, we survived. Many of our competitors didn't make it through some of the downturns we experienced. From my experience, the best of strategies is a contrarian's view of seeing opportunities when others see failure, as well as investing and starting companies in a downturn. The rules of the game can be quite different in such situations when things are looking bad for many and when others only see the negative while ignoring the positive possibilities. It is in such times when the rules of the game can be changed, and when one can create the best of opportunities, as my experience in starting three great companies has shown. The ability to discover the right formula, when everyone else is thinking alike, makes all the difference. Our formula included the survival strategy (see a later chapter for more).

Never Overdo Things

Related to this belief in seeing opportunities during times of difficulty is the philosophy of not overdoing things no matter what the industry performance or economic outlook is. There is a great tendency to over-invest in good times and under-invest in bad times. There is also a great tendency to be over optimistic in good times and over pessimistic in bad times.

The philosophy that many successful entrepreneurs follow is one of moderation, which is not to be overly optimistic in good times or overly pessimistic in bad times. One should keep the investment going in good or bad times, but my advice is, don't overdo things when everyone thinks more should be done, and don't under-do things when everyone thinks less should be done. It is quite typical to follow the herd instinct both in good and bad times, and those who win are the ones who lead the herds, not follow them. As the leaders of the herd make the first moves, not waiting to see what others do, they are the ones who get to pick the cherries first.

Never Panic

Entrepreneurs should always be prepared to invest even in a downturn, and they should not panic when the industry makes huge turns. As I described earlier, starting companies in the so-called bad times could be the best of strategies. This stems from the belief of not being overly pessimistic in bad times.

If you can plan to be in a survival mode in a downturn and keep your cash flow positive while also taking the opportunity of a slowdown to continue to update and upgrade your capability and technology, you may never have to worry about the huge gyrations of the ups and downs of a business cycle. What may seem like huge gyrations of the industry to others will look like the normal course of business for you if you follow this philosophy, because you will be doing something constructive in such a downturn. So when others start to worry and take a conservative approach in a downturn, the entrepreneurs should open their eyes wide to look for the opportunities others are not seeing. When others are enjoying an upturn, the entrepreneur should start preparing what to do for the next downturn, and how to survive it.

Another way of looking at this issue is whether the cup is half full or half empty. Most entrepreneurs see a half-filled cup as a head start, and all they have to do is to fill up the other half. They think that it could have been much worse, and the cup could have been completely empty. But even if the cup is empty, the entrepreneur will perceive an opportunity to fill up the empty cup by doing things differently. And this brings me to the second belief entrepreneurs have, which is, being optimistic and believing they can change the world.

Fig. 3.2: Perceiving Opportunities

Belief No. 2: I Can Change the World

Like what cowboys say, if it ain't broken, fix it anyway. Things have to change all the time, and if others cannot do it, I can.

This belief is what continues to drive entrepreneurs to greater heights. The fact that they could do things unimagined by others stems from this belief that they can change the world. Being optimistic, they believe they can achieve almost anything in this world, and beyond. They may seem egoistic at times, but it is this attitude that drives them to compete with giants and to change the rules of the game. They redefine the rules of engagement and how business is conducted, often catching the incumbents off guard.

Change is the Only Constant

While most people follow the principle of: "If it is not broken, don't fix it or don't meddle with it", entrepreneurs are always questioning the norm and seeking changes. It is this constant quest for change that drives entrepreneurs to innovate and come up with innovative solutions, to develop intellectual property and define new business models. They therefore believe in the exact opposite of the norm, and that is, "If it is not broken, fix it anyway". In doing so, they come up with new ideas, thereby creating new companies that become formidable enough to compete with more established companies.

> **This Present Moment** used to be the **Unimaginable Future**
>
> **Stewart Brand**
> The Clock of the Long Now

Entrepreneurs also believe that the world needs to be constantly changing. In fact, if you observe the behaviour of most entrepreneurs, they seldom thrive in a status quo environment. They actually do much better when things are constantly changing. When things stop changing, entrepreneurs become bored and look for new things to do. They also sense a challenge coming when others fail, or others fail to execute on a plan. In fact, they always feel that they can do it better than others can, when in actual fact they may not necessarily be able to do so. The most important thing is that they think they can do it, and it is this mindset that allows them to do extraordinary things, which they themselves may not have thought possible at the beginning. As mentioned earlier, according to Stewart Brand, "The present moment used to be the unimaginable future." Entrepreneurs are constantly challenging themselves as they do not see the limit of what can be achieved. Such a mindset distinguishes entrepreneurs from others. Many fail to adapt quickly to change and are not agile enough to move fast as the environment changes. Entrepreneurs are agile and adaptable.

Some very good examples of entrepreneurs who changed the world by the companies they created are Ikea that changed the way furniture is sold, Starbucks that changed the way a coffee shop operates, Microsoft that changed the world of computing; and Creative Technology that changed the world of sound for personal computers.

Belief No. 3: I Am Fearless and Relish Challenges

Sometimes, a task may seem quite dangerous, yet entrepreneurs seldom fear they will fail or be hurt when they take on the challenge of fighting against the odds. This sense of fearlessness has allowed kings, emperors, and warriors to conquer countries, coupled with the belief that they could conquer and rule the world. This same sense of fearlessness has allowed insurgents or newcomers to topple giant incumbents – entrepreneurs who come in and fight with giant companies and beat them at their game. As an example, Netflix killed Blockbuster with a completely new business model – sending videos tapes or disks by normal snail mail (compared to Blockbuster's model of in-store renting of videos) and later for Netflix, using technology – streaming of videos as a means to deliver movies. There are many such examples of how fearlessness allowed entrepreneurs to defeat larger companies.

Fearless Entrepreneurial Conquerors

In the business world, entrepreneurs see themselves as warriors and emperors, conquering the business world or their industry. Again, as we have seen in history, many emperors never really achieve their goal of ruling the world, but that did not stop them from trying. Similarly, entrepreneurs fearlessly think of conquering all. This fearless attitude and mindset keep them fighting against all odds. They will stop at nothing until they achieve their goals or until they are defeated in the process.

No emperor ever conquered the whole world but they kept trying. Similarly entrepreneurs keep going, continuously to pushing themselves to achieve greater heights. They seldom feel they have arrived at their destination. Obviously, in the process, they can and will make many enemies, particularly from their competitors, and sometimes even with their peers and some stakeholders, but this does not deter or stop them because of their great sense of confidence and fearlessness. Their behaviour may look reckless to many outsiders, yet it is a rare occasion when entrepreneurs feel they don't know what they are doing. Because they have very little fear for most things, they are able to take the most radical of steps. They are able to make the most significant changes, to the point that the ordinary person, may not understand why entrepreneurs do what they do.

Thriving in Chaotic Environments

Because entrepreneurs are fearless and desire constant change, they can thrive in chaotic environments. This does not mean they have to have a chaotic environment to operate in, but rather, when others fail in a chaotic environment, they are able to make sense of things and achieve a positive outcome.

In a non-chaotic environment, entrepreneurs sometimes feel bored, so will think of new and different ideas. They are not afraid to make changes even if others think it is better to retain the status quo. Fearlessness is a belief that guides entrepreneurs and turns them into brave warriors.

Breaking Rules

The entrepreneur is typically willing to break the rules, an aspect of their risk-taking nature. In fact, they are not afraid to break the rules in order to "test the waters".

While there may be many out of bound or OB markers on his journey, the entrepreneur is willing to push the boundaries. However, this is not usually done recklessly, but as a calculated move to find the new limits. By "testing the waters" this way, they are the first to discover new territories and discover new ways of getting things done. They discover that things are not so bad after all, even as they cross the line. This further increases their confidence to push further, becoming more and more fearless in the process.

This does not mean that everyone who crosses the line disregarding the rules gets away with it. Many may have failed in trying, were caught and punished. But those who crossed the lines and survived, created many new things and made many new discoveries. For instance, they may discover new business models or new technologies and innovative ways of doing things.

One last point regarding this issue of fearlessness, and of testing and breaking the rules is the famous NUTS or the No U-Turn Syndrome. (I must attribute this NUTS syndrome to the founder of Creative Technology, Singapore's famous entrepreneur, Mr. Sim Wong Hoo, who first used it in his book about the mindset of people in Singapore.) What NUTS basically says is that in countries where entrepreneurship thrives, people will typically assume it is okay to push the limits, unless the law explicitly says you cannot do it. So, if the rule or law does not make mention of it, then by all means go ahead and do it. In less entrepreneurial economies, the reverse mindset is true, i.e., do it only if the rule or law allows it. If the rule or law does not explicitly state it, then assume you cannot do it. This differing mindset makes a world of difference to the way people go about doing things.

Asking the Police Force to Break Rules

When I was a Member of Parliament and was known as an entrepreneur, I used to be called upon to give talks at conferences, business meetings and gatherings of entrepreneurs and to students in the universities and schools, to share my entrepreneurship experience. I was once invited by the Commissioner of Police to deliver the keynote address at the Singapore Police Force's annual planning seminar in 2003. This is what I said:

"Risk taking is also about (and I know among the police this is a risk I am taking in saying this) not following rules that do not make sense. It may be about disobeying the orders at times and then worry about explaining it later, as long as they were not ill intended or not done out of malice or not criminal like fraud and cheating. Sometimes, on the ground, you have to make a choice of fixing it if it is not broken, as opposed to fixing things only if they are broken. In other words, it is about anticipating what others did not and it is about leading changes, even if others think you are wrong, as long as you think it will lead to good things."

Now this must have shocked the Commissioner and the management of the police force, I was telling them sometimes you may have to just go beyond your protocol and SOPs, but I meant what I said. I encouraged the police to adopt an entrepreneurial mindset and to think out of the box when needed.

Well 10 years after I made my speech, in 2013, Singapore suffered the first ever riots at Little India. It was a sad day and while there are many explanations of why things went out of control that day, my assessment is that the officers on the ground were waiting for instructions and because we never experienced riots in Singapore modern times, the commanders probably did not know how to handle the situation. Perhaps the police officers on the ground should have put on their entrepreneurial hat by going against their SOPs and do what was needed to disperse the crowd and bring things under control. Such an approach might have saved the day and the police officers could explain later to the commanders why they did what they did. The frontline people could have practised greater initiative and not waited for instructions. Now this is my layman view of what could have been done on that fateful day in 2013. The authorities may not agree with me and I may even be wrong about this.

Of U-turns

On Singapore roads the U-turn sign means that vehicles can only make a U-turn when a sign tells them to do so. If there is an opening on a road divider but there is no U-turn sign, it is assumed you cannot make a U-turn. In many other countries, there is only a "no U-turn" sign to stop vehicles from making a U-turn in dangerous areas. In all other areas where there are no signs or other road markers, vehicles are free to make U-turns anywhere.

Chapter 3 Summary

The Three Beliefs of Entrepreneurs

THE THREE BELIEFS

Fig. 3.3: Three Beliefs of Entrepreneurs

Entrepreneurs are guided by three beliefs:

- I seize opportunities where others fear failure

- I can change the world

- I relish challenges.

Guided by these beliefs, entrepreneurs:

- See opportunities when others see obstacles

- Can find the right formula for success at the worst of times

- Understand that moderation is the key to success and not to be overly optimistic in good times or overly pessimistic in bad times

- Know how to change the rules of the game to compete with giants and win

- Adopt a fearless attitude and mindset, fighting against all odds to achieve goals
- Can thrive in chaotic environments
- Test boundaries, unless the law explicitly forbids.

CHAPTER 4

THE THREE REALITIES OF ENTREPRENEURSHIP

Those who choose the path of entrepreneurship must be prepared to face certain realities. I have identified three realities which entrepreneurs must come to terms with so that they can face the challenges and excel in their journey. These realities are:

1. Risks and failures are necessary
2. Creativity and innovation matter
3. Timing makes a difference.

Reality No. 1: Risks and Failures are Necessary

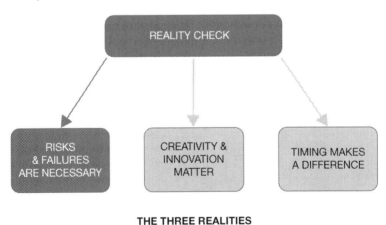

THE THREE REALITIES

Fig. 4.1: Risks and Failures

The one reality about becoming an entrepreneur and about running a company is that it is all about risks and returns, the basic building blocks of a capitalist economy. And of course, related to this is the issue of facing failure.

We often hear about how entrepreneurs are risk takers, and that without taking any risk there is little chance of becoming a successful entrepreneur. This is very true, but the question is, does taking risks automatically ensure success? Or are all risk takers entrepreneurs? To what extent should an entrepreneur take risks? Is it all about risks and nothing else? Let's examine this issue of risk which is very much misunderstood.

It's Not About Blind Risk Taking

It is important to clarify risk taken in the right context in order to understand the way entrepreneurs think. I doubt any entrepreneur would advocate blind risk taking. One does not go on a blind adventure just because he or she is an entrepreneur. Similarly, one cannot call oneself an entrepreneur just because one decides to take all sorts of risks without due consideration for the outcome. The reality is that taking blind risks only results in catastrophic failure. So, what is it about risk taking that we need to understand with regard to entrepreneurship?

Firstly, an entrepreneur is typically willing to tread into dangerous territory where others see a threat. As I mentioned previously, an entrepreneur sees opportunities and is fearless of failure when others see threats or the great possibility of failure. In that context, entrepreneurs are willing to take on more risks than others. Even if they do see a great chance of failure, they might still be willing to take that risk to create success. On the surface, it might look like reckless risk taking, but in the mind of entrepreneurs, they would have pondered the consequences and taken the steps to minimise the possibility of failing – in other words, they take a calculated risk.

The reality is that in any venture or adventure, there are all types of risks. Many people will want all existing risks to be mitigated before they explore any opportunity. Such people are rarely entrepreneurs. Some people would like to put in place measures or hedge themselves before they move in. They move in after as many of the perceived risks as possible have been reduced, and therefore increase their chances of success. Such people are good managers and will do well in managing growth once the company has gone beyond its infancy stages, but they are not the true-blue entrepreneurs. In many cases, they would have waited for others to reduce the risks or waited for circumstances to change so that the risks have been similarly reduced before they move in. These people as I said make good managers.

However there are others, who will look at the list of possible risks, and as long as they cover themselves and avoid or mitigate *some* of the risks, will go ahead. Entrepreneurs take on the task of starting something new or changing things by challenging the status quo or the incumbents. All the risks that can be reduced will be reduced or removed while those that still exist will be addressed as they move along. This is how entrepreneurs start their journeys – addressing some risks but not wait for all to be addressed.

True entrepreneurs, however, will not stop doing what they do even when the risks they have identified are not yet resolved. They may change direction, but they do not stop and wait for things to clear up. They, of course, will actively seek to clear up the issues themselves – to solve the problems or remove the obstacles (the "no problem that cannot be solved" mindset). However, if there is a full minefield of risks ahead of the entrepreneur, it does not mean that he or she will ignore them and do nothing about it. The reality is that entrepreneurs do not take blind risks. They will only move if they are sure that they have at least cleared for themselves a path to tread after they have addressed some of the risks.

Entrepreneurs, unlike most people, do not require all the possible risks and issues to be completely resolved before starting on the entrepreneurial journey. In order to move forward, they only need to resolve "just enough" which is typically of a level much lower than that of non-entrepreneurs. As I mentioned, the entrepreneurs will continue to address the rest of the risk factors as they move along their journey. As they get started, they keep an eye on the risks that were not addressed, but do not allow those other risk factors to stop or slow them down – unless along the way some of these risk factors become so high and greatly threaten the possibility of success.

In summary, the big difference, therefore, between an entrepreneur and a non-entrepreneur is that the entrepreneur is willing to live with a few risks (but not all the risks). His or her threshold of risk taking is much higher, and the first move to start is made even if the risks are not fully addressed.

Handling Failure as It Happens

It is very rare for an entrepreneur not to plan for failure. In fact, typically, most are aware of the impact of failure on their lives and that of their families. They are, however, prepared to face the consequences of failure. Their threshold of how they handle a failed life is a lot higher than that of non-entrepreneurs. They are willing to accept a much bleaker alternative and are willing to start again simply because they believe in themselves even if it means doing the most basic jobs to support the family after their failed attempt.

The unfortunate thing about entrepreneurship is that people in general seldom realise that the possibility of failure is much higher than the chance of success for any venture. Because only the successful ventures are publicised and failed ventures rarely discussed openly, others may think becoming an entrepreneur is easy. They therefore may not realise all the risks, and may fail to address these before moving forward, resulting in being blind-sided, and failing because of their lack of preparation, especially in sufficiently addressing risk factors before starting. This is one area that can stifle the promotion of entrepreneurship – high failure rates because people do not understand the reality about risk taking.

One of the reasons many start-ups fail is the lack of awareness of the strong possibility of failure and what should have been done to address failure of execution. And when failure actually happens because of the lack of preparation at the start, people may not realise why they failed. The negative outcome of this will be that the people who failed this way will become much more conservative after an incident of failure and will then not be willing to try again.

The reality is that those who try again after a failure are the ones who will have a better chance of success the next time round, simply because they will have a better picture of why they failed and be more realistic in their future planning. This is of course based on the premise that they learned from their past mistakes and failures. We all know that for every success there are many failures, perhaps up to 10 or 20 times more. Knowing the reality of risk and failure can help entrepreneurs do better by being more prepared before they start.

The Tri Star Story

In early 1997, my brothers and I decided to start our own company based on my brother's expertise and knowledge. However, we knew it was difficult to start because to run a trading company, we would need substantial funds. In his assessment the minimum requirement was way beyond what our family members raise. Undeterred, I felt we could at least start small, but I also agreed that a minimum sum was needed for the business to be viable.

We counted our savings and asked my parents and sister if they could contribute. They agreed. I offered all my savings, and because we were still far from the minimum needed, I also put up my house as security to obtain trade financing facilities. Next, we looked for bank financing. Coincidentally, it was the beginning of the Asian Financial Crisis, and no bank was willing to risk funding a start-up, especially one that already had so many competitors in an industry with a low barrier to entry. By pledging my house, we managed to convince just one bank to finance us, and that too, only after we had put all of our life savings as a deposit with the bank. The consequence of failure would have been the loss of my house. Looking back, it may have seemed reckless, as I had not even considered where my family would go should the bank decide to acquire the house in the event of a business failure. However, the thought of failure was not foremost in my mind. It was my belief that we could create a big successful company. I am glad the plan paid off. Tri Star has been doing fine despite the Asian Financial Crisis and the two subsequent recessions that have hit Singapore since. We expect to survive the Covid-19 global debacle, too.

Culture and Environment

The issue of risk taking is also related to culture and environment. If we study the level of entrepreneurial activity in different countries, we can see that entrepreneurship development varies according to how the country's economic environment has been developed and structured, the culture of society, and how failure is viewed and treated.

For example, in a country where the cost of living is very high and there are very few lifestyle alternatives, failing can be such a big burden and loss that the threshold for taking risks increases greatly. The cost of failure is so high that getting back to even the basics of life becomes too painful. In such an environment, entrepreneurship development can become problematic as opposed to an environment in which one can easily pick oneself up and take on a cheaper and more frugal alternative for living if one loses all assets as a result of a failure. Similarly, if the model of success lies in getting a stable government job or working in a big established company as an executive, fewer people will tread the path of entrepreneurship, since it is not considered "respectable". Anything other than the "safe and admired" jobs are considered unattractive and just too risky. This is the big issue Singapore faces because the cost of failure is very high due to the very high cost of living. The model of success as propagated by the government is one where a person who is a government scholar is rewarded the most. This leads people to develop a mindset of taking up a "safe career" in government or big Government Linked Companies (GLCs) or big MNCs.

The issue of tolerance to failure is another important factor in developing the risk-taking attitude of entrepreneurs. How society treats those who fail and whether failure is celebrated or frowned upon will make a big difference in whether people will be willing to take more or fewer risks. In countries where failure does not push entrepreneurs to great hardship, we see many more willing to try again and do another start-up. Societies that consider failure as part of a journey and not the end of the journey thereby remove any stigma of failure.

However, in countries where societies treat failure as the end, people are less willing to take risks because of the high cost of failure. For example, countries where bankruptcy laws are very onerous (as in Singapore which severely punishes the person made bankrupt for a business failure), society will develop risk aversion.

The day you seem to have failed is the day people make you look like a failure. They look at you differently. But entrepreneurs must not make the mistake of looking at themselves differently, and entrepreneurs should not be influenced or affected by how others see them. Entrepreneurs should see failure and success with equanimity, treat failure as part of the process, and never lose sight of their goals and objectives. Entrepreneurs have to keep on trying, and the day they fail is the same day they restart the whole process and start a new entrepreneurial journey.

Reality No. 2: Creativity and Innovation Matter

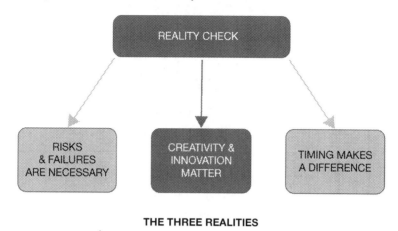

THE THREE REALITIES

Fig. 4.2: Creativity and Innovation

Thinking Out-of-the-Box and Transforming Ideas into Businesses

Entrepreneurship is synonymous with creativity and innovation. You need both creativity and innovativeness to be a successful entrepreneur. One of these traits alone will not ensure success. Most people have always thought of creativity and innovation as one and the same, but I see these two attributes a little differently. I will now elaborate and explain the subtle difference.

The only reason one can be called a successful entrepreneur is because he or she has been able to create something out of nothing and is able to overcome the odds to create a successful business. There are two steps necessary in creating successful businesses or in completing successful projects. The first is getting that bright spark or the idea, which is of course quite difficult to do and does not happen to everyone. The second is putting a realistic and executable plan together with the right resources to execute the plan. To do all this, the entrepreneur requires both a creative mind as well as an analytical mind – the creative mind to conceive the bright idea, and the analytical mind to transform the idea into a business with disciplined execution of plans to achieve particular goals. It is therefore incorrect to think that entrepreneurship is only about creativity.

Creativity

Creativity has a lot to do with a curious mind and a mind that thinks out-of-the-box. Curiosity leads to experiment with different ideas and alternatives. Curious people think about things others will not normally think about. They are willing to question the status quo. They ask questions differently from others. Instead of just asking, "Why?" they typically also ask, "Why not?" By not placing a limit on what they can do or think of, and by not practising self-censorship of their mind, they are able to come up with ideas that very few can dream of. Talking about dreams, yes, creative people have to be dreamers, and they dream of not just airy-fairy things, but also about ideas that can revolutionise industries, economies, countries, and even the world.

Innovation

Innovation is related to having an analytical mind. It is an innovative mind that transforms the ideas into a business model and then into a business plan and strategies. The business plan which covers many areas also consists of clear, itemised and executable plans, which can also be easily communicated not only with people involved in a start-up, but also with potential investors, employees, board members, customers and suppliers – in short, one that can be understood by all the venture's stakeholders.

Being innovative also requires one to be thinking out-of-the-box all the time, creating new business strategies and new business models and using whatever resources at their disposal to achieve success. This will require nothing less than unconventional thinking. To do all of these well, the entrepreneur needs to be innovative – having an ability to analyse, develop structured ways of doing new things, develop new capabilities, and apply new ideas in new ways. These are things an analytical mind does best. So innovative thinking is the next step after creativity or after conceiving an idea, and innovation is what really creates a successful entrepreneur. An innovative mind is needed when an entrepreneur has to solve problems along the way, especially when things do not happen according to plan. Entrepreneurs have to be innovative problem solvers to overcome obstacles affecting the business. Creativity alone will not help solve problems. Employing an innovative mind to use creative ideas is what entrepreneurs do best.

Reality No. 3: Timing Makes a Difference

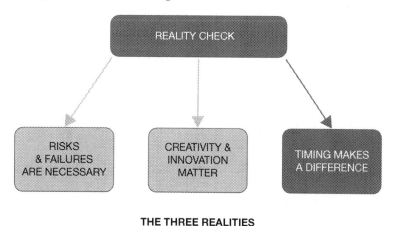

THE THREE REALITIES

Fig. 4.3: Timing

In Chapter 5, "The Alignment of Your Stars" I discuss why your stars must be aligned before you can achieve success. But before I touch on this, I would like to share one very important reality for everyone. This reality is one of whether or not the timing is right for you. We can call it luck, or we can call it a skill of identifying the right timing to start and grow a company, or for that matter, to do anything in life.

Often, I have seen good people with very good ideas putting in the best of efforts, but still end up failing to create something significant. Unfortunately, this is the stark reality of life.

Is Lady Luck Shining?

Some look out for a star that is shining brightly for them. What they really mean is that they are looking for the right timing. Is it a skill that can be acquired – the skill of identifying the right timing to do the right thing? I would like to say, yes; to a certain extent, skilled entrepreneurs are able to sense and look out for the best opportunities. They can then plan and time the execution of their work to achieve the best possible outcome at the best possible time. This is what I will elaborate on in the next chapter.

For example, I could have started UTAC much earlier in the year 1995 or 1996, but I waited till the end of 1997 to start the company. I started planning for UTAC way back in early 1995, writing my business plan that year while keeping an eye on the developments in the semiconductor industry. I waited for the right timing as I had analysed that anything earlier would have been the wrong timing for such a company. In the case of UTAC, I was right, and the company went on to be one of the best in the industry – it was a fairy tale start-up by all accounts. But having said that, there is always one last element of timing, which I feel nobody can see or predict.

No matter how well one plans or how hard one tries, there are many examples of when the timing turns out to be wrong. And this is because that one element (and I don't know how to define this element) of timing was missing. It is best to simply accept the reality that it was not meant to be, and that one should look beyond the current situation rather than lament over whatever one may call it – bad luck, bad timing, the stars not shining, or any other negative thoughts. In other words, accept that changes have to be made rather than to try to press on when the timing is dead wrong.

If the entrepreneur can accept this reality, it will be easier to accept an incidence of failure and move on to find success in another way or at another time. I always believe that things do not remain static. Time changes things, and as the saying goes, "every dog will have its day". It is best to move on and consider any failure a lesson learnt as part of what is needed for a long journey before eventual success can be achieved.

Light at the End of the Tunnel

I always like to think that there will be light at the end of the tunnel and that everything happens for a purpose. Most importantly, when things do not turn out as planned or timing is not right, it is probably a blessing in disguise, and you should move on. The star of the timing will eventually shine upon you and you will find the time is right.

My Experiences with Timing

Let me share a couple of stories about timing which I experienced with two of my companies, UTAC and Tri Star Electronics.

UTAC achieved excellent performance within such a short time that we attracted the attention of a number of bulge bracket firms ("Bulge bracket" is a slang term that describes the company or companies in an underwriting syndicate that issues the largest number of securities on a new issue) that wanted to lead our IPO plans by the end of the year 2000 (in our third year of existence!). We chose Solomon Smith Barney as our lead investor and hired the best USA and Singapore legal firms and advisers to prepare for the IPO. But our lead underwriter slowed us down and instead put another semiconductor firm ahead of us, thus causing us to delay our listing.

We then removed the lead and hired another bulge bracket firm to replace them – Morgan Stanley. We worked hard and got approval to concurrently list on NASDAQ and the Singapore Stock Exchange by 4Q2000. As we were preparing for the listing, as luck might have it, the tech bubbles started showing weakness and by April 2001 had burst. We missed the window for an IPO because tech companies took a long time to become attractive to investors again. Timing wise, had our first lead manager not delayed UTAC's listing because they wanted to bring another firm ahead of us, we could have raised money before the tech bubble burst. On hindsight, perhaps we should have done better due diligence and not chosen the wrong lead underwriter. Our IPO listing might then have been completed by the end of 2000.

Tri Star Electronics also saw a phenomenal growth after its inception in 1997. The company saw revenue growth every year and in 2014 the total group sales in Singapore and our overseas units was around US$300m. Tri Star was not funded by any VCs, just family money and support by banks. Something happened in 2014 that many did not realise had a great impact on a number of countries in Africa. The oil price dropped from a peak of US$115 in June 2014 to below US$50 by the end of 2014 and continued to drop to around US$30 by 2016. This devastated the economies of those countries that were highly dependent on oil for their economic growth. Two badly hit countries were Angola and Nigeria, both big oil producing countries. And these two countries were also our two major revenue generators for the previous few years. When the oil prices dropped, so did the currency value drop for both these countries.

When the crisis hit, our management team contemplated what to do – quickly exit and extract our money or wait. Based on our past experience of Africa, we decided to wait. That was a decision that impacted us quite badly and resulted in losses due to the huge erosion of currencies and our inability to remit money back to Singapore.

Many companies, not just Tri Star, were hit badly. Many collapsed, but Tri Star went through a very rough patch. Nevertheless, four years later, by 2019, Tri Star managed to recover (we are planning to survive the Covid-19 crisis at the time of writing this book). On hindsight, we should have acted fast and not waited and brought back our money fast – "money in hand is worth two in the bush".

Never give up, and never think you will never find a right timing for yourself. Believe that you will eventually have your day in the sun and your glory will come. There is no point in lamenting; it will just slow you down with negative thoughts. The true entrepreneur should never give up trying. As the saying goes, "do not cry over spilt milk" when things do not turn out as planned. The milk may be gone, but you should look for new milk. Try, try again, and again.

Some people seem to have all the luck and get the glory and credit for things that other people have already done, while others who work very hard and are actually really good at what they do, seem to have no luck and fail to achieve the ultimate success. Yes, I have seen many people who seemingly so effortlessly attain glory – many times, as a result of other people's hard work. They happen to be in the right place at the right time. And there are those who have to work very hard, yet are not credited for what they have achieved – yet someone else comes along to take the credit for their efforts.

If it is not meant to be at a certain point of time, then it is not meant to be. But I believe the world comes full circle. Although you cannot change things, you should never give up, as everyone will have their chance and their success. It may come at a different time and in a different way. It's simply difficult to decide when the timing is right.

Sometimes you may have to cut your losses and move on. Yet sometimes to give up prematurely is also wrong, as success may be just around the corner, and the calm may come after the storm.

It is a judgement call that entrepreneurs have to make, and the good ones are typically right. A little pressing on could have converted the wrong timing into a right one and giving up would be such a big waste. It is a tough call, so think and act, and then don't ever regret.

The Three Realities of Entrepreneurship

Entrepreneurs must face three realities:
1. Risks and failures are necessary

2. Creativity and innovation matter

3. Timing makes a difference.

- Entrepreneurs do not take blind risks. They will only move if they have at least cleared for themselves a path to tread on after they have addressed some of the identified risks.

- The big difference between an entrepreneur and a non-entrepreneur is that the entrepreneurs are willing to live with a few risks (but not all the risks).

- An entrepreneur's threshold of risk taking is much higher than a non-entrepreneur's, and they will make their first move even if the risks are not fully addressed.

- Culture and societal attitudes towards failures affect the level of risk taking among entrepreneurs.

- Creativity is about having a curious mind that allows one to experiment with different ideas and alternatives. Instead of just asking, "Why?" they typically also ask, "Why not?"

- Innovation is related to having an analytical mind that can transform ideas into strategies, strategies into a business model, and a business model into a business plan.

- Creativity and an innovative mindset are essential for entrepreneurship, but it is innovation that makes businesses successful. A creative mind thinks of the ideas but is not necessarily able to implement the ideas and convert them into a business. The innovative mind takes the creative ideas and thinks of ways to convert these ideas into businesses.

- Timing makes the difference between success and failure in business. A good idea and a good business plan with the best strategies and efforts will not create success unless the element of timing is right.

CHAPTER 5

THE ALIGNMENT OF YOUR STARS

To ensure success, the stars need to be aligned. What do I mean by the alignment of stars? It is said that hard work is only 50 per cent of a success formula, while the other 50 per cent depends on your luck. I used the term "alignment of stars" in the previous chapter, and I will now explain what this means. I am sure the first thing that might have come to mind was that I must be referring to this thing called LUCK. You might wonder, "Is Lady Luck with me this time?"

Some people consult astrologers and priests to advise if their stars are aligned, if it is time for them to embark on something new, like getting married, starting a family, or making an important trip. Astrologers might also be asked for an auspicious day to start a new business. *Feng shui* experts or geomancers can advise on a location for a place of business, the seating arrangements, and how to decorate the rooms. It might have crossed your mind that these are examples of "alignment of stars". But no, this is not what I meant.

Feng Shui at Work

When I started UTAC, many of my investors and partners were Taiwanese, while one was a large Singapore government-owned company with a Singaporean Chinese at the helm. When we bought a building to operate our business, this large Singapore Government Linked Company (GLC) sent a geomancer to look at the building and to advise me if it was right for the company. I was surprised when the *feng shui* expert gave me his name card, which showed him to be an employee of this GLC. I almost couldn't believe that the GLC had actually employed someone specifically to look at these things. This geomancer decided where I should sit, the kind of decoration I should use, and more significantly, he asked us to break up a solid concrete fence to create a new gate for me to drive in and out. When I told the Taiwanese about this, they told me they believe not in *feng shui* to achieve success, but in hard work. However, to please everyone, I said to myself, why not and I decided to follow the instructions of the *feng shui* master. The things I did – broke down the fence, created a new gate, installed a small fishpond in front of the building, built my office at a designated place, and started the renovation work before the Chinese Ghost month, which began in August 1998 – all for good luck. I did what I did to keep everyone's peace of mind and it didn't hurt me a bit.

My idea about the alignment of stars is a little more scientific than the examples quoted. But before I elaborate on this, I would just like to say that doing all the things I mentioned, like seeing an astrologer and geomancer are all personal beliefs. If you believe these need to be done, then by all means proceed with peace of mind that is so critical when you embark on your tough journey ahead as an entrepreneur. So, consult your *feng shui* master if that is what you want to do to feel comfortable.

Stars as Ingredients of Success

So what stars am I talking about? The stars I am talking about here are basically the necessary ingredients for your business to succeed. Depending on how the business model is developed, there can be differing ingredients needed to increase your chances of success.

Each of us may have differing views as to what ingredients we believe are necessary in achieving success. Of course, different types of businesses and business models will definitely have differing success factors or ingredients that will determine success. Let's look at the example of starting a restaurant – what are the key success factors for a restaurant business. There may be many but at least these three should be included:

1. Good Cook and Good Recipes – These are the most important: without good tasting food, customers will never come back.

2. Good Location – You must be in a location with good traffic, not one that is in an isolated place.

3. Good Customer Service – You want customers to have a good experience and to come back and to recommend others.

Unless all or most of the above three factors exist, your chances of a successful restaurant are greatly diminished.

The starting point for any entrepreneur, therefore, is to identify the success factors for the venture being considered – what is the business model and the key drivers that will create a successful business. Once you have identified these ingredients or drivers for success, start the business when and if all these ingredients (or most of them) are in place, in order to increase the chances of success. The more the number of necessary ingredients that are in place, the greater will be the chances of success. Identifying the right ingredients or success factors is thus the most important task for a good entrepreneur.

I prefer to define all these factors or ingredients needed for achieving success as the **Stars** needed for the business being started. If you do not know what the **Stars** for your business are, then I am afraid you will not have much chance of success since you will not know whether the necessary conditions for success are in place. For instance, how can you possibly create a successful company if you do not know what is needed to construct the whole business model? At least the very critical elements must first be in place before you can expect the business to take off.

So, before you start on your entrepreneurial journey, you must identify the necessary ingredients or **Stars** for your type of business. You must at least have a mental model of what these **Stars** are. Just as it is necessary to have all the right ingredients present in the right amounts and added in the right order for a dish to come out right, it is similarly necessary for all the success factors to be present in the right order at the right time for the business to come out all right. And having all these right factors in the right order is what I mean by the "**Alignment of Stars**".

Before starting the company, all the stars must be fully aligned, otherwise the company will not be off to a good start. After you have begun your journey of starting the company, you must ensure that all the stars continue to be aligned. Things change all the time and some of the factors that existed when you started your business may no longer be relevant as the business environment changes. Even if all your **Stars** were aligned when you started your company, make sure you keep monitoring to ensure all or most of the **Stars** remained aligned throughout your journey. As long as the stars are aligned, your chances of success are much higher. If any one or a few of the stars are not aligned or are missing, then the chances of your success will be greatly reduced. You will then have to pause and understand what needs to be done in order to realign as many stars as possible. Often, people get so caught up in what they do that they don't pay attention to the status of their stars. A misalignment of **Stars** may lead to eventual failure if the entrepreneur cannot identify what went wrong and rectify it.

No matter what type of business you are in, there are in my opinion, three very **Basic Stars** that must exist, and that must, at all times, be aligned. If you lose sight of any one of them, be prepared for a rough ride.

Basic Star No. 1: The Star of Opportunity

The first questions you should ask are these: Is there really an opportunity for you in the business you are trying to create? Can the market absorb your product or service and your new company, or are there already too many

STAR OF
OPPORTUNITY

STAR OF
TEAM

STAR OF
INVESTOR

ALIGNMENT OF YOUR STARS

Fig. 5.1: Star of Opportunity

players? Is yours a solid plan that can convert the opportunities into a real business?

In the dot.com days, there were many copycat entrepreneurs. There were already many players, and many more tried to compete in a particular space of an industry. The result was that all those without the fundamental market and strategy failed. Many entrepreneurs during those days did not properly identify the real opportunity yet they started companies. But as we all know, if there is no real opportunity, you will fail.

You must ensure you know the industry and the market environment. Be convinced there is a real opportunity for your company to tap, in the markets you want to compete in. If it is an existing industry, the market must be able to handle a new entrant. Sometimes, entering into a crowded market with a new business model that creatively destroys existing business models and existing incumbent companies may work. This simply means the **Star of Opportunity** is still there for a new company. Whether it is a new product, a substitute product, a new technology, or a new market, wisdom and experience should tell you that you cannot assume you have something that the market will immediately accept and adopt, for it is never so easy. Your ability to identify business opportunities is very important, without which your venture will become a non-starter. Your business and the market must be aligned to what is really needed and what people want.

We have witnessed companies that mistakenly assume technology alone would make a product a success while the actual outcome might have been that the market was not really ready to accept this new product. The technology might be great, but as long as the market is not ready for it, and as long as the market opportunity has not been fully developed, it means the **Star of Opportunity** was not aligned to your technology. The actual outcome might be a failed product launch. Unless there a real opportunity determined by the market, you might not be successful. Or your company might require a much longer time to take off, longer than set out in your business plan. You, of all people, need to be convinced that there is really an opportunity for what you are trying to establish. If you yourself are not convinced, you will not be able to convince the other stakeholders to join you. I will explain who these critical stakeholders are when I discuss my next two basic stars.

Compared to when I wrote the first edition of this book in 2007, today there are many tools available to help one better identify a market opportunity. This book has a chapter dedicated to this. Let me briefly talk about how entrepreneurs can develop a product-market fit before starting a full blown company. A product-market fit refers to the extent to which the product satisfies the market or customer needs or demand. In other words, a company can gather early information as to how well the product will be accepted by the market and the customers, when launched. One of the tools used to do early stage market validation is the Business Model Canvas (BMC). This tool is jointly created by Alex Osterwalder, a Swiss business model guru, and Professor Yves Pigneur. The BMC helps identify the value proposition which is a measure of the clear benefits that the product or service brings to the consumers.

The other good reference on how to do the product-market fit is the book *The Lean Startup* by Eric Ries. The book shares the structured methodology that one can use to identify the Star of Opportunity, the Minimum Viable Product (MVP). This refers to the basic version of a product which will allow the start-up to gather enough information about the customers' preferences with the least amount of effort.

So today, we have many tools available to help you identify your **Star of Opportunity.**

Entrepreneurship is About True Belief

Now that you know the **Star of Opportunity** is necessary for you to get started, it also follows that entrepreneurship is not about doing fancy things or about people trying their luck and hoping they will be lucky enough to make it (although I did talk about some people having all the luck and appearing in the right place at the right time). Entrepreneurship has to be about a true belief that what the entrepreneur is planning is going to be a true winner. It is about a belief that the product or service being planned will be able to sell well and be readily accepted. It is about being able to compete effectively with many incumbents – existing competitors, existing products and services being substituted, and customer preferences, amongst others.

True entrepreneurship is not about copying others and hoping you will succeed just because others have. It is not about an emotional outburst resulting in someone starting a company without long-term plans. It is not about a transient activity nor a part-time hobby which does not interest the market.

The **Star of Opportunity** is really there if the entrepreneur sees the long-term viability of the project, is strongly committed to it, and has the passion to make the project succeed. Above all, the **Star of Opportunity** must fit in with what the market and the consumers want, and it must be about the company making real revenues and profits. Anything less than what I have mentioned will mean that the **Star of Opportunity** does not really exist and therefore the chances of the project taking off will be very slim.

Basic Star No. 2: The Star of the Team

Once you have correctly identified the opportunities and believe there is space for your business, the next question is, do you have the right people

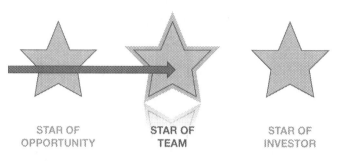

ALIGNMENT OF YOUR STARS

Fig. 5.2: Star of the Team

and enough of the right people to join you in your venture? This important ingredient for success, called the people or the team, is my second necessary star, the **Star of the Team**.

You Can't Do It All by Yourself

Starting and growing a company to become a significant player is never about doing it alone. It is always about a group of people coming together as a team, moving in the same direction, believing in each other, and having the same frequency to become integrated enough to look like one lean and mean fighting machine. You have to create this fighting machine because in any new venture you have to fight many battles with your competitors, many of whom have been around for a long time and are well entrenched as incumbents. Without a solid and integrated team, and without everyone believing in each other, the team can crumble under pressure and fail to execute a start-up.

Often, there are start-ups that depend on only one person. This is fine for a small "provision shop" type or a "mom and pop" type of business, which does not aspire to grow beyond the neighbourhood. This will, however, never work for anyone who wants to build a world-class business capable of competing with the many existing players.

You Need a Diversified and Integrated Team

I mentioned earlier and will again cover more about this point – an idea alone is not a business. The idea needs to be converted to a proper business model. When the start-up is formed, the business operates in many dimensions with many operating units – including those for technology, marketing, operations, and finance. We all know that no one person can do all the above effectively. The entrepreneur needs to have an idea of most of these but can't possibly be an expert in everything. Even the best entrepreneurs may have strengths in a few of these domain areas, but seldom do they have excellent skills in all the areas of business. Therefore, unless the entrepreneur can assemble a well-diversified but integrated team, it is unlikely the start-up will be able to grow quickly to become a world-class company.

What do I mean by a well-diversified and integrated team? The members of the team should complement each other. Not everyone needs to have the same strengths. No one is perfect in this world, and while they may have some weaknesses, as long as their strengths can help create a strong team, the entrepreneur should focus on how to tap the strengths, and at the same time handle the weaknesses.

In Chapter 1, I briefly used an analogy of the hand to describe the kind of strength you can achieve through a diversified team. Not all five fingers of the hand are the same. On its own, each finger can only do certain functions, but when all the fingers come together to form a hand, there is great strength, and many more things can be done with a complete hand. With any one finger missing, the hand's strength is diminished. So, the first thing about an integrated team is that the combined strength of the team should be far greater than the individual strengths added together. The team must derive great synergy when they are together.

The second aspect about a good integrated team is that, if the team had worked together before, it will be easier to convince other stakeholders, especially potential investors, that indeed the team will be able to work together and execute the start-up well. While this is not always possible, it is best that at least the core members of the team should already know each other before they start their company. The advantage is that they do not have to then spend time getting used to each other.

As we all know, there are many stages to the formation of a team, from the time the team starts working together until everyone gets comfortable working together to achieve continuous good results. If we look at the many successful companies around the world, we can identify a core group of people who would already have worked together before they started a company. In fact, many are good friends and are therefore able to handle the stressful times together on their entrepreneurial journey. Running a start-up is not easy. Everyone is under pressure most of the time. Unless the team can handle the stress, it can disintegrate very quickly.

The third aspect of an integrated team is that the members will already know what needs to be done in running the company. For example, in a manufacturing company, if the operations person already knows what is expected of him and the engineering person already knows what needs to be done, no one needs to be given instructions all the time. When a task is given, each of the team members will immediately do their part without spending too much time checking with the rest. At the same time, when team members perform their task, they will already know that the others will similarly do their part without worrying that someone will drop the ball along the way. This is possible because of the trust the team members have in each other and the trust they have in each other's abilities. This trust, which typically takes a long time to build up, is possible because the integrated team members have already, in the past, worked together for some time and built their confidence in each other. This way, like clockwork, the team can execute things in a very short span of time.

The other point to look out for when forming a team is this – don't get all "yes-men" to join you. This will lead to group thinking which will not be useful for the start-up because there would be no diversity of ideas and no one challenging one another. Ideally, as mentioned in an earlier chapter, the entrepreneur should identify who among them is the "Dreamer, the Thinker and the Doer". You will need all three attributes to build a strong integrated team who knows where their contribution is most valuable. While the best entrepreneur may have all three attributes, you will still need to have others in your team who can complement and supplement your input to start and scale up your new venture.

The **Star of the Team** is definitely a necessary condition for the execution of the business plan and for the running of a successful company. Failure to put a good team together will rarely excite potential investors. A good plan with a poor team can lead to failure, whereas a poor plan with a good team can still result in success.

Basic Star No. 3: The Star of the Investor

The third important basic star is: Do you have the right mode of financing or the right type of investors? Are the investor's interests aligned with yours? Is the money you are getting Smart Money?

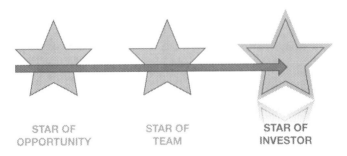

STAR OF OPPORTUNITY   STAR OF TEAM   **STAR OF INVESTOR**

ALIGNMENT OF YOUR STARS

Fig. 5.3: Star of the Investor

Choose the Right Investors

What do I mean by Smart Money? It is my belief that if you have a solid plan and a good team, you already have the first two basic stars aligned and you will be able to attract the money. The money will simply smell or sniff you out. This is true even in the less vibrant entrepreneurial economies around the world. In any corner of the world, no matter how harsh the environment might be for entrepreneurship, companies will be able to attract the financing needed if the plan is good, and especially if the team running the company is good. The entrepreneur should therefore be more selective in choosing the right investors for the business.

If you have a solid plan and you have a strong faith in your ability to execute because you have a good team behind you and the opportunities are very clear to you, then you can be sure that you will be able to find money to support you. You should never compromise on the type of investor you want to bring in to join you. If all of your other stars are strongly aligned, investors will look for you, so you should not fear being unable to find the money. Be prepared to look beyond your shores if you have to, like I did when I was trying to start UTAC.

Seek out an investor or financier who will add value to your company and who can bring more than money to the table. Do not jump in at the first sign of money waving at you. In the dot.com days, there were many instances of "not so smart money" chasing after gold, resulting in an almost corrupted system where projects that had no chance to make it were funded at ridiculous valuations. As I said, investors should bring more than money to the table. They could help in many areas, including providing expertise your team may not have, a reputation that backs your company, a network of business deals, and many others. It is this type of currency, in addition to the hard cash the investor provides, that brings on board a number of other value-added factors we call **Smart Money**.

Besides value, it is also important that the investors and the team are well aligned and have the same objectives. Otherwise, if you and your investors start having divergent objectives, it can become a living nightmare with investors breathing down your neck at every turn of your business and with every move you make.

The question therefore is this: Are all of you, the stakeholders in the company, operating on the same frequency? Therefore, the final star, the **Star of the Smart Money** or the **Star of the Investor** is necessary for you to fuel your growth and help smoothen your way. The **Star of the Investor** must be aligned, because if it is not, it will become an obstacle to the other two stars you have already aligned, thus stifling your growth. There have been cases where investors and the entrepreneur moved in different directions resulting in an ugly situation of deadlocks and legal fights. Everyone ends up a loser in such a scenario. Never rush for the money from the first person who comes along but wait and choose the money carefully. Ensure you can work well with each other before proceeding to build a partnership.

The Star of Investor

I personally learnt a useful lesson when I started UTAC. UTAC was basically an initiative I had been planning for many years before I actually executed it. In late 1994, I began planning the start-up. Along the way, I was introduced to a number of Taiwanese investors who became interested to invest. This, of course, was my first start-up, and I had no experience on how to attract investors, how to value a company, what amount of money I should raise, and many other things an experienced entrepreneur should know. Because the plan was convincing, these key Taiwanese investors courted me very keenly, and I allowed them to coordinate the fund-raising process in Taiwan without placing any conditions. I had little choice because there were mainly sceptics in Singapore who did not believe my team could pull off a start-up, and therefore very few Singapore-based investors were willing to commit any funds.

To cut a long story short, because I did not pay attention to the quality and number of investors I was dealing with, I ended up raising US$138m all at one go, much to my team's and my disadvantage. We had 40 investors, big and small, and as I had gotten too comfortable due to the excellent "courtship" displayed by the potential investors, I had neglected to protect my team's position. (Later in this book, I talk about the VC Trap, and I urge all entrepreneurs to be aware of this before they seek investors for their start-ups.)

So, when the company started operations, my team achieved record-breaking results, which impressed the investors. They made comments like, "This is one of the best start-ups we have ever participated in, and the results are beyond our expectations." Because the same investors had also invested in a similar company in Taiwan, and one of them was running that same company, another investor actually asked him, "How does it feel when the little brother (meaning me), does better than the bigger brother (meaning the investor running the company in Taiwan)?" They sang mighty praises. But when the crunch came, and the company faced a critical situation, requiring more funds after an aborted IPO, the investors' true colours emerged. In brief, the level of professionalism my team and I displayed did not mean very much to some investors who wanted to do things for their own good even if it meant disadvantaging all the other shareholders. The final outcome was disastrous – I had to leave my own start-up company, one that I created. I will talk about why I had to leave my own company UTAC a little later. But the fault was mainly mine, as I had not done my due diligence to ensure that the Star of the Investor was aligned to what I aimed for.

To be fair, the key investors in UTAC were gung-ho, knew how to judge the opportunity, and could make decisions fast. This was something I was comfortable with. However, getting an alignment of minds, of operating philosophies, and of certain professional and ethical standards are actually very important things to look out for in an investor. When choosing an investor, it's important to ask if everyone will be able to work with each other in both good and bad times. So, when we started Infiniti Solutions, my team was very clear about choosing the right type of investors and also about limiting the number of investors to one or two, or at most three. If we could not get our Star of the Investor aligned, we would not embark on the start-up.

Other Stars

What I have described are three very basic stars, and as I mentioned earlier, there can be many more stars necessary for the entrepreneur to create a successful business. These other stars are the other necessary ingredients, which have to be added together to form a company or a business. Some of these stars are the necessary technology, the necessary location, the necessary regulatory environment, and similar things.

Each business will have its own unique, basic requirements of critical success factors, and the entrepreneur has to be able to identify these correctly. So there can be more than the three basic necessary stars I described here, which need to be present and aligned before a business can be successfully executed. For example, to start a restaurant business, the location has to be a necessary star, and so too the team (i.e. the cooks, the restaurant manager, and other key staff). Or in another example, the regulatory environment will become a basic star, should one want to start a banking business in a country. Without getting the necessary approvals from the government, it is impossible to start a business.

In summary, each business will have its own unique stars, and the entrepreneur must do a good job in identifying all of these as early as possible. The better the task in identifying all the necessary stars, the higher the chances of success for the start-up.

Make Sure the Stars Remain Aligned Throughout the Journey

Although you ensure that all your stars are identified before you commence your entrepreneurial journey and they are all aligned when you start up, they may become misaligned along the way. If one is not watching the stars regularly, things can start to go wrong, and the company can get into real trouble. So, don't forget to have enough monitoring points to check the status of the stars of your business. If the stars are misaligned, quick action is needed to realign them, otherwise you will greatly reduce your chances of success. I am not saying you will surely fail. You may still succeed if one or more of the stars is misaligned or starts disappearing, but you will have a much more difficult time in trying to make things work for you.

The BuyItTogether Story (Of Missing Ingredients)

Let me share the story of BuyItTogether, my first internet start-up co-founded with a group of young computer engineers who graduated from Nanyang Technological University, Singapore (NTU). This was a very smart bunch of engineers who had very good technical and programming or coding knowledge. They shared their idea of group buying through the Internet.

The idea was simple. It is based on habits of Asian shoppers who typically bargain with retailers for lower prices especially when they want to purchase more than one product. For example, a shirt may cost $15 but the shopper will ask for a discount if two shirts are purchased. The brilliant team idea was to bring strangers together as co-shoppers to buy as a group (i.e. buy it together). With the power of the Internet, we could put up a product for sale and invite more buyers to come online, indicate their willingness to buy the same product and the price they are willing to pay. As the number of buyers grew, we could go back to the merchants to secure higher discounts so that every buyer would benefit. This was called "reverse auction" where the price reduces as more buyers bid for the product on sale. This was a winning idea and I invested US$1m over the few years we ran the business. The team met in my house every Saturday to discuss the business plan, strategy, and execution. We were quite sure that as the Internet economy grew, we would become highly successful.

Here was the problem. We were 15 years too early. It was a great idea, but the Star of Timing was wrong. Why? A number of ingredients were still missing. First, the Internet bandwidth was still not ready for huge volumes of traffic and transactions. Second, software was very expensive. We had to write the codes from scratch. This task was very well done by the computer engineers in our team. But operating a software (called Apps today) was very expensive, especially buying the database software and other plug-ins. Third, the world was not yet ready for Internet payments. Payment gateways were not safe and there were many cases of fraud that kept potential online customers away. We had an idea for a Unicorn company, but it was 15 years ahead of its time.

Fast forward 15 years later, Internet speed is great, software cost and cost of writing Apps have fallen drastically, and most importantly, the current generation is very comfortable making online payments (thanks to very well-developed security tools to protect the consumers).

These were the three missing Stars or ingredients when we started BuyItTogether 20 years ago. I have a business model of BuyItTogether later in this book for readers to understand the concept further.

Final point – Groupon which came many years later, I believe, was initially modeled after BuyItTogether.

So, remember, you need to ensure all the relevant Stars are aligned if you want your venture to succeed.

I would like to make one last point about stars. At the different life cycles of your business, other than the three basic stars, new stars may be needed to operate the business, and some of the original stars you started with may have to be replaced by new ones. As the reality of execution sets in, as obstacles are faced and cleared, and as the operating environment changes and competitors create new challenges, the entrepreneur has to modify and adapt the plans and identify new critical success factors that may not have been identified earlier on. Therefore, new stars may arise along the way. It is key therefore to understand what stars are needed for your business at a particular point of time.

The stars must be well aligned, and as the company progresses, you must constantly monitor the alignment. The ability to identify the right stars is the mark of a good entrepreneur. The ability to continue to monitor the stars and react fast to get them aligned, if they get misaligned along the way, is how the entrepreneur ensures success. Not knowing the right stars for your business means you are not ready to embark on your entrepreneurial journey. If you do start your venture despite not knowing what your stars are, your chances of failure will be very high. Knowing and getting your stars aligned will increase your chances of winning and achieving success.

Chapter 5 Summary

The Alignment of Your Stars

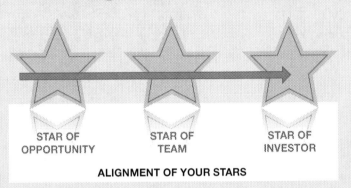

STAR OF OPPORTUNITY   STAR OF TEAM   STAR OF INVESTOR

ALIGNMENT OF YOUR STARS

Fig. 5.4: Alignment of Your Stars

- Success in a business is determined by the alignment of stars, which refer to the necessary ingredients and success factors for a business to succeed.

- You must identify the necessary stars for your type of business before you start.

- Ensure that all the stars are aligned throughout your journey of entrepreneurship.

- The three basic stars that must exist before a business can be successful are:

  1. The Star of Opportunity

  2. The Star of the Team

  3. The Star of the Investor

- Analyse the business opportunity before you start and ask if there really is an opportunity.

- The Star of Opportunity must fit in with what the market and consumers want, and it must be about the company making real revenues and profits.

- The Star of the Team refers to having a good integrated and diversified team to execute the business plan.

- The Star of the Investor refers to selecting the right investor to pump money into your business. The investor must have the same frequency of thinking as the entrepreneur.

- Always look for Smart Money when choosing an investor.

CHAPTER 6

YOU NEED THE PASSION

In Chapter 1, I listed one of the traits of entrepreneurs as **"Entrepreneurs love what they do and do what they love – with passion."** Unless you love what you do you will not enjoy what you are doing. And the best job to do is the one you love – which means, your start-up is one that started as a result of you doing what you have enjoyed doing (e.g. coding, entertainment, engineering, etc.).

Some people ask if entrepreneurship is another form of career choice. Just as you can develop a liking for a certain type of job, is it possible for you to also develop a liking for entrepreneurship? Sometimes, when one starts in a job, it may not be exciting at first, but as time goes by, a liking develops, and one can find excitement and passion about the job.

So, the thinking process among some people might be that one may not have to like being an entrepreneur, but it might not be a bad career option if other options are not available, as one can slowly adapt and become a good entrepreneur. Can this be true? Can you develop the passion like I did as a fresh graduate in my very first job with Texas Instruments Singapore – to do what you might not think you like, but subsequently learn to like?

Elsewhere in this book, I also discuss whether entrepreneurship can be learnt or if it is something inborn. This is another controversial issue concerning entrepreneurship, for which there are many views. In this chapter, the question I would like to address is one of passion. What role does passion play in determining whether a person becomes successful as an entrepreneur?

What is Entrepreneurial Passion?

Passion is something psychologists can describe better than most of us can, but it is useful to get some basic understanding of what passion is all about. Many experts in fact point out that at the centre of entrepreneurship and the reason entrepreneurs become highly successful is because of passion for what they undertook as a personal challenge to create something new. In other words, passion is at the heart of entrepreneurship. Research on this link between passion and entrepreneurial behaviour, indicates that the perseverance, determination, willingness to take higher risks, and willingness to "suffer" more than others, are all driven by passion. Some experts also seem to indicate creativity is a product of passion.

Entrepreneurs who are indeed highly passionate also are more motivated, more confident about what they do, are able to convince others to believe in their projects and tend to be more persuasive. They have internalised what they believe of the project as their personal belief. Yet while passion is critical, entrepreneurs must also be able to convert their passion to something that can be easily communicated to others – in other words, the passion must also be seen in the business plan communicated to others.

One must also realise while passion is very important, being overconfident is an unintended product of the display of passion. The entrepreneur must remain grounded to realities, the environment, the timing so that he or she develops a believable plan. Some entrepreneurs who display high levels of passion tend to also translate this to overconfidence. Being very confident is important and other stakeholders want to see this in an entrepreneur, but when extreme passion clouds some of the decisions made, those may start looking unrealistic. However, it is still better to appear overconfident than lacking in confidence, so I encourage every entrepreneur to start your entrepreneurial journey when you are passionate about something. Always remember the world out there may not understand why you are so passionate, so keep the passion burning but be prepared to look grounded when you deal with others who do not share the same passion and belief as you.

The Role of Passion in Entrepreneurship

Entrepreneurship is all about having the passion to do it. If there is no passion, then one cannot be successful in achieving something significant, or sustaining any initial success for the long term. Without passion, entrepreneurship becomes a chore. Entrepreneurship is a personal choice, whether as a career or to further a cause of doing what you truly believe in. It is this passion that brings out the best in a team of entrepreneurs to achieve maximum potential. Without passion, an entrepreneur can attain no success.

Let me elaborate this point – **"Entrepreneurs love what they do and do what they love – with passion."**

The difference between your success and failure is determined by your level of passion. This passion drives the level and intensity of your actions to create success out of an idea or concept. Your energy level is determined by the intensity of your belief in the project. In turn, this belief is driven by your level of passion about the journey and the outcome of your endeavour. So, someone can attempt to become a good entrepreneur, but the final outcome will be determined by this one all-encompassing value or trait in a person, and this trait is called **passion**. How passionate you are about what you have undertaken, how well you convey your passion through effective communication with others, and how much they believe that you yourself truly believe in what you want to do – these are all very important outcome drivers in the practice of entrepreneurship.

An Entrepreneur's Pressure Cooker Environment

I believe that the life of an entrepreneur can become unbearable at times of great difficulties and uncertainties (which is quite typical for all companies starting up and trying to grow), especially if the entrepreneur is doing it without the right passion. As every entrepreneur will tell you, the journey is never an easy one, and you have to be prepared for very stressful times, particularly in the first couple of years. Plans seldom play out as expected and many obstacles will come in the way of the start-up. Possibility of failure can demoralise even the most passionate of entrepreneurs. It is during these stressful times that we see the difference – those who persevere and make it, or those who cannot take the stress and prematurely fail. In a very big way, the passion you have is the determining factor between success and failure. I am not saying all those with passion will never fail – many do fail. There will come many times in the life of an entrepreneur that the journey seems to be coming to an end and when obstacles seem unsurmountable. Many feel like giving up as life becomes tough, even if success is around the corner. We all know that only those with the right level of determination will be able to push through, to survive and eventually emerge to make things work. Such strong determination can only be strengthened by one's level of passion.

Some entrepreneurs embark on a start-up because it is fashionable to do or they want to make a lot of money or some other reason. In bringing in other stakeholders to join them or to invest, such entrepreneurs may convey the impression that they are indeed passionate about what they are doing – they may be very good presenters and tell good stories. But this façade cannot possibly last long. The amount of effort needed and the amount of pain, stress and anxiety an entrepreneur needs to endure will constantly be high and stressful. Without a high level of passion, very few can possibly last the long distance under a "pressure cooker" environment. Life in general will become miserable trying to cope with insurmountable difficulties.

For those who intend to embark on the entrepreneurial journey it is essential to understand that they should do it out of passion and not for glamour, money, or as an alternative career choice. Entrepreneurship is much more than a career choice, because it typically requires devoting a greater part of one's life to further a chosen cause – doing it for the wrong reasons will result in misery. Those with the passion will actually enjoy even "pressure cooker" type situations. They will let things cook as long as needed until they successfully create what they set out to achieve.

Finding Passion in My Work

When I was in my final year at the university, I got a job offer from Texas Instruments Singapore as a product engineer. My job involved writing test programs, doing product analysis, and working out corrective actions to improve product reliability, quality, and yields. I turned them down because I was really interested in becoming an IC design engineer. But my future bosses knew better. Every fresh engineering graduate wants a fancy design and development type job. They enticed me to join them as a product engineer first, and they would later recommend me for a transfer to a design type job (which by the way was non-existent in Texas Instruments Singapore in those days). One of the engineering managers told me that if after a year I did not like the job, she promised to get me a transfer to a design job. Agreeing, I accepted the job offer.

As my bosses guessed right, after a few months, I enjoyed the work given to me. I got the chance to become a problem solver in the company and was assigned to different jobs. I showed passion in what I was doing and enjoyed my work. Sometimes, I worked from 8 a.m. till midnight, and sometimes up to the early hours in the morning. My mother thought I was mad to work the way I did, and that being a graduate I should have a nine to five job. She asked me to find another job. I explained it was my choice to put in the long hours, and I enjoyed my work.

After about 11 months, my boss decided to promote me to a section manager. He told me they were offering me a promotion despite me being the most junior in my department and warned I would have a hard time managing engineers more senior than me. Without hesitation, I replied, "Yes, I accept the promotion." Then my boss asked me whether I still wanted the IC design job, to which I replied, "No." They knew I would develop the passion for the job as

I went along, and they were right. I spent the best part of my early productive years from the age of 25 till 37 in Texas Instruments, doing nine different jobs in the 13 years I was there (as a result of lateral moves and promotions).

Passion and Entrepreneursip

When I joined forces with a group of fresh graduates to start a dot.com venture in 1999, I thought I had partnered a group of very enthusiastic young people who believed in what they wanted to do and had the passion to establish what we thought would be a great company.

My first impression was that they were very creative in the way they established contact with me to communicate their desire to work with me on a start-up. At that time, I was quite prominently promoting entrepreneurship, which gave me a lot of visibility, so some people sought to make me their partner. Thus, I partnered them, and we started a company with some initial ideas we thought would be great winners in the dot.com world.

As we began the process, the hard work started, and because it was a tough environment, results were not easily achieved. Each time, when I energised the team to work on some interesting initiatives, I would see initial excitement, but then that excitement waned quickly as the hard work did not produce immediate results. This went on a few times, and I started to wonder about the level of passion these people really had for what we were trying to do. Finally, one day, I had a heart-to-heart discussion with them about why they had lost interest and momentum in what we should have been doing quickly. After much discussion, one of them let slip that "we do not feel the pinch because it is not our money." I was surprised, but I should not have been, because I was paying these guys a good salary at the same time as a good equity position, so they did not feel the pinch. Well, I told them I would immediately solve the pinch problem by cutting their salary by 50 per cent until we saw some results.

But the real problem was really about passion. Were these guys in it because they really believed in the idea and really wanted to become entrepreneurs, or was it because it was a fashionable thing to do in those days, because of the level of prominence given to young "successful" entrepreneurs. (I will talk about this in Chapter 19 "Lessons Learnt During the Dot.Com Era".)

I quickly realised that what was missing, in addition to the pinch factor, was the trait of passion. The team were excited and committed to do the start-up but lacked the kind of passion to thrive. The reality is that if the motivating reasons are other than the passion and the belief in what they are doing, life can become very tough. As soon as I realised collective passion was not clear for our team, I decided to either wind down the company or sell it to someone who was more passionate about it.

The good news is that we managed to exit from the company in February 2000, just before the dot.com crash of April 2000.

Don't be an Entrepreneur for the Wrong Reasons

What I am saying may seem a very obvious thing, but my observation is that many have failed to realise the subtle difference between true entrepreneurs in it for the right reasons, and those doing it as an alternate career choice. Failure to understand this results in disappointments and quick failure if one becomes an "entrepreneur" for the wrong reasons.

From time to time, we have seen a surge in the number of people wanting to become entrepreneurs. The many quick success stories, such as what we saw during the dot.com era, encourage others to want to achieve the same – this is an attitude of "if others can do it, I can do it too". Promotional efforts by agencies, and especially by governments, excite those who want to give entrepreneurship a shot because it appears the "in thing" to do. Many people jump onto the bandwagon, some for the right reasons, but many for the wrong reasons. This was especially so for many young graduates who wanted to start their careers as entrepreneurs and thought of it as an alternative career choice especially during the dot.com era. Many failed to realise that you don't just create companies from thin air. A company is born out of a bright idea, especially a very unique idea, which is then transformed into a business model and finally implemented as a business. And all the Stars must be aligned for you to create a successful business. This is the only way to create long-lasting companies.

The journey is never an easy one. Once you have found the right idea and the right business model – and if and only if you have the passion – will you be able to create the business and be called an entrepreneur. There is no shorter way, as you will realise from any literature about entrepreneurship. You will discover this is the case with every entrepreneur you speak with. They will not forget to tell you about this thing called **passion**.

Chapter 6 Summary

You Need the Passion

- Entrepreneurship is all about the passion – Entrepreneurs love what they do and do what they love.

- The difference between success and failure is determined by passion.

- Passion drives the actions you take to create success, influences your energy level, and the intensity of your belief about your business idea.

- Passion helps entrepreneurs to survive the "pressure cooker" environment to emerge as winners.

- Don't be an entrepreneur just for the glamour, the money, or as an alternative career choice.

- Be an entrepreneur because you are passionate about growing your idea into a successful business.

CHAPTER 7

THINKING WITH YOUR HEART NOT YOUR HEAD

I wrote this chapter after I had finished writing most of the other chapters of my earlier book. I felt there was something still missing. I could not pinpoint what it was until a casual conversation one day with a friend from Saudi Arabia triggered the thought in me. (See the story about "Mother's Wisdom" below.) Sometimes, we might look at the outcome of certain decisions and wonder what logic was used to make the decision resulting in a certain outcome. Such decisions might even have defied logic, yet a good result was achieved. So why and how was the decision made?

A Mother's Wisdom

An Arab friend told me that mothers are indeed very amazing people. He shared a personal experience with me about his wife. He was once carrying his son while walking with his wife. After a few minutes he felt the heavy load and his arms started to ache. He then asked his wife how she could carry their son for such a long time and still not feel or look tired. She gave him an excellent reply, "You men carry your children with your muscles, but we mothers carry our children with our hearts. That's why we never feel the pain or tiredness when we carry our children."

How true this must be. When you do something with your heart, anything becomes possible – mind over matter as they say.

In my many years of studying this, I learned that entrepreneurs have a special skill; they typically have the knack of coming up with solutions that others cannot even think of. Even the best of brains might not have been able to solve a particular problem or issue, despite in-depth analysis and applying all the logical decision-making skills. Entrepreneurs possess something special when it comes to thinking and making decisions. This also sometimes leads to the conclusion that entrepreneurs are born, not made, and therefore they have a special skill in solving difficult problems and in coming up with solutions.

This chapter explores how the entrepreneur thinks and makes decisions, what special skill entrepreneurs are supposedly born with, what kind of logic they apply when they make decisions, and whether there is any magic to how they think and do things.

Gut Feel

Indeed, there is something special and different about the way entrepreneurs make decisions, and there are many terms that have been typically used to describe this special thing. Some call it a gut feel, where entrepreneurs are able to sense something or smell something others typically might not be able to. You can also call it intuition or intuitive thinking.

When I was working in an American multinational company, we used to call it "firing from the hip", which involved making a decision without going through a very thorough analysis of the situation or the circumstances that can affect the decision and the outcome. In fact, as an engineer, I was taught that "firing from the hip" was wrong, and that any decision needed to be preceded with a very thorough analysis of data and facts, including a structured decision-making process. And many managers use the concept of "Manage by Facts" – through analysis of data, using structured decision-making tools.

As engineers, it was easy to understand why there needed to be structure. However, during my days at Texas Instruments, we had witnessed certain people who "fired from the hip" and typically looked more disorganised than others, yet they achieved very good results. At the same time, for many operations and engineering problems, we achieved many good results by applying logic and a structured approach to analysing and solving the problems. In fact, without certain structured decision-making tools, many problems could not have been solved.

Yet not all decisions needed the application of such tools, and sometimes, a judgement needed to be made. This is when "firing from the hip" could help. But "firing from the hip" worked only for certain people; most people made bad decisions when they "fired from the hip". I used to think it was luck that made such people successful, but later I realised these people who used to "fire from the hip" were entrepreneurial in their thinking and approach. They just had a certain special way of coming up with solutions.

I once met with the head of a very large American company, worth billions of dollars. Over dinner, I asked him how he managed to do so well in a difficult region. He gave me a simple answer: "I don't think with my head. I think with my heart." In other words, he uses gut feel to make certain decisions. He explained that certain things just cannot be logically resolved, and by using his heart to make a decision, he knows that he would have invoked his passion when making a decision. And this is what makes entrepreneurs different from others. We make the most important decisions by using our heart to think rather than depending on our head to decide. And when we do this, people tend to think there must be a magic touch that entrepreneurs are born with. But really, many times, such people are guided by their gut feel; they were thinking using their hearts, making sense of things quite differently from the logical thinking process we are all familiar with.

Another term used by some people who can see things differently from others and who seem to be able to make quick decisions without going through a very thorough analytical process, is, "I feel it in my belly," or "I feel it in my stomach." This is another term for "I have a gut feel." So, when they say they feel it in their belly, they are using not logic, but their heart to think. Some call it a "sixth sense" – the ability to see what ordinary people cannot.

Thinking with Your Heart

Throughout my years of experience as an entrepreneur, whether when I worked as an engineer at Texas Instruments, as the Director of Operations some years later or as an entrepreneur starting a few of my companies, I have relied heavily on using my instinct and "heart" to think. And I must say, most (not all) of the decisions I made this way turned out alright. I managed to solve many problems, win many business deals and created success when many thought I would fail.

I guess some of this ability develops with experience, some level of confidence not being afraid to make mistakes, and being prepared to change quickly if things don't go the way you expected. Over time, each of us can develop some level of thinking with our heart as you will learn from this chapter.

Let me share a story about one of my greatest wins with my start-ups, namely, UTAC. I went against all conventional wisdom and against all advice by my Singapore-based investors (who are typically risk averse anyway) and relied heavily on my gut feel to make a decision which has been one of the greatest assets for UTAC till today. See the story box "A Good Deal Won".

A Good Deal Won

When I started UTAC, I wrote a business plan requiring 200,000 square feet of building space in Singapore, which could last the company for at least its first five years of business before it expanded its operations. When our company began, my team started looking for a building of the size we had planned for, something in the range of 200,000 to 250,000 square feet. We had looked at a number of buildings, and most fitted excellently with our plans.

Just as we were negotiating the purchase of a building, a new opportunity arose. Micropolis, a disk drive maker, had gone out of business, and the company's liquidators were looking to dispose of all the assets. They had a 400,000 square feet modern, fully fitted factory, which I estimated to have cost the owners at least S$60m to build. I went with several of my team members to look at the building, and I had a special feeling about it. Somehow, I could sense it would be a perfect fit for what I hoped to achieve for UTAC. But there was one glaring problem I had to contend with – the Micropolis factory building was just too large for our plans – double the space we had initially planned for. In addition, we also expected it to be double the price we planned to pay for our intended building.

Many of my team members opposed my plans to make a bid for the building, because they thought we would be overdoing things and there was no way we could afford the building. Some of my shareholders were very uncomfortable because of the size and also the fact that the building was "bad luck" since Micropolis had failed in it. However, my gut feel told me the building would be a perfect fit, and the detailed analysis I did to come out with the 200,000 square feet building requirement did not necessarily have to be correct. I also felt we could get a very good price for the building, and my gut feel was that we should bid for the whole 400,000 square feet by paying about the market price of a 200,000 square feet building. Some thought I was crazy and that there was no way we would win the building.

At that time, we were in the advanced stages of negotiating for a 200,000-square foot building, and had to employ some delay tactics with the owner of the smaller building so that we would still have an opportunity to acquire the smaller building if we failed in our bid for the Micropolis building. Of course, my feel was not just based on empty considerations. I thought if I could offer cash for the building, the liquidator would be pleased because the liquidator's job would be made easier with an upfront cash deal. My heart was telling me this would be a very good deal, and a very good way of jumpstarting our new company. I was quite fixed on getting the bid done.

With the agreement of a couple of my major shareholders – the entrepreneurs among my shareholders – who must have also "sensed something in their bellies" about the Micropolis building, my team started preparing for the Micropolis building bid. We kept things very secret and even submitted the bid just five minutes before the closing of the tender.

To cut a long story short, my feel of what the liquidator was looking for and the price we needed to pay turned out to be correct. We got a 400,000 square feet building for the price of a 200,000 square feet building, so my shareholders had no reason to block the deal as we would be acquiring a very cheap property, which would allow the company to start quickly. My team members were happy because we had obtained a very well-fitted factory, which would make our job of starting our operations much easier, without draining too much cash by buying a large building, and more importantly, we would not have to worry about expansion for the next five to eight years.

Had I gone with my logical thinking and thought with my head, there would have been little reason for us to bid for the Micropolis building. My heart told me it was the best building, that I could get it despite the odds, and despite many people telling me it was impossible.

My heart was right, and today, UTAC must thank me and my team for making a visionary decision that has allowed the company to expand to beyond our original plans. In addition, the value of the building must be much more than what we paid for in 1998. Today, UTAC has moved into another building since the original Micropolis building has reached its capacity.

Entrepreneurial Judgement

Entrepreneurs use a lot of judgement to make decisions. What then, is this judgement? It is a form of process in decision making, but not a very structured process. Based on the success of many entrepreneurs, judgement is definitely not something plucked out of thin air; it comes about after considerable thought, using a fuzzy process for decision making. It's fuzzy because of the lack of structure, because a lot of gut feel is applied, and also because the vital thinking process is done mainly using the heart and not the head.

The process of thinking with the heart is continuously refined with greater experience. As one gains more experience, evaluates the outcomes of certain decisions, and sees the results of certain problem-solving approaches these become lessons learnt. These shape a person's thinking process and help develop better skills that are internalised as "thinking with the heart".

Rules of thumb are developed to help in the decision-making process. In fact, entrepreneurs and businessmen typically love to use rules of thumb. However, it is very difficult to document all of these, and equally difficult for anyone to communicate or discuss why they have a certain gut feel about something. It is an internalised skill and ultimately developing into something called a **fuzzy logic**. This "thinking with the heart" process appears very complex and cannot be easily understood by the ordinary person. This is the reason why entrepreneurship seems to be something a person is born with and not learnt – because entrepreneurship requires a people to think with their hearts, which is not something easily done or understood. On the other hand, fuzzy logic is also developed after a series of lessons based on the entrepreneur's experiences, and therefore it can be learnt.

From Small to Big

Entrepreneurs often do a great job of conceiving an idea, developing it into a business, and then starting the business. They do it best at the start-up stage when the number of people involved is small.

Start-ups have to go through many changes before the final company structure can be established and for the company to grow. This is easily handled by entrepreneurs who do best using judgement and gut feel because no one can easily see the final structure.

When the company finally becomes bigger and more successful, the old approach of using judgement to make decisions becomes more difficult because there is now a need to communicate the decisions to many more people. In fact, proper corporate governance and a structured approach become requirements for the company. As the fuzzy logic used by the entrepreneur cannot be understood by all, it becomes necessary to set up proper rules and regulations, specifications and operating procedures to ensure the smooth running of the company.

But guess what? This is exactly why the entrepreneur starts to fail. He or she is required to use a structured process to make decisions. Unless he can communicate with the other stakeholders the reasons and the process used to make a certain decision, the company procedures may not allow the company to accept his decision made through "gut feel" that only the entrepreneur can understand. Thinking with the heart becomes unprofessional and unacceptable. Yet the very reason why unique decisions were made and the company became successful in the first place was because of the thinking with the heart approach, which has now become unacceptable!

It is at this stage of company's growth that many entrepreneurs start to look ineffective. In many cases, the entrepreneurs who had created very successful companies did not end up operating the companies as the companies became big. So-called professional management teams are often brought in mainly by the major investors and the board because the entrepreneurs seemingly start to fail and can no longer make effective decisions.

Apple's Steve Jobs – Thinking with the Heart

Steve Jobs was one of the most highly successful entrepreneurs in the world. He started Apple in a garage in 1976. It is today one of the greatest companies in the world.

However, Jobs had to leave Apple in 1985. Some say he was fired by the board, and some say Jobs resigned. While Jobs was a highly creative person, creating one of the best technologies and products, somehow he had problems managing when the company became bigger and as more structures were put in place.

John Sculley who was hired to become the CEO of Apple, must have put in more structures, as he used to manage a large MNC like PepsiCo. Jobs wanted to continue to experiment and invent new things, but he had already failed with two products – LISA and Apple 3. Sculley and the board probably could not tolerate the approach Jobs was taking because Jobs was **"thinking with his heart"**, something Sculley and the board could not understand.

So, Jobs started looking ineffective in his ability to manage a big company that increasingly required a more structured way of thinking and decision making. He was therefore forced to leave his own company, one he passionately started.

One last point – Sculley in a speech in 2013 (reported on *CNET Online*, by Daniel Terdiman, 9 September 2013) said at that time of Jobs' "firing" that "he (Sculley) didn't have the business expertise at the time to fully understand what visionary leadership was." In 2011, Sculley also called Jobs "the greatest CEO ever" because perhaps he finally realised how effective Jobs was in **"thinking with his heart"**.

This idea that the entrepreneur cannot make effective decisions as a company grows is a big misconception. The fact is that entrepreneurs look ineffective because they are no longer allowed to make decisions by the judgement process or by thinking with their hearts. Should they be allowed to still decide things the way they are best at, everyone will benefit from the outcome. Just look what Steve Jobs did after he returned to Apple. He made Apple even greater than before and it remains one of the greatest companies in the world. Sculley had realised Jobs' brilliance, and the Apple board learned to understand Jobs' process of decision making by "**thinking with the heart**".

The challenge therefore is, how to fit everyone into a growing company, how to allow the entrepreneurs to still provide the direction, and then have a group of professional managers translate those decisions into actions that can be executed in a structured way as required by the operating procedures and according to proper corporate governance. If this kind of relationship and decision-making process can be developed, we will see stronger companies emerging. It is difficult to do, and therefore, often, once a company grows very big, the original group of people who started the company will no longer be directly involved. So, my advice would be to set up a structure that still values the entrepreneurs' skills – allowing them to continue to think with their hearts – and you will see an even better outcome for your company. In the long term, let them become mentors, advisors or visionaries, not CEOs. Apple finally realised the value of the entrepreneur and brought Jobs back to the company from which he was fired a few years earlier.

I have personally gone through the experience of changing my decision-making process from one that used my heart to think to one that used my head to think. I discovered that the more structured the process I used and the more I relied on as complete a set of data to make a decision, the less satisfying the outcome has been. In fact, when I stopped relying on my gut feel and started depending on a much more structured process to satisfy others who were also important stakeholders of my company, I became less effective with my decisions.

After a prolonged period of less than satisfactory results, I analysed what went wrong and realised my problem was that I did not utilise the biggest strength I had, which was to **think with my heart**. Each time I reverted to **thinking with my heart** again, I achieved good results. So, each time I find myself going into a downward spiral of performance because of the excessive structures put into the company, I remember how I did it best in the first place, thinking with my heart. I then start to become more gung-ho using my heart to help me make decisions and in not letting structures limit my decision-making process.

When the Head and the Heart Disagree

There will be many times throughout your entrepreneurial journey when you will face this dilemma on how you decide on things. The dilemma is to decide whether you rely on a lot of information and data before making a decision – a more structured process, applying logic and **thinking with your head**, or do you decide on your gut feel or by **thinking with your heart**, the way you did when you first started your journey as an entrepreneur.

On the one hand, the structured process the company may have implemented as the company grew, where you need to manage by facts, depends on a lot of data and logic to make decisions that others in the company will also understand and agree with. On the other hand, you may have a gut feel about certain things, you apply your heart to help you think clearly and you may want to decide something that may be counter to what a more structured decision-making process may have led to. We can say that there will be situations when both your heart and your head cannot agree – you may be stuck and find it difficult to decide. Let me share one such experience below. I failed to allow my heart to make the final decision and therefore paid the price for it later.

Head and Heart Disagreeing – The Infiniti Solutions IPO Story

One experience that remains very clear in my mind is a fund-raising exercise I handled for my company. This was the IPO for Infiniti Solutions. We spent a lot of time preparing for the IPO fund raising after we received the approval to list on NASDAQ in 2004. When done professionally, fund raising is a very structured process. We started well but after some time, my heart told me we were not doing the fund raising in a manner we should have followed. But my head told me it was the right and logical thing – if I looked at all the facts.

Throughout the process of preparing for the IPO, something inside me told me it was not the right thing to do, but nevertheless I ignored my heart and allowed my head to rule. A few days before I left for the USA to kick off the formal part of the IPO process, I also had a funny feeling, which made me think that it might not be the right thing to do, but it was too late to turn back. When my team members and I were in New York, we had a dinner with an analyst who talked about the industry and the environment. At the end of the dinner meeting, I felt very edgy about starting the formal IPO process the next day. One of my team members also had the same gut feeling. We felt like aborting the plans, just a few hours before the formal launch of the exercise.

It would be a setback because we had taken many months to prepare for IPO. From New York, we called a banker in Singapore to tell him we were considering pulling out of the fund-raising exercise. He instead started sharing data with us to convince us it was the right thing to do and that we should proceed. I let my head take control of the situation, and we proceeded with the fund-raising exercise. Once

> we started, we could not turn back. Despite the tremendous effort we put in, WE FAILED. We aborted the IPO after the full roadshow process, just the day before the company was to be listed on NASDAQ!

Had I listened to my heart and my gut feel, we would have been in much better shape. Of course, the difficulty was that there were too many stakeholders involved, and I would have had a hard time telling them that my heart and my gut feel were telling me something was wrong. How could I communicate this to them? Not everyone can understand that "**thinking with the heart**" can be effective.

Going Back to Basics

After the missed IPO fund-raising exercise, the company went through a very tough period due to a tight cash situation. Everyone was breathing down our necks. We needed to make decisions that our stakeholders could agree with. But things got worse as I stopped using my heart to think. Finally, when I really felt the pressure of not achieving results, I decided to go back to doing things the way I knew best. I started relying more and more on my gut feel and judgement, following which the outcome was excellent. With renewed confidence, our company moved forward, and once again started producing the results we wanted to see. I am a firm believer that we should always think with the heart because it will allow you to make a quick decision that will make the difference.

As I have mentioned earlier, it is not pure luck or just guesswork when you make a decision as an entrepreneur – you take calculated risks. These calculated risks are taken using our **hearts to think**. Thinking with our hearts is really a set of decision-making processes that are not very structured but use a set of fuzzy logic, a logic that evolves as we experience new things and develop skills along the way.

The Reality – The Head Consulting the Heart to Make Decisions

In the real world, it is very difficult to say how one should be making decisions – whether by using the head or the heart. There is of course no right or wrong answer – sometimes you use your head, and sometimes you use your heart.

In my opinion, the best of decisions will always require a combination of both thinking with the heart and the head. The correct process is when the **head consults with the heart** to apply a structured process alongside the gut feeling. The sum total is probably the fuzzy logic I mentioned earlier. So fuzzy logic is a semi-structured decision-making process that uses the heart and the head to think. To pinpoint how entrepreneurs make good decisions, the answer is that they can do so when their head is in consultation with the heart in solving problems.

The decision-making process may become slower because you have to include a little more structure in the decision-making process, but perhaps it will be a better decision than using only your pure gut feeling. And although it will be less structured than using only your head to make decisions, it will be much faster than purely using the structured process. Sometimes, you will need to use more of the head to think, and at other times, more of the heart, depending on the situation and circumstances under which you have to make a decision. I believe you will always need to find the right balance between the head and the heart, which changes as you progress with your start-up.

In the early stages, perhaps you will need to use more of the heart and less of the head, and in the later stages of company growth, you might use more of the head and less of the heart to think – rarely should you use only one way to think. Even in the later stage, depending on what the circumstances are, things might change. So for example, for a stable company, when things suddenly change and do not go according to plans, like the circumstance as described for my company Infiniti Solutions, you must be prepared to shift from using more of your head to more of your heart, but you should always work with the head consulting the heart to make the right decision.

Fig. 7.1: The Yin and Yang in
Entrepreneurial Thinking

In the case of Apple, Steve Jobs lost out to John Sculley when the company needed a more structured approach of decision making (thinking with the head). Jobs in the meantime started his other companies and must have learnt his lessons on why he failed in Apple. When Jobs was later brought back to Apple to serve as the CEO, injected his entrepreneurial way which included thinking with both his head and his heart, the outcome is the tremendous success Apple that has been able to achieve again.

In brief, the head must always consult with the heart – finding the right balance of how a decision is made is a special skill all good entrepreneurs must have.

I must attribute this concept of the head and heart consultation to Venerable Master Chin Kung, a religious leader, in his explanation of spirituality during a conversation I had with him. When I read his explanation, it dawned on me that this is exactly how entrepreneurs make decisions.

In Chapter 1, I touched briefly on how entrepreneurs think differently from managers – Effectual ("Entrepreneurial or Thinking with the Heart") versus Causal ("Managerial or Thinking with the Head") thinking processes.

An entrepreneur is MOST effective when he uses both Causal and Effectual Thinking depending on the situation and timing.

<u>Chapter 7 Summary</u>

Thinking with Your Heart Not Your Head

- Entrepreneurs have a special skill; they can come up with solutions that others are not able to despite in-depth analysis and despite applying all the logical decision-making skills.

- Entrepreneurs are guided by a special sense called gut feel. It is the ability to sense something or "smell" something others typically might not be able to.

- The most important decisions are best made by using our "hearts to think" rather than depending on our head to decide.

- Entrepreneurs use a lot of judgement to make decisions. It is an unstructured and fuzzy process of decision making.

- The judgement is not something plucked out of thin air; it comes about after some thought, while using some gut feel.

- The process of thinking with the heart is refined with greater experience and the acquiring of new skills and knowledge.

- An entrepreneur starts to fail and become ineffective when he is required to use a structured process to make decisions. This is one reason why entrepreneurs start failing as CEOs when companies become big.

- The best decisions are made when the Head consults with the Heart – use both effectual and causal thinking methods in a balance.

SECTION A: Summary

The Art of Entrepreneurship – Entrepreneur's Mind

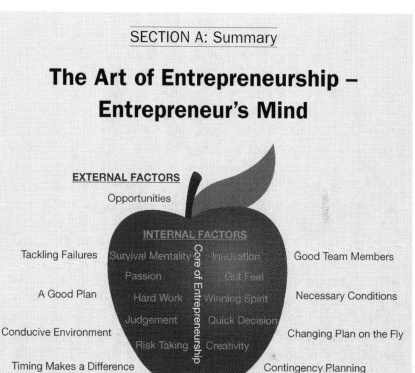

EXTERNAL FACTORS

Opportunities

INTERNAL FACTORS

Tackling Failures   Survival Mentality   Innovation   Good Team Members

Passion   Gut Feel

A Good Plan   Hard Work   Winning Spirit   Necessary Conditions

Judgement   Quick Decision

Conducive Environment   Changing Plan on the Fly

Risk Taking   Creativity

Timing Makes a Difference   Contingency Planning

Core of Entrepreneurship

CORE OF ENTREPRENEURSHIP

Fig. A.1: The Entrepreneur's Mind

In this section, I have attempted to capture how entrepreneurs think, what are their traits, how they make decisions, what is it in them that increases their chances of success, how they handle difficult situations, and failure. These are all very abstract factors for which I have attempted to create theories on aspects of being an entrepreneur.

I started with an introduction of entrepreneurship and covered some theories around entrepreneurial thinking. I summarised the key traits of entrepreneurs, which may not be the same as how others may have written about traits of entrepreneurs. But these are all based on my personal experience and my observations of entrepreneurs.

Next, I discussed the mindsets entrepreneurs operate with. I distilled the key thinking processes, including how entrepreneurs behave and how they are guided in life. I tried to make some distinction between creativity and innovation, which I think are not exactly the same, though others have made it seem like both are one and the same. Much of the rest of this section covers the operating philosophies of entrepreneurs that guide their thinking and actions.

The entrepreneurial journey is not an easy one, but when you have the passion – no matter how difficult – it can be a very enjoyable process. However, success is never guaranteed, and you will be mistaken if you think that by doing all the things I talked about you will be assured of success. The fact of the matter is that failure is a more likely outcome than success for most start-ups. What is more important for you and me is the journey and how we make decisions. A failure should be seen as a lesson for future success. But do you give up because the likelihood of failure is higher? Of course not. The best of entrepreneurs never give up and have a high tolerance level. How then do you create success? Put simply, you have to reduce the chances of failure. While you cannot possibly cover all bases, you can minimise the chances of failure by lowering the risk factors and by ensuring the right ingredients are available to increase your chances of succeeding.

It is very useful to understand what attitudes and behaviours entrepreneurs have and how they do things. While you will never be able to read the minds of entrepreneurs and understand everything about them, by learning and understanding the traits that differentiate entrepreneurs from others, you too can learn how to become an entrepreneur.

You need a more in-depth understanding before you can conclude that you know everything you need to know about entrepreneurship. As the saying goes, "a *kung-fu* master teaches as many skills as possible to his disciple but there will always be something or some skill that he does not impart and keeps for himself." The trick then is to try to figure out what this other hidden thing is that you need to know, and to develop it by yourself into something that might be unique for you alone. This is something I cannot capture in this book.

This section should have given you a good feel of what goes on in the mind of an entrepreneur and should equip you with the necessary knowledge to move on to the next stage, the "doing it stage".

The Technical Aspects of Creating a Business

In Section A, I covered the mindset aspects of entrepreneurship, The Art of Entrepreneurship. In Section B, I will cover the science or the technical aspects of entrepreneurship, which is the nuts and bolts of creating a business.

From the time you have an idea to the point you develop a business model, start a company, bring in team members, write your business plan and raise money, there are many steps, and it is important that you understand what you have to do, what tools you have to use, and how you will need to manage the whole start-up process.

Since I wrote the first edition of my earlier book, I have gone through many more rounds of starting-up companies, investing in some and mentoring many others. Many new concepts and tools have emerged that did not exist when I started my first company. I therefore have added many more new sections and new chapters to Section B – The Science of Entrepreneurship. Feedback I got for my first edition was that my fund-raising coverage focused on raising large funds at later stages and I did not share how entrepreneurs do it in early stages. I have updated this edition to cover much more of the early stages of doing a start-up – how you take your idea and develop it into a business model, raise funds, form teams and manage your start-up.

I start off Section B by bridging the Art of Entrepreneurship with the Science of Entrepreneurship. In Chapter 8, I discuss the very essential step of what it takes to create a business out of an idea. This is perhaps the most difficult part of starting a new company. An idea alone is not enough; you need to convert the idea into a business. Often, the first-time entrepreneur does not have enough experience of how to successfully start and navigate the various processes necessary for starting and growing a company. I added a new chapter that was not in my first edition and this is something I teach at the university – Strategy Development for New Ventures. In this chapter, I have added a number of concepts and tools that will help the entrepreneur to systematically transform his idea into a business model. I then go on into minute details of all the steps which you will have to take to start your company to the point where you will be able to attract other stakeholders, especially investors. These are based on my many experiences with the start-ups over the years. I believe this will aid a new entrepreneur in mapping his entrepreneurial journey from the beginning. I trace the steps that entrepreneurs go through in starting with an idea, translating the idea into a plan, working with team members and investors. I will cover details of how to write a good business plan and also the very important topic of pitching. The Pitching chapter is also new and is something I developed to teach my future classes at the university. I learned about pitching from the first company I worked for – Texas Instruments (TI).

SECTION

B

THE SCIENCE OF ENTREPRENEURSHIP

I have strengthened many chapters that were in my first edition and added many of my experiences with fund raising over the years after 2007. I have also added my experience as an angel investor so that the reader will see fund raising from both angles – from the investor side and from the entrepreneur side. I discuss what entrepreneurs should look for when they are trying to raise funds and partner with investors.

The initial chapters of Section B cover the early stages of fund raising. The later part of Section B is focused mainly on fund raising as a more structured process, especially at the later stages where every entrepreneur will have to do many formal rounds of fund raising.

One of the most difficult aspects of being an entrepreneur is fund raising. As most entrepreneurs are not quite savvy about fund raising. I have devoted many pages in this book to talking about it, especially from the perspective of the entrepreneur. I have also attempted to spell out what investors look for in their decision-making process of whether or not to invest in the entrepreneur and his start-up.

I cover the detailed steps for a very formal fund-raising round. I share my rules of thumb on fund raising and finally a chapter titled "The VC Trap" based on my experiences of how entrepreneurs can get caught off guard when dealing with investors.

The whole of Section B includes writing the business plan, finding the right type of financing and funding for the start-up, selecting the team members, and aligning all the stakeholders to a common goal and direction. In other words, it is about getting all your stars aligned. I've learnt that this is a long path you have to take; there is no shorter way.

CHAPTER 8

TRANSFORMING AN IDEA INTO A VIABLE BUSINESS

After you have conceived and developed the idea, and once you are sure your stars are all aligned, what's next? What else do you need to do to start a successful business? Many people do not realise an idea they have conceived may not necessarily make a successful business. It is very important for us to be able to distinguish between an idea and a business. Ideas are of course great and do not come to us all the time. Creative people can think of and also visualise ideas that ordinary people may not be able to imagine. There have been many examples in history where great ideas resulted in great companies. The real question is this: is an idea all it takes to create a successful company? To phrase it another way, is an idea sufficient as an ingredient for a successful business to emerge? My contention is that while an idea is definitely a necessary ingredient for creating a successful company, it is not a sufficient ingredient.

You need much more than an idea to create a successful business. I am not downplaying the value of the idea, and as I mentioned earlier, ideas do not come to just anyone, and ideas are definitely very valuable commodities in the context of entrepreneurship. However, an idea in its original form is actually still very far off from realising a successful company or business.

From Idea to Businesses

An idea by itself does not automatically transform into a business, and this is one thing many people have failed to see. The real fact is that after the idea has been conceived, someone must then be able to transform that idea into a workable business, the most difficult part of the whole entrepreneurial process. To successfully perform this transformation requires a few more steps through defining the necessary ingredients or stars. The entrepreneur will also have to define a meaningful business strategy and an executable implementation plan, gathering the right people and resources followed by actually implementing the plan. During the implementation process, many challenges will emerge, often unanticipated, which will force the plan to be modified, fine-tuned, or even drastically changed along the way. And doing both – the modification and implementation of the plan – at the same time, is really very challenging. It takes many more steps than the idea, for one to claim to have created a successful business or company as an entrepreneur.

If we study all the successful as well as unsuccessful companies, it will become obvious that the difference between the successes and failures was really determined by how well the entrepreneur managed to convert the original idea into a working business with all the bells and whistles that make businesses tick.

Looking back in history, we can find some examples of businesses that became successful due to the vision and expertise of someone other than the originator of the idea. The person who can transform the idea into a business is the one who should really be defined as an entrepreneur. Recall in an earlier chapter, I spoke about how a successful team consists of a Dreamer, Thinker and Doer. And I also said that all entrepreneurs must try to gain all three attributes to succeed. The creative person who thought of the idea, without making the transformation happen, is therefore just the Dreamer or perhaps the Thinker, but he or she may not necessarily be a successful entrepreneur. There is nothing wrong with this since not everyone can be everything in this world. The partnership of the creative person with the innovative, entrepreneurial person – the Doer, also results in successful companies being created. This distinction between the person who can create ideas and the true entrepreneur who can transform the idea into a business is an important one, and if fully understood, can help enhance the chances of successful start-ups.

The Process of Transforming an Idea into a Business

I teach a Masters Course, MSc TIP (Technopreneurship and Innovation Programme) at the Nanyang Technological University in Singapore. One of my lectures is called "Creativity, Innovation and Opportunity Recognition". In that lecture, I talk about the three Stages of Opportunity Recognition – from idea generation, transformation of the idea to a business model and then the business formation. I will elaborate on each of these three key concepts.

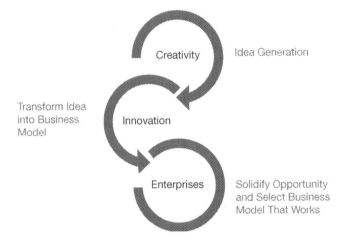

Creativity

Idea Generation

Transform Idea into Business Model

Innovation

Enterprises

Solidify Opportunity and Select Business Model That Works

Fig. 8.1: Concepts of Creativity, Innovation and Opportunity

1. CREATIVITY

According to the Cambridge Dictionary:

> **Creativity**
>
> *noun* [U]
>
> **The ability to produce original and unusual ideas, or to make something new or imaginative.**

If we agree that creativity is the birth of something new, original and imaginative, can we really learn these things? The conventional belief is that the ability to think creatively is genetic. In my opinion it is not. By the same token, people say entrepreneurs are born not made. I disagree, and say entrepreneurship can be learned. At least within the realm of business, virtually everyone has some capacity for creativity and innovative thinking.

In 1968, George Land devised a creativity test (which NASA used to select innovative engineers and scientists). Land did a longitudinal study of 1,600 five-year-olds, and then tested the same children every five years until they reached 15 years of age. The results were astonishing (see Table 8.1).

Table 8.1: Creativity Test Scores, by Age

Creativity Test Scores:		
Test results amongst 5 year olds	:	98%
Test results when 10 years old	:	30%
Test results when 15 years old	:	12%
Same test given to 280,000 adults **(Average Age of 31 years)**	:	2%

And in the words of George Land – "What we have concluded," wrote Land, "is that non-creative behaviour is learned." (Source: George Land and Beth Jarman, *Breakpoint and Beyond*. San Francisco: HarperCollins, 1993.)

In addition, let me summarise some findings by Louis Mobley from the IBM Executive School, that he shared in 1956!

Louis R. Mobley, IBM Executive School (1956) – Six Insights into Teaching Creativity

1. Traditional teaching methodologies like reading, lecturing, testing, and memorisation are worse than useless.
2. Becoming creative is an *unlearning* rather than a *learning* process.
3. We don't *learn* to be creative (it is not by reading only). We must *become* creative people by experiential learning.

4. The fastest way to become creative is to hang around with creative people.
5. Creativity is highly correlated with self-knowledge.
6. You have permission to be wrong – there are no bad or wrong ideas.

We can conclude that creativity is not learned but unlearned. As we get older, we restrict our minds, get boxed up based on our experiences and stop thinking out of the box. If we want to be creative, we should be fearless, allow ourselves to dream and let our minds run free from time to time.

2. INNOVATION

Let's now discuss innovation. In an earlier chapter, I briefly talked about the subtle difference between creativity and innovation. Let me repeat it here.

Creativity – conceiving the idea, thinking of new things, new initiative (needs a curious and creative mind)

Innovation – ability to transform idea to business model, to strategise, execute, communicate and implement the plans (requires an innovative and analytical mind)

Creativity – needs a curious mind

Innovation – needs an analytical mind

Both require you to think out-of-the-box

Interestingly, research on innovation concluded that innovative ideas are not a function of creative thinking or the mind alone, but they are also a function of behaviour. The good news therefore is that we can all be innovative if we change our behaviours – in other words we can learn innovation.

You can pick up many ideas on how to become innovative by reading the book titled *The Innovators DNA* (written by Jeff Dyer, Hal Gregersen, Clayton M. Christensen, Harvard Business Review Press, 2011). The authors suggested five skills of Disruptive Innovators:

- Associating,
- Questioning,
- Observing,
- Experimenting, and
- Idea Networking.

Another book about developing innovation skills was written by Michael J. Gelb, titled *How to Think Like Leonardo Da Vinci* (Deli Pub, 2003). His "Seven Da Vincian Principles for Innovation" are summarised in the box below.

Seven Da Vincian Principles for Innovation

1. **Curiosity (Curiosita)** – unrelenting quest for continuous learning.
2. **Demonstration (Dimonstrazione)** – test knowledge through experience, persistence, and willingness to learn from mistakes.
3. **Sensation (Sensazione)** – The continual refinement of the senses, especially sight, as the means to enliven experience.
4. **Smoke (Sfumato)** – Becoming open to the unknown. A willingness to embrace ambiguity, paradox and uncertainty.
5. **Art and Science (Arte/Scienza)** – Whole-brain thinking. The development of the balance between science and art, logic and imagination. Think with your heart and head.
6. **The Body (Corporalita)** – The cultivation of grace, ambidexterity, fitness, and poise. Balancing the body and mind.
7. **Connection (Connessione)** – A recognition of and appreciation for the interconnectedness of all things and phenomena. Systems thinking.

We can safely summarise that we can indeed cultivate creativity within us, and that with a creative mind, we can come up with new ideas that can potentially be developed into business opportunities.

3. STARTING A COMPANY – IDENTIFYING THE OPPORTUNITY GAP

The final stage of "Transforming an Idea to Business" is to select the final business model, solidify the business plan and gather all the resources to start your venture. I call this – Identifying the Opportunity Gap (remember the first Star – **Star of Opportunity**?). The entrepreneur will be able to exploit the Opportunity Gap to create significant value and competitive advantage for the company.

To able to exploit the opportunity gap, you have to understand your market and operating environment and have very good domain knowledge of the industry you are entering. Understanding the market and environment, the winners can redefine the rules of the game to create a business model that can beat incumbent or other competitors. Of course, the environment is never static. As customers' needs and demands change over time, you will need to know what their latest needs are to create a good market fit for your product or service. Don't underestimate your competitors – they too will not remain static. You must assume competitors are always improving and innovating to compete. Finally, once you have done a self-analysis of your strengths and weaknesses (do a full SWOT) and addressed all of these, you can identify where the "sweet spot" of the Opportunity Gap is and therefore identify the Winning Opportunity.

So, we have learned how we can bring an idea from the creative stage, to work on it through an analytical and innovative mind to identify the opportunity gap. If you can transform your idea into a business this way, your chances of success will be greatly enhanced. Remember this one important fact – that the environment is never static, don't become complacent. I like this quote by Jack Welch, the legendary former CEO of General Electric.

> **"When the rate of external change exceeds the rate of internal change, the end is near."**
>
> **Jack Welch, former CEO, General Electric**

Let me end this section by summarising with a few stories of how some of the best companies and inventions were created, applying some of the innovation concepts that I covered in this chapter. You can research their individual stories to understand them in more detail.

Opportunity Recognition

1. Smaller, Faster, Cheaper Solutions
– *Thomas Edison's Light Bulb*

Edison was not the first inventor of the incandescent light bulb. There were many already present, but they were economically not practical for widespread use. He saw an opportunity to create a practical and cheaper bulb. That idea drove him to innovate.

2. Observe Patterns and Value Created in One Location and Transfer to Another Location
– *Starbucks Story*

Howard Schultz was the GM of a company selling coffee-making machines and observed that one coffeeshop was buying more machines than Macy, one of the largest USA retailers (Pattern that was out of Phase). He joined Starbucks, went to Milan and experienced the culture of expresso bars – particularly, the way in which people interacted. He then transplanted this value to Seattle.

3. Evolving Vision
– FedEx – from 1965, it took eight years to tap opportunity
Fred Smith, a pilot, wrote an economic paper at Yale University about overnight delivery service. He participated in the Vietnam War and saw the logistic issues on ground and air, and cast a vision based on many years of experience.

4. Idea Inversion
– The GPS
Turn things upside down and look at the world differently from the original path we were on. Look at things from a different angle, from a completely different perspective. Suspend all your beliefs for a while and think differently. Originally scientists used the Doppler Effect to track the position of satellites relative to a position on earth. Someone then thought, why not do the reverse? Using a known satellite position, a navigator could determine his location anywhere in the world.

5. Listening to Customer
– Ford Car
Henry Ford famously said, "If I had listened to the customer, I would have bred a faster horse" (instead of developing a car). Listening to the customer is important but finding a right balance is important too. Don't just listen but observe and identify what they really need. Identify needs/problems customers want solved (not just listen). Re-invent and solve the problem and go back and validate with the customer until the problem is solved.

6. Isolating Value
Key ingredient when looking for opportunities – identify value for the innovation you are working on. Don't lose sight by narrowly focusing on your product/service/technology. Value should be from the perspective of the customer, not from your perspective.

The Transformation Process is Tough

Unfortunately, this subtle issue of transforming an idea into a business has not been well understood. People have been taking for granted that once an idea is conceived, they can create a business that will automatically work. This is an erroneous assumption. The sooner we realise this, the more successful we will become as entrepreneurs. Therefore, the ability to spot a winning company at its very early stages depends on the ability to spot the person or team of people who can effectively transform an idea into a business. In other words, the ability of the team to execute the plan is crucial to early success.

In my personal experience, converting the idea into a business strategy and a workable business model is the toughest. There are so many aspects of doing business to consider, such as the people to be part of your team, gathering enough resources, raising the funds, developing the marketing plans, the competitive analysis, the risk factors, the financial plan, the market survey, etc. There are so many things to consider.

It is not only the thinking or the planning that is important, but also the ability to convert the concepts, plans and vision into a total plan that makes sense. In a later chapter, I will talk about how you can use some planning tools to bring the plan together before you write the Business Plan. Following this, the plan must be sensibly communicated to all the stakeholders involved in the company's creation. Putting everything into a business plan requires more than a creative mind. It requires some experience, innovation, as well as the ability to communicate clearly what others may not be able to communicate well. Drawing up a business plan requires skill, and sometimes outside parties may be needed to help put one together. The completed business plan, while being another very difficult step, is also not the end of the journey. It does not necessarily create successful companies and successful entrepreneurs. It is just the next important step after conceiving the idea.

After the ideas and plans have been penned down in a business plan, the next step, which involves the implementation of the plan, is yet another very difficult stage in the whole process. It is common to hear about how implementation would have been made easier if the planning phase had been better conceived. For most management models, the prevailing advice is that one should not take shortcuts in the planning process but be as detailed as possible to avoid hiccups during the implementation phase. While this is true to a certain extent, it is also true that for start-ups and new companies, particularly for those testing out very new ideas, the plan will have to be modified many times before a successful company can emerge. Often, unexpected occurrences happen, requiring modification of the plans to further ensure better chances of getting the desired results.

Enterprise Creation

We have discussed Creativity's role in coming up with new ideas and how we can use Innovation to transform the ideas to viable business models and business plans. Creativity is an act of creating new ideas, imaginations and possibilities, while Innovation is the introduction of something new and effective into the market. The output of innovation is something tangible and quantifiable and measurable that is a new addition to the market (product/service, a start-up). This process needs resource and money and entails risk (whereas Creativity is an imaginative process without the following attributes: quantifiable output, resource consumption and high risks).

Once we can successfully do this transformation process, we are now ready to form the enterprise (the start-up) that can become a viable business that creates value for all the stakeholders. There are many tools that are available today to create the initial product/service and the initial business. The Business Model Canvas, the Lean Start-up Methodology, developing a Minimum Viable Product (MVP), prototyping and beta testing – these are tools to help you create the enterprise based on an original idea which you used to identify the opportunity and can be realised through innovation.

The Need for Special Skills

Special skills are also needed when implementing and adapting the plan as the business develops. Great bandwidth and tremendous energy are required in the first few years of the company's life. In fact, the ability of the entrepreneur and the team is one of the most important criteria that potential investors will look for before they decide to invest. I will discuss this in later chapters, but what investors, especially the savvy ones such as venture capitalists, will look for is the ability of the entrepreneur and the team to make the idea work as a business; they will look for evidence of this ability through the business plan presented to them. Savvy investors will be able to figure this out very quickly as they read the business plan. They will look for evidence of whether the entrepreneur has identified all the necessary actions to transform the idea into a business.

Most start-ups and most entrepreneurs fail because of the inability to transform an idea into a business. I will be bold enough to say that 90 per

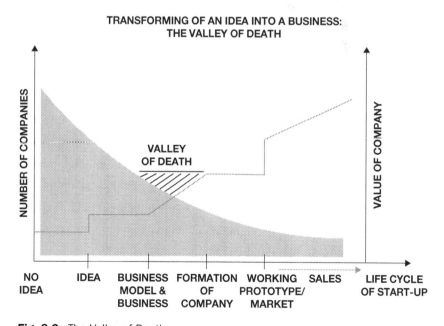

Fig. 8.2: The Valley of Death

cent of start-ups don't make it any further because they don't successfully manage this transformation.

As is illustrated in Figure 8.2, of the number of companies that start out, many rapidly fail and those who survive the "valley of death" will have a chance of creating growing value. The "valley of death" is crossed over when an idea is successfully transformed into a business. Therefore entrepreneurs should focus on building the right bridges to cross over the "valley of death". And these bridges are the strategies, plans, and skills needed to transform an idea into a workable and viable business.

Transformation of the idea into a business requires more than creativity. It requires the other set of entrepreneurial skills, those that I discussed previously in Section A. In summary, if people think an idea is all it takes to be a successful entrepreneur, they are mistaken, as the tasks to implement the idea are a lot more difficult to accomplish. Since it is at this transformation-of-an-idea-into-a-business stage where most will fail, it is important to understand this at the start so that more realistic expectations can be set for everyone involved, and the right preparations can be made to help increase the chances for success.

Chapter 8 Summary

Transforming an Idea into a Viable Business

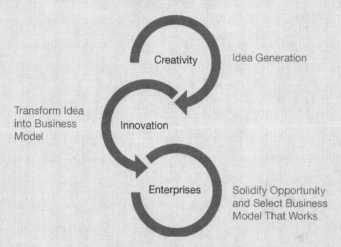

Fig. 8.3: Concepts of Creativity, Innovation and Opportunity

- An idea is not a business. The idea has to be transformed through innovation to a business model and only later into an enterprise.

- Creativity cannot be learned but is unlearned.

- An innovative mindset helps transform the idea into a business.

- The transformation of an idea into a business involves defining a meaningful business strategy, having an executable implementation plan, followed by the proper implementation of the plan.

- Most start-ups fail at this stage – they fail to transform a good idea into a good business, i.e. they fail to build a bridge to cross over the "valley of death".

- It is not only the thinking or planning that is important, but also the ability to convert the concepts, plans and vision into a process that makes sense.

- The business plan must be sensibly communicated to all the stakeholders involved, to convince them that the business is viable.

- Develop an innovative mindset to make the journey from a creative idea to a business model and then to a creating start-up.

CHAPTER 9

STRATEGY DEVELOPMENT FOR START-UPS AND NEW VENTURES

Start-Ups are Not Small Versions of Big Companies

As I mentioned earlier, I lecture at the University and my module is called – Strategic Management for New Ventures & Technology Firms. In this class, I cover strategic management in big companies – typically covering 12 lessons in an MBA course. But I devote only one out of 12 such to focus on how strategy is developed by start-ups and emerging firms, not big companies.

Whether you are running a big company or starting a new venture, you have to develop your strategy and business plan to succeed. You must do a certain amount of strategic planning. Strategic planning in large companies is a long-drawn process that involves many people in the company starting with the CEO and down a few levels in the organisation. It can take months to develop. Of course, entrepreneurs starting out don't have the luxury of time nor resources to do the same type of strategic planning.

We must realise that start-ups are not small versions of big companies and therefore the strategic management process is not the same. The time taken for the strategic planning process is different and the people involved are not the same. Furthermore, the amount of information available for planning differs for both – big companies have much more information or data to help in their planning process while start-ups have very little or uncertain information.

Let's look at the activities of both large companies and start-ups to understand how each manages their key activities. Some of the key preoccupations for each of the types are summarised in Table 9.1.

Table 9.1: Key Management Activities

Area of Focus	Larger Companies	Start-Ups
Managing Money	Annual Budget	Burn Rate
Marketing	Leadership Position	Product/Market Fit
Sales	Sales Growth	Customer Acquisition
HR	Hiring/Retention of Talent	Finding a Team
Finance	Efficient Financing	Attracting Investment
Publicity	A&P	Pitching

Let's examine more details of how different parts of each organisation manage their activities and processes. This will give the entrepreneur a good feel of what needs to be done at the start-up stage and later when the start-up becomes a large company. It is best to have that understanding as early as possible so that a proper system can be put in place early to prepare for growth.

Table 9.2 gives the entrepreneur a good feel of how different it is to manage a company in a start-up stage compared to a grown company. In the Apple story, perhaps Steve Jobs had remained stuck at managing Apple like a start-up although the company had grown enough to be listed on the stock exchange. And perhaps John Sculley came into Apple wanting to run Apple too much like a matured corporation when in fact Apple was still making a transition from a start-up to a large company. It is useful to know the differences to avoid disappointments at all stages of a company's life cycle.

Table 9.2: Organisational Management of Large Corporations Compared with Start-Ups

Area of Focus	Large Corporations	Start-Ups
Organisation Structure	Structured Functional Areas/Clear Lines	Informal and Multi-Functional
Management Style	Policymakers/Top Down	Democratic Process/ Consultative
	Longer-Term Plans	Day-to-Day Decisions
Complexity of Environment	Stable	Turbulent
	Less Competition	Many Competitors
	Many Markets, Many Customers	Single (small) Market, One (few) Customers
Operations/ Processes	Long Lead Times	Fast Lead Times
	Complex and Structured Processes	Flexible Processes
	Established Technology	Disruptive Technologies
	Long Market Reaction Time	Quick Market Reaction Time
Decision Process	Analysis and Thorough Discussions	Gut Feel, Test and Correct
	Many People Involved	Few Key Decision-Makers
	Take Longer, Steady Pace	Quick Change
Change	Incremental Innovation	Radical Innovation
	Avoid Risks	Risk Taking, Fail Fast
Focus Areas	Productivity	Solve Customers' Problems

Entrepreneurship is Hypothesis Testing

Starting a new business is essentially an experiment – for the entrepreneur as well as the investor and other stakeholders. And in any experiment, you have a hypothesis, you test the hypothesis to then come up with the rules. Similarly, for a start-up, the hypothesis testing ends with a business model.

The development and testing of hypotheses is an important way to deal with very high levels of uncertainty. Start-ups face great uncertainties and therefore should start with hypothesis testing to verify if their assumptions about the technology, the market, the product or service can indeed create a viable company. Entrepreneurs therefore are like scientists; they conduct an economic experiment with their start-ups to test a hypothesis (business model). As in engineering and science, there is a lot of trial and error throughout the entrepreneurship process. Like scientists, entrepreneurs test their theories about the business and use the feedback to modify their experiments until they nail down the key ingredients for success.

Chances of failure increase if one does not understand the market and customer feedback that requires adapting or changing the business model. Failing early is not necessarily a bad thing. Such experimentation involves a product/market fit early. As entrepreneurs frequently get this wrong, it is important to learn what does not work, go back to the drawing board to develop a workable plan (business model). Entrepreneurs must not get stuck with their original plan or theory – these must be tested and modified as new information becomes available. Trying only one experiment – i.e. starting-up with just one original plan will likely result in failure. If we keep experimenting and the plan keeps changing from its original form, is having a strategic plan important for start-ups? The answer is a definite yes, because a strategic plan will allow the entrepreneur to focus and to identify what not to do if they want to succeed the next time.

To succeed, the business model and the business plan need to be fluid. Entrepreneurs need to continue to modify assumptions of their hypotheses, test them and solidify their business model and business plan. The start-up must experiment extensively, test many new ideas and identify the path of greatest potential success. Testing and experimenting extensively will also help identify and mitigate risk, optimise resources and increase chances of success. This will help prevent expending too many resources and money on the business model and plan. (50/500 rule – I will elaborate on this rule a little later.)

While it is good to be passionate about an idea, like a scientist who tests a hypothesis and proves it wrong and either modifies his hypothesis or drops the idea, an entrepreneur too must be prepared to continue, pivot or modify the business model or completely drop the idea if it does not work.

The Nine-Stage Strategic Planning Process for New Ventures

So how does an entrepreneur go about developing a strategy – from the time he conceives an idea to the point the start-up is formed and then beyond that, to the stage when the company grows and scales up to become a bigger company? In my class, I share a **nine-stage Strategic Planning Process for New Ventures**. The nine stages are:

1. Idea Generation
2. Identify Opportunity Based on Idea Generated
3. Convert Idea to Business Model to Tap Opportunity
4. Opportunity Analysis to See if Model is Sound
5. Write Business Plan Based on Final Business Model
6. Use Business Plan to Secure Funding
7. Gather the Resources (Team, Stakeholder, Assets, etc.)
8. Start-up the Venture
9. Execute, Scale and Grow.

The nine stages can be further grouped into three main sub-stages:

1. The Opportunity Recognition Phase (Pre-business Plan)
2. The Strategic Planning Phase (Business Plan done at this stage)
3. The Strategic Management Phase (closer to managing a big company).

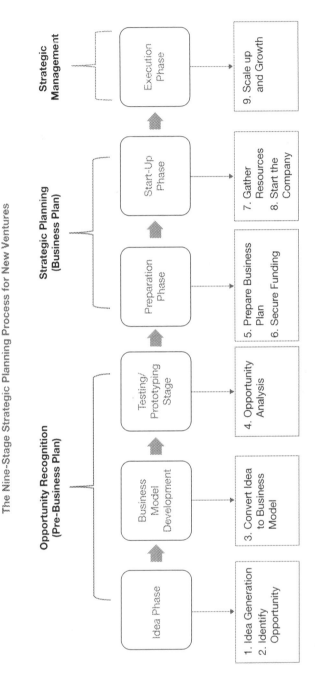

Fig. 9.1: Strategy Development for New Ventures

1. IDEA GENERATION

Here I am going to repeat the difference between being creative and innovative. Recall that there is a subtle difference about thinking of an idea and transforming that idea into a business. The first stage starts with an idea, which requires creativity. Don't discount any idea.

   a. Nothing is impossible – don't shrug off an insane idea.

   "If at first the idea is not absurd, then there is no hope for it."

   – *Albert Einstein*

   b. When you think of an idea, immediately write it down.

   – *The original idea is always the best, not after you have rationalised it.*

   c. There is no such thing as a silly idea.

   – *Like a child, don't be afraid to look silly.*

   d. If there is an idea you thought will work, don't be afraid to do it.

   – *Don't give up because of criticism by others.*

2. OPPORTUNITY RECOGNITION

This is where an innovative mind comes in – you convert the idea into a business model by identifying the opportunity gap and moving fast to tap that opportunity. Let me share some steps you can take to help you recognise and identify an opportunity based on an idea you may have generated.

Steps for Opportunity Recognition/Identification

-   **Target customers:**

   a. Identify a problem or a need significant enough to introduce a solution through a new venture.

   b. Who are the potential customers?

   c. Do you have the best solution to the problem?

- **Business model**:
  a. Does the business model have a clear path to make money?
  b. What does the company sell and how much will the customer pay?
- **Sustainable competitive advantage**:
  a. An analysis of what it takes to grow the business
  b. Positioning the business to be competitive
  c. How sustainable is your business in the long term?

3. BUSINESS MODEL DEVELOPMENT

There are many tools available to help you convert your idea into a business model.

The Business Model Canvas (BMC)[1] – The first stage of developing the BMC is to develop Product/Market (Customer) Fit, using the Value Proposition Canvas (VPC).

Product FIT: The goal is to come up with a model of how to deliver a product or service in response to the customer's need. The elements of this analysis are:

i.   What are the key ingredients or elements of the whole product?
ii. How will the company deliver the product/service?
iii. What will it cost to produce? Is the customer willing to pay at that price?

Customer/Market FIT: The goal here is to develop a model to identify how a company will win customers and gain market share. The key elements of doing this are:

i. Demand creation, and how to achieve it
ii. Demand fulfilment – the most convenient way for the target customer

---

[1] BMC was developed by the Swiss business model guru Alexander Osterwalder and management Information Systems Professor Yves Pigneur. They defined nine categories for the Business Model Canvas which they refer to as the building blocks of an organisation.

iii.   Identify any barriers to winning customers – have these been addressed?

Sustainable Competitive Advantage: How can you be competitive enough to win over market share from other competitors? Why will customers switch over to your company? The key elements to do this are:

i.   Understand the competitive landscape

ii.   Know your strengths and weaknesses and compare to competitors

iii.   Identify the barriers to entry and raise the barriers higher

iv.   How much of a lead do you have and how to lengthen that lead?

4.   OPPORTUNITY ANALYSIS

Once you have identified the Product/Market (Customer) fit, you should start testing the market to see if you have indeed identified the correct model, correct strategies and have the right resources to deliver to the customer before you nail down the final business model. This is where the concept of hypothesis testing that I described earlier in the chapter is used. The way to do this is by quick prototyping and testing. I call this the 50/500 Rule (see story box below). Based on the outcome of your testing, select the best opportunity and summarise and identify the key ingredients (Aligning Your Stars) for success. Once you are confident you have identified the key ingredients for success, go ahead and fine tune and finalise the business model.

a.   Identify a product/service that customers want

b.   Identify customers who will buy

c.   Identify the best way to deliver the product/service

d.   Identify your competitive advantage to win

e.   Identify a business model that will sustain the company.

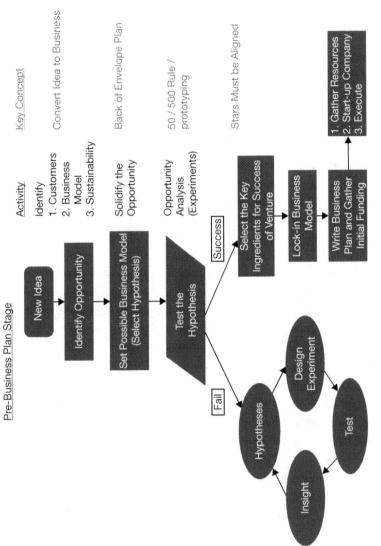

Fig. 9.2: The Nine-Stage Strategic Planning Process for New Ventures

In other words, you have a full BMC completed after this stage. I will not elaborate on the rest of the stages in this section which are covered in a different part of the book. For completeness, let me list the rest of the steps here:

    f.   Write a business plan based on the final business model

    g.   Use the business plan to secure funding

    h.   Gather the resources (team, stakeholders, assets, etc.)

    i.   Start up the venture

    j.   Execute, scale and grow.

Figure 9.2 captures the nine-stage strategic planning process that start-ups and new ventures should use.

The 50/500 Rule (Beta Testing the Market)

I developed a rule for myself on how I would grow my company step-by-step. It has been very useful in guiding me through my entrepreneurial journeys. I coined this the 50/500 rule and developed it when I was working with a group of fresh graduates on a dot.com company. It was my first experience in the dot.com world. I realised that some entrepreneurs might not understand the realities of how to start and grow a business and had a tendency to overdo things too early in the process.

Our dot.com (Internet) company set about to do demand aggregation over the Internet. We were the first in Asia to do this, almost in parallel with a few companies in USA and Europe. The idea was simple. When we go out shopping in a group and we all decide to buy the same item, we approach the shopkeeper to bargain for a better price since we are buying more than one piece. Sometimes, the shopkeeper agrees because the sales volume might justify the bigger discount. Taking this philosophy online, we thought of bringing strangers over the Internet to aggregate their demand and then use it to look for merchants or suppliers to bid for this potential aggregated demand at a lower price. It is akin to a reverse auction. If it worked, the business could become phenomenal and many buyers and suppliers would come onboard to use our portal.

With this thought in mind that hundreds of thousands of people would be coming onboard and that thousands of merchants and suppliers would also be using our portal to bid for the sales we could facilitate, my young partners wanted to build a large infrastructure to support a huge business. Such a large infrastructure would be needed for the portal, which would require sophisticated software, supply chain management, secured payment channels, customer service, delivery, etc.

We could spend a lot of money building a huge infrastructure in anticipation of the long-term vision of generating a few hundred million dollars of sales. However, should the business fail, we would have wasted a lot of money. At the same time, should the business model be changed as circumstances change, we would have to spend a lot to modify and adjust the infrastructure. To build a solid infrastructure we would have to spend a couple million dollars – not a small sum, I thought.

My idea was to slowly scale up the business and not just jump into what we thought would be the final business structure. Because the demand aggregation business we were trying to build required customers and suppliers, I decided we should test our business by first seeing if the model would work with around 500 customers using our portal at any one time, with only around 50 suppliers bidding for our business. We could easily handle 500 customers without building huge infrastructures – through a simple portal, outsourcing some functions, and with our team members doubling up as customer service and sometimes doing delivery.

Similarly, if only 50 suppliers were registered to bid on our portal, dealing with them would become easier for the small team. Now, if the business model could be proven for the 500 customers and 50 suppliers, we could then quickly develop a much bigger infrastructure with the confidence that the business model had a greater chance of success. It might seem a little wasteful if the model worked and we had some redundant infrastructure, which we would have to abandon should we migrate to a bigger system (for example, the portal would probably need to be completely revamped to take care of the much bigger business).

But looking on the other side of things, should the business fail, or should the business model need changing, we would not have wasted too much money in anticipation of a big business. So, we went on to test our business model targeting 500 customers and 50 suppliers, and I called this the 50/500 rule.

Simply put, I believe in scaling up a business appropriately and not overdoing things right from the beginning. I have always operated with this 50/500 rule of testing the business model before deciding on building up the businesses I have been involved in to avoid any waste of money should the model not work. It is in fact a lot more difficult to make U-turns or to change things if one starts with a large infrastructure. By following the 50/500 rule, changes will come about faster, thus ensuring the development of a more robust business.

Let me touch a little on the concept of Design Thinking. You will come across this term quite often when you read about entrepreneurship. What is design thinking? This is what I found on the Internet:

Design thinking is a human-centred approach to innovation that draws from the designer's toolkit to integrate the

needs of people, the possibilities of technology, and the requirements for business success.

In other words, it is a creative thinking and problem-solving process that follows the pattern of how designers do things to create new designs, whether building a machine or product designs. Design thinking is increasingly becoming a popular way to innovate. There are many books written on design thinking which aspiring entrepreneurs should read.

Let me end with a summary of some of the pitfalls and failures when doing strategic planning for start-ups and new ventures.

Potential pitfalls when doing strategic planning for new ventures:

1. **Focusing on form instead of substance** – Focused on planning but not keeping an eye on running the business.
2. **Missing the market** – Targeting the wrong market at the wrong time.
3. **Over planning** – Spending too much time planning but neglecting to tweak on the run.
4. **Lengthy business plan** – Trying to capture too many details makes the business plan difficult to read – keep it concise and easy to read.
5. **Not all team members involved** – Don't leave it to a consultant, get team members involved so that they have skin in the game.
6. **Rigid business plan** – A plan that is inflexible and fails to adapt to early assumptions and the changing environment.

Chapter 9 Summary

Strategy Development for Start-Ups and New Ventures

- Bearing in mind that start-ups are not small versions of big companies, it may not make sense for a start-up to develop a strategic plan the way big companies do.

- Entrepreneurship is hypothesis testing – it is an economic experiment undertaken by the entrepreneur to test whether an idea can become a great business.

- Entrepreneurs can follow a nine-stage strategic planning process grouped into three business stages, as a guide to build stronger and longer lasting companies.

The three business stages are as follows:
1. The Opportunity Recognition Phase (Pre-business Plan)
   - Idea generation

   - Identify opportunity based on idea generated

   - Convert idea to business model to tap opportunity

   - Conduct opportunity analysis to see whether idea is sound.

2. The Strategic Planning Phase (Business Plan stage)
   - Write business plan based on final business model

   - Use business plan to secure funding

   - Gather the resources (team, stakeholders, assets, etc.)

   - Start up the venture.

3. The Strategic Management Phase (closer to managing a big company)
   - Execute, scale and grow.

- Recognise the potential pitfalls when doing strategic planning for new ventures – focus on the substance, make it simple and flexible, must be market driven and involve all stakeholders.

CHAPTER 10

THE PROCESS OF STARTING A COMPANY – EARLY STAGES

In the first edition of my book, this chapter covered the stages of the company after the idea stage – starting the company, taking off after the start-up stage and finally focusing extensively on the fund-raising process. In this second edition, I have decided to break the chapter into two parts. The feedback on my first edition was that my fund-raising sections were too focused on the company raising funds at a later stage and not on the earlier angel and seed stages. Let me explain why I inadvertently did that. You see, I did two consecutive start-ups where my first external round of fund raising came from big VCs and I raised US$138m for my first venture UTAC in 1998 and then US$36m for Infiniti Solutions in 2001/2002. So, my experience had been with major fund raising. But as an angel I have invested into close to 25 start-ups since 2000, thereby gaining experience in investing at the very early stages. I will share my experiences for early-stage fund raising in this chapter and leave the major VC-type fund-raising lesson to later chapters.

Starting and Taking Off

What does it take to transform an idea into a business, or perhaps first into a plan before creating a business? In this chapter, I will describe the practical step an entrepreneur will have to go through from the ideas stage to the stage the start-up is formed, before gathering resources and raising the funds to sustain the company. I covered some key concepts and methodologies for the strategic planning process for new ventures in the previous chapter, and also discussed how we can transform an idea to a business in another earlier chapter. In this chapter, I will go through the practical steps for entrepreneurs right from the beginning of an idea to the growth stage. It may seem like overlapping, but as you go through this chapter you will realise that it is about putting into action what I had discussed earlier.

Starting with the idea, next you pen it down and communicate it with others. You then need to elaborate on the plans and strategies, look for the money, and finally, complete all the necessary documents and agreements. It is only after all these most difficult tasks have been completed that the business would have finally taken shape.

These three areas of starting, taking off, and fund raising all entail very different experiences and require different skills and abilities. It is therefore important that the new entrepreneur knows what he will have to go through before a company can finally be created. It involves many steps. If you want to be successful as an entrepreneur, it will be critical for you to master all these steps. I have identified a total of 13 steps that are worth sharing. I have distilled six of them to discuss in this chapter. I will cover Steps 7 to 13 in Chapter 12.

Step No. 1: Getting the Idea and Writing a Conceptual Plan
– "The Back-of-the-Envelope Plan"

An idea is usually conceived in some creative mind. While sometimes the ideas come in flashes and may not appear coherent at first, after a period of time, the ideas solidify, and become organised in the mind. The next stage, therefore, is to formulate a mental model and a mental plan of how the idea can be developed into a possible business, and how the opportunities can be tapped successfully.

While the idea and the mental models may remain in the mind for some time, it is quite typical for the entrepreneur to pen down the ideas and briefly draw the product, invention, or the possible business model and plans. Because the final mental model can be developed at any time after the flashes of ideas solidify, the broad plan typically gets written on any piece of paper the entrepreneur can lay his or her hands on. This is therefore called the back-of-the-envelope plan or a napkin plan (of course with technology, the back-of-the-envelope could be a tablet, a notebook computer, or any other portable device). By doing this, the idea and a raw plan are captured on paper. Even if the flashes cease, the captured idea remains visible and can be further developed into the next stage. This back-of-the-envelope plan is also used to communicate more visibly with the other team members and potential stakeholders about the possible opportunities.

An example of a napkin plan that a group of young computer engineers worked on with me to develop our first dot.com or Internet business in 1999 is given in Figure 10.1. If you look at the plan, we were 15 years too early with a great idea – Group Buying. Groupon came and did something similar 15 years later. We were too early because the world was not ready for Internet buying until much later (technology, payment, security, logistics).

Step No. 2: Getting the Team Together for Buy-In
– The Believers, the Sceptic, and the Convincible

The second step of the process always begins with a group of people the entrepreneur knows and trusts. Because it is too early to be discussing the ideas and potential plans with just anyone, it is important that the initial group should be trustworthy – one that is more likely to join in or support the plan. Letting the ideas and potential intellectual property out of the bag too early can result in tremendous loss, and even result in the project never taking off the ground.

Sometimes, even the most trusted people who are willing to explore the possibility of joining the start-up may not necessarily be able to see the opportunities and how the obstacles can be overcome. It is therefore very important that there be at this stage a small core group of people who have a frequency of thinking almost similar to the entrepreneur, and who can understand the essence of the plan that is being developed. And they must also have some amount of appetite for taking risk.

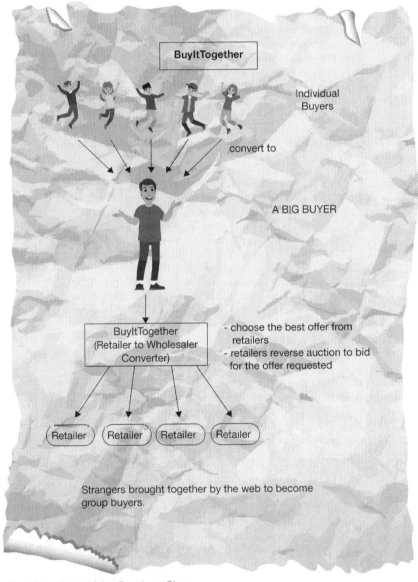

Fig. 10.1: Back-of-the-Envelope Plan

BuyItTogether

Key Points

1. Why it will work -> When we go shopping as a group, we normally bargain with shopkeeper for better price if we buy more than one item -> Go for group discount.

2. New sales channel -> Retailers effortlessly have new channel to sell things in bulk – retailers become wholesalers.

3. Web-middlemen -> Use web to aggregate demand – bring strangers as a community of buyers. Web used to enhance efficiency of buy/sell channel.

Success Factors

1. Build up community of buyers
2. Good partners in supply chains – especially merchants/sellers
3. Portal to allow aggregation and real time reverse auction
4. Work with logistic company

Information Needed

1. Cost of developing portal and how long it will take
2. Type of products which can sell on internet – do market research
3. Any competitors – first mover advantage
4. Sources – merchants to tie-up with

Internet Buying will explode and Aggregate Buying will make things cheaper

Fig. 10.1: *(Continued)*

This does not mean all of them should think alike, but more that they are able to easily understand each other, even if they may have differing views. Getting the wrong people too early in the discussions could kill the project prematurely.

In any team, there will be the believers and the sceptics, and also those who can be convinced by more in-depth sharing of views and plans. It is important that all their views be taken in perspective without letting any one of them dominate the process.

The goal is to form a team that will buy into the idea and the plan. Having all the optimists dominate the discussion can be self-defeating in creating a situation of over-confidence, resulting in the failure to consider possible pitfalls. In contrast, listening only to pessimists and sceptics could result in neglecting to look at the alternatives or possible ways around potential obstacles. The project could get killed too early with this type of thinking. Also if too many people require a lot of in-depth explanation and convincing, it could result in a weary exercise, tire out the believers, sapping their energy and making it more difficult to bring the project to the next stage.

It is best to have a good balance of all types of people in the founding team, but perhaps slightly over-weighted with more optimists than pessimists. How one works with each differing type of person in the team has to also vary. There is no one right or wrong way of dealing with all the people involved. The approach and time taken to work with and deal with each type of person will also need to differ for the best outcome. Some are highly independent while others need more guidance in certain areas.

Step No. 3: Writing an Initial Business Plan (Mini Business Plan)
–Building More Details than "The Back-of-the-Envelope Plan"

The purpose of the initial business plan is to communicate professionally what you have conceived, to others who may not be as familiar as you are about your project and of the opportunities you seek. The initial business plan is also important at the very early stages of a start-up because it has to also be used as a means to convince the team whom you want to attract to finally join you. They will need to know that things have been well thought out and that there is a believable plan, which can be executed to achieve success. To the team, the business plan is also a guide to how your business will be conducted to avoid any misunderstandings later. It provides some structure and certainty out of the very uncertain prospect of a new venture.

The plan should be able to communicate the vision, goals, markets, opportunities, and strategies to achieve the goal, tactics, how to secure financing, and what is the long-term goal of the company. At this juncture, the business plan is really a guide to be used by the team in convincing more people to join the venture, as well as to begin doing a reality check of whether the start-up will indeed look interesting to external parties. It also acts as a guiding roadmap for the company's initial activities.

The above two paragraphs were what I wrote in the first edition of my book. Let me expand a little more to add new concepts that have since been developed. Being a mini-business plan, it is useful to capture all the key elements or ingredients that will bring success to your venture: There are many tools for this and one is the Business Model Canvas (BMC) that serves to highlight the winning formula for your company: identifying your customers, why they will want to use your product or service, how you are going to win customers, how you will deliver your product/service and some key operational and financial details. I will elaborate more in a later chapter about this. But suffice it to say that at this Step 3, your initial "back-of-the-envelope or napkin" idea has now evolved with more details providing a better picture of how you are transforming your idea into a business model and into a viable business. You can now communicate better with all stakeholders who need to know and want to know about your start-up.

Step No. 4: Putting in Your Money and Getting Started

Rarely will you find someone who is willing to fund a brand-new project. In particular, everyone must realise that venture capitalists or VCs will rarely fund companies that are not already funded by someone else unless the idea or the technology behind the project is earth shattering in nature.

Companies most typically get started with the entrepreneur putting in his own money. Of course, the other best source of very early stage funding comes from family, friends and relatives, in addition to the self-funding by the founding team, particularly by the entrepreneur.

The 3 "Fs"

Sometimes, people call this initial group of investors the "3Fs" – family, friends, and fools. When no one else has confidence in you, these are the people who will at least help you out. Note that "fools" are used because at this stage, the start-up is highly risky and the chances of failing are relatively higher. Most likely the money put in will be lost – hence it is like fools parting with their money. I will elaborate about these 3Fs later in this book.

Additionally, there are people called angel investors, who invest in very early stage projects. They are typically very rich individuals who have the spare cash and want to see part of their money multiply through early investments. They know the risks involved and are willing to lose their money, but they also know that if the start-up becomes successful, they will reap huge gains. Most of the time, such outside investors will want to be reassured by the entrepreneur's own investment and sacrifice in starting the company. As the saying goes, "put your money where your mouth is" – an entrepreneur must be able to demonstrate this to attract outside money. Why should someone else risk their money if the entrepreneur has nothing to lose? In fact, some VCs go to the extent of assessing the entrepreneur's *pain factor*. In other words, they assess what the entrepreneur has to lose should the company fail. This pain factor is very typical in the mindsets of VCs, and particularly so after the dot.com experience.

It is at this stage where start-up can now test the viability of their business model and product/service with some initial customers by building a minimum viable product (MVP). With initial money for the start-up, it is able to build a prototype, validate (or invalidate) the business model, pivot and after discovering the possible ingredients of success develop a final business model that can be translated to the final business plan.

Step No. 5: The (Real) Business Plan

At this stage, the proper business plan should have already been prepared to become a robust document. In fact, the initial business plan is something that comes before the whole core team is assembled. The first cut would typically have been prepared by the few people who have been involved during the back-of-the-envelope stage. Once the rest of the team is assembled, the plan is developed further to capture all the thoughts of the team members. While the business plan is best developed by the founders themselves, some start-ups do engage outside experts like consultants to help them strengthen the business plan to make it look attractive to potential investors. I personally think there is no need to engage consultants as no one knows the business better than the founders. Potential partners will depend on this business plan to understand your company and decide whether to become one of your stakeholders – so it is important that the business plan be a really good one.

A well-written plan is one that can communicate the vision, strategies and tactics the team is planning for the company. If prepared correctly, it will ensure the best chance of attracting serious investors. The business plan at this stage should be a document that is ready to go to very savvy investors, particularly the VCs. It therefore has to be very professionally prepared and has a proper structure that will allow you to communicate what your start-up is all about to all stakeholders. It must be understood that most VCs will not have the time to go through very lengthy plans. So, it is best to have a concise plan, which is able to attract attention and draw excitement among those who look at the plan for the first time. Table 10.1 is a sample of what the contents page in a business plan looks like. In a later chapter, I delve into greater detail about the business plan and what constitutes a good business plan.

Table 10.1: Business Plan Table of Contents

1	Executive Summary		1
2	Industry Background		
	2.1	The Type of Industry Your Company is in	3
	2.2	Your Company Position in the Industry	4
	2.3	Competitive Landscape	5
3	Company Background and Management Team		
	3.1	Industry, Company History and Business Description	6
	3.2	Pain Point and Problem You are Solving	7
	3.3	The Opportunity and How You Solve the Problem	9
	3.4	Organisation Chart and Shareholding Structure	10
	3.5	Profile of Senior Management	11
4	Products/Service		
	4.1	Technology & IP	13
	4.2	Product/Service Details	14
	4.3	Value Proposition	15
	4.4	Product Development Roadmap	16
5	Company's Goals, Objectives, Mission and Vision		
	5.1	Company Vision/Mission	18
	5.2	SWOT & Competitor Analysis	19

Table 10.1: *(Continued)*

	5.3	Goals, Objectives and Plans	20
6	The Market, Marketing Strategy and Plan		
	6.1	Market Study and Segmentation	21
	6.2	Marketing Plan and Marketing Strategy	22
	6.3	Marketing and Sales Budget Consideration	24
7	Operations Strategy		
	7.1	Operations/Execution Plan	25
	7.2	R&D and Product Roadmap	26
	7.3	Resource/Facility Acquisition and Set-Up	27
	7.4	HR/Hiring Roadmap – Filling Skills Gaps	28
8	Financials		
	8.1	Financial Statements – Historical and Five-Year Forecasts	29
	8.1	Fund-Raising Plans	30
9	Risk and Contingency Plans		32
10	Exit Plan		33
11	Appendices		34

Step No. 6: Fund Raising

One of the most difficult tasks for any entrepreneur is raising funds. I have done business in many parts of the world – Singapore, Silicon Valley, China, USA, Southeast Asia and many countries in Africa. The one common challenge I hear from every start-up and every entrepreneur is access to financing. I too faced this challenge for my start-ups. As I mentioned before, for UTAC, I could not find any investors brave enough to invest in my start-up and I found most of my money in Taiwan. Taiwan, like Israel and the Silicon Valley, is much more entrepreneurial than many countries, including Singapore.

In the year 2013, I had the privilege to speak to the United Nations General Assembly representing Singapore for the Thematic Debate called "Entrepreneurship for Development". Listening to all the speakers from different nations, what I learned is that the whole world is facing the same issues when it comes to start-ups or entrepreneurs. It does not matter if it is Australia or Angola, USA or Uganda – financing or funding was always the number one problem.

Before you embark on your fund raising, it is important that you have a good strategy that defines some important factors. These include the reason you are raising the amount of money and how the money will be used, how much you need for the first round of fund raising, who are you targeting to raise the money, and by when do you need the money. It is best to identify the fund-raising strategies, not just for the initial stage but also a roadmap of future fund-raising plans and strategies. There could be certain milestones for fund-raising plans at each stage. I will share more about this in a later chapter where I discuss "The Rules of Thumb" for fund raising.

Entrepreneurship is a Global Common Language

Entrepreneurship and Social Justice

1. Even as the world progresses, poverty continues to plague mankind. According to the World Bank, 2.5 billion people live on less than US$2 per day. I believe we can solve this poverty problem through entrepreneurship.

2. We must believe entrepreneurship is not only about wealth creation; it is also about the pursuit of social justice. Social justice can definitely come about by creating good jobs for all, giving equal opportunities through meritocratic systems and social entrepreneurship.

3. On 26 June 2013, I attended and participated at the United Nations Thematic Debate called "Entrepreneurship for Development" held in New York. Members of the United Nations were gathered to discuss how entrepreneurship can help solve the world's development problems. What struck me most during the debate was that the world is indeed going through an Entrepreneurial Revolution. Whether the discussion was from America or Zambia, whether it is the East or the West of the world, whether it is a developed nation or an emerging nation, all geared up to participate in the Global Entrepreneurial Revolution talking the same language of Entrepreneurship for wealth creation and social justice.

4. Here are some of are the common things that cut across nations, cultures and societal attitudes:

   a. Financing and getting smart money for funding start-ups

   b. The need for a good eco-system of rules and regulations facilitating start-ups

   c. The need for equal opportunities for all

   d. Focus on a global market

   e. Leveraging on technology for productive growth.

Let us now examine the steps of early fund raising as depicted in Figure 10.2. The figure is a rough guide to show when and where you should raise funds. Don't be concerned about the exact numbers and the exact stages – the diagram serves to give us a feel of the whole process of fund raising. Let me briefly discuss each stage.

Early Fund Raising
The Pre-Seed Stage

This is also called the bootstrapping stage. It is where you use whatever little money you can acquire to stretch the company as far as you can to achieve some measurable milestone to gain interest from future investors. This first source of funds has to come from yourself and the 3Fs or the Three Fools that I mentioned earlier. In addition to the 3Fs, you should also show you believe in your project by putting in your own money. When I started my third major company, Infiniti Solutions in 2011, I put in US$500k to bring my team together to get started. We then managed to raise our first round of US$36m (actually this is not bad for a post September 11 and post dot.com bubble burst era). The first US$500k allowed me and my team to start the preparation work for Infiniti Solutions. Valuation at this stage is very difficult to determine and is a matter of judgement.

New Platforms for Fund Raising

Let me briefly share some new platforms that are available for entrepreneurs and start-ups to use to raise funds at the early stages. These did not exist when I wrote the first edition of my book but today are very well-established and popular. However, my previous book did introduce a platform that I developed – called the "Deal Flow Connection". It brought investors and start-ups onto a common web platform to "meet" and then later discuss investment deals. The web platform was like a marketplace bringing all the stakeholders together. I guess that was the prelude to what is well known

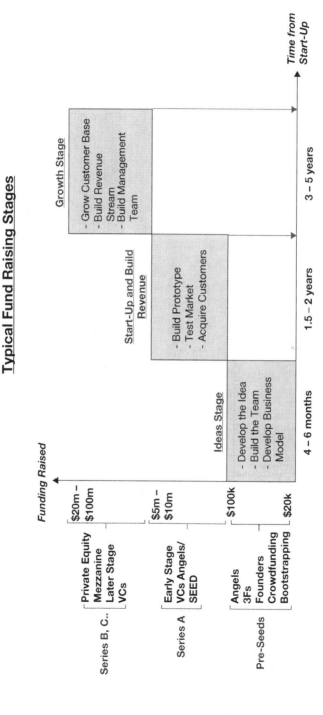

Fig. 10.2: Typical Fund Raising Stages

today as Crowdfunding. So, while the formal next stage for raising funds after you have done the bootstrapping and the 3Fs round, is the Seed stage. Today start-ups have access to a whole new world of opportunities to raise funds from strangers using crowdfunding platforms and websites. There are different varieties – some allow you to take a loan, some are pre-orders of your product while others are equity investment types. Theoretically, through the web, you can today reach any potential investor from any part of the world (I say theoretically because there may be government regulations that may restrict such fund raising, so you should be aware if it is legal or not before using any of these platforms.) You can find hundreds of such platforms all over the world, so I will not name any in this book.

A couple more options that many start-ups use today for early funding are Accelerators and Incubators. While the primary role of these is to provide an initial working space, mentoring, use of common facilities, including Makers Labs, some also provide initial funding to the start-ups. Start-ups have to be prepared to give up some equity for these services and the initial funds provided.

An emerging form of early-stage fund raising is the Initial Coin Offering (ICO) or Security Token Offering (STO) that builds on Distributed Ledger Technology (DLT). Most ICO's are like Kickstarter Crowdfunding. The start-up creates a pool of tokens (also called coins) which represent the IOU that he can use to redeem the product or service at a later stage. The buyers of the tokens hope that the value of their tokens will appreciate when the product or service becomes popular in the future. For STO, the start-up creates a pool of tokens that represents the equity of the company. This is the same as the equity assigned to the stock in a publicly-traded company. Hence the token is considered as a Security Instrument and needs to comply with all existing Securities & Futures regulations.

Using DLT, these tokens can be traded from digital-wallet to digital-wallet without going through any regulated exchanges. Hence the fund-raising process can be much cheaper and faster, especially with speculative investors and traders favouring DLT's reach and liquidity.

To use ICO and STO for fund raising, one must understand the nature of **Distributed** Ledger Technology (DLT) and how it is different from the current **centralised** regulation concept. It is best that professional and legal advice be sought before using DLT for fund raising.

Seed Stage Funding

So you have planted the seeds for your start-up by bootstrapping and now you have to raise money from external investors. Research has shown that close to 30 per cent of start-ups fail because they run out of money during the bootstrapping stage. This stage should therefore be treated very seriously and hopefully you have achieved some measurable results to show to potential investors (like your business plan, your team, if possible, a prototype or design of your first product). At this stage the potential investors are Angel investors, high net worth individuals, the 3Fs, and early stage VCs. These days, crowdfunding platforms may come in useful. The valuations will now improve as you have achieved some milestones. Even formation of a company and having a team on board is a milestone achieved. Depending on the nature of your industry and company, valuations can now be in the few millions of dollars to enable you to raise a few hundred thousand to a couple of million dollars.

Later Stages of Fund Raising

I will briefly introduce the later stages of fund raising in this section. In a later chapter, I will cover in detail how a start-up can engage in these later stages of formal fund raising.

The Formal VC Stage – Series A

After the Seed stage, the start-up should have made more progress and by now, should be able to demonstrate the ability of the team to execute the business plan. The product or service should already have passed the Beta stage and is now ready for production and actual use by customers. You must already have a reasonable customer base before you see Series A funding. Raising the Series A money should be to bring your company to a more rapid growth and to head towards profitability. It is important that the entrepreneur does not wait for Seed money to run out before looking for Series A investors. Ideally, immediately after the Seed stage funds are raised, you should start networking and send feelers to potential VCs at every opportunity. From experience, you will have to engage between 20 to 30 potential investors to end up with two or three who are finally interested to consider your start-up. So cast the net wide if you have to. The potential investors at this stage could be Angel investors who have a bigger appetite, or a group of Angels pooling their money. But the most important investors at this stage are VCs. Valuation can be in the tens of million dollars at this stage and the start-up should raise between $5m to $10m as a rough guide. Do note that while at the Seed stage, most investments are pure equity type, but at this stage and all the subsequent stages, different structures are typically used. Convertible notes are quite typical, where the money put in looks like an interest-bearing loan but the investor has the right to convert the full or partial amount to equity at some pre-agreed price.

Advanced VC Stages – Series B, C, D …

The next stage of fund raising typically involves securing much larger amounts of money to fuel an even more rapid growth of the company, which at this stage may no longer be seen as a start-up. For all fund raising after the Series A, you will typically be looking for large VCs and institutional investors who will bring in smart money and networks to help your company grow further. It is important that the VC or investor you choose during Series A can remain an anchor investor for these other series of fund raising and that he has a wide network who can join in future fund-raising rounds. At this stage, your company would be considered a successful company that could lead to good future exit for all investors. The valuation can be quite high – ranging from around $50m to a few hundred million dollars; you can raise huge sums of a few hundred million depending on your valuation.

The investors at these rounds are typically late stage VCs, private equity companies, mezzanine funds, hedge funds, etc.

Pre-IPO Stages

While the above (Series B onwards) are all pre-IPO stages of fund raising, sometimes the company may raise some bridging financing to bring the company to an IPO or an acquisition event – in other words towards an exit for all investors. This can be in the form of equity, debt, convertible notes and can come from banks, mezzanine funds and late stage VCs.

Valuation of Start-Ups and Companies

This is one of the most important points entrepreneurs need to know – how to value your company when you are raising money from external investors. While I suggest entrepreneurs familiarise themselves with how they can value their company using one of the many valuation methodologies, I also advise that at the very early stages, it is very difficult to come out with exact valuation numbers just because most of the valuation models depend on some financial performance and projections. But at the very early stages of the start-up, you may not have revenues, and you have forecasts that very few will believe at face value. So, it is a matter of judgement. For this reason, I say that valuation of a start-up (and perhaps for even established companies) is more of an art than a science. But to convince the investors of the valuation you need, you will want it to be a science by building on valuation models that show that your company is worth a lot. The investor will want it to be more of an art or a judgement and they will discount as many factors as possible that you would have used to justify your valuation. While I say the valuation is more of an art in the early stages, you must still rely on a number of models based on some financial projections to arrive at your valuation number. You cannot simply pluck a number from thin air to quote to your potential investor. So, take note of the following when negotiating a valuation number with an investor:

1. Valuation is both an art and a science (as I mentioned above).
2. As you will need some type of formal structured computation, choose a model that can be justified when you work out the valuation.
3. No two companies can ever be the same and hence what is used to value one company may not be suitable for another. Many entrepreneurs try to justify a huge valuation by comparing themselves to some "already successful" companies. Nevertheless, as transforming your idea into a business is tough, do not compare yourself to a company that has already made it.
4. Because valuation is both an art and a science (more of an art in the early stages), do not be too dogmatic about a magic valuation number. Let that valuation number be a rough guide and a starting point for you to use to initiate negotiations with the potential investors.

Remember this, your company will only have some value if you have an investor interested in investing in you. Otherwise it will all be theoretical. Therefore it is not only a valuation number that you will need to work out but also the need to show to potential investors your intrinsic value that will interest them to initiate an investment discussion. What are these intrinsic values – they are your team, your IP, your experience, your networks, and your ability to attract customers to want to use your product. In other words, you must be able to show that your **Stars are Aligned**.

Valuation of Start-Ups and Companies

How did some companies start?

- It is useful to know that many good companies really did not start with an external equity investment by VCs.
- They relied on their own money and on those of friends and families who also did not expect to get back their money.

> Examples:
> - HP started with US$538 in 1938.
> - Microsoft and Apple had capital of US$5,000 in the 1970s.
> - Starbucks started with US$4,050 by three shareholders (and a bank loan of US$5,000).

What should the entrepreneur look out for when determining the valuation of the start-up? You need to remember a few things. First, both the entrepreneur and the start-up have different objectives in the valuation exercise. The entrepreneur is always looking for the highest valuation in order not to be diluted too much when the external investor puts in the money. While the investor wants to ask for the lowest possible valuation to own a good share of the company. It is a competition between the two of them. So, who convinces whom? Well, as I have mentioned before and will mention many times again, it is all an art.

Different Valuation Methodologies

There are many valuation methodologies to choose from, depending on what stage the company is at. It is useful to know as many of these valuation models as possible to select the most suitable one as your company progresses through the growth journey. You can read books on the details of each of these methodologies but let me briefly summarise some of the more popular ones:

    a. Venture Capital Method
    b. Berkus Method
    c. Scorecard Valuation Method
    d. Risk Factor Summation Method
    e. Cost-to-Duplicate Method
    f. Discounted Cash Flow Method
    g. Valuation by Stage Method

h. Comparables Method
i. The Book Value Method
j. First Chicago Method

I don't intend to explain each of these methods as you can search online. Just remember that each method depends on the stage of the start-up or the growth journey that the company is in. At the very early stages, more judgement is used to derive the value, at a later stage more of the financial performance is used to derive a more accurate valuation.

Chapter 10 Summary

The Process of Starting a Company – Early Stages

There are 13 steps to transform an idea into a business. Steps 7–13 are covered in Chapter 13.

STARTING

Step No. 1   Getting the idea and writing a conceptual plan – the "Back of envelope plan"

Step No. 2   Bringing the team together for buy-in: the believers, the sceptics and the convincible

Step No. 3   Writing an initial business plan – business model and mini business plan.

TAKING OFF

Step No. 4   Putting in your money and getting started

Step No. 5   The (real) business plan

Step No. 6   Early fund raising
- Pre-seed
- Seed
- Series A

This chapter also describes the various platforms for fund raising, valuation of startups and the different valuation methodologies.

CHAPTER 11

THE BUSINESS PLAN

The business plan is the most important document that captures the essence of what your business is all about. The business plan is the identity of your company – the industry you are in, the problem you are solving, how you are solving it, your strategies, goals, and the people behind the company. It is an important document used to guide all the stakeholders in the execution of the plan. A well-written business plan is one that captures the thought process of the entrepreneur and the company's founders and tells a convincing story to third parties. In particular, it is the only way to convince potential investors to look at your company and to decide whether or not to invest with you. The entrepreneur should therefore put in the best effort to prepare an impressive business plan. If the entrepreneur does not have the capability or knowledge to write the business plan, professional help should be engaged.

In this chapter, I will briefly cover some of the important components that make up a typical business plan. I will touch mainly on the technical details of what constitutes a business plan. In a later chapter, when I discuss the issue of what investors look out for when deciding to invest in a company, I will go into more details of the salient aspects the entrepreneur should understand about the business plan.

Not only is the business plan important as a communications tool to third parties, but it is also equally important for the entrepreneur, the founders, and the company's management team. It acts as a guiding light to how the company is to be operated and how plans are to be executed. The business plan helps the company be more organised. It should guide everyone on how activities in the company are to be executed, what should be done first, and subsequently, to serve as a roadmap of the activities planned.

A Living Document

The business plan should be treated as a living document to be constantly updated as new information becomes available, and as the environment and the company's situation changes. Based on my experience, for all the start-ups and the ones I invested in, without fail, whatever is written in the original business plan has to be continuously modified as company operations are underway and new conditions affect the outcome of all the company's actions. A rigid business plan that cannot withstand the stress of many changes will be considered a weak plan. The flexibility of the business plan should therefore be an important factor, which has to be built into the document during its preparation.

The business plan is also a useful document to measure success. Some people consider the business plan to be a battle plan for the company. Typically they are very confidential documents that should never fall into the hands of a competitor. The business plan should only be released to third parties, including potential investors, if the entrepreneur is sure confidentiality will be maintained. Finally, the business plan also helps the entrepreneur plan how money should be spent and when the money will be needed.

One key aspect of a good business plan should be the uniqueness of your plan and your company. What differentiates your company from the many others? Have you been careful about the details and is your plan realistic? These must come out clearly in a good business plan. The entrepreneur should consult someone who has a good handle of the financial aspects of a business to be involved in preparing the financial plan. This is because the financial plan and the assumptions behind each number quoted in the plan will be carefully scrutinised by the third party reader. Most of the time, investors quickly zoom in to this part of the plan because it provides the best objective measure of how the company will emerge and how successful the company is expected to be.

Before I go through the details of each section of the business plan, Figure 11.1 summarises not only the business plan but also the related documents and activities that are derived out of the business plan.

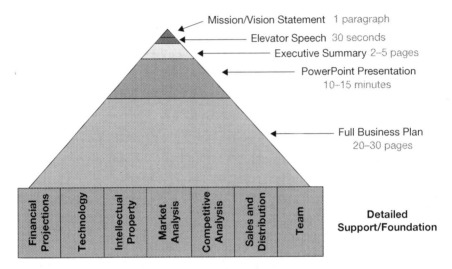

Fig. 11.1: Aspects of a Business Plan

Let's go into greater detail. What I am sharing is what I have been using for my start-ups and also teaching at my Masters Class. The business plan structure can vary, with different sections appearing at different places but the basics remain the same.

By reading this chapter, entrepreneurs will have a good feel of what they should include in each of these sections to create a robust and attractive business plan. But let me start with the first few features of a written plan that many books fail to highlight.

The Cover Page and the Content Page

Many entrepreneurs don't focus on the cover page, thinking the content inside is more important than the external look. But we must realise even the look can communicate important messages. Let me elaborate.

The cover page should contain these few elements:

- Name of company
- Company logo and colour scheme (branding from Day 1)
- Title and date (Title is "Business Plan")

- CEO/Founder's address and contact details
- Confidentiality statements.

The next thing that some entrepreneurs overlook is the Contents page. Again, while you may think this is a minor point, it could make a big

STRICTLY PRIVATE AND CONFIDENTIAL

- BUSINESS PLAN -

Infiniti Solutions Pte Limited

A Semiconductor Test and Assembly
Global Company

Contact:
Inderjit Singh
E-mail: inderjit@infinitisolutions.com.

July 18th, 2001

Information provided in this business plan is unique to this business and confidential; therefore, anyone reading this plan agrees not to disclose any of the information in this business plan without prior written permission of the Company

Fig. 11.2: A Sample Cover Page of a Business Plan

difference when a busy investor picks up your business plan, glances at it and wants to go straight to certain sections to make a quick initial assessment. If it is difficult to navigate, the investor might just not bother and both you and the investor would have lost an opportunity.

Table 11.1: Sample Contents Page

1		Executive Summary	1
2		Industry Background	
	2.1	The Type of Industry Your Company is in	3
	2.2	Your Company Position in the Industry	4
	2.3	Competitive Landscape	5
3		Company Background and Management Team	
	3.1	Industry, Company History and Business Description	6
	3.2	Pain Point and Problem You are Solving	7
	3.3	The Opportunity & How You are Solving the Problem	9
	3.4	Organisation Chart and Shareholding Structure	10
	3.5	Profile of Senior Management	11
4		Products/Service	
	4.1	Technology & IP	13
	4.2	Product/Service Details	14
	4.3	Value Proposition	15
	4.4	Product Development Roadmap	16
5		Company's Goals, Objectives, Mission and Vision	
	5.1	Company Vision/Mission	18

Table 11.1: *(Continued)*

	5.2	SWOT & Competitor Analysis	19
	5.3	Goals, Objectives, and Plans	20
6	The Market, Marketing Strategy and Plan		
	6.1	Market Study and Segmentation	21
	6.2	Marketing Plan and Marketing Strategy	22
	6.3	Marketing and Sales Budget Consideration	24
7	Operations Strategy		
	7.1	Operations/Execution Plan	25
	7.2	R&D and Product Roadmap	26
	7.3	Resource/Facility Acquisition and Set-Up	27
	7.4	HR/Hiring Roadmap – Filling Skill Gaps	28
8	Financials		
	8.1	Financial Statements – Historical and Five-Year Forecasts	29
	8.1	Fund-Raising Plans	30
9	Risk and Contingency Plans		32
10	Exit Plan		33
11	Appendices		34

The Main Contents
SECTION NO. 1: Executive Summary

Typically, for any third party reading a document, the first two or three paragraphs will make a tremendous difference as to whether they will be interested to read on. The first few paragraphs of the business plan should therefore tell an interesting, convincing, and compelling story. The whole business plan can be quite a bulky document. Not every investor will have the patience to read the whole plan. They need to be enticed to do so, which can be effectively achieved with an Executive Summary. Needless to say, the executive summary needs to be very well written. It must be concise but at the same time capture all the key points to give the reader a good feel of what the business is all about and what the key success factors are. Its most basic function is to catch the reader's eye, compelling him to dig into more details of the proposal. In essence, the executive summary should, in a concise manner, capture the rest of the business plan, in particular, with a description of the company and business, a brief on the management team, a roundup of the market and the marketing strategy, how the competition will be tackled, and end with a summary of the key financials. Finally, the executive summary should also emphasise the company's uniqueness.

One final point – the executive summary is not an introduction section of your business plan. It is a mini business plan capturing all the key elements of the problem being solved or pain points being addressed, your solution, your market, your customers, your team and all else that is detailed in the full document. You must assume the reader and the potential investor will not go beyond the executive summary to understand your company. If the executive summary fails to attract the attention of the reader, you may lose a potential stakeholder or investor. So, make sure the essence of the whole business plan is captured in the executive summary, in two or three pages.

SECTION NO. 2: *Industry Background*

In this section, you should clearly state which industry you are in, and what part of the industry your start-up is in. For example, for UTAC, the industry was the semiconductor industry but specifically my start-up was in Semiconductor Assembly and Test (SAT) outsourcing or as some may call it, on the backend assembly and test services industry.

The investors reading your business plan will want to know the size of the industry – in other words, what is the market size that is available. You should gather data from reliable sources to give the reader a sense of the size, shape, trends and key success factors for your industry and the segment your start-up is participating in. It is critical to show the outlook of your industry, too – are you in a growing or stable or sunset industry? This section should also mention the key players in the industry who will be your competitors, and what are the features of the industry that will allow you to differentiate from others.

Basically after reading this section, the reader must have a good feel of what your start-up is all about and how you fit into the whole industry and why you will have a good chance of succeeding. Written well, it will give confidence to the reader, especially potential investors that the entrepreneur indeed knows the industry very well. And VCs typically will have industry experts who will scrutinise this in detail to see if you really know what you are talking about.

SECTION NO. 3: *The Company Background*

The details now begin. This part of the business plan communicates how the company got started, who the founders are, and what drove the founders to start the company. It also communicates the company's stage of development. In some cases, it is just the beginning, and in other cases, the company has already been formed and some activities have already begun.

An important question that needs to be addressed here is, "What business are you really in?" It is surprising that many entrepreneurs fail to give a concise and succinct answer. If the business had been clearly defined and the battle lines clearly drawn, one should have no problems answering this question. Therefore, entrepreneurs should make a business case in this section and have a very clearly defined description of what the business is really all about. In addition, you should also discuss the market and what value your company brings to its customers.

Over the years, I have read many business plans, and frankly, very few are good. Most are substandard and quite a few are confusing where I just cannot make out what the business is really all about. After proceeding to the second section, I just lose interest and give up reading. It goes to follow that I never invest in such companies.

SECTION NO. 4: *The Company's Vision, Mission, Objectives and Goals*

It is crucial for the third party reading the business plan to understand where the entrepreneur and the company are heading. The key question is whether clear goals and objectives have been set. These then become the means of measuring the success of the entrepreneur and the company. This section also allows others to judge the nature of the people promoting the company – whether they are realistic, if they are dreamers (which may not necessarily be bad), if they have a long-term vision of things, etc.

In this section, it is useful to state the long-term company goals and describe quantitative measures of what these goals will be. Then, the long-term goals should be broken down into short-term goals and measurable outcomes. Sometimes it is very difficult for people to visualise how the entrepreneur or the company is going to achieve the long-term goals, but when these are broken down into shorter-term goals to be achieved at certain intervals of time, it may become easier to see how the company will arrive at its longer-term goals and objectives.

The long-term thinking and aspirations of the entrepreneur and the management team must be included. The best way to do this is to spell out the Vision Statement and the Mission Statement. These two statements should not be taken lightly. These, together with the values the company intends to operate with, will give a feel of the company's heart and soul. The Vision and the Mission Statements will also help the current and future management team members develop the strategies and future plans for the company. If correctly defined, the Vision and Mission Statements should remain evergreen, so a lot of thought should go into their development.

SECTION NO. 5: The Management Team

One of the most important criteria for investors to decide whether or not to invest in any company is the quality and capability of the management team. It is widely believed that the best of plans, if executed by a weak team, may not necessarily bring success and can in fact result in the company's failure. On the other hand, a poor plan executed by a very good management team can still bring success.

A good team will be able to identify the weaknesses and find new solutions to ensure good execution. It is therefore very important that this part of the business plan captures the strength and potential of the management team, convincing the reader that this team is among the best to do the job.

The details that should be included in this section are the background and qualifications of key personnel, including those who may have yet to be identified and have yet to join the team. In such cases, the plan should clearly spell out the attributes of the people that the company intends to hire. Details of their past experiences will be very important, especially if they have had previous experience with start-ups, or if not, how their experiences can contribute to the team in handling a start-up. The domain expertise of each team member should also be specified. A track record can provide useful details and should be clearly recorded in this part of the plan. It does not matter whether all or some of the team members have been involved in failed attempts to start companies. What is more useful is the experience the team has acquired. In most cases, failure is looked at as a good prerequisite to creating success the next time around. So, in this section, entrepreneurs should not shy from talking about successes and failures.

Something less obvious that should also be detailed is how all the individuals in the team can perform in an integrated and cohesive manner capable of withstanding the great stresses new companies face. The complementary nature of their skills should also be identified. Often, the entrepreneur underestimates what it takes to create a successful management team. The biggest issue typically lies in not realising that one or two people cannot possibly do everything.

SECTION NO. 6: *The Product or Service Offered*

Specifically, the products and services the company intends to provide and how these will be produced and delivered need to be spelt out. It is useful to simplify the description of the product and services at the start of this section, and then slowly introduce more details a little later on. Commonly, the entrepreneur fails to realise that his or her understanding of the business may not necessarily be the same as others. In fact, the description should start in layman terms, allowing any ordinary reader to easily understand the contents. The potential investor will definitely not be as knowledgeable as the entrepreneur. The use of technology and how the intellectual property will be created, protected, and utilised also needs to be discussed. Additionally, a brief description of the technological advantage would be useful.

One key aspect that must become apparent from reading this section is the value proposition your company is planning to offer, which will compel your potential customers to switch suppliers, products, or services by way of substitution. What must appear here are the compelling reasons why all the current products and services in the market are not fully satisfying the customers and how your products and/or services can better satisfy them. Also, what are the key differentiators of your new company? The differentiating factors must come out very clearly for others to be convinced that the company will succeed, especially if there are already many competitors. The market being addressed needs to be well-defined. It will be useful to include general market statistics and market survey data to support some of the assumptions being made about how the business will shape up and grow. The market segmentation and targets need to show that your management team is focused, targeted, that you also have a well-defined plan and are not just hoping for luck to make things happen.

The product or service roadmap needs to be spelt out to give the reader a good feel that yours is not a one-product or one-service company. It is important to communicate to others the long-term thinking of your company and its key personnel, and this can be demonstrated by mapping the product or service roadmap to the technology roadmap. This will then drive the resource allocation and investment decisions of the company during its complete life cycle.

An analysis of the industry and the environmental conditions that will dictate the outcome of the industry winners or losers should also be included in this section. A SWOT analysis could be useful in showing that the management team and the entrepreneur have indeed studied the issues systematically. Lastly, an analysis of the factors involved in creating successful businesses should also be included.

SECTION NO. 7: *The Market, Marketing Strategy and Plan*

The company's strategies and plans need to be detailed. In the previous section, the main goals should have been described in broad terms, while in this section, the entrepreneur should spell out a much more detailed strategy that will help achieve the earlier-identified objectives and goals. Unique tactics to capture market share through better value propositions or greater differentiation, which will make the product or service being offered more attractive than those currently offered by competitors, should be outlined. One of the weakest parts of most plans is the marketing strategy, due to the entrepreneur's failure to fully understand the market and the industry dynamics. Failure to prepare a good marketing strategy will hinder the entrepreneur in pinpointing exactly how the customers can be won, particularly in a market already crowded with many players. The usual items covered in this section are:

  a. The market segmentation, the total available market (TAM), and the market share the company intends to capture

b. The plans and tactics to capture the market share or create new markets
c. The value proposition and the differentiation
d. The defensive strategies to keep competitors away
e. The offensive strategies to win market share from competitors
f. How customers will be won and kept – the important customer service factors once customers have been engaged
g. The cost of customer acquisition – the advertising and promotion strategy, the structure of the marketing and sales organisation, etc.

In summary, the plan should show how the company intends to reach out to potential customers and convince them to enter into a partnership with the company, or in the simplest outcome, to induce the customer to want to buy the products or services offered.

SECTION NO. 8: *The Operational Strategy and Plan*

This section involves perhaps the most controllable factor in the whole business plan. It outlines the execution of operations, including developing new technologies, R&D roadmap, products, beta testing, prototyping capacity planning, resource utilisation, and capital spending. Once the product or service roadmap has been defined and aligned to the technology roadmap, the execution plan can be developed. This will include the resource acquisition and resource allocation strategies. Capital spending can then be estimated, and this in return drives the cash requirements over a certain period of time. This section becomes the key driver of the financial plan. The assumptions made in the operational strategy and plan will determine how money will be spent and cash flow managed. Once the operations and the marketing plans have been developed, proceed to the financial plan.

SECTION NO. 9: *The Short-Term and Long-Term Financial Plan*

This is the part of the business plan where investors will spend the most amount of time, after they are convinced the company has indeed developed a good product and strategy to grow and attain profitability. The company's pulse can be measured by its financial status, which consists of a few critical financial statements. These numbers are a prediction of how the company will look when execution begins. The assumptions used to drive each financial number should be clearly described. While all the preceding sections of a business plan build up the set of assumptions used to drive the financial numbers, it is useful to summarise some of the more critical assumptions in this section so that the third party reading the business plan has a better feel of how the numbers were developed. The financial numbers therefore become a proxy of the execution ability of the entrepreneur and the management team. There are three types of financial statements, which as a minimum should be clearly developed for the financial section of the business plan. They are the income or profit and loss statement, the balance sheet, and the cash flow statement.

The Income or Profit and Loss Statement

At the end of the day, everyone is in business to make money. If any entrepreneur says they are not in it for the money, then they are probably in the wrong business. They should instead be doing charity work. Even if the entrepreneur is not driven by money alone, as a minimum, he should be driven by the need to create wealth for the company. The income statement (or the profit and loss statement) captures the success of the business, showing how revenue will be streaming into the company as the plans get executed. It also measures how the money is being spent and how efficiently the money was spent by way of measure of the various cost items in this statement. It therefore measures how effectively the business is being conducted according to the gross profit margins (GPM) and net margins.

The income statement will also show the growth of the business through the revenue growth rate for various time periods. For this purpose, the financial projections should be stated over a period of time. Such time can vary from business to business, but typically the financial plan should cover a period of three to five years. One should show a monthly or at least a quarterly breakdown for the first and second year and then a full-year financials for the rest of the three- or five-year financial plan.

The Balance Sheet

The balance sheet captures the status of all the company's assets, including its cash position and liquidity. It measures how capital is spent and how the business is being financed. For example, certain equipment could be bought, while others could be rented or leased, and the balance sheet will give a flavour of how efficiently the capital and resources have been deployed. Here, the company's loans are reflected, as well as its status of equity. The balance sheet gives a running summary of how the value of the company's equity grows or shrinks as its business performance changes. It also captures all the liabilities the company has incurred and how these stack up against its assets, thus illustrating whether the company will be able to meet all its obligations.

The Cash Flow Statement

This is another important financial statement the entrepreneur should be very familiar with and pay particular attention to. This statement helps the company plan for its cash needs. Despite the best of profits, if a company's cash flow is messed up, the company can still collapse. Many people use the cash flow statement to measure the company's pulse and survivability.

The cash flow statement should be realistic and show how the cash will be utilised over a period of time. It should show how long the company will last, especially if the rate of cash injection is not as fast as the rate of cash use (or cash burn). It also shows how the cash in the company is being utilised during each of the time periods stated. Some uses of the cash include operations, investments, and bank loan repayments, etc.

The bottom-line that people will look out for is whether the business is cash flow positive or negative. Being cash flow positive means the company is generating excess cash even after using cash for all the necessary company activities. Cash built up will become excess cash or reserves in the company to be used for other significant expenditures or for a rainy day should the need arise in the future. Being in a negative cash flow position means the company is draining its cash reserves. In such a situation, it is important to determine how long it will take for the company to run out of cash. This statement, which already measures the cash burn rate of the company, will give a good feel for how long the company can last with the remaining cash, and thus help trigger certain actions like going out to raise more cash to fund the company or to resort to drastic cost reductions to reduce the cash outflow so the company's life can be extended with the fixed amount of cash left on its balance sheets.

Other schedules of financial statements that should be included are the capital spending roadmap, the financial policies adopted (e.g. US GAAP, depreciation policies, exchange rates, etc.), salary rate chart, and benefits for employees, etc. The key thing is to be able to answer any questions readers may have of how the company's performance will be measured and affected should things change.

Typically, it is important to breakdown the financial statements into a few time periods. The granularity or details of the statements can be slightly different for different time periods. It is usual to have a month-by-month breakdown of the financials for the first 12 to 18 months, and then perhaps quarterly financials for the next two years. All in all, there should be around five years of financial statements included in the business plan. Beyond the third year, there is little point in breaking down the time periods of the financial statements to quarterly or monthly numbers. It is okay to just show how the yearly numbers will look like for the distant future. Realistically, very few people can forecast so far out into the future, so there is little point in trying to be so detailed for the distant future.

Finally, I would like to again emphasise that the two key financial measures the entrepreneur should never neglect: first, the gross profit margins, which measure the value-added aspects of the business and the key players, and second, the company's cash flow. Many companies fail to pay attention to the cash flow situation, and these typically end in failure. Cash is king, as the saying goes, and the entrepreneur should never forget this in any business undertaking.

SECTION NO. 10: *The Risk Factors and Contingency Plans*

While the business plan and financial projections may be based on certain assumptions and be conditional on certain situations and environmental factors, the reality is that one can never predict and forecast all these conditions and assumptions especially further down the road. So, things may not necessarily play out as expected.

In fact, some people say the business plan becomes obsolete the day the company is launched and therefore needs updating as new conditions prevail. It is important that the risks involved in running the business be identified in the business plan so there is some amount of confidence that the entrepreneur and the management team have thought of backup plans, should things go wrong or not happen as expected. The entrepreneur should spell out all the possible risk factors that can directly affect the company as well as those that can indirectly affect the outcome of the business and the projections and forecasts. These risk factors should be carefully analysed and the impact of each factor quantified. Then, for each of these factors identified, contingency plans should be worked out.

Contingency plans are very useful for the entrepreneur, because, should things go wrong and if he or she has already predicted this possibility of things going wrong, at least there would already be a possible backup plan to address the new situation. Otherwise, when things do not actually go according to plan, the people involved would have to urgently start thinking of plans and end up doing things in a rush. We all know that when anyone is faced with such a rushed or critical situation, it becomes very difficult to start conceptualising a plan. Your mind will already be occupied with trying to hold together the things that are falling apart. Typically, when people are in firefighting mode, they have very little time for long-term planning, or for that matter any type of planning.

A third party reading the business plan would be very interested to see if the entrepreneur and the management team had been realistic in identifying the risk factors as well as what could go wrong, and also how they plan to address such issues when and if things do go wrong. The business plan should therefore have a comprehensive discussion of as many possible risk factors as possible.

Some examples of risk factors, which are typically included in most business plans are:

a. Market risk – This involves uncontrollable things that can affect the market and the company's ability to address the market.

b. Execution risk – The team's inability to execute the business according to plan, whether in producing the product on time, or in terms of successfully engaging customers, raising funds, etc.

c. Technology risk – The company's inability to create the technology, or the situation in which technology that was assumed to exist did not come into being on time.

d. Environmental risk – These are typically uncontrollable but will affect the business, such as the state of the economy, condition of the industry and competitive landscape.

e. Regulatory risk – The effect of government and governance on the company's operations and business execution.

SECTION NO. 11: *The Exit Strategy*

While this is not a typical section in most business plans and may typically be covered within the financial section, it is useful to note that this issue of potential returns and an exit for the investors, especially the VCs, is an important one close to the heart of any investor. The value of the returns or form of returns can differ in different types of investment proposals, but the investor will want to know how much returns will be possible and also when the returns can be withdrawn from the company. I say the forms can be different because many entrepreneurs view a public listing or an Initial Public Offering (IPO) as the only form of providing investors an exit to realise their returns. While this is quite a typical and preferred form of exit expected by VCs, other investors may prefer to have dividends or profit sharing as a means of returns. To be realistic, an exit by way of a trade sale should also be considered. So, it is important to identify what form of exit would be best for the type of company being set up.

The returns and exit questions are not just for investors to worry about. It is also of great concern for the entrepreneur, the management team, employees, and all other stakeholders of the company. It is useful in this section of the business plan to identify what returns and exits are possible for each of the stakeholders. It becomes a form of motivation for all these players.

A clearly defined exit strategy will become a good guide for all involved to make a judgement as to when in the company's life cycle a certain type of return can be given to the stakeholders, or when in the execution phase can an exit be planned. The milestones and conditions for an exit can be clearly stated in this part of the business plan. Some examples of milestones include a certain level of profitability, a certain level of revenue being achieved, or a certain level of acceptance in the market. Some other examples of conditions could be the level of cash left, the future cash needs, and the consensus of all key stakeholders before an exit strategy can be executed.

SECTION NO. 12: And Beyond – Attachments, Appendices and Annexes

Supporting documents and any non-essential details should be included in an appendix section, as the main body of the business plan should not be bogged down with too many details.

As discussed at the beginning of the chapter, the business plan should be as concise and focused as possible. For example, you should avoid the tendency of giving too many lower level details of an operations strategy and plan, too detailed a description of the technology, or too much of a minute-level breakdown of how the financial plan was developed.

While it is useful to give as much information as necessary for a third-party reader to get a good feel and understanding of the company and the plans, the risk is that details may drown the key points the reader should have picked up. Worse still, the reader may lose interest because he may not have the time or aptitude to go through and understand all the details. It is therefore more useful to have a very brief and concise description of what needs to be communicated in each of the preceding sections of a business plan. If it is necessary to include details to provide a better understanding of certain things, these can be included at the end of the document as attachments, annexes and appendices. In fact, it is a good idea to do this, because some readers, particularly the VCs and the more sophisticated investors, may want to consult experts on certain things like the technology, market assessment, operational plans or the assumptions made. The investor may rely heavily on such expert opinions before making a decision on whether or not to invest in the company. If details are provided in the business plan attachments, the experts can make a fast judgement without having to spend too much time interviewing and discussing things with the management team.

Although details are good, the entrepreneur should resist from adding too much information, especially information that will not help much in the reader's understanding of the business. Unnecessary details could in fact have a negative impact and give the impression that the entrepreneur does not know how to write a good business plan. So, doing everything in moderation is the best guide I can give.

The Business Plan

A good business plan is not one that is very technical in nature. It should be easily readable and able to communicate the essence of the business simply and concisely. It should be like a short story that you can read from front to back in one sitting, after which you should quickly gain a clear understanding of the whole story line.

The business plan should capture important facts of the company and the people behind it.

Section No. 1—The Executive Summary
Section No. 2—Industry Background
Section No. 3—The Company's Background
Section No. 4—The Company's Vision, Mission, Objectives and Goals
Section No. 5—The Management Team
Section No. 6—The Product or Service Offered
Section No. 7—The Market, Marketing Strategy and Plan
Section No. 8—The Operational Strategy and Plan
Section No. 9—The Short-Term and Long-Term Financial Plan
Section No. 10—The Risk Factors and Contingency Plans
Section No. 11—The Exit Strategy
Section No. 12—And Beyond

Remember you must treat the business plan as a living document that will need to be constantly updated as you get new information. Without fail, the business plan becomes "obsolete" the day you start your company. Don't be so rigid in following the business plan and be prepared to change and modify the plan as you gain more insights about your business.

CHAPTER 12

PITCHING

Why is Making a Good Presentation Important?

I started my career in Texas Instruments (TI) which was a great company to learn from. In fact, many of us jokingly used to call TI, a Training Institute (TI). For me I learned two very important lessons which helped me in my entrepreneurial journey. First, as an enthusiastic engineer solving many technological problems, I learnt that as an engineer, we can always find a solution to any problem. I had the opportunity and was given the leeway to solve problems in any possible way, gaining the confidence that there is nothing that cannot be solved. I called this the First Mantra of Entrepreneurs and covered this in an earlier chapter.

The second very important lesson I learned in TI was, how to make a good presentation. Because we had to make regular presentations to all levels of management in the company, we had to polish up on presentation skills. Many a career was made or broken because of presentation skills. You will always get an opportunity to present yourself to important people so when you do have a chance, you must make an excellent first impression that will leave a lasting impact on those present. I must say I developed the knack and skills of making good presentations while at TI.

Achieve Success with a Good Pitch

When I started my first company, I faced tremendous difficulties raising funds in Singapore and found the opportunity to pitch to Taiwanese investors. When I went over to Taiwan I had a room full of potential investors, around

50 of them. The presentation was one of the most important milestones of my entrepreneurship journey.

In my pitch, I highlighted many points, as how a good pitch and business plan should be, to attract attention and interest from potential investors. This presentation, which I made a special trip to Taiwan for, was done while I was actually still working for TI. As my potential team members were also mostly still working at TI, I did not want to take a risk by putting their names on my Business Plan nor on my pitch deck. So, in my presentation to a room full of potential investors, I did not even name a single team member. It was important, otherwise all of them risked losing their jobs if TI found out! Instead, I showed the planned organisational chart to the potential investors, indicating that I had identified a good team, and for each of the key positions, I called them Mr. A, Mr. B, etc. I knew it was my last chance to find the money at the time I needed it – it was a like a life or death situation for me. So I applied all my presentation skills to deliver the pitch of my life. I made just one presentation: the outcome was that I had offers of more money than I needed and had to turn away some. We raised more than US$100m from Taiwan alone! After I raised the huge amount, I came back to Singapore and secured the remaining money to make a total of US$138m raised at the seed stage!

A Good Presentation

I hired a young engineer in the department I was heading in Texas Instruments Singapore. He was one of the better performing engineers with good problem-solving skills. I knew he would find the solution and have the information on the problem tackled ready by the time I needed it to present to my boss. Although he was of a small build and looked timid, I was quite sure of his leadership skills and his ability to lead one of the sections of engineers in my department. I wanted to promote him to section manager some two years after he joined. I made my case to my boss, the division director, but my boss was not impressed based on what he had seen of the young engineer's presentation skills at our regular throughput meetings. I was adamant about the promotion, so my boss challenged me to get him ready to present at the monthly meeting of all department managers so that these department managers could give their opinion on my recommendation.

I asked this engineer to brush up on his presentation skills as it was an important component of his career progression. I made the mistake of not spending enough time to train him. So, on the day of our monthly meeting, the engineer made his presentation, and I don't know what it was but perhaps he was nervous, and his presentation was poorly done. I sat there embarrassed and cringing and saw the anxiety and impatience on my boss' face as I knew the engineer blew his presentation. At the end of the meeting, my boss got all of his managers to stay back and as soon as everyone left, I had a shelling of a lifetime. He was so upset and questioned my judgement as a manager and told me that if I thought that the engineer was ready for a promotion then I am a lousy manager and did not know how to train my team.

I felt bad and resolved to prove my boss wrong and immediately set out to train this engineer in his presentation skills. I set a regular schedule beyond working hours to personally coach him. It was quite hard on him but I had to ensure that he learned how to manage and train his future team members. I had to postpone the promotion for three months to get him ready for that one critical skill he lacked – presentation skills. If I failed to get him up to par, I would have failed in training my team and I would have let this engineer down. After about three months, I was confident that the engineer had polished up his presentation skills and took a huge risk by lining the engineer up for a presentation, not to my boss but to the managing director at one of our quarterly department presentations. I spent a lot of time helping the engineer prepare the presentation material and also did a few dry runs to let him practise. On the day of the presentation, my boss was not in the office but all other top management team members and all department managers from my boss' division were present.

The presentation started with an engineer from another department. That engineer blew his presentation and the MD looked upset. Then came a second engineer from another department and he too did a bad job and the MD was starting to lose patience. Then came my engineer's turn. I sat at the back of the room to observe and guess what, he made an excellent presentation. I was watching the MD and could see that he was impressed. We continued with another two presentations for the day and they were also not well done. At the end of the presentations, the engineers and section managers left, while the department managers and division directors stayed back for a debrief. The MD started by telling us all off that he was upset with the standard of presentations except one (my engineer's) and then went on to say all the reasons why he found that presentation good. I was overjoyed and sat at the back of the room writing word for word what the MD said about my engineer and his presentation. The MD was the toughest cookie and if anyone could meet his criteria for a good presentation, then he must be good. I was overjoyed not only that the engineer finally got it right but also because I proved my boss wrong about what he thought about the engineer's ability to be a manager and my ability to train a manager. The next day when my boss was in the office, I marched into his office, grinning from ear to ear and sat down and told him that I was ready to promote the engineer and that the only problem my boss had with the promotion was solved. Then I opened my notebook and went on to read to him verbatim what the MD had said about that engineer. I told my boss he did not have to take my word for it but he could go and ask any of his managers if what I said was not true. My boss finally conceded defeat, and I managed to promote the engineer at the end of the month. This engineer later went on to join me in my start-up at UTAC and was one of my vice-presidents and did a good job in supporting me in making UTAC a success.

The first customer I engaged in UTAC was Siemens Semiconductors. I must say that I succeeded in gaining their business because of an impressive pitch I made to their global director in charge of packaging and testing, who was based in Germany. I managed to make an appointment with him while I was still operating in my temporary office and was negotiating to purchase a building for my company. We had no factory, no equipment and no production floor, no technicians, no production operations to show and yet we had the audacity to sell a manufacturing service. Siemens global director visited my temporary office and I made a presentation to him about my plans and how I felt I could support Siemens' production needs. At the end of the presentation, the gentleman laughed and said that I was selling him services based on a paper plan and when we did not even have a factory yet. I replied that I was confident he will not regret his decision if he gave us the business. Well can you believe it – HE DID – and I went on to buy a building, purchase equipment and hired the people, and within four months started production for Siemens. Looking back I realise it was the pitch I prepared and how I delivered it that made all the difference. I got the attention of my first customer, as I did the many investors when I made a pitch to the VCs in Taiwan.

I would therefore urge entrepreneurs to brush up on presentation skills and learn to make good pitches. Sometimes you just have one shot at it for a particular investor so you have to put your best foot forward. The good news is that there are many ways you can develop the skill of making good presentations and develop good communications skills. Don't underestimate this. In fact, these skills will be important not just to attract investors; but also useful to attract all stakeholders – potential team members, customers, and other partners. It is better for you to work on it before you start meeting others. Remember – first impressions count and are very important; don't make the pitch until you are sure you are ready. It is better to wait a little longer than to blow it the first round.

Understand What Everyone is Looking for

Before we go into the details of what makes a good pitch, it is important that the entrepreneur knows what everyone is looking for. Start by knowing yourself – what are you looking for in an investor to partner you. Then try to understand what the investor is looking for in you and your company.

You must find an investor who is aligned to your goals and thinks with the same frequency as you (recall the **Star of the Investor**). The investor should bring "smart money" to the partnership – in other words, not just in putting in money but also in being able to bring a lot more value to you and your start-up. Some key attributes entrepreneurs should look for in potential investors are as follows:

What do entrepreneurs want of investors?

1. *Enough money – deep pockets*
2. *A good reputation and track record*
3. *A good network to help the business*
4. *The ability to work well together*
5. *Ability to understand the business and add value*

To prepare well and to ensure you communicate the right things that the investors want to see in your start-up, you must know how the investor will be assessing you and your company. What are the most important aspects of your business plan that must come out clearly in your pitch? What are the hot button issues that the investor needs to be convinced to take the next step? What is it that will get the investor excited about you and your company? Some important areas that investors look for are as follows.

What do investors want of entrepreneurs?
1. *Good team with right combination of skill sets*
2. *Unique idea or business model or intellectual property (IP)*
3. *Sizable market served*
4. *High growth potential*
5. *Any early wins or near wins.*

As you can see, each stakeholder has different objectives. If you know what yardstick the potential investors are going to use, you can then prepare and show the investors what they are looking for. I am not suggesting you cook up a story – that will be lying, and one should never lie to a potential partner or for that matter, to anyone.

Let's now get into the nuts and bolts of what a good pitch should look like.

The Pitch

There are two important components in making a good pitch:
a. First, the content of your pitch; and
b. Second, the way you deliver it (including your interpersonal skills).

I would say that the content part is slightly easier as you will have the knowledge advantage of what you are going to present. If you are passionate about what you are doing, you can easily impress the listeners. The challenge is how you put together a presentation which communicates the message concisely and clearly. You can get help from experts on this but really, it is going to depend on you to be able to present the ideas pictorially or in writing. Don't assume the listeners have the same technical knowledge as you – the best presenters make their presentation seem easy to understand by the way they put it together. The second part of doing a good pitch is how you deliver it. I feel this part is tougher compared to preparing the content of the pitch, because not everyone is naturally inclined to communicate effectively. But the good news is that you can be trained to do it and if you feel you are not quite up to the mark, you can engage experts to help you improve. Notwithstanding help from experts, I will share here some of the things you need to look out for in delivering the pitch.

Content of the Pitch

A good pitch should last around 20 to 25 minutes that usually entails about 15 to 20 slides at a maximum. Don't flash too many slides as it might bore the listeners and also give the impression that you don't really know how to handle non-technical presentations. So what are the essential points you have to include in your pitch? There are many possible points but let me suggest a few that are key:

1. Introduction – your company name, logo and key legal messaging (e.g. confidentiality)
2. Attention grabbing-slide which in one slide describes the space your company is in and what you are doing
3. What problem are you solving and/or what opportunity are you seizing – show excitement
4. Market size and customers you will target
5. Your solution – i.e., product/service and why you can solve the problem better and why the customer should choose you – your competitive advantage
6. Your unique technology or business process and what IP you have and future roadmaps

7. Business Model – how you fit into the industry you are in – how disruptive
8. Market development and marketing strategies
9. Your Team and your current and planned organisation
10. Execution plans – business development, operational and technical
11. Risks and contingency planning – how well you have thought through the obstacles
12. Financials – the burn rates, sales, P&L, over a three- to five-year period
13. Valuation, investments sought, exit strategies and returns (if presenting to investor)
14. Conclusion and Summary – your company's vision, goals, and why you are a winner

Let me go through each of these and highlight what you will need for each of these sections of the pitch.

1. **Introduction – your company name, logo and key legal messaging (e.g. confidentiality)**

   Clearly display your company name, any logo or tagline and also the presenter's name. State clearly the confidentiality of your material on the first and all pages of the presentation. It is useful to have a good tagline which in one sentence describes what you do. If you cannot think of one, it's ok as you should be heading quickly to your next slide which has to get the attention of the listeners.

2. **Attention-grabbing slide**

   You should in one slide describe the space your company is in, the most important value proposition and why you are a winner. If you feel you will look like one of the big players one day, feel free to say that, but be sure you can back it up later with credible information. When I started UTAC, I pitched that UTAC will become one of the big five players by a certain time. When I started Infiniti Solutions,

I said I will be the Flextronics of the semiconductor industry (well we did not make it that far).

3. **What problem are you solving and/or what opportunity are you seizing – show excitement**

    Don't spend too much time explaining the industry especially if it is a well-known industry. Don't spend too much time talking about the obvious things in the industry you are participating, unless you know the listeners have no clue about the industry, which is highly unlikely. Explain the problem clearly, especially showing why it is a big enough problem which if solved can bring good returns. Spend more time talking about your solution. Start by describing the potential market and the problems today in tapping that market – what are the current obstacles and why the current competitors are not doing it correctly. Then share how you are solving the problem, why you can do it better and why the customers will want you and how you will get to them. Don't make tall claims – be realistic that there will be obstacles.

4. **Market size and customers you will target**

    I hate it when someone tells me that "all we need to do is to capture 1 per cent of the market and we will have $1b of revenue". Anyone can say that, but the real question is how you are going to get to that 1 per cent of customers. Never use this line. The percentage you capture should be calculated bottoms up not top down i.e. show your plans of winning customers and add it all up to see what your final number is. Focus on the how and not on the what.

    It is important that there is a real demand. Can you show why your customers will see your product or service as an essential need that is not satisfied? If you can get some credible sources (some market research companies), make sure you quote them here.

You must show that you know what the TAM (Total Available or Addressable Market) is defined as total size of market available for the product or service. (The market must be big enough to make it attractive.) Explain which part of the market you will be targeting that is the Serviceable Available Market (SAM) and why and how you will ensure you can capture the part you have identified. This is the SOM (Serviceable Obtainable Market) or share of market you can capture. Keep an eye on changing trends on the market – make a statement about what your opinion on the trends are and how it will impact you.

5. **Your solution – i.e. product/service and why you can solve the problem better and why customer will choose you – your competitive advantage – compared with competitors**

   Show the innovative nature of your solution and why it is different from others. Use simple diagrams explaining your product or service. It is good if you have a prototype, a physical product or a video to show pictorially. Use analogies if the technology is too difficult to understand. Clearly explain the nature of your solution to the market problem you are solving, and why customers will love the solution. Also demonstrate what differentiates you from existing solution providers and those who may also be able to do so.

   In this section, you should identify all current and possible competitors. Those who say they have no competition are either lying or have no clear understanding of the industry or are just too naïve. They will always be others who are bigger, have more money and have been already working on it and can catch up if they focus on the same thing. Do not assume you will be way ahead of others. The competition is always not very far behind you. So, identify current and potential competitors as accurately as possible and describe briefly their strengths and weaknesses, what trouble they can create for you and how you will overcome them.

6. **Your unique technology, IP, or business process and future roadmaps**

   Your key strength and unique proposition will be the technology or the process or the innovation or an innovative business model, so you must be able to explain why yours is the best. Share whatever patents you have or are in the process of filing. Talk about your unique competencies which make you an authority in the area of technology or innovation. As I said before, this should be explained in as simple terms as possible. Break down the complex parts of your technology or innovation to simpler steps so that those without the in-depth knowledge can also understand. But remember, don't overdo the technology part and get too technical. Make it as simple as possible and assume the audience is a layperson. On the other hand, don't oversimplify till the essence of your innovation and technology is lost. Technical people typically overdo this portion of the presentation and get so technical that it becomes difficult for the listener who may not have the same level of technical knowledge to understand. Technology is ever evolving as are business models and processes. Be sure to share the technology or company roadmaps to show that yours is not a one-product company and that your technology or business models have a long roadmap of revenue generating solutions. But remember one thing – do assume that your intellectual property will be lost if you are too generous with details about your technology or trade secrets, so always remember to give what you are prepared to lose. Don't assume the listeners will protect your interests.

7. **Business Model – how you fit into the industry you are in – how disruptive are you**

   You must be able to show your idea will be transformed into a business model and then a business. How do you plan to acquire customers who will pay for your product or service and then how will you grow the market? What is your revenue model and how scalable is it?

Some Revenue and Business models:

a. *Buy/Sell* – the most common one where you make a product or produce a service and sell it directly to customers for cash.

b. *Subscription* – where customers pay a recurring fee for the use of a product or service – common for online service (e.g. online newspaper subscription, some software).

c. *Franchising* – where you have a business which can be duplicated in different locations or platforms and the business owner pays you a fee for doing a similar business – you get paid an upfront fee plus a recurring yearly (typically) fee (e.g. McDonalds, Subway, 7-11, etc.).

d. *Freemium* – you offer something free to attract customers to your site – you make money by selling value added services or other products which are not free (e.g. free admission to an event and customer pays for other services offered).

e. *Advertisements* – you provide a free service and have many customers and you charge advertisers to access your customers on your platform.

f. *Commissions* – you help other sell their products on your platform and you get paid a commission (e.g. brands consigning their products to a supermarket, people selling courses through your website, payment service providers charging a fee for products and services which are purchased and paid using their services, e.g. PayPal, credit cards).

8. **Market development and marketing strategies**

You must have a good feel of the market – a good grasp of numbers is important – and show your growth plans. Start by talking about your market penetration strategies: what will be the challenges you will face in gaining your customers, especially in the initial stages. If you already have early adopters, this is the best time to mention your customers and how you won them over. If you have any good feedback from potential customers, you should also share these here.

Show how you will scale up and how realistic is your growth plan. What are the growth drivers and have you sufficiently addressed the growth drivers? Most people fail to show numbers – it cannot be an abstract thing, something tangible is important. Show that you have done sufficient market research. You must state your assumptions.

Your pricing strategies could include:

1. Give some part free and charge for value added services.
2. Entry pricing for early stages.
3. Realistic pricing – may be higher than competitors because your solution is better.

As you grow, how will you reach your potential customers – what channels can you tap on and how? Describe the type of advertising and promotion strategies you will adopt. Don't forget to share the challenges you will face throughout your growth journey.

9. **Your team and your current and planned organisation**
Give a brief profile of yourself and your team members. It will be useful to show how each team member's previous experience is directly relevant to your start-up. Relate how the team came together, and if you have had previous experience working together, talk about it because it will be an important factor. Explain why your current team can handle everything now and at what stage you will need new team members and the type of people you will need. Don't launch into a long resume for each person but say a few words which kind of summarises the key highlights and significant achievements of each key person – spend no more than 20 to 30

seconds describing each person. If you can't, your investors will not be impressed.

10. **Execution plans – business development, operational and technical**

   Describe your implementation plan for technology, market development, operations, etc. Start by showing where you are right now and how you are going to achieve your targets. It is useful if you have some initial customers but if not, then how likely you will get some soon. Realise that you will have to deliver on what you promised, so be sure you will be able to achieve a good proportion by the timeframe you promised. It is ok to be aggressive but don't be unrealistic. It is better to exceed your plan than to miss by a mile. Your execution plans will also be scrutinised by the investors to see how well you understand the market and technology and how likely you will be able to do what you say. But don't give too many details – leave the details to question time.

11. **Risks and contingency planning – how well you have thought through the obstacles**

   You must go through some of the major areas of risks – some are controllable and some are beyond your control. State them clearly and have a plan on how you will react when each happens – i.e. how you will mitigate each of the risks you have identified. Don't spend too much time going through every risk factor; identify a few major ones and show others as a footnote – so that the listener will know you have enough depth. One key question in the investor's mind would be: what is it that keeps the entrepreneur up at night – what are some of the key worries. Building entry barriers is an important way of addressing some of the risks – i.e. what is so unique about your technology or process that will make it difficult for competitors to attack you. Things can go wrong from a number of directions, so you have to have a good feel of these. You must be able to communicate how you will handle risks. The listeners should walk away thinking that you have done enough homework that you will be able to handle any surprises when you start running the company.

For each of the risks, you must have solid contingency plans that you must communicate convincingly (see the chapter on Business Plan for more on risk and contingency planning).

12. **Financials – the burn rates, sales, P&L, over a three to five years period**

Frankly, the financial projections are always wrong. I have not come across any start-up which shows results close to what they had shown in their initial projections. So, 100 per cent accuracy is not important but being realistic is more important. Don't be too aggressive but also don't be too conservative. Be slightly more aggressive than the realistic plan (if you want better valuations). Scalability of business is very important. You can show a slower start but by the third year if you don't start showing high growth, the company will not look attractive. Don't go into too much detail – show the plan first from a bigger picture point of view: your burn rate; how your revenues will build up; when and what sales will it take for your company to hit the break-even point? Show your costs and expenses, and whether you have factored things realistically. What are the revenue drivers and what are the cost drivers? Explain the revenue model to show that you know your business and your industry.

13. **Valuation, investments sought, exit strategies, and returns (if presenting to investor)**

This can be one of the most challenging sections of your pitch for two reasons. First, valuation, and amount you need, can be quite subjective; you must be able to come up with a convincing story of why you put those numbers down. Second, this is what it really boils down to for the investors – they want to maximise the returns on their investments and assuming they like the rest of the story. (You can assume they would have got experts to drill down to the details of the technology, business model and the business plan and would already have a pretty good understanding of your company before you even start your presentation.) Investors will be very interested to discuss this portion for their own interest, so you can bet they will pay a lot of attention to this part of your presentation.

You must be able to explain why you are raising the amount you indicate and also show how you plan to allocate the money. What proportion will go to people, technology, marketing, prototyping, etc.? Be sure to show a milestone chart of what you plan to achieve and deliver at different stages of the company growth once you bring in the money. Also make sure you can deliver on what you promise. While it is not a good idea to seem too conservative, it is better to under promise and over deliver. You have to find the right balance and more importantly convince the listeners why they should believe your plan. (See the chapter on Three Rules of Thumb for fund raising.)

Valuation is a tricky subject. Ensure you have a believable model and you can justify your numbers and methodology. The most important thing to remember is that you must get your numbers right so that you can get the best value for yourself while the investors feel that they too got a good deal. Don't argue too much with the investors, take note of their concerns and come back later with a stronger story. The valuation answer does not need to be settled at the first meeting.

Finally, if you are presenting to investors or even potential team members who will get reasonable stakes in the company, you must be able to show them how much money they will make, how they will make it and when they will make their money. Let's be realistic, it's not only you who should make money, the rest should also have a cut of it and investors are there just to make their money by betting on your company. Use examples of other similar companies if possible so that it will be easier to communicate. Also, don't bet your returns on only one exit point – show a couple of alternatives in your exit strategies so that everyone knows they have options and are not dependent on an IPO only (many entrepreneurs make the mistake of pitching the IPO as their only exit mechanism).

14. **Conclusion and Summary – your company's vision, goal, and why you are a winner**

   You must end with a strong ending slide which recaptures the key elements of your company – what your company is about and why you will succeed. It may be useful to remind the audience of your vision and goals and how you plan to achieve these. Just one or at most two slides for the ending should be sufficient as you have already told your story. This portion must briefly summarise all the important things you have already delivered in your presentation. As attention grabbing as the starting slide was, this must also be an attention-grabbing parting slide – the life and soul of your company should be captured to leave a lasting impression.

Now, the above content part looks like a lot. But can you and should you prepare a lengthy pitch? Remember the investors will be looking at many pitches regularly and won't have the patience to listen to an hour-long pitch. Keep it short and leave as much time as possible for the Q&A. I mentioned in the beginning of this section that the pitch should be somewhere between 20 to 25 minutes at maximum. How can we break this down so that the most important parts of your pitch have greater airtime? As a guide, I suggest time allocation as shown in Figure 12.1. Use this as a rough guide. You have to decide which parts you want to spend more time on, and which less, depending on your unique situation and the uniqueness of your venture. <u>*Key message*</u>: **Present the whole message in 15 to 20 minutes, plan on 15 minutes, save the rest for the conclusion.**

Plan a 15 minute presentation	**– Don't overrun**
1. The problem you are solving	– 3 minutes
2. Your solution to the problem	– 3 minutes
3. The market you are targeting	– 3 minutes
4. Your unique proposition	– 3 minutes
– *IP, business model, team*	
5. Making money	– 3 minutes
– *Your financials and investors' returns*	

Fig. 12.1: Pitching – How Much Time to Spend

Pricing is an Art Not a Science

One of the jobs I did at Texas Instruments Singapore (TIS) was to manage all TIS's external sub-contractors. My job was to qualify sub-contractors, secure capacity for our company and also be responsible for all pricing negotiations. One of the sub-contractors we secured was called EEMS based in a city called Rieti, Italy. (This was actually a former Texas Instruments (TI) factory that I used to visit for meetings many times when it was still a TI facility. TI sold it some years later to Italian investors who formed a company called EEMS that provided semiconductor assembly and test services.) When TIS needed capacity, I travelled to EEMS in Rieti to meet up with the CEO, Enzo D'Antonio, a seasoned industry veteran. My key goal was to negotiate good prices for the assembly and test services we needed. As a young senior manager (I was 34 years old), and being an engineer, I prepared a lengthy presentation doing numerous calculations to justify why I needed the prices before I started business with EEMS. When I arrived for the meeting at the EEMS factory, Enzo got me to start my presentation. I spent about an hour showing all my analysis and calculations to justify a lower price than what EEMS was proposing. He did a very smart thing as he got me to show my cards first (it was hard to beat a veteran). But this was not the most important lesson I learnt that day. As I ended my presentation he asked me, "Inderjit, are you done, do you have anything else to show?" I said no and I was expecting a similar lengthy presentation from Enzo to justify the prices he was proposing to charge TI. And I was preparing to rebut his calculations and justification.

But to my shock and surprise, Enzo pulled out only one slide to show me and the slide said, "**Pricing is an Art not a Science, Costing is a Science**". And that was it. Then Enzo went on to explain to me that he did not want to go through a lengthy discussion and understood my needs and will think about it and get back to me. We had a good friendly discussion (I was expecting a tough negotiation process). We took a break, and Enzo came back with an alternative price, I negotiated further, and he gave me a little more reduction. The discussion was friendly and Enzo already knew I had some room to move. He judged me well and we ended the meeting shortly – I got what I wanted and Enzo got what he wanted. We then went for a friendly dinner before I headed home the next day.

This is one of the most valuable lessons I learned for anything we do in life – **Pricing is an Art not a Science** and I used this throughout my entrepreneurship journey. So, remember this when you are negotiating valuations for your start-up.

Enzo and I remained friends for a long time and as I said, somewhere before – never burn your bridges – when UTAC IPO was aborted (and this is many years after the meeting with Enzo in EEMS at Rieti), Enzo and I met and we discussed possible mergers of our two companies. The merger did not happen, but I was happy to meet a mentor who taught me a very valuable lesson: **"Pricing is an Art not a Science"**.

Delivering the Pitch

Since we know the important contents to put into a pitch, let me share the other important aspect of the pitch – the impression you give when delivering the pitch. Make sure you show passion and excitement and also transfer your excitement to the investors listening to you.

First and foremost, as an entrepreneur, you must deliver it yourself. You must be the main presenter of the pitch. I therefore encourage entrepreneurs to get help if they are not good presenters. The investors and other stakeholders, including your customers, will want to hear from you directly and not through some other team member. At some point you have to take the lead, so it is best that you do it early. I will share some ideas on how you can deliver a pitch effectively.

1. ***First Impressions Count***
   - Your opening statement is important – do you have a good one liner (e.g. "we have reinvented cooking technology").
   - Your opening posture is important – confident or nervous?
   - Your opening message is important. In one sentence, deliver the gist of your business plan. If you cannot explain it in 30 seconds, then you will not impress the listener. Many times, when I hear entrepreneurs present their plans (to get me to invest), if I have to keep guessing even well into the

presentation what exactly the company is doing as a core business, I get bored and most likely will not invest. Here is an example of how you can present your whole company in one sentence:

Our company [*company name*]

Has developed / is developing [*product / service*]

That solves the problem [*define problem*]

For [*target market*]

So an example might be (state a full example of a successful company – e.g. *XYZ has developed a phone which operates using your body warmth to deliver the wireless signal that solves the problem of looking for a Hotspot when you want to go online*).

2. ***How Do You Capture Your Audience's Heart?***

Unless you capture the audience or listener's heart, you will lose them as you progress. Keep revealing "goodies" as you progress in your presentation. You need to realise that your presentation needs to flow in a manner where you start with something that is interesting but brief, quickly get the attention of the listeners and then slowly add more meat to entice them to hear more and more. It's rather like the way you peel an onion – expose layer by layer till you get to the core. Don't give it all away in one go! So how do you capture their hearts? You need to tell a good story which is related to your message:

get the listener's attention quickly

–   know what interests the listeners most and makes them happy to hear you addressing their interest

–   change the tone and momentum every 5 to 10 minutes.

(Dr. John Medina, molecular biologist and author of *Brain Rules*, recommends introducing significant changes in a presentation every 10 minutes, in order to keep an audience's attention.)

3. ***Simple and Concise Message***
    It is sometimes good to have the skill of being concise while delivering a message. Some people are just too long-winded. Saying too many things may cause the listener to miss the punch lines. Make sure you have great punch lines for each slide. Remember:
    -   Aim for simplicity and clear messages when you explain each slide. Don't read verbatim what is written on the slides. Most people don't like it because they can already read what is written. It's best that you say it in different words, kind of a summary of what is written.
    -   Assume the listener is a lay person (but don't oversimplify to lose the message).

4. ***Avoid Too Many Words***
    Your slides therefore should also have just a few words. Most listeners hate to read too many words on a slide and get lost halfway, so avoid lengthy sentences. Instead, have more pictures and every slide must look interesting and different from the previous one. Some things to note:
    -   Have good pictures and limited words – best ones are when there are no more than 10 words per slide (not easy to achieve)
    -   Pictures should be the focus and not the words
    -   Make each slide look different and deliver a new message.

5. ***Slides Should Not be the Primary Focus. You Should be***
    The best thing is that the listeners are looking at you most of the time you are presenting and need to only glance at the slide to understand what you are saying. This is another reason to keep the slides simple – so that the listeners understand quickly and pay attention to you, not have to read the slides to figure out what is happening. If they are not spending most of their time focusing on you, the message will likely get lost. Remember – the slides are to aid you in delivering the message. You are the focus – don't let the slides overtake you.

6. **Be Humble**

   Try not to boss the listener around. Most of the time, at this stage you need the other party more than the party needs you, so don't be arrogant and put them off. Humility does not mean you don't have to seem confident and confidence does not mean you need to appear arrogant. Get this balance right. Some tips:

   - Respect everyone and don't seem arrogant and think you are the best person in the room. Don't start by saying you already have investors to put pressure on the VC, leave this to the end and that too, only when you feel you are being pushed to a corner. If you don't have offers, don't lie; just say you are going to speak with others.
   - Never lie, be honest and stick to the facts. If you cannot answer a question, just say so.

7. **Your Team Should Participate**

   - Don't let one person do all the talking if your team is present. One person can do the presentation but the others should also be involved in answering questions. If one or two team members could do some parts of the presentation, ensure a smooth transition each time (if you have too little time, then you may have no choice but to limit to one presenter).
   - Investors will feel comfortable if they have a better feel of your team, not just with one person.

8. **Rehearse**

   Practice makes perfect – don't ever forget this. Whether it is a company presentation to top management or pitching for funding, the more you have practised, the more confident you will be and the more prepared you will be. So how do you practise?

   - Present without anyone to get the feel of the flow and where exactly you need to pause, highlight, etc.
   - Present to your team members and ask them to scrutinise your delivery.

- If possible, present to a third party who is not part of your team and seek their feedback (someone you believe will give frank feedback).
- It is ok to edit your presentation – take feedback seriously, don't be defensive.

9. *Keep an Eye on the Audience*

This is Presentation 101 – you have to maintain eye contact with your audience. This will help you seem confident to the listener and it will help you get feedback:

- Keep eye contact so that you can sense the audience reaction – do they love listening to you or are they bored.
- Eye contact can help you see if they are nodding in agreement or are they showing signs of disbelief. Depending on the feel you get, adjust yourself immediately; don't wait till the end of the presentation to get the message from the audience.

10. *Don't Assume the Audience Knows as Much as You*

Put yourself in the shoes of your audience, believe that they will be sceptical and don't assume they will believe everything you say. Have a foolproof story ready before you meet anyone. Foolproof means something even a fool will understand (not quite that but you know what I mean – simple and easy to understand).

11. *Prepare for Q&A*

Your presentation is just one part of the whole pitching process. The real exciting part will be the Q&A session. The VCs will already expect that you would have practised your pitch before meeting them or that you had expert advice on doing up a good pitch. Their best way to test if you are indeed competent in what you do and know the details of your content are to ask questions about what you presented and ask difficult questions that may not even be part of what you presented but are related to the topic.

Be prepared with a list of potential questions which the investors might ask. Have good answers ready. Don't give academic answers –

understand the questions and don't go off-tangent. You are supposed to know your company best. Involve your whole team in preparing the list of potential questions and work together to prepare good answers. You may still be posed with questions you never expected. When that happens, it pays to be honest: if you don't have a good answer, just say so and inform them you will get back to them after you have gone into further details. Telling them something wrong is worse than telling them you don't have the answer.

12. *Reinforce Key Messages*

You must keep the audience focused on your few key messages. Emphasise these every few slides, but say it in different ways so that subtly the message sinks in by the end of the presentation. This is not the same as repeating the same thing over and over again – people will get bored listening to the same message, so be creative in how you do this.

13. *Don't Show Dejection*

If at the end of the presentation and the Q&A, the listener tells you that your company is not impressive or he or she is not interested, don't display dejection and don't show a sour face. If not this time, maybe some other time. You never know when your paths will cross again and it is best that all part ways looking confident, than having sour feelings. Respect their decision as they should respect your decision. It is not the end of the world if they make you feel your idea is something that will never work. People told me I was dreaming when I started UTAC; today it is one of the largest companies in the world in what they do.

Chapter 12 Summary

Pitching

The pitch is one of the most important aspects of your journey as an entrepreneur. Usually, you only have one chance and it can make or break a deal.

The basic principles of a good pitch are that it must:

- Tell a good story

- Not have too many slides, or too many words

- Be simple and easy to appreciate, so that a layman can understand

- Have content which is aligned to the purpose of the pitch and the audience

- Be able to support any claims or assumptions made.

Understand what all stakeholders are looking for before you prepare your pitch.

There are two aspects of making a pitch, focus on both:

- The content – the 14 key sections of your presentation

- The way you deliver the pitch, including interpersonal skills

Keep the pitch short – not more than 15 minutes

Pitching can be learned. First impressions count. So it is important to Practise, Practise, Practise.

CHAPTER 13

GETTING READY FOR FORMAL FUND RAISING

In the first edition of my book, I wrote about the entire start-up journey, beginning with an idea, to developing a business model, making a business plan and all the way to raising funds. As I mentioned in Chapter 10 of this edition, I have now broken the old chapter (The Process of Starting a Company – Early Stages) into two chapters, the first of which focused on the six early stages of the start-up formation, including fund raising. This second chapter is focused on formal fund raising, typically when the start-up has taken off and is in the growth stages. For continuity from the six Steps covered in Chapter 10, this chapter will start from where I left off, at Step 7.

Before looking for funds, you should update your business plan to include the latest status of your company, as well as reflect the latest realities and new exciting possibilities. At the growth stage, you should have working products and services, a proven your business model, paying customers and shown that you have been able to execute on the initial plans. All financials should be updated, with new goals and targets that are shaped by your experience so far, with more informed projections for future growth. Include your latest organisation chart highlighting key team members and their achievements.

Step No. 7: Preparing for Fund Raising
–Engaging the Broker for Fund Raising

As previously mentioned, once your company has overcome all the initial hurdles and pains of the initial start-up phase, the company should sooner or later be ready for growth. To fund the growth stage, you will have to typically raise larger amounts of money and therefore you will have to rely on a more structured process. While going through the early stages, you should start to also prepare for the formal and major round of fund raising which most of the time involves going to VCs and institutional investors. In fact, you should avoid going to angels and individuals at this stage. There are a number of reasons. Firstly, individuals may not be able to fund the larger amounts you need and you may have to raise from a few individuals. This is not a good idea as you may end up with too many shareholders which will be challenging to manage.

Secondly, you will want at some stage to bring in some big name shareholders, whether VCs or institutions, as their brand name will increase your brand value, not just for future fund raising rounds but also to look good when you speak with other stakeholders – whether customers, banks, suppliers – or to attract future employees. Thirdly, VCs and institutional investors bring along with them networks that can come in very useful for your company – they may be able to introduce customers, banks, suppliers and other support that you may find difficult to obtain on your own. Fourthly, larger institutional investors can continue to provide you follow-on funding, so you minimise the time and effort to look for future funds. This is when you should really focus on getting "smart money".

UTAC Had Almost 40 Shareholders

As mentioned, when I started UTAC, I raised money mostly from Taiwan. The money came from a large number of VCs, institutional and individual investors. This is how Taiwanese investors invest – when they see a good opportunity, they will bring along their friends and network to share in the investment. While I coordinate with a group of three key investors, they gathered many more to join, thus explaining how I managed to raise more money than I wanted to at phase 1.

While it was nice to raise so much money, the downside was that I had to deal with almost 40 shareholders from day one. That presented a challenge as it required much attention and effort to address their needs and requests. Also, whenever shareholder resolutions are required, imagine coordinating with 40 shareholders to sign documents. It can be quite a nightmare. The entrepreneur should be fully focused on running and growing the company. Spending too much time entertaining investors is a distraction. So, my advice is to try to keep the number of shareholders to a small manageable number.

When looking for institutional investors, this stage of fund raising has to be conducted professionally. Not only do you need to present your company as an attractive investment opportunity, but the institutional investors also need to feel assured that they are backing a professional organisation. Therefore, it is wise to seek help from experts to prepare for this round. Another important consideration during this round of formal fund raising, is that your founding team also needs to benefit from the exercise and not be shortchanged. It is useful to have a middleman – typically an investment banker – to act as your broker. This person should have a good understanding of your industry, your company and your team. The team's aspirations and objectives must be at his fingertips. Unless the broker understands what your hot button issues are and what you are willing to compromise, he will have a very difficult time doing a good enough job of representing you for the exercise.

One question you might ask is: how can you afford a broker with the limited cash. The best answer is not to spend too much upfront, but to pay the broker only upon successfully raising the next round of financing. At the very best, give the broker a small retainer but backload on the success fees to minimise cash drain. With this arrangement, the broker too will be motivated because the real compensation for him would be the success fee.

Step No. 8: Getting Attention from Investors
– *The Teaser*

Prepare a summary of your business plan. It is not simply an executive summary, but something that can "tease" the target VC or the target institutional investor. This three to five-page teaser must make your plan and your company appear so attractive that the target investor just cannot wait to meet up with you. Refer to teaser example I have provided in Figure 13.1. This is an actual teaser I used when starting Infiniti Solutions, my third major start-up. The teaser has to be very skillfully prepared such that the essence of your plan is captured, the size of the opportunity spelt out, while illustrating the company's vision and value of the team. The teaser must be able to make the company look so unique that VCs are hungry for more information.

I would also caution against sending the teaser to too many people. Be targeted and do enough homework to shortlist the investors who are likely to be interested in your industry and project. For example, there is little point in sending a teaser to a company that rarely invests in capital-intensive companies, or those who only invest at the pre-IPO stage. The better you do your homework, the more effective you will be in attracting the right parties to look at your company. Look for the "smart money" this time so that the investors can help accelerate the growth of your company.

You also do not want to spend too much time talking to too many investors nor trying to convince non-believers – those who do not understand or do not have the appetite to invest in your type of business. Remember the whole fund-raising process can take up a lot of key management time and this may distract the team from doing their duties efficiently. Company performance can be affected while time is spent with too many potential investors, many of whom will want to discuss detailed plans and have multiple meetings to understand your team and your company better.

In summary, target smart money and make sure you align your Star of the Investor correctly – do not go for just anyone in the horizon. Also, you do not want too many people to be exposed to your idea, especially if it is very unique. Remember that VCs will deal with many other entrepreneurs and companies and letting out information to too many people may result in your idea going to your potential competitors, whether intentionally or otherwise.

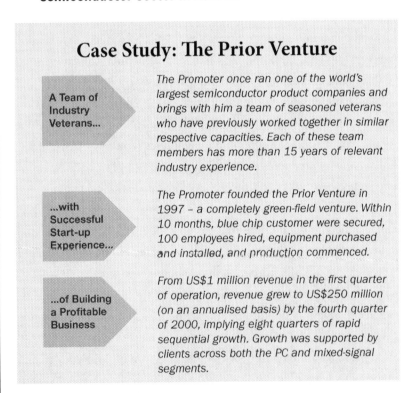

A Unique and Rare Opportunity to …

1. **Back one of the most successful team of veterans in the semiconductor sector in Asia …**

Case Study: The Prior Venture

A Team of Industry Veterans…

The Promoter once ran one of the world's largest semiconductor product companies and brings with him a team of seasoned veterans who have previously worked together in similar respective capacities. Each of these team members has more than 15 years of relevant industry experience.

…with Successful Start-up Experience…

The Promoter founded the Prior Venture in 1997 – a completely green-field venture. Within 10 months, blue chip customer were secured, 100 employees hired, equipment purchased and installed, and production commenced.

…of Building a Profitable Business

From US$1 million revenue in the first quarter of operation, revenue grew to US$250 million (on an annualised basis) by the fourth quarter of 2000, implying eight quarters of rapid sequential growth. Growth was supported by clients across both the PC and mixed-signal segments.

Fig. 13.1: The Teaser

...and a Solid Track Record...

By the second month of operation, the Prior Venture was profitable. By the second quarter, it had cumulatively broken even since in start-up. The Prior Venture consistently demonstrated one of the highest profit margins in the industry and was subsequently listed on NASDAQ in early 2001 with a current market capitalisation of US$1 billion.

2. **... that has recently successfully filed five patents for the new technology invented and is now testing the prototype ...**

The Technology: A Quick Snapshot

- Cuts down design to prototype samples from 20 months to six months
- Cost of production reduced by 80% compared to other typical technologies
- The team of 20 engineers has among them 50 years of industry experience
- Six customers, already signed on, will test the new product in three months

The Unravelling of Value:

- "Design win" concept – The technology will accelerate the launch of products from the prototype to the mass production stage. Arguably, this is the stage where the technical and engineering relationship is most intense. We intend to capitalise on this technology to win customers rapidly.

Fig. 13.1: *(Continued)*

- Current downturn – still a tremendous need for engineering and prototyping work.

  "... Those suppliers who can cut down product introduction time will win the business. We are trying to rapidly get there."
  Ref: ABC SE Test Ltd 1Q results press release dated 04/25/2001.

1. ... to become a leading semiconductor product player:

The Genesis of a Future "Walmart" in the Semicon Industry:

- The vision: To be the largest supplier in our industry
- What we are building:
  - A full turnkey solutions provider with a global presence
  - Competing on value added services, particularly engineering expertise and technology
- The people. An integrated team of veterans, both in Asia and the United States
- The strategy: Exploit patented technology and then grow and acquire competitors

Fig. 13.1: *(Continued)*

Key Investment Theme

- **PROVEN TRACK RECORD OF THE TEAM:** The team has excellent credentials and experience in the field of semiconductor design and technology, and has worked in big multinationals and in a start-up, which proved successful with its rapid growth, high profitability, and well-established relationships with over 50 customers.

- **ALREADY TESTING PRODUCTS:** The Company is not in the conceptual stage; it has already developed the products and secured blue chip customers.

- **EMERGING DEMAND FROM NEW FABS AND FOUNDRIES IN ASIA:** The rapid growth of wafer fabs in Asia will drive a big growth in the demand of the Company's products and technology.

- **ACCESS TO BLUE CHIP CLIENT BASE:** The team has long standing personal relationships with the key decision makers at the blue chip fabs, IDMs and fabless companies are proposed to be targeted in the business plan.

- **EXPOSURE TO HIGH IMPACT TECHNOLOGIES:** The company intends to continue to focus on high-end technologies. The base technologies will have enough spin-off applications for the next seven years. No other competitor can claim this.

- **CLEARLY DEFINED EXIT STRATEGY:** The proposed business plan targets a listing of the Company by year four. The Promoter believes that by such time the Company's revenues could have grown to US$300 million and investors may be able to achieve an attractive IRR on exit.

- **SIGNIFICANT BARRIERS TO ENTRY:** There are very few technocrats in Asia who have the ability to set up a high technologies in Asia. The patented technologies will prevent many from entering the same space for a few years to come.

Fig. 13.1: *(Continued)*

Background to the Company

The company is headed by an individual with 19 years experience in the semiconductor technology sector and who is also a well-known technopreneur in the region. He founded a similar green-field venture in Singapore in 1997 and grew it from a start-up operation into a company with an annualised revenue run rate of almost US$250 million by the end of 2000. In the Prior Venture, he was able to assemble team of 100 staff, acquire facilities and equipment, and sign up the first customer within a short span of ten months from inception. Before founding the Prior Venture, he worked with a large Japanese semiconductor company in the USA where he served in a number of positions, including the Chief Technology Officer. He received his PhD from the U of N and on MBA from U of S.

The core management team comprises veterans from the industry, each with an experience of 5–20 years. Currently, this includes a team of veterans both in Asia and the United States. The Company is also confident of attracting several senior managers, engineers, and technical specialists to build the depth and breadth of its management team.

Business Strategy

The core business of the Company is to:
- Provide turnkey products and services to electronic companies
- Undertake strategic acquisitions in certain semiconductor companies (subject to certain investment goals and procedures to be structured by the Board), after the initial growth of its own products and services. The business plan

Fig. 13.1: *(Continued)*

for the Company is divided into three phases as outlined below.

- **PHASE I:** Complete the prototype and test the products with the customers already engaged. Expand internal growth with the initial base of customers.
- **PHASE II**: Will be spread over the subsequent three years, and during this phase the Company will focus on rapidly growing the customer base, expanding internal capabilities and capacities, and also develop its presence across Asia, the USA, and Japan.
- **PHASE III:** By year four, the Company expects to have grown to a size, and with its track record will tap the capital market to fund its next stage of growth. The Company will then embark on an inorganic growth strategy by acquiring technology companies around the world.

Timetable and Process

The Company has already concluded its First Round funding. The Company is now undertaking a private placement process to raise capital (of between $35 million to $50 million) for the Second Round, involving both new strategic investors as well as its existing partners. The amount raised will be used to fund capital expenditures over the next 12 months, which includes completing the purchase of the Lab, strengthening the engineering and management team, and setting up a production facility in Asia.

The Company is seeking to conclude the private placement process before end of August.

Interested parties will be requested to sign a confidentiality agreement, and thereafter, will be provided with a copy of the Business Plan and be requested to bid on the following basis.

Fig. 13.1: (Continued)

- Confirm interest in committing to the capital expenditure requirement of the Company, as detailed in the Business Plan, and
- Explicitly state, the percentage shareholding sought in the Company in return for the investment committed, in this funding Round.

Fig. 13.1: *(Continued)*

Step No. 9: Confidentiality During Fund Raising
– The Non-Disclosure Agreement (NDA)

What is a Non-Disclosure Agreement or NDA? It is an agreement between two or more parties who are sharing with each other information considered classified by one, some or all of them, whereby each party is required to continue to keep the information classified whether or not they do business with each other. This is a very useful document for entrepreneurs who should ask potential investors to sign, and in some cases, also employees who have access to sensitive information, which if leaked to outsiders, particularly to potential competitors, could result in your company significantly losing competitiveness.

It is a good practice to get an NDA signed and properly documented because one can never know when in the future the documents will be needed in case the other parties use the information to put your company in a disadvantageous position. Many big VCs will tell you they never sign NDAs. To them I would say, "Then we cannot talk to you." But it is also a question of how desperate you are. If you have a great plan, one so unique that anyone seeing it will want to invest, then you should let go of those potential investors who do not want to sign an NDA. If, however, you really want to engage such parties, and if they really hold their ground in not signing the NDA, then perhaps it would be best to have a different set of documents prepared for them. All the material shown or given to such a VC or potential investor should be limited to protect your trade secrets and intellectual property. It is best to hold your ground and limit the exposure of your plans to only those who sign an NDA, or at the very least, a letter of undertaking that they will not divulge your intellectual property to others.

I experienced this once when helping a company I invested at the seed stage to raise funds from VCs. We prepared a very attractive teaser and sent it to a few VCs – some big and famous ones from the USA. Two of them refused to sign the NDA stating it was not their company's policy because they saw many start-ups. I then replied that if they did not sign an NDA, we would not make a presentation. After a few days, one of them called, saying they would sign a simple agreement. The company eventually invested in the start-up. Like a poker game, who blinks first will lose.

Step No. 10: Your Chance to Impress During Fund Raising
– The Pitch (Presentation)

To have a good plan that communicated badly is of little use. It is not easy to arrange an audience of good investors. When you have that opportunity, you have only one chance to impress. So, when the potential investor agrees to meet with your team, it is important to make an impressive pitch.

The pitch is typically a good summary and an eye-catching part of the business plan. It is important that the pitch be aligned with the business plan so as not to confuse the investor. As in any good presentation, it must flow well, have good graphics, good punch lines, etc. The people in your team making the presentation need to have very good presentation skills. Those who have worked in large multinational companies and have had very good experience in making management presentations will find their skills coming in very useful. For those not quite exposed to such presentations, it is recommended that they receive some coaching and also to do some dry runs with the broker. If your team has no experience in making presentations, it is best to seek some external help. I have seen many cases of very good ideas and plans that fail to interest investors due to poor communication skills during the pitch.

The content of your pitch should follow closely that of the business plan. After the pitch is over, the VCs will go back and digest the information further. The key points to communicate are:

1. The opportunities
2. The uniqueness of your approach and how you will beat the competitors
3. The background and the track record of your team
4. How you intend to use the money raised
5. A financial plan that is realistic and shows prudence
6. The short-term and long-term plans, as well as your company's direction.

See Chapter 12 on pitching.

Step No. 11: Agreeing on the Terms of Investment
–*The Term Sheet*

Once the investors have obtained a good feel of the company, especially after a presentation where they fully understood the business plan and have had a chance to meet the founders and the team, those interested will now want to quickly talk about the terms of their potential investment. The terms of investment are typically captured in the term sheet.

If the project is really very unique, many investors will be knocking on your door. It is very important not to react too quickly to initial requests by potential investors to sign the term sheet. Any signs of excitement and eagerness may lead to investors having the upper hand, leaving the entrepreneur with fewer options or resulting in a less than favourable deal. Why do I say this? First of all, they may get the impression that there are no other investors and you are excited to get their money. In such a situation, they will call the shots on the valuation and terms of the investment. The second problem with excessive eagerness is that the potential investors will quickly try to cut you off from talking to other investors so that they can take control of the situation and curb your ability to get better deals from other investors.

Often, potential investors will throw a very big carrot to entice you. They will offer very attractive valuations in the hope you will stop talking to other investors. Once you have cut off other potential investors and left your fate to the one or two first mover investors, then the games will start, where the investors will look for all the possible reasons to start cutting down valuations. The process can be drawn out, and one can easily become so entrenched and trapped by it that in the meantime other interested parties or investors would have moved on. At this point, there will be very little room for you to manoeuvre, leaving you at the mercy of the investors' terms and conditions.

It is therefore very important to not acquiesce to the first investor who comes along, but to keep a few engaged and excited, and only at the right time, further along the process, to choose the one or two you really want to partner with. This is called the competitive process without which you will be at the losing end.

Some potential investors will want you to sign an exclusive agreement with them, which means they will not allow you to discuss the deal with anyone else while they are evaluating your deal. They do this to avoid the competitive process themselves. You should avoid exclusivity agreements unless there is a very special offer, or if the potential investor is prepared to offer a very high valuation compared to the others in return for an exclusivity agreement. In general, I would avoid an exclusivity deal unless it is for a very short duration, which will allow you to catch up with other potential investors who might have been locked out of your deal during the exclusive period.

The essence of the final investment agreement is captured in the term sheet. The commercial terms must be very well spelt out and will become the basis for an official agreement between the investors and you. It is better for you to structure the term sheet before the potential investors structure it. Always endeavour to be in the driver's seat, so that very early in the process, the potential investors will have a good insight and feel of what your team is looking for. See Figure 13.2 for a sample term sheet.

Step No. 12: Reaching the Final Agreement with the Investor
– *The Deal Negotiations*

Negotiating the deal with interested parties is quite an interesting process. It is a critical part that involves each party taking care of its own interests. It is important to create a competitive process, as I mentioned earlier. In other words, by not quickly narrowing yourself down to one potential interested investor, you will remain in the driver's seat.

Summary of Terms (7/10/2002)

This term sheet summarises the financial terms of a proposed private placement of equity securities of ABC Pte Ltd [the "Company"]. The term sheet is for discussion purposes only, there is no obligation on the part of any negotiating party until a definitive Investment Agreement is signed by all parties. This term sheet is subject to the satisfactory completion of due diligence.

A. AMOUNT AND INVESTORS:	MNC Ventures	US $5,000,000
	SUB-TOTAL	US $5,000,000
B. TYPE OF SECURITY:	Redeemable, Convertible, preference "A" shares ("RCP "A" Shares")	
C. PRICE PER SHARE & CAPITALISATION:	$20 ["RCP "A" Shares Original Purchase Price"]. 1,000,000 total pre-financing fully-diluted Ordinary Shares and Options issued.	

Fig. 13.2: A Sample Term Sheet

		This financing: 200,000 shares of RCP "A" Shares issued as follows:
		Thus US$5,000,000 buys 20% of the company.
D.	**VESTING SCHEDULE:**	Shares held by the Founders shall be vested ratably over the 60 month-period following 1 December 2001.
		Unless the Board determines otherwise, employees' Ordinary Shares shall vest 20% at the end of the first year of full-time employment, and at a rate of 1/60th per month thereafter, with respect to shares granted prior to an IPO. There shall be no accelerated vesting of employees' Ordinary Shares in the event the Company is acquired or merged.
E.	**COMPENSATION:**	No Company employee shall receive annual compensation in excess of US$50,000 (except those receiving commissions from approved comp plans) without consent of all of the directors until the company is merged, sold, or completes an IPO.
F.	**DIVIDENDS:**	The holder of RCP "A" Shares shall be entitled to receive dividends at a rate of 8% per annum on their purchase price in preference to any dividends payable to the other holders of Ordinary Shares, whenever funds are available, when, if and as declared by the Board of Directors.
		The Company shall not declare or pay any dividends or capitalise its retained earnings or reserves and distribute them as fully paid up Ordinary Shares ("Bonus Shares") until after the conversion or redemption of all the RCP "A" Shares or unless the RCP "A" Shares participate in the proportionate share of the dividends or Bonus Shares on the basis that each RCP "A" Share (solely for the purpose of dividend and/or Bonus Shares) will be treated as if it has been converted to an Ordinary Share.

Fig. 13.2: (*Continued*)

G.	**RETURN OF CAPITAL:**	In the event of a return of capital other than on liquidation, the return of capital shall, as far as shall be practicable and permissible under law, proceed in accordance with the liquidation preference.
H.	**LIQUIDATION PREFERENCE:**	In the event of any liquidation or winding up of the Company, the holder of RCP "A" Shares will be entitled to receive in preference to the holder of Ordinary Shares an amount equal to the Redemption Amounts, or if such net proceeds are insufficient to make full payment of the Redemption Amounts, the net proceeds are to be distributed ratably amongst the holder of RCP "A" Shares in proportion to their respective Redemption Amounts RCP "A" Shares will be participating so that after payment of respective preferential amounts to the holder of RCP "A" Shares, the remaining assets shall be distributed pro-rata to all shareholders on a common equivalent basis.
I.	**CONVERSION:**	The holder of RCP "A" Share will have the right to convert RCP "A" Share at the option of the holder, at any time, into shares of Ordinary Shares at a conversion rate of 1-to-1. The conversion rate shall be subject from time to time to anti-dilution adjustments as described below.
J.	**ANTIDILUTION:**	Proportional anti-dilution protection for stock splits, stock dividends, combinations, re-capitalisation, etc. The conversion price of the RCP "A" Share shall be subject to adjustment to prevent dilution, on a full ratchet basis, in the event the Company issues additional shares of Ordinary or Ordinary equivalents (other than reserved employee shares) at a purpose price less than the applicable conversion price.
K.	**VOTING RIGHTS:**	The holder of RCP "A" Shares will have a right to that number of votes equal to the number of shares of Ordinary Shares issuable upon conversion of the RCP "A" Shares.

Fig. 13.2: *(Continued)*

L.	**REDEMPTION RIGHTS:**	i.	In the event that by 30 June 2005, it appears that the Company (or a listing vehicle including the Company) will not be listed on any recognised stock exchange or securities market by 30 June 2005, the RCP "A" Shareholder may give one (1) month's prior notice in writing to the Company of their intention to redeem their RCP "A" Shares, in which event the Company shall by 30 June 2005, or such other date as the RCP "A" Shareholder may agree, either seek a buyer for all the RCP "A" Shares at a price not lower than the Redemption Amount, or redeem the RCP "A" Shares at the Redemption Amount.
		ii.	In the event that a listing of the Company (or a listing vehicle including the Company) on any recognised stock exchange or securities market is deemed feasible, but the Existing Shareholders elect not to or act in a manner that makes it not possible to proceed with the listing, the RCP "A" Shareholder may give notice in writing to the Company of their intention to redeem their RCP "A" Shares, in which event the Company shall redeem the RCP "A" Shares at the Redemption Amount.
		iii.	The Company shall be obliged to redeem the RCP "A" Shares in full at the Redemption Amount when so requested by the RCP "A" Shareholder at any time on or after the occurrence of any material breach of any of the warranties jointly or independently given by the Company and the Founders, and where such breach has not been remedied within a period of 30 days after receipt of written notice given by RCP "A" Shareholder.
M.	**REDEMPTION AMOUNT:**		The Redemption Amount shall be the Investment Amount plus cumulative dividends at the rate of 10% of the Investment Amount per year, accurring from the date of issue of the relevant RCP "A" Shares to the date of redemption of such RCP "A" Shares, which shall be exclusive of any dividends declared by the Company. The appropriate adjustments the Redemption Amount will be made in the event of any shares splits, bonus issues or rights issues in the capital of the Company.

Fig. 13.2: *(Continued)*

N.	**BOARD OF DIRECTORS:**	The Board of Directors will consist of 5 seats. MNC shall be entitled to elect 2 members for the Company's Board of Directors, and the Founders collectively shall also be entitled to elect 2 members. The fifth director shall be the Company's Chief Executive Officer.
O.	**RIGHT OF FIRST OFFER:**	Any new issue of shares (whether ordinary or such other class of share) by the Company (other than an issue of shares pursuant to an employee share option scheme) shall be offered first to existing shareholders (of all classes of shares) in the proportion of their shareholding in the Company (solely for the purpose of determining the shareholding, the RCP "A" Shares shall be treated as if they have been converted to Ordinary Shares.)
		In addition, the Company will grant the RCP "A" Share Shareholder any rights of first refusal or registration rights granted to subsequent purchasers of the Company's equity securities to the extent that such subsequent rights are superior, in good faith judgment of the Company's Board of Directors, to those granted in connection with this transaction.
P.	**CO-SALE:**	The Company, the RCP "A" Share Shareholder, and the Founders will enter into a co-sale agreement pursuant to which any Founder or other investor who proposes to sell all or a portion of his shares to a third party, will offer the RCP "A" Shares investors the right to participate in such sale on a pro rata basis or to exercise a right of first refusal on the same basis. The agreement will terminate on the earlier of an IPO or fifteen (15) years from the close of this financing.

Fig. 13.2: *(Continued)*

Q.	**RESTRICTIONS & LIMITATIONS:**	So long as RCP "A" Shares remain outstanding, the Company shall not, without the vote or written consent of the RCP "A" Share shareholder, authorise or issue any equity security senior to the RCP "A" Shares as to dividend rights or redemption rights or liquidation preferences. Furthermore, the Company shall not amend its Articles of Incorporation or By-laws in a manner that would alter or change the rights, preferences or privileges of any RCP Shares without the approval of the RCP "A" Shares Investors. Written consent of RCP "A" Share Shareholders shall be required for (a) any merger, consolidation, or other corporate reorganisation, or (b) any transaction or series of transactions in which an excess of 50% of the Company's voting power is transferred or in which all or substantially all of the assets of the Company are sold.
R.	**PROPRIETARY INFORMATION & INVENTIONS AGREEMENT:**	Each officer, director, and employee of the Company shall have entered into a proprietary information and inventions agreement in a form reasonably acceptable to the Company and the RCP "A" Share Shareholder. Each key technical employee shall have executed an assignment of inventions acceptable to the Company and the RCP "A" Share Shareholder. Each Founder will have made appropriate representations and warranties as to no-conflict with prior employers.
S.	**PURCHASE AGREEMENT:**	The investment shall be made pursuant to an Investment Agreement reasonably acceptable to the Company and the RCP "A" Share Shareholder. The agreement shall contain, among other things, appropriate representations and warranties of the Company, with respect to patents, litigation, previous employment, and outside activities, covenants of the Company reflecting the provisions set forth herein, and appropriate conditions of closing, including an opinion of the counsel for the Company.
T.	**MANAGEMENT:**	The Company shall hire a CEO and a CFO within a six (6) months period following 1 December 2002.

Fig. 13.2: *(Continued)*

U. **LEGAL FEES & EXPENSES:**	The Company shall pay all reasonable fees and expenses of counsel to the investors and the Company.

The foregoing Summary of Terms sets forth the good faith agreement of the parties set forth below. By accepting this term sheet, the Company agrees to refrain from solicitation, consideration, or acceptance of alternative proposals to finance, recapitalise or sell the Company for a period of thirty (30) days from the date of the Company's signature below. This offer expires on Thursday, Oct 10th, 2001 at 12 p.m.

MNC Ventures   **ABC Pte Ltd**

By: _____   By: _____

Dates: _____   Date: _____

Fig. 13.2: *(Continued)*

Never forget that investors, particularly the VCs, are not engaged in charity work. Their objective is to make the best return for their investment. They are therefore motivated to cut you down as much as they can. Because each party is trying to get the best deal, there will be times when both parties will feel frustrated and angry with each other. Never lose your cool and try not to show either your enthusiasm or your anger, because, should the investor finally invest, everyone becomes a partner. If there was any bad blood created during the negotiations, it will tend to linger and become difficult to overcome as the company operates. There will be many more battles to fight moving forward, and having a partnering spirit is very useful in discussions with shareholders.

At the end of the day, whatever the negotiations are, have a mindset that you can maintain should the investment go through. Do not go overboard, and do not do anything to burn your bridges even if the investment falls through.

A very important part of this process involves a broker. I have found it very useful to engage a broker to step in as a buffer between the entrepreneur and the investor. Creating a buffer zone during negotiations gives you a chance to re-think as opposed to having to back off from a decision or a position when you are dealing directly with the investors. The broker can play the buffer role. With a broker, you can also play a good guy versus bad guy game, where sometimes you play the bad guy in the negotiations and the broker plays the good guy trying to make parties compromise, or alternatively, vice versa where you play the good guy to make the investor feel that you are more flexible and compromising than the broker. While a broker may cost money, the outcome could make quite a big difference in the eventual valuations.

Once again, keep as many investors interested for as long as possible. Start negotiating with all of them to keep the process going until you gain a better insight into how they will be valuing your company and how you can strengthen your position. You can even learn from the approach of one investor and use it against another. Narrowing down your choices too quickly will mean you will exclude a wider range of options.

Some team members may want to close the deal quickly for fear of losing potential investors. Beware as it is a grave mistake to ever show such eagerness. The process can be very tiring and could even lead to internal team conflicts because of the eagerness of some and the aggressiveness of others. The key point to remember is that VCs will only take care of their own interests and you will have to take care of your own. Never think that the VC wants to help you or think they are willing to give up some value just because they want to help you. This never happens. The sooner everyone realises that he has to take care of his own interests, the better the outcome will be. Business is business. No one will do you any favours or help you by giving you special treatment. The mindset should be to create a win-win situation for all. Once the decision has been made and the agreements signed, there is no point looking back wondering if you could have had a better deal. If you handled the process right, you will feel everyone had a good deal.

Step No. 13: The Final Stage of a Formal Fund Raising
–Closing the Sale and Purchase or Investment Agreement and Shareholder Agreement

Once the negotiations of the term sheet have been concluded and the key commercial terms of the investment have been agreed upon, the next important step is to put it all down in the form of a formal, legal and enforceable agreement, which all parties need to sign. This consists of two agreements: a Sale and Purchase (S&P) agreement and a Shareholder Agreement (SHA).

These two are very important documents that will govern the way each shareholder will behave by spelling out the rights of and remedies available to each party– do not take this lightly. If you do not pay attention to the details, I guarantee it will come back and bite you when you least expect it, whether things go better than planned or when everything starts to fall apart. While you should take care of all the usual legal issues, be careful not to make the agreement too precise too quickly. The more issues you open up during the discussions of the final agreement, the tighter the agreement becomes. As I mentioned earlier, the investors or VCs are not there to help you, but to protect their own interests. So do not ever feel that they will have a balanced agreement done for you. Start from a position that they will take care of themselves, even at your expense. Think that they will go all out to create a one-sided agreement that only takes care of their interests. So, you too must make it as one sided as possible in favour of yourself. To do this effectively, you need to engage a lawyer to handle your part of the negotiations. Make sure your lawyer clearly knows what your expectations and hot buttons are, to help you defend your interests.

Negotiations should be started with the two lawyers, the one representing you and the one representing the investor. Let the lawyers do as much as possible without involving yourself, the investor, or the VC. Ask the lawyers to distil a list of unresolved issues that they could not nail down during the lawyer-to-lawyer meetings. Once the lawyers are done with round one (and there will be many more rounds), the list of outstanding issues that they could not resolve should be highlighted to all the parties.

After everyone has digested and understood those issues that the lawyers could not resolve, the next step is to arrange a four-way meeting with the investor or VC's representative, you and your team, and the lawyers from both parties. At this meeting, everyone will work through the unresolved issues. Everyone should be "locked" in a room for a marathon meeting for as long as it will take to thrash out all the issues. If a particular issue cannot be resolved, it should be distilled or put into a "parking lot". This list of unresolved issues will now be much smaller than the original list. Henceforth, these unresolved issues should be taken up separately without the lawyers' present.

The next step is to have a four-eye meeting – a meeting of minds and hearts between the potential investor and the key decision-makers of the team. At this stage, there will have to be some give and take between both parties. Everyone will be required to give up a little to arrive at a compromise or a middle ground acceptable to all parties.

If the top representatives from both sides cannot agree the process may drag on. At the end of the day, you must ensure you have some room to move, otherwise it will be very difficult to close the deal. It is very useful to have a bag of "goodies", which may not be worth much to you but is a sign of your goodwill for the sake of getting the deal done. By giving some of these "goodies" away, you can make the other party feel as if they have succeeded in winning a good deal. Whatever you do, do not give the "house" away, because if you do, the whole experience of running the company could be painful. You will always feel you gave away too much, leaving yourself less incentive to make sacrifices for the company. Once an acceptable agreement has been reached, both parties should send it to their respective lawyers, instructing them to incorporate what has been agreed upon into the necessary legal jargon for the final agreement.

I have one final point to make on this part of the process: The cost build up can be quite high if you do not rein in your lawyers. Ensure that you keep a tight control of both the process and what your lawyers do. Some may be inclined to go to certain extremes as a means to show their client how well they are taking care of their interests. The problem is that the lawyers often try to handle commercial issues, which they should not. The commercial terms should be fully controlled by the entrepreneurs and the investors, while the lawyers' job is to fit the commercial issues and commercial terms into a legal framework. Whenever the lawyers stray into the commercial areas, clients should intervene to instil discipline.

Finally, it is important that one member of your team understands and has the patience to plough through all the words and paperwork being generated during this part of the process. If not, you will not realise the type of commitments you might have made in signing a potentially onerous agreement.

Is this the end? Of course not. Now that you have acquired the funds, the company can start operating to grow the business rapidly. Attention shifts to the execution of the plan you presented to the investors. Typically, the institutional investors and VCs will require to have board seats in your company. Through the board they will be able to monitor your progress closely and also influence decisions on the company's plans. This is generally useful especially if the investors can bring value to help the company execute their plans. However, in some cases the VC can hamper decision making to the frustration of the entrepreneurs and the management team.

Chip Design Company

I once invested in a Singapore-based chip design company. The technology was great and if it worked, it would have changed the way telecommunications devices worked. A group of friends and I put in more than US$1m in this company and we were involved at the board level to guide the company. The group of us who invested at the Seed stage were angel investors and entrepreneurs and we had a flexible arrangement where we discussed with the founders and management team on the direction of the company and how they executed the plans. There were no such companies founded in Singapore but there were many in the Silicon Valley and Taiwan and other parts of the world. After some initial success, we managed to attract a very big VC (DFJ – Draper Fisher) to put in a few million dollars. DFJ required a board seat and the person on the board was actively involved in managing the company. There came a time when the DFJ team was not happy with progress, and they forced the company to hire a CFO who would be chosen by DFJ to be their eyes and ears in the company and who would ensure decisions of the board are followed. Before long, this CFO was the de facto "CEO" and was driving the company direction and activities. This made the founder team uncomfortable, but they had little choice since this was a condition of DFJ's investment. The point I am making is that after the VC invests, they may play a dominant role in the company and the founders need to be prepared for this when finalising the terms of the investments. To end the story, after a few years, this company failed and was closed.

Getting Ready for Formal Fund Raising

I have outlined 13 steps to transform an idea into a business, followed by raising funds for the company. The first six steps were covered earlier in Chapter 10.

In this chapter, I elaborated on the remaining seven steps of fund raising. These are the typical formal steps start-ups go through in doing later stages of fund raising:

- Step No. 7 — Engaging the broker for fund raising
- Step No. 8 — Preparing and targeting the teaser to attract smart money
- Step No. 9 — The Non-Disclosure Agreement (NDA)
- Step No. 10 — The Pitch
- Step No. 11 — The Term Sheet
- Step No. 12 — The deal negotiations
- Step No. 13 — Closing the sale and purchase or investment agreement

The whole fund-raising process can be lengthy and take away time from running the company. Be mindful that you don't neglect executing your business plan while engaging in the fund-raising exercise.

CHAPTER 14

THREE RULES OF THUMB FOR FUND RAISING

If you ask any entrepreneur, he will tell you what a challenging task it is to raise funds for a start-up. As it is not everyone's cup of tea, it is also one area where many entrepreneurs fail. In fact, it is probably one of the first tests of whether the entrepreneur can successfully transform an idea into a business. After all, without money, the business may never ever get started. The fund-raising exercise is also probably one of the first interactions the entrepreneur has with his future investors.

The entrepreneur should never underestimate the effort needed to start and complete the whole fund-raising process. It is definitely a very tough and energy-draining exercise, which can easily frustrate even the toughest of entrepreneurs. I have seen many entrepreneurs taking this exercise lightly, getting hurt in the process, and in the worst-case scenario, failing to raise any funds resulting in the premature end to the start-up.

While many people have differing views on how the fund-raising exercise should be conducted, I have identified three useful rules of thumb for fund raising. Remember that the funds you are planning to raise will come from someone who wants to invest in you and your company to make a huge return at a later date. So never lose sight of the fact that you have to show everyone quite convincingly how those returns will be achieved. If investors are convinced, you will receive their money.

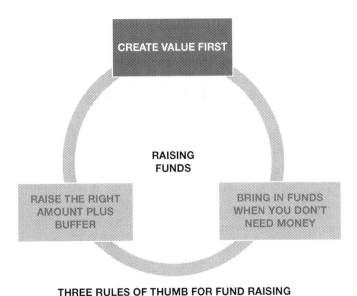

THREE RULES OF THUMB FOR FUND RAISING

Fig. 14.1: Fund Raising: Create Value First

Rule of Thumb No. 1: Create Value First Before Finding New Funds

The first rule of thumb for entrepreneurs is to always create value before going for the next stage of fund raising. There are many ways entrepreneurs can begin funding their start-up. Some put in their own money or take on credit card debts, and others borrow from their family and friends. It is quite typical to start with the "3Fs" when starting up, and these 3Fs are family, friends and fools. I mentioned earlier this third "F" is called a fool because of the high risks of investing in start-up companies and losing money. I am sure it is meant as a joke, because people part with their money in anticipation of making money and not to fool around. Generally the 3Fs are the most sympathetic towards the entrepreneur and really want to help even if the risks are very high.

To be frank, these days, unless a start-up has some funds from one of the Fs, others outside this circle will rarely give you money. Of course, if the required sum of money is too much, beyond what the 3Fs can support, then you will have to look beyond this group. It will be easier to convince angel investors who have a higher risk appetite (but expect a much higher return) and can make an investment decision much faster than any institutional investor can.

If the entrepreneur can manage with money from only the 3Fs, I would suggest they do not go to the next stage. The reason is simply what this rule of thumb says: you should create more value before raising new money. Raising the next round too early will dilute the equity held by the entrepreneurs and founders too early. Exactly how the 3Fs funds are structured can vary. In some cases, it is a loan given in trust, expecting the entrepreneur to pay it back one day. Others offer it as a friendly loan, not expecting to make any returns. In some cases, the 3Fs simply want to help and are willing to write off the amount should the entrepreneur fail. At best, the money is converted to equity at very good valuations giving the 3Fs huge returns should the company succeed.

After the initial money from the 3Fs is in hand, the focus should be on setting up the company with a few key people coming on board, preferably on a full-time basis. This initial stage includes a design of the product or service with a prototype to prove that the idea works. Even if you don't have the product, putting a team together itself is additional value added. Coming up with a business model and some initial designs or blueprints is also new value added. All these will help create a better valuation.

The next round of fund raising should start once a working prototype can be produced to demonstrate the product or service and how it will work. Angel investors would be the next best group of investors to attract for the reasons I mentioned earlier. They will typically invest smaller amounts than VCs taking on tremendous risks at this stage of funding, typically called the seed stage. Angel investors will be able to quickly decide whether or not they want to invest, without spending too much time doing due diligence on your company and on you. The more professional investors like VCs typically spend a lot of time on due diligence.

This quick due diligence fits in well with what the entrepreneur desires. One should not spend too much time entertaining people doing detailed due diligence of the company and the team at a very early stage. A long-drawn due diligence process will distract the founding team from the real task they should be focused on – executing the business plan by working on the products and service and also testing the market potential – Product/Market Fit. So, at this stage, the start-up should deliver a prototype or initial product/service that can indeed prove that the problem can be solved with the solution being proposed. This then would have added more value that can be used to help increase the valuation of the start-up at the next stage.

Only after the project gains momentum and the start-up has gained more traction, achieving more results and value in the new company, may it be the right time to go after bigger institutional investors like VCs.

The key objective for the entrepreneur is to enhance the company's value before embarking on any new rounds of financing. As the company's valuations increase, the investment of the original founders and investors will be less diluted as a result of new investors paying a higher price for each share in the company issued at the later stage. There is of course a balance and a judgement as to how much money should be raised at each stage.

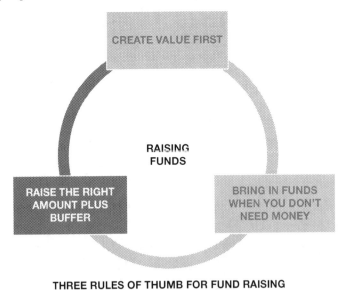

THREE RULES OF THUMB FOR FUND RAISING

Fig. 14.2: Fund Raising: The Right Amount

Too much gets you too diluted, resulting in you and your team owning less of your company at too early a stage. Too little, and you risk having insufficient money to bring the company to the next stage of development, and perhaps in the worst-case scenario, lead to a premature collapse of the company due to a lack of funds. This now brings me to the second rule of thumb for fund raising.

Rule of Thumb No. 2: Bring in Just Enough Funds Plus a "Small" Buffer Each Time

Ideally, the entrepreneur should bring in the right amount of funds into the company at the right time. So, while the first rule of thumb is about the right time to bring in certain types of funds, the second rule guides the entrepreneur on how much should be raised at different stages. In order for the entrepreneur to maximise value for himself as well as for all the other early investors, the amount of money that should be raised depends on the value already created in the company. It also depends on how much more money is needed for further value creation to bring the company to the next fund-raising stage. This rule of thumb states that the entrepreneur should bring in just enough funds plus a little buffer, and then, as much as possible, stretch every dollar raised.

Raising too much money too early in the company's development will mean a huge dilution for the entrepreneur, the founding members of the company, as well as the early stage investors. Raising too little will mean that the company may not have enough money to create further value needed to bring the company to the next stage of fund raising. So how much is enough and how much is too much?

This is a matter of skill and judgement. In many cases, entrepreneurs tend to either overdo their fund-raising exercise by bringing in too much money or under-do it by bringing in too little, thus not giving them enough runway to reach the next level of the company's development. In fact, raising too little money could also prove disastrous, particularly if the company runs out of funds and desperately needs new funds to be injected. Once potential investors know that the company is in desperate need of money, new investors will demand low valuations to put in their money. Even existing investors may take the opportunity to squeeze the desperate entrepreneur and his team members by clawing into their shareholdings in the company.

When this happens, it is then a matter of who blinks first. It is quite typical for entrepreneurs in such a situation to be pushed into a corner and accept new terms and conditions at new valuations imposed by the investors. This reduces the entrepreneur's stake in the company that may be quite significant. Raising funds is an important skill to have and requires discipline. How much do you raise each time? What is the "buffer" to be raised? Most get it wrong.

Over the years, I have learned from both personal experience and that of other entrepreneurs that this funding buffer is not a small buffer. It is a big buffer. It is best summarised based on what one very experienced investor once told me: it will typically take *twice as long* to execute the plan and use

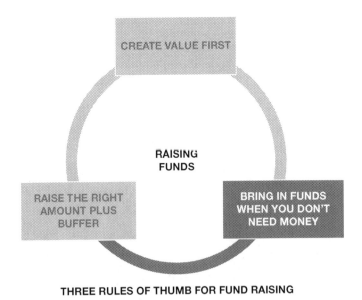

THREE RULES OF THUMB FOR FUND RAISING

Fig. 14.3: Raising Funds When Not Needed

twice as much money than shown in the original business plan. In other words, whatever the entrepreneur judges to be the time and money needed to bring the company to the next logical stage as shown in his business plan, it should be assumed that the plan really showed the amount to be half of what is truly needed. Thus, one should assume that it will take double the money than conceived on paper, two times more resources, and twice as long to complete. To cover the large buffer amount, you should therefore raise double the money you think you need.

Rule of Thumb No. 3: Raise the Funds When You Do Not Need the Money

Once the first two rules have been mastered, this third rule of thumb should become second nature for all savvy entrepreneurs but which many forget to do. According to this rule, the entrepreneur should raise funds when the company does not need funds. Is this not a contradiction you might ask? If you do not need the money, why would you want to raise more?

This third rule of thumb may seem to contradict the first two rules, but it is a very important discipline for entrepreneurs. I say many entrepreneurs forget to do this, because understandably, when the company still has funds, comfort sets in and fund raising is neglected. As we do not have complete control over all the factors that determine the success of our company, then we know things can go terribly wrong when you least expect it. The whole environment we are operating in is dynamic. We should be prepared for unforeseen situations that will challenge the assumptions made when launching the company.

In reality, most people cannot accurately time the market. By this, I mean not many people can determine when the best and most conducive time is for the industry they are in, and therefore they cannot possibly tell when the industry conditions will take a turn for the worse. So when you think your company has taken off and that you want to wait a little longer for more good results before you go for the next round of fund raising, the issue is that your timing and that of the industry and market sentiment seldom align. It is not easy to catch the right market timing. While you may not be ready to do the fund raising at a certain time when the market is ready for you, the problem is that when you are ready, the market might no longer be willing to consider you. Time and tide wait for no man, as the saying goes. Catching the right time is one of the most difficult things to do.

I have learned to believe in this third rule of thumb, which is, you have to raise money when you do not really need it. In planning the execution and growth of the company, the entrepreneur should keep a close eye on how the cash is being utilised and plan way ahead of time for some form of new fund raising before the money runs out.

Sometimes, the market might be very buoyant, and investors typically move by herd instinct. We have seen this during various eras, whether it was the dot.com era, the recent Fintech era or when any other "flavour of the month technology" became popular. In such a situation a lot of money chases start-ups to invest in, especially if the technology or business model happens to be the current craze. During such times, it may be an opportune time to get some money during such a craze when valuations become ridiculously high.

In a scenario where many potential investors might be interested in certain types of companies, of which yours happens to be a good fit, you might want to consider raising additional funds anyway to increase the company's war chest. In such a situation, the valuation would be attractive for the company. Dilution of valuation is less of a factor compared to the situation in which the company missed the boat and is in dire need of raising new funds when really needed, causing valuation to be depressed. When the investors know that a company is desperate for funds, they will take the opportunity to cut the valuation in their favour.

It is not an easy skill to judge when the time is right. When you already have money and do not really need more, you tend to become complacent.

In a good market, money is abundant, and investors will be looking for good deals to invest in. In this case you will not be desperate, while the investors will be desperate to invest if yours is indeed a good investment deal. This is quite a satisfying position to be in for the entrepreneur. Unfortunately, this position is not easy to achieve and requires a lot of skill and experience.

Often, if your lucky stars are aligned, the benefits are tremendous. It is therefore very important to know WHEN to look for money. Be on the constant lookout and go ahead and raise money for your company when you do not really need it. If you have the discipline and are not distracted by complacency, you can do it – raise money after creating value, raise just enough, and raise funds when you don't really need the money. Many people might think you are overdoing it, but when the time comes, you will have the last laugh.

Looking at the Wrong Places at the Wrong Time

One other mistake many entrepreneurs make in trying to raise funds is looking at the wrong places at the wrong time. This happens due to their lack of experience and lack of proper guidance. Typically, it happens at the very early stages of the company, especially before an angel investor or a VC invests in the company.

Once experienced partners enter the company, they provide valuable advice and guidance for the entrepreneur to go to the right place for the right type of financing. For example, I have seen many cases in which the entrepreneur looks for debt financing when he or she should really be looking for equity financing, and vice versa. Another example is in some entrepreneurs seeking VC financing too early when they should really have gone for 3Fs or angel investors. In many cases, if the entrepreneur approaches the wrong sources, the funds never get raised, which leads to an even more desperate position for the entrepreneur. Therefore, it is also important to know WHERE to look for money.

When and Where

Fund raising can be a very tricky exercise. Some of the issues include what the right valuation is, who the right investor or financer is, how much to raise, what type of financing mode is needed, and when the money should be raised. It all boils down to the questions of WHEN and WHERE. Those who figure out the answers will be well rewarded, while those who fail will in most cases regret the outcome. It is worth studying the examples of successful and unsuccessful entrepreneurs and companies to have a feel of what is right or wrong for you, the entrepreneur. You should carefully study the three rules of thumb to help you in your fund-raising efforts.

Learning from Personal Experience

I have varying experience in fund-raising exercises. I have raised funds from family members, angel investors, venture capitalists, as well as private and public companies, mostly for equity financing of various companies I started. I also have raised debt financing, both big and small, from finance companies, banks, and other institutions. The companies that received this funding include those at the early stages, growth stages, as well as stages at which the company was considered large. The amounts raised range from US$0.5m for seed-stage funding, US$3m for growth-stage financing, US$10m to US$30m debt financing, US$36m for equity financing, and all the way up to US$138m for my UTAC start-up. Personally, I also have done angel investing of various sums, some big and some small, at the early stage as well at the later stages of company growth. I have provided debt as well as equity at low as well as ridiculous valuations.

These experiences have enabled me to learn a thing or two about fund raising and how everyone behaves in the process. In the case of UTAC, I overdid things by raising too much money at the early stage. It should have been done in stages and at varying valuations so the founders and the early-stage investors would not be disadvantaged by huge dilutions. The rate at which UTAC developed showed me I should have really raised only 60 per cent of the US$138m in the first stage, created some value, and then proceeded for the next round of fund raising. As I said, it was my first experience as an entrepreneur.

In the case of Infiniti Solutions, my team funded the seed stage ourselves, with a very small amount from a venture capitalist. And then we went on to raise another US$36m when we were ready to execute the company's growth. We also raised enough, but I must say, given that we had to go through two downturns in succession, we had to stretch every dollar raised. I should have raised money when I did not need it. I could have done it as planned in my business plan, but got distracted with an early IPO plan for the company. Had we stuck to our original plan where we were supposed to do another private VC round two years after we started, life would have been much better.

I also learned it isn't easy to practise the three rules of thumb outlined. Had I followed them, success would have come a lot easier. In future, I will continue to be guided by my three rules of thumb for fund raising.

Deal Flow Connection

Through my experience in raising funds for my many ventures, I knew how difficult it could be for entrepreneurs in Singapore. Hence, I volunteered to form a National Committee to study the local financing landscape and find solutions to enhance the financing environment. The goal was to develop new tools of financing so that Singapore could have a much better entrepreneurship and start-up ecosystem as seen from more entrepreneurial regions like the USA, Israel and Taiwan. One of the biggest stumbling blocks for Singapore as I experienced was inability to raise funds even for great start-up ideas (like UTAC which is a huge success but which did not find local investors). My goal for this National Committee was therefore to develop a vibrant financing and fund-raising environment so that future entrepreneurs do not have to struggle and face the same obstacles I did when trying to raise funds.

As I did my work, I realised having many options for financing alone might be insufficient. We needed an avenue to bring the entrepreneurs and the companies looking for funding to the right places, since entrepreneurs often look for money in the wrong places. I used to give talks about entrepreneurship in Singapore and as a result, many entrepreneurs used to speak with me to assist them to raise funds. In one case, a company tried to raise equity for their project financing needs. They tried and failed so they asked me for my advice. The company was dealing with a government entity and had confirmed orders. I realised they should be going for debt and not equity financing. I helped connect them to a bank and they secured the money. There were other cases where entrepreneurs complained they could not get bank debt financing. But banks don't finance start-ups with debts because of the high risks involved. I linked them up with angel investors and some successfully attracted investment funds. I then thought that if what I did for a few companies could be replicated into a more formal channel or a more institutionalised manner, many more companies could be helped.

The idea was to set up a financing matchmaking infrastructure where entrepreneurs and companies are matched to the right types of financing and funds. For any such matchmaking to work, you need matchmakers, so if we could create a community consisting of people looking for money, people who could provide the money, and people who could act as the middlemen to bring the two together, we would have a powerful tool to facilitate and make the fund-raising exercise much more efficient.

The outcome was what we call the Deal Flow Connection (DFC). This is a platform supported by a portal consisting of a community of the three groups of people I mentioned above. We realised that one of the most important components of the DFC community were the matchmakers, whom we called the intermediaries. The more intermediaries we had, the more deals we could facilitate. These intermediaries could act as consultants or brokers, to do all the legwork for the companies looking for money.

By having a common marketplace for the entrepreneurs, the investors, and the intermediaries, we managed to create an efficient channel for fund raising with the potential to become a commercially viable platform that perhaps could become a business by itself in the future. This platform was run by a government agency (SPRING) in the beginning and after a few years, we spun it off to operate as a private company. Now this was sometime in the year 2005, something that was new and ahead of its time. Today Crowdfunding platforms have become a norm. I called it "Deal Flow Connection" at that time. I could easily have called it "Crowdfunding".

Three Rules of Thumb for Fund Raising

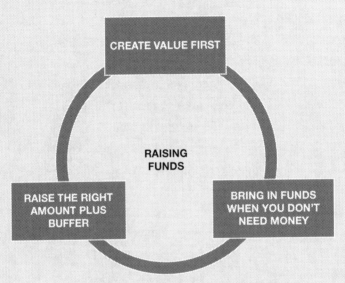

THREE RULES OF THUMB FOR FUND RAISING

Fig. 14.4: Three Rules for Fund Raising

Rule of Thumb No. 1
- **Create value first before finding new funds**
  - The amount of money that should be raised depends on the value already created in the company, and also on how much more funds are needed for further value creation to bring the company to the next fund-raising stage.

Rule of Thumb No. 2
- **Bring in just enough funds plus a small buffer each time**
  - Do not over-raise or your valuation will be diluted too early.

- Always be prepared that it will take double the money than conceived on paper, two times more resources, and twice as long to complete. Do not under-raise the amount needed to bring the company to the next stage, otherwise the company might prematurely cease due to a lack of funds.

Rule of Thumb No. 3
- **Raise funds when you do not need the money**
  - You should raise funds when the company does not need the money. In such a situation you can call the shots and investors will realise you are not desperate.

CHAPTER 15

WHAT SHOULD ENTREPRENEURS LOOK FOR?

The process of creating a successful company is not simple nor easy. From the time that the idea is conceived, to converting the idea to a business model, forming the team, gathering the resources and raising funds, many steps are involved and many are very difficult ones. Just because you started a company does not guarantee that the company will be a successful one. So, entrepreneurs need to be mindful of what it takes to be a successful entrepreneur.

While many factors go into making a person an entrepreneur (the art of entrepreneurship), many more factors are needed to build companies that last a long time. In this chapter, I will cover areas the entrepreneur should look out for when starting a company. In fact, these are what the entrepreneur must be confident of doing should he want to venture out to start a company.

I believe that failure to address and cover the bases that I am going to list here will result in weak companies and failure in the long term. The factors I am about to discuss will also help the entrepreneur and the start-up to identify good partners, find good people for the team, select the correct type of investors, partner the right suppliers, and most importantly identify and cultivate the right type of customers. When you can correctly identify all of these factors, we can say your Stars have aligned. For fund-raising purposes, if you correctly follow what is covered in this chapter, you will easily find the right investors for your start-up.

Here are some salient points to increase your chances of finding the right partners and therefore increase the chances of success.

Start-Up Criteria No. 1: Look Not for Heroes, but Team Members

I talked about this in a previous chapter, where I mentioned that investors will look out for not only a team of people with a strong background and good track record, but also one that is strongly integrated. From the entrepreneur's perspective, he should also ensure that the team is well diversified and can help cover all the areas needed to run a company. However, one should not overdo it by bringing in a large number of people, each to cover one area of a company's function (i.e. marketing, engineering, finance, operations, planning, etc.). It is, of course, convenient to bring in one person for each area and therefore cover all possible bases. But it is best that you bring with you, in the early stages of the startup, a core group of people who can work with you where each can cover a few domain areas so that the team is not so large that it becomes difficult to manage. The other downside of having a big team too early is that it burns up too much cash early in the process.

If you have a lineup of good people who can form an A-one team, investors may be impressed by your ability to assemble good people. The best thing to do would be to line up all the people whom you can convince to join you and show the list to the potential investor. Then bring them into the company in phases, and in particular, time their entry according to the expertise the company critically needs and what it can afford at each point in time.

Typically, in the early stages of a start-up, it is useful to have each team member doubling or tripling up his or her role. For example, in a number of the start-ups I managed, I played the role of CEO as well as CFO, in addition to handling some technical responsibilities. Similarly, I have had individual team members handling at least two roles, such as both engineering and operations and perhaps the planning function.

The second and equally important point about bringing in team members flexibly is that you cannot afford to erect high walls between departments too early in the process. The entrepreneur, who himself will have to get involved in almost all the aspects of running the business, should also assemble a team that is willing to be flexible enough to be involved in areas other than what they were originally expected to handle. In large organisations, it is quite typical for each department head to just worry about his area and leave the other department heads to worry about their own. This is a highly unproductive and risky way of building a company, particularly in the early stages.

Each team member must not feel offended nor create restrictions if any other team members gets involved in his or her defined responsibility. Due to the speed at which things need to get done at the start-up stage, Such crossing of boundaries facilitates fast reaction and fosters a culture of teamwork, which is necessary to create long-term success. The entrepreneur must be very careful in choosing team members who can accept a flexible job role at perhaps half the market rate of salary, who allows others to help him or her in the job and who is willing to help others in their jobs.

As the needs of the company evolve and depending on what each team member can contribute, it may sometimes be necessary for some team members to change their primary job roles from time to time. For example, a person doing R&D may need to understand how to market the technology and product, and thus switch roles to do marketing.

The team must be willing to accept changes as well as be adaptable enough to take on another job which they may not have sufficient strength in, although they will have some knowledge in. It is even more useful for team members to have the initiative to voluntarily crossover or help other team members without being prompted. Team members should have the basic interest to see each other succeed. Any help offered from other team members should be seen in a positive rather than negative light.

During the start-up phase, the entrepreneur should also consider including a few Jack-of-all-trades team members, to handle issues that might otherwise fall between the cracks. If the team members are specialised, they might fail to see perspectives other than their own areas of expertise. In addition, certain grey areas may not be properly addressed. An attitude of overall responsibility for the whole team is a very important trait for entrepreneurs and the start-up team. At the end of the day, all members should seek success for the whole team, rather than individual success – the motto being, "All for one and one for all". There is no point assembling a group of heroes and champions who may not be able to work in a team. An integrated team will bring greater success than a few good individuals will.

Start-Up Criteria No. 2: Alignment of Stars

While starting a company should be driven by passion, it should never be the result of an emotional outburst. Building a company is a long-haul exercise. If its creation stems from emotion, it will not last long since emotions do not last long. While emotions may play an important part in why a company is created or what sparked the idea, it should still not be a reason for forming a company. For example, sometimes, a person may be forced to leave employment at a company against one's will, and as an emotional response, decide to form a company to compete head-on. The question we should ask is whether such a company will be successful or last long.

There is nothing wrong with someone wanting to start another company in the same field of business as his previous company, especially if it will be utilising prior knowledge, but the company should be started for the right reasons, not for reasons that are emotional in nature. If the reasons are right, then by all means, the company should be started to allow the entrepreneur to create another success.

I discussed the alignment of stars in an earlier chapter and I would use this as a guide in deciding whether or not the company should be started. The three basic stars I spoke about are:

- *The Star of Opportunity*

  Is there really an opportunity in the industry for your new company? Is there room in the market for your company or business especially when there are already many players? Is the new start-up not just a knee-jerk reaction and does it have long-term viability? Can you visualise the company 10 to 20 years from now? If your answers to all these questions are yes, then by all means start the company and you will have some chance of success.

- ### The Star of the Team
  Do you have a strong team and the right people to run this company? Is yours an integrated team or can it become an integrated team? Do you have enough diversified people to form a strong team? Are good people willing to follow you into the battlefield? Is your team committed and not just involved? In other words, do they have the so-called pinch factor, full-time commitment, and a belief that is strong enough to go the full mile with you? Again, if your answers are yes to all these questions, your chances of success are further enhanced.

- ### The Star of the Investor
  Do you have strong investors who are on the same frequency as you and can also add value? Do the investors believe in your team? Are they willing to back you in good and bad times? Are they in it for the long haul and are you sure they won't abandon you halfway through the game? Will you be able to handle the investors' involvement, and do you understand enough of what they want so that you meet their expectations? If your answers are all yes, then you have further increased your chances of succeeding.

If all your stars are aligned, then you have a very good chance of success. You should forge ahead to form your company and aim as high as possible. If any one star is missing, then your chances of success are lower. Therefore you should plan to hedge against the missing elements so that you will still have a winning chance.

Start-Up Criteria No. 3: Domain Knowledge

For most entrepreneurs, their existing domain knowledge and expertise will become the determining factor of success for their start-up. Rarely can one create tremendous success by crossing over to a completely new area of business that the would-be entrepreneur has never experienced before. Although many have tried, the incidences of failure for such people have been very high.

One question we should ask is, if your skill is in the semiconductor business, can you do well in the furniture business? Without understanding how a furniture business works, it will be near impossible for one to succeed, especially when competing with companies and people who already have a long history and expertise in the furniture business. In a later chapter on the lessons learnt during the dot.com days, I will explain how many dot. com enthusiasts tried to start retail businesses without any initial domain knowledge on the wholesale and retail industry. Such computer engineers who went into the retail business on their own were doomed to fail right from the start. Had they teamed up with people who understood the business, they could have improved their chances of success. Similarly, to run a company, you need a team with all the necessary skills to start and manage an ongoing business. Domain knowledge in the various aspects of the business is needed.

Importance of Domain Knowledge

BuyItTogether, the first internet company that I co-founded with a group of computer engineers from NTU, Singapore, was a great company that focused on retail of goods online. I share more details about this company later in the book but one lesson I learned as an entrepreneur is this – if you don't have the domain knowledge of the business you are getting into, then avoid doing that business, or make sure one of your co-founder has the necessary domain knowledge. I am an electronics and electrical engineer and the rest of the co-founders were computer engineers. None of us understood sales or retail and the related supporting infrastructure to handle all parts of the supply chain. While it was a brilliant idea and we knew how to develop the software and the engine, it took us a long time to get a handle on all the other aspects of managing a retail and last-mile delivery ecosystem.

We soon realised that we should have brought in someone with the right domain knowledge who may have allowed us to grow faster.

I was approached by a friend of mine to be involved in a spinoff from the National University of Singapore. The company in the biotechnology field was involved in cancer drug research. I led the initial round of US$1m investment with a group of friends, and I put in the highest amount among all. I was also asked to chair the board of the company to keep an eye on and guide the start-up. Even though I had business experience, I had zero knowledge about drug discovery and cancer. It was reckless of me to put so much of my money into an area that I did not understand. I lost all my money that was invested in the company.

So my advice is this – whether you are an entrepreneur or an investor, without having enough domain knowledge, don't jump in so quickly unless you can partner someone with the domain knowledge whom you trust. In investment, if it is a small amount, and you want to participate, perhaps it's ok, but if you are going to have to lead and play a bigger role and you don't have the relevant domain knowledge, then don't.

The entrepreneur should therefore be realistic about the businesses he or she chooses to enter. Rarely can one be successful without a fundamental knowledge of the business, including an in-depth feel for the success factors. While assembling a team of people who understand the business is the right thing to do, the key people need to know enough about their area of business so they can meaningfully drive the company. Not only will the entrepreneur have to convince himself or herself that success is attainable, but more significantly, the investors must be convinced the team can do a good job with or without the necessary domain knowledge.

As a side discussion, I share the Singapore experience of how many of the Government Linked Companies (GLCs) as they were called in the past (today they are called TLCs – Temasek Linked Companies) had civil servants and military officers parachuted to run these companies, that for all intents and purposes are private companies, many of which are listed on the Singapore Stock Exchange. Military generals or senior civil servants were appointed as CEOs of many of these companies. While these people are not entrepreneurs, they seem to succeed in running these companies. But if we look deeper, their success was due more to the tremendous funding (easy money), help in market access (many times through government agencies) and help with regulatory issues. But can these companies remain strong in the long run? I highly doubt it, and I am sure post Covid-19, we will see reality bite. My point is that, without the domain knowledge, one may have been very successful in one area (in this case as a civil servant or an army general), but it does not guarantee success as an entrepreneur. We have seen a number of bad failures for a number of GLCs in the past few years. One of our founding cabinet ministers, Dr. Goh Keng Swee (the architect of the Singapore economy) interestingly observed this very early on, but it was not heeded by subsequent government leaders. In 1972, he said, "One of the tragic illusions that many countries of the Third World entertain is the notion that politicians and civil servants can successfully perform entrepreneurial functions. It is curious that, in the face of overwhelming evidence to the contrary, the belief persists."

"One of the tragic illusions that many countries of the Third World entertain is the notion that politicians and civil servants can successfully perform entrepreneurial functions. It is curious that, in the face of overwhelming evidence to the contrary, the belief persists."

Dr. Goh Keng Swee,
Former Singapore Deputy
Prime Minister, 1972

However, I must add that the pioneer ministers, government leaders and civil servants indeed were themselves "entrepreneurs", not only because they succeeded in starting up a nation but they also helped start many of the successful Singapore GLCs – SIA, SingTel, DBS, etc. And of course, it is not right to over-generalise – there are some success stories.

Start-Up Criteria No. 4: Set Measurable Long-Term Objectives and Break Them to Visible Near-Term Targets

While the business plan sets out your goals and objectives, it is important to be able to communicate them to not only your investors, but also your team members. All these goals and objectives need to be measurable. The entrepreneur and his team must be able to quantify the results so the outcome can be easily measured. In addition to needing realistic plans, it is very important to also show sufficient details on how they are to be executed, taking into consideration all the environmental conditions that may exist and that may change over time. Of particular importance is the set of contingency plans that will give the stakeholders the comfort that the team had at least thought of all the possible pitfalls and prepared recovery plans should the pitfalls occur, even if in actual fact a totally unexpected incident could derail the company's plans.

It is also useful to break up the objectives and goals into a few categories so that the plans look realistic. For example, it will be very difficult to convince people that you will become a one billion dollar company, say in ten years from having just qualitative plans and goals. It is more realistic to draft your revenue plans for each of the ten years, and then for the first one or two years, breaking down the forecast and projections on a monthly basis.

Similarly, in forecasting the company size and the investment needed, you should not plan on investing for the end game. Rather, it is best to show the investment in stages so there is a more realistic and meaningful plan of starting small and then scaling up as the company progresses along its growth curve. This may include investing in technology, hiring employees, making assumptions on the office and building size, etc.

Based on the 50/500 rule that I mentioned in an earlier chapter, the business should have a rational roadmap of scaling up. Simply put, scale up a business in stages and not over-extend at the beginning. I have always operated with this 50/500 rule of testing the business model before deciding on building up the final structure. Such an approach is to avoid wasting money should the model not work. It is in fact a lot more difficult to make U-turns or to change things if one starts with a large infrastructure. By following the 50/500 rule, changes will come about faster, thus ensuring the development of a more robust business. So, in your business plan make sure you have a beta test, or a 50/500 rule planned to show you are being practical and not reckless in trying to start out big right from day one.

Start-Up Criteria No. 5: Start with a Global Mindset

In today's rapidly globalising world, the entrepreneur has no choice but to start thinking of his business in global terms right from the start. In fact, today's customers believe the work can be done in any part of the world, as long as they can get their products and services completed in the desired cycle time. With communications so pervasively strong and with continual improvement in technology, where the jobs get done has become increasingly irrelevant.

In fact, the reality is that for almost any business, the whole supply chain and chain of activities will be broken up such that the right activity will happen in the right place at the right time. For example, in the semiconductor company, the high level product development, marketing, and core business will take place in the USA or some other well-developed market close to the key customer bases, but the chip design may be in India because of the strong software and design expertise of the people there. The wafer fabrication may occur where the cost and technical expertise are the best, like in Taiwan and Singapore, while the assembly and testing may occur in places where such core competencies and costs are most developed, like in Singapore for high-end products, and Philippines and China for low-end products. Finally, the logistics and distribution may occur in centres like Singapore.

As you can see, this is how the world is right now. Hence, there is little point in thinking you can go against the grain and do everything all in one place as companies often did in the past. Unless the entrepreneur and his team can have a global mindset right from day one, they will most likely not succeed. And investors will be looking at whether you have planned your business to be able to address a global or at least a regional market.

Due to the Great Disruption we have experienced during the Covid-19 era, globalisation will be restructured but how much it will change remains to be seen. The thinking of thinking "Global" is actually think global and act local, i.e. how you can create a business that is customised for a local market no matter where that market is. The company that gets the model right will win.

Start-Up Criteria No. 6: Be Prepared to Fail, Converting an Idea into a Business is the Most Difficult Step

Transforming the idea into a working business is the most difficult step in the whole process of starting a company. All entrepreneurs should therefore pay special attention to address this question of how he or she plans to achieve this. Your investors and other stakeholders must be convinced you have a workable plan and that all the possible risk factors have been mitigated or at least considered, and should things go wrong there will be an appropriate reaction and response. Since most start-ups actually stumble and trip at the phase of transforming the idea into a business, the entrepreneur should place special emphasis on developing a realistic and well-considered plan.

Related to this is also the issue of planning for failure. Entrepreneurs owe it to other team members to discuss the contingencies and what to do should things go wrong, including how the company and its stakeholders will be affected should failure knock on the door. It is quite reckless not to plan for such failure.

Start-Up Criteria No. 7: Assemble a Good Board or Advisory Board

Many entrepreneurs, especially those embarking on the journey for the first time, tend to be frustrated when potential investors look for a previous track record as one of the assessment criteria before they make a decision to invest. The question the entrepreneurs must ask is, how is one ever going to get started for the first time if the investors require a track record? Besides, many entrepreneurs do not manage to succeed the very first time. The issue is that for every successful start-up, there are many more failures. Investors therefore understand that unless the risks of failing are reduced through factors like a good team, previous experience, and extraordinary ideas, any investment comes with tremendous risk. How then do we address this problem of inexperience? Well, as I mentioned before, the team members' previous work experience and a convincing plan will help immensely.

One more way to compensate for an entrepreneur's lack of experience is to invite reputable and experienced people onto the start-up's board. If your company's potential is impressive, many credible people may be willing to back your team up. If you cannot find such people on your own, you should ask your potential investors to help look for people who can compensate for your team's shortcomings by becoming active members of the board.

In looking for board members, it is useful to have a diversified group that can contribute a variety of ideas and suggestions to help guide the management team in the execution of the business. Try not to find people of the same mould to join the board. For example, some individuals could be strong in corporate governance, others in technology, and yet others in marketing. Having "yes men" on the board could be self-defeating in the long run. It is better to have a board that can help look at different perspectives and challenge the management team internally, rather than to discover they have a weak plan when they compete in the open market. In reality, it is a balance. Having an unfriendly board, resulting in the entrepreneur and management team spending too much time trying to explain things internally, will leave less time to spend on external issues and productive work, further resulting in a very tiring exercise.

Ideally, the board members should have almost the same frequency of thinking as you but be independent enough to challenge you if they don't agree with your strategies and when they see you heading down the wrong path. If you assemble a strong and credible board, they can greatly enhance the value of your company and also greatly influence investors into injecting money into the company. Additionally, a good board also brings business networks to the table and can prove useful in the company's growth or opportunities to test their products and services.

You may not always be able to attract top talent and highly successful people to immediately join your company as a board of director. They may not have the time, nor want to take the reputational risk at such an early stage of your company. Nevertheless, that does not preclude them from having the interest to help you but not wanting to be responsible for the fiduciary duties of being a formal board member. The next best option is to invite such people to be advisors to your company. You can form a board of advisors – a group of people with differing and complementary skills and expertise who can add a lot of value in advising you on how you can manage the company or also help you with the wide networks they may have. Successful people will prefer to remain as advisors rather than to take a formal position as a board of director. So do look out for such people who can help you. The good thing is that the advisory board can comprise a much bigger number of people than the formal board of directors. The advisory board is not typically involved in day to day or regular meetings. The entrepreneur can call upon the advisory board members to advise on specific issues when the need arises. While it is good to have full advisory board meetings from time to time, the entrepreneur can call upon individual advisory board members or a small group to discuss specific issues.

Whether you assemble a formal board or an advisory board, you will have to compensate them with some shares in the company. Paying cash is not a good idea for two reasons: first, highly qualified people you want to invite will likely already be successful and don't need cash incentives; second and equally important, you should not be spending money at early stages on compensating them. You should conserve cash as much as possible. A third reason is that having equity will mean everyone's interests are aligned and everyone will want the start-up to succeed to benefit from the increased valuation of the company later on. In any case, many of the people who are willing to help you may also be incentivised to see you succeed and not really count on making more money for themselves. If you can find such successful people, you will be lucky, and it will go a long way to help you create success. How much in shares do you allocate to board members or advisory board members? This is a judgement call – it can range from 0.5 per cent to 3 per cent, most of the time vested over a few years.

Start-Up Criteria No. 8: Prepare for the Due Diligence Assessment

It is key for investors to have a good understanding of the business they will be investing in and also to make an assessment of whether the team is capable of starting and executing the business. In order to make this assessment, the investors will have to investigate the start-up as well as the team proposing the start-up. This process is called due diligence. It is one of the most important processes that will help determine whether or not the investor will invest. All the information gathered during this due diligence exercise will help the investor put together the investment document that will be presented to the decision-makers on the VC side, upon which the decision-makers will deliberate and evaluate the investment viability.

Each investor has their own investment criteria, but the process does not differ among them. They will always do a due diligence assessment and will always prepare the investment document or proposal, which they will hand to their decision-makers, typically called the investment committee.

To help the people representing the investors prepare a good case for investment, the entrepreneur and founding members of the start-up should make every effort to provide as much information as possible during the due diligence phase. In fact, the process should be embarked upon with the attitude that you are going to help the person writing the due diligence report look good by doing a thorough job in assessing the viability of the investment. Often, the due diligence process ends up making the founders become too defensive, as the investors start asking very tough and probing questions. The entrepreneur should view this probing constructively and help address all the issues that may be raised, no matter how negative they may seem. If you are well prepared, there is no need to be defensive.

Being transparent, open, and proactive during the due diligence process will allow the investors to gain a good feel of the company and the people they will be dealing with should they invest. It is best to make an early discovery of each other's weaknesses and potential problems of working together. If it is evident the entrepreneur and the investor will not be able to work together, it is better to part ways early rather than having the investor make the investment, only to result in both parties arguing with each other along the way, thus hindering the company and destroying value.

The due diligence process could be a very tiring exercise because of the depth of information that is needed and because the entrepreneur and the team have to meet many people (financial experts, industry experts, human resource experts, technology experts, etc.), to answer many questions, thus distracting the team from the real work of running the company. You should remain patient and start with the expectation that it will be a tiring, draining, mentally exhaustive, but necessary exercise. Also, always remember the due diligence assessment benefits everyone, including the entrepreneur. Most of the time when a third party looks at your company with a detailed lens, you too will discover some areas where you can strengthen yourself – your plan, your team, your business model, etc.

You Must be Ready Yourself

So, you can see that unless you are sufficiently ready, you will decrease your chances of success. The entrepreneur should therefore have a checklist (even if it is a mental checklist) of what should be present before embarking on an entrepreneurial journey. You must create the environment for success and be sufficiently prepared if you want to have a less bumpy journey. You must know yourself, identify your strengths and weaknesses, and rectify any shortcomings to increase your chance of succeeding.

What Should Entrepreneurs Look for?

In this chapter, we discussed what entrepreneurs should look for to increase the chances of success.

- Successful companies have a strong and diversified team behind them.

- Members of the team are expected to accept a flexible job role with a lower compensation if necessary. Additional members can be brought into the company in phases and at the right time.

- The company must be driven by passion and not emotion.

- The alignment of three stars – the Star of Opportunity, the Star of the Team, and the Star of the Investor – determines if a company should be started.

- Domain knowledge and expertise are the determining factors of success for start-ups.

- Set long-term objectives and near-term goals for the company and make sure they are measurable.

- Use the 50/500 rule to grow your business in stages.

- Think global from the start. Unless the entrepreneur and his or her team can have a global mindset right from day one, they will not be able to create a world-class company.

- Invite reputable and experienced people onto the board. A diversified board can contribute a variety of ideas and suggestions to help guide the management team.

- Investors conduct a stringent due diligence process when considering an investment. Provide as much information as possible and be transparent, open, and proactive during the due diligence process.

CHAPTER 16

WHAT DO INVESTORS LOOK FOR?

When you are courting an investor to entrust their money to you, the one question every entrepreneur must ask is, "What do investors look for when deciding to invest?" It is very important to answer this question before an entrepreneur sets out to seek external investment, especially VC money. Of course, each VC has its own set of criteria which they use to evaluate the viability of any investment, but at the end of the day there are a few aspects in common. If entrepreneurs can understand these few criteria, then it will be easier for them to raise funds. In fact, understanding what investors look for may even lead the entrepreneur to decide that a fund-raising exercise may be futile and therefore should be abandoned. In this chapter, I will share some insights from the point of view, both of an entrepreneur trying to raise funds, as well as of an investor deciding whether or not to invest in companies.

Investment Criteria No. 1: A Strong Integrated Team

A strong and integrated team is without doubt the most important criteria investors look out for, because at the end of the day, whether it is a good or bad plan, the team will have to execute it. The best of plans will be ineffective if the team is incapable of executing it. On the other hand, a good team may be able to transform a poorly conceptualised plan by spotting the problems and turning it into a good executable plan.

If we look at how companies progress from a start-up to the growth stage and into an ongoing business, in almost all cases the plans that were originally drawn up are changed and fine-tuned many times. In some cases, the actual form and structure of the company may look very different from what was envisaged at the beginning of the company's formation, at the time when the idea was conceptualised or when the company was a start-up. This has to be so because the plan, and particularly the business plan, is really just a guide and a "living document", which needs to be updated along the way. As plans are carried out, there will invariably be changes in the environment, market, or other circumstances, that dictate and necessitate a change in direction. Obstacles also result in new situations. The plan therefore needs to be flexible enough to be adapted, as sometimes the changes happen on-the-fly or almost at real-time. More importantly, the team must be flexible enough to accept and embrace changes as the company develops. Therefore, investors will spend a substantial amount of time making assessments of the team members to decide whether the team is able to work in varying conditions, particularly in a stressed environment.

Related to the issue of the team's ability to execute the plan is whether the team is strong enough to ride out tough times without cracks developing internally. When the environment is tough and everyone is under stress, the team members may not necessarily be able to withstand the pressure and relationships may become frayed. If this happens, teamwork may be affected and execution will suffer. Therefore, being able to put together a team alone is not quite enough. What is even more important is putting together a strong and integrated team. The keyword here is INTEGRATED.

What do I mean by integrated? I discussed this earlier in Chapter 5, "The Alignment of Your Stars", but this topic warrants further discussion. On one hand, the team leader or the founder can assemble champions from across various companies and industries. Just like in a soccer team, one can assemble a David Beckham, a Cristiano Ronaldo, a Lionel Messi, a Maradona, etc. The key question is whether the star players can indeed work together since soccer is very much a team sport. It is never about an individual who is good but not able to gel or work with others. It is therefore useless to have in the team a group of heroes who cannot work together. Starting, building, and running a company is a long-haul undertaking, and like a marathon, you need the team to work with each other under challenging conditions and still achieve the desired outcome. If all the heroes in a team start fighting with each other, the team will crumble. Another analogy is one of an army. You cannot have a successful army made up only of generals. You will need all the other ranks, each with a different duty and role to effectively create a good fighting machine.

For a long-term sustainable organisation, the team must have the ability to understand the strengths and weaknesses of each team member, so that everyone can complement each other to achieve synergy and avoid conflicts even in very tough conditions. How well the team is integrated or how well the team is able to become integrated is one of the most important criteria for investors. In fact, this is an important point for all parties, including the founders and the team members themselves, if they want to have fewer heartaches and headaches as they go about forming and growing their companies.

Whether or not the team has worked together in the past, it is important that they collectively demonstrate an ability to remain integrated under all conditions. Of course, if most of the team members have had previous work experience together, it will be viewed as a strong asset, giving potential investors the assurance that the team should have no problems working together in the new company.

Investment Criteria No. 2: The Assumptions in Your Business Plan

The second important criteria that potential investors will look for is the quality of the business plan. Particularly the quality of the assumptions you made in writing your plan. The business plan is an important document that captures your thought process and your understanding of the business, reflecting the quality of your plan. By looking at the business plan, the VC will make an assessment of your understanding of the industry and ascertain what the key drivers are. They will assess your understanding of your industry's key success factors, and from there, judge if you have identified a winning formula for your company.

Knowing what the VCs and other investors look for in a business plan will greatly help you put together an effective plan and help increase your chances of closing deals with them. Beyond doing proper research and penning down the details of the business plan as I described in the previous chapter, investors scan the business plan for a number of salient points, namely: opportunities, threats, market size and market share, customers, marketing strategy, competitors, suppliers, risk analysis, financial plan, and cash flow.

A Good Team Makes the Difference

When I was planning the set-up of my first company, UTAC, I was still working in Texas Instruments as the director of operations, managing much of the entire operation with some global responsibilities. Working with me was a group of managers I considered among the best in Singapore. They all had very good domain knowledge, and more significantly, they had built up a very strong working relationship and understanding of each other. After many years working together, the team had gone through a few rounds of ups and downs together. The stressful periods did result in frayed relationships at times, but eventually built strong bonds over the years. More importantly, the team had learnt to read each other SO well that sometimes, very little needed to be discussed while they focused on execution of actual work matters.

When I was planning UTAC, I knew it was vital that a significant number of my team members in Texas Instruments should join me in the venture. Had I not been able to convince them to join me, UTAC may never have been formed. So, when we started UTAC, there was very little pressure in trying to develop an understanding of how the team would work. We had a good idea of what we had to do.

Our confidence lay in our knowledge of how to run the business and also the comfort that each team member knew what he had to do without needing anyone else to tell him. To us, running the business and operations was as familiar as the back of our hands. Our challenges were therefore reduced to that of having to raise funds and find customers. The team aspect of the equation was already solved. We trusted each other and each other's judgement. This did not mean we never argued. On the contrary, we argued many times, but we knew this was part of the process, and after all was said and done, we still sat down for a drink and kept our relationships strong.

One funny thing happened when part of our same team later went on to start our next company, Infiniti Solutions. The four of us who founded the company all had a long history of working together in Texas Instruments as well as in UTAC. However, we also had a new team member. During one heated meeting in which we discussed the terms of investment by a VC, some of us wanted to be more aggressive in negotiations while another team member was very conservative and played the devil's advocate. We just could not agree on the approach to take with the VC. In the meeting, voices were raised and it looked like we were going to get into a fight. Of course, the four of us from the original team knew exactly what was going to happen, but our new member was so worried we would end up in a fight that he immediately stood up and asked for a time out, putting his two hands in a T-format. The rest of us almost laughed as we knew what the final outcome would be – we would have reached a position the whole team subscribed to. After that meeting, we all went for tea at a nearby Indian coffee shop.

- **Opportunities**

  In your business plan, try to address the following issues: Have you identified all the possible opportunities? Have you been realistic in identifying the areas you can participate in, particularly if you are targeting an industry with many existing players? Are you doing it for the sake of doing it or is there a real opportunity for a new player like you to tap into and benefit from? What is so unique about you and your plan? Are you a "me too" entrepreneur? The more you differentiate yourself from others, the more convinced others will be of your ability to succeed. The more clearly you have defined the opportunities, the easier it will be for others to see them, too.

- **Threats**

  Have you been realistic in identifying the possible obstacles that will impede the execution of your plan, and how do you plan to overcome these obstacles? Have you been thorough in identifying these threats? Your ability to identify all the possible threats will show how well you understand the industry and how widely you have thought about things, hence ensuring a better chance of succeeding with your plan. Your ability to convert the threats others may see in your industry into opportunities for your business will further strengthen your credibility as a true entrepreneur.

- **Market Size and Market Share**

  Have you conducted the relevant market surveys and understood the size of the market you want to tackle? How realistic have you been in identifying what proportion of the market you want to gain and are your plans realistic enough to achieve market penetration? Did you consider the fact that your competitors may also be thinking of capturing the same market share? Is there double counting of the market opportunities? Your ability to clearly identify your market and how you plan to address the market is one important area others will assess.

One impractical approach some people use when discussing what market share they hope to capture, is to come up with an arbitrary percentage. For example, they will show the size of the market in the entire universe and say, "If I can capture just a small percentage of the market, my business will be so big." For example, market data might show that there are 500 million mobile phone users in the world today. The new company intends to sell software to be used in phones for $1 each. Then they will say, "All I need to do is capture 5 per cent of the market share, which will make my revenue $25 million." Looks easy? But how do you really do the "all I need to do is capture" part? It is the most difficult part, and while 5 per cent looks like an easy target for a product that sells for only $1, it is never that easy to sell something. Entrepreneurs should avoid using such a simplistic approach to tell investors what market share they intend to capture and what level of business they can generate. The investors have heard it all; avoid it and come up with a better analysis of how you intend to do it. Have a realistic plan.

- **Customers**

Who are your potential customers? Have you identified enough of a pipeline that you have a better chance of executing and engaging at least a first group of customers early? Have you understood the customer's needs and what they will be looking for in you as a supplier? Have you developed a realistic plan as to how you can engage the customers? Why would the potential customers engage you? Have you identified the success factors for winning customers? It is not an easy task to capture market share by engaging customers. It is important to assume that customers have built some loyalties to their existing suppliers. It is not an easy task to take customers away from existing competitors who already have established relationships with their customers. Factors such as loyalty, trust, and proven track record should not be taken lightly.

- ***Marketing Strategy***

  In line with your plans to engage your potential customers, have you been able to develop a meaningful and exciting marketing strategy? Is your marketing strategy differentiated enough to allow you to beat your competitors? Do you understand how to build a strong marketing and sales team? Many companies fail badly in this area; thus, it is important to spend the time to flesh out a good strategy and put in place the best resources to execute the strategy. Without an effective marketing strategy, the best product in the world will lead you nowhere. In fact, more companies fail because of a poor marketing strategy rather than a poor product strategy. Entrepreneurs tend to underestimate the importance of the marketing role in the whole chain of activities of a business. Often, they assume a good product or service will be able to sell by itself. Most of the time, this is not the case.

  I have seen marketing as typically one of the weakest attributes among many entrepreneurs. If the entrepreneur has a weakness in the area of marketing, he or she needs to find someone who can plug this gap in the management team. The investors will definitely make an assessment of whether there is a good marketing person in the team.

- ***Competitors***

  Have you understood the industry well, especially who your competitors are or are you operating in a vacuum? Have you identified the success factors of your competitors and therefore understood how you can work around those factors to win customers away from your competitors? How will you as a new player be able to beat your competitors who will be after your skin the moment they discover there is a new entrant? I mentioned the factors of loyalty and an established track record as being difficult to overcome; customers will have to see a much more compelling reason to switch suppliers than a promise of a better product. While a new start-up may identify a compelling reason why their potential customers should switch suppliers, it should not be assumed that their competitors will remain at a status quo position. The competitors will also be improving themselves, and they too will have secret weapons to help them win in the marketplace.

- **Suppliers**

Suppliers are your partners for success. Identifying the key suppliers who can help you succeed is important. Will the suppliers be willing to support you, and will they have confidence in you? What is your value proposition for the suppliers to want to work with you? Will your suppliers be willing to bet on your plans? Often, suppliers are neglected as an important success factor in many business plans, as well as in many operating businesses. The fact is that suppliers can make a very big difference in how a company executes the business.

For example, sometimes suppliers are willing to give very good payment terms, which will help minimise the company's cash drain. In other cases, suppliers can help a company with the technology that comes with the equipment they provide, which can then help better in the execution of the production process. Suppliers who develop partnership relationships with their customers will also give advance information about new products, equipment and technologies, which may make a difference in how a company executes its business. For instance, if there is new and much more capable equipment in the pipeline, good suppliers may advise you to wait for the new equipment to be released instead of purchasing older equipment, which may become obsolete sooner than expected. There are many other benefits to be derived from partnering a few key suppliers.

- **Risk Analysis**

There are many types of risks, and every business faces them. The key question is whether you have identified the right risks that could affect the success or failure of your company. Have you been thorough and realistic in identifying the risks and also in identifying how you plan to address or divert away the risks? Have you identified the right contingency plans should things turn out differently from what you had anticipated? Do you have a recovery plan should things start to go terribly wrong? In almost all cases, companies never follow the original path indicated in the original business plan. Things change, and as reality sets in, many changes need to be made.

Unless the business plan had identified the areas in which things could go wrong and a planned change of the execution takes place if such adverse events indeed occur, a new company will rarely succeed. All of this should be clearly illustrated in the risk analysis section. Others looking at your plan will also have a feel for the type of risks your business will potentially face. It is useful to align your risk expectations with that of the investors.

- ***Financial Plan***
The financial plan measures the lifeline of your project or company. Your ability to prepare a financial plan that can communicate how you will be utilising the incoming funds is important. Have you been able to show a realistic set of financial numbers that tie in with what you have outlined in the qualitative section of your business plan? Have you considered all the nitty-gritty details of how the expenses will be paid? Is your financial plan realistic compared to industry norms? This is one part of your plan on which investors will spend quite a substantial amount of time.

The financial plan basically reflects how successful you will be when you put the rest of your business plan into operation. It measures the outcome of your plan and therefore gives the investors a feel for how rewarding their investment is going to be. With the financial plan, the investors will do their rate-of-return analysis and decide how viable an investment in your company will be for them. Remember, they are not putting in their money because they like you or because they are doing charity work – they are in it to make money, and the more they can make, the more excited they will be to invest in your company.

- ***Cash Flow/Cash Burn***

   This is one of the most important parts of your financial plan. Many businesses fail because they fail to plan and execute their cash flows well. The investor will therefore be very interested to assess your ability to control your cash flow. In the initial stages they will look at your burn rate, how well are you utilising your cash and how long you can last with the cash in the company, both before and after their investment. Many start-ups have ridiculously high burn rates, spending money on unnecessary things. They will also assess when and how well you can generate a positive cash flow when your business starts to run. Investors worry a lot about how cash is utilised in the company. It is therefore very important to pay special attention to the cash flow plan.

Investment Criteria No. 3: Feasibility to Transform the Plan into a Business

I have previously discussed how difficult it is to convert an idea into a business, and this is therefore one of the areas investors will pay particular attention to. The key aspect they will look out for is how realistic your plan is. Many entrepreneurs will put up fantastic plans and show aggressive numbers. The issue lies in how you can convince your potential investors about your ability to deliver the numbers. While the entrepreneur is typically, very confident of tremendous success, he or she needs to realise that the investors will always look at a more conservative scenario and are rarely willing to go straight for something very aggressive. The plan you present to your potential investors therefore needs to provide sufficient clarity on how it will be executed and must look realistic and doable.

   A past track record will greatly help the investors decide whether the team is able to execute. The problem many entrepreneurs run into is that they are running a business for the first time, which makes convincing investors a lot more difficult. The best thing to do is to show the investors your achievements and entrepreneurial ability in your previous work, whether or not it was a start-up. As I mentioned previously, you can be entrepreneurial in any environment, be it a small or big company, in the government or in any other work or service. It is therefore important to show these abilities by way of examples. By showing how you have in the past executed projects and overcome obstacles, you can demonstrate to the investors why you have all the traits of an entrepreneur and will be able to do a good job even if you are starting a company for the first time.

It is therefore very important to make your plan look realistic. One way is to break the whole journey and plan into a few smaller journeys. Having some near-term milestones and targets that then become the stepping-stones for the next phase of growth, could be one way of convincing investors that the team has thought through the various steps involved. Scaling up the company only after executing several shorter-term, more realistic targets is one way that can help convince investors your goals can be achieved.

For example, a retail e-commerce start-up can be handled in many ways. One involves going for the maximum infrastructure investment and preparing your company to handle millions of customers and thousands of suppliers all at one go, and to have the very best customer relationship management system. On the other hand, one can also start by testing the start-up on a smaller scale by building a smaller infrastructure, which will cost much less to build and manage. If the company takes off, a bigger infrastructure may then be built at a much higher cost and implemented in a few stages. In this way, should the company fail, the cost incurred for the testing phase would be much lower, or should the business model need changing, the cost of the changes will not be too high. I will give an example of this in the next chapter. By executing the business plan in stages and scaling up gradually, you can show investors you have a down-to-earth team at the helm. The investors will then feel more confident in allowing your team to manage the money they will be pumping into the company.

Investment Criteria No. 4: Fund Utilisation

Related to the issue of scaling up and not over-extending too early in your company's life cycle is explaining how your team intends to utilise the funds they have raised. It is very important to show in your plan how realistically you are intending to spend your funds. The investors will make a judgement of how good your plan is by looking at how you are allocating the money raised.

For example, if your team intends to spend a disproportionately high amount of money on paying the salaries of engineers and staff, it will give investors the impression that your team is not conscious of cash burn and is not safeguarding the valuable cash they have raised. Or if your team had planned to buy the best breed of technology and use a Mercedes when they could have done an equally good job with a mid-range Korean car, then again, the investors will view your team as having unrealistic thoughts. It is therefore important for your business plan to be thorough enough to give the impression that your team is planning a very efficient utilisation of the funds raised.

The other issue about fund utilisation is whether your team is thinking of the money raised as their own? There is a tendency by many would-be entrepreneurs to get too aggressive in spending the money raised. They tend to do this simply because the money is not their own. The investors will make an assessment as to whether you will be treating every cent you raised as if it were your own money. If so, then the details in your plan will show this. For instance, are you paying yourself and your team members too much? Are you planning to spend a lot of money on a big office furnishing it lavishly? Or are you planning to fly in business class rather than coach? All these are very important things investors will definitely look at.

The other thing about money raised is the *pinch factor*. Investors will look out for how much money you and your team put into the company. In fact, investors will ask the founding team to put into the company something of their own, by way of cash investment, as a show of commitment as well as to ensure you have something at stake and will feel the pinch should the company collapse and you end up losing your money too.

How much should you put in? The investors will assess this based on how much you can afford. If your net worth is high, the investors will insist on you putting in higher amounts, but if your wealth level is not that high, they will accept a lower amount. It is all a relative measure, related to what you own. So, what may be small to one person may be large to another and this is what the investors will look at. The key is, if you have a significant amount of financial involvement and therefore have too much to lose, it gives investors the confidence you will not be reckless with their money.

Investment Criteria No. 5: Global Thinking

Increasingly, investors are looking at the scale of thinking and the dare-to-dream ability of the team. As the world globalises, investors want to know whether the team has considered how they plan to conquer the world. This has to figure in the plan. Although in the USA, an entrepreneur may be forgiven for thinking of the USA as the world that needs conquering because it is a big market and is a good place to test new ideas, products and services. Entrepreneurs elsewhere in the world will need to make a convincing story about how they intend to market their products and services outside their country of domicile. This is particularly important for very small markets like Singapore, Israel and Malaysia.

Entrepreneurs must therefore ensure they have considered from Day One how to create a global business. This may not be an easy task for a team that may not have had the appropriate exposure to international markets. Therefore, the entrepreneur needs to add one or two team members who have the right global exposure.

Gone are the days when an entrepreneur could take his or her time to first exploit the domestic market, and only upon finding success on the home front, start planning to tackle the regional and global markets. You have to have this global plan figured into your business plan right at the beginning. Investors will not be keen to support a company conceived along the lines of a provision shop, which is a small neighbourhood shop that caters to the needs of nearby residents. A provision shop rarely thinks of attracting customers from beyond the neighbourhood. Such a shop can have its own success and give the businessman sufficient comfort for a period of time, and sometimes even for a long period of time if no new competitors decide to set up another provision shop nearby. Similarly, a provision shop mentality is one in which the entrepreneurs never think of becoming bigger than that one shop they started. They may have thought of only conquering the neighbourhood, and having successfully done so considered themselves as successful. Thinking of growing bigger outside their neighbourhood is rarely their priority.

So, while in some cases it is necessary to start small, as in the case of a provision shop, unless your plan has also outlined how you and your team intend to grow your business beyond the small shop and beyond its own country's shores, your chances of attracting serious investors is slim. Of course, I have to qualify this by saying there may be special cases suitable only for a domestic market, which can still prove to be profitable and bring good returns for investors. Such businesses may still attract funding, but in a globalising world, these types of companies are becoming increasingly rare.

Investment Criteria No. 6: Commitment Level

I have mentioned this as part of the mantra, "There is no short-cut to success." No investor will invest in a team that is itself not fully immersed in the start-up. Some entrepreneurs may want to start a company as a part-time effort while still enjoying the income and comforts of another job they may already hold. This will not work and will not impress any investor. Investors will need to be convinced that you and your team will spend all your time – all 24 hours of it – on your company. If you fail to show this commitment, the investors will be confident that you and your team are indeed passionate in building the start-up.

Investment Criteria No. 7: Investor Returns

Investors are not providing charity. Neither will they put in money because they love you or your team. They are in it to make good money for themselves and will therefore make every effort to take care of their interests even if it is compromising yours. It is important to be aware of this when you initiate the process of looking for an investor.

As each party has to take care of their own interests, it is better to think of the fund-raising process from the point of view of professional investors like the VCs. When engaging in any business deal, never let yourself become soft or worry about how you will hurt other people's feelings or if you will look too money-minded when fighting for your rights. Like anything else, for both parties, the fund-raising process is just like any business deal. Each party in a business deal has to start by thinking of a win-win outcome for both sides, without compromising one's own interests. At the end of the day, when the deal is done, all parties involved must feel that they won. Having a win-lose outcome, regardless of whether it is the investor or the entrepreneur on the losing end, would be a long-term loss for both parties because the negative thoughts of the losing side will prove destructive in the long run.

It follows that the fund-raising exercise should be a value-maximising exercise for both parties, and each should negotiate aggressively for the best possible outcome. If everyone does this, when the negotiations finally come to an end and a deal is struck, both parties will feel a lot more satisfied that they had tried their best and arrived at an outcome acceptable to all. Once this deal is done and sealed, both parties should close the negotiation chapter – no matter how they may have felt during the process – and start a new chapter of partnership.

Knowing that everyone wants to maximise their own value means you will need your plan to demonstrate good results and good growth in the shortest possible time. Investors measure their returns by the rate of return measure called the Internal Rate of Return (IRR). They will need to see that the IRR for the investment can meet a certain minimum level before they decide to invest. You therefore need to know what IRR the investors are looking for. Not knowing what they expect might leave you guessing, and you may not know how to position your plan to excite the investor.

Before you start approaching investors, you need to know if your business plan demonstrates an IRR level that fits the needs of the investor or VC you are courting. Sometimes, entrepreneurs prefer to show a conservative plan to ensure they will be able to demonstrate a track record of beating their plans; however, this conservatism could backfire and compromise the valuation of the company. You might end up shortchanging the founders by getting their shareholdings too diluted as a result of a low valuation. Showing a plan that is too aggressive might also backfire especially if it looks unrealistic to the point that those reading the plan won't believe you. In such a situation, the potential investors will themselves make a judgement on the numbers, reducing them to what they think is realistic, which again results in a lowering of the valuations. The latter aggressive approach will create a negative perception about the ability of the management team to make an accurate judgement of the situation. In essence when you show a challenging plan, you must ensure it's achievable, and be confident you can stand up to defend it in front of anyone. Doing it right will allow you the chance to maximise your valuation.

Knowing What the Investors Want is Important

As you can see, there are many criteria the investors will look for before they invest. Not knowing what investors want will put the entrepreneur at a disadvantage when discussing a possible investment. It is best to do some homework about what the investors will be looking for. Then make sure your house is in order so that when the due diligence is done, the investors will find what they are looking for. It will increase your chance of success in fund raising. According to Sun Tzu's *Art of War*, "Know your enemy and know yourself; in a hundred battles you will never be in danger."

What Do Investors Look for?

Understand what investors look for to increase your chances of getting funded.

- A Strong Integrated Team.

- How Realistic are the Assumptions in the Business Plan – Depth of understanding and thoroughness of coverage.

- Feasibility to Transform the Plan into a Business – Can the team make the transformation?

- How Funds will be Utilised.

- Market and the Global Reach.

- Commitment Level of the Entire Team to the Start-up.

- Returns Investors Can Make by Investing in the Start-up – Both the entrepreneurs and the investors should be seeking to maximise their returns.

CHAPTER 17

THE SEVEN VC TRAPS

While there are many ways of funding start-ups, a time will come when almost all start-ups will have to raise significant sums of money, which typically will come from VCs. It is therefore useful to understand how this is done and what to look out for when dealing with VCs.

Although VCs are a great source of funds to help entrepreneurs finance their companies, it is important to understand what drives their decisions, how they operate, how they behave and how they will decide. At the end of the day, everyone (in this case I am refer to the entrepreneur and the investor) has a role to play. As long as each of the players in the whole ecosystem of entrepreneurship understands each other's role and what each is looking for, I am sure the entrepreneur can better align his or her expectations with that of the VC and other players. Failure to understand the intricacies of the roles, responsibilities and relationships between the various players will without doubt result in disappointment. This could even lead to a point where the performance of the entrepreneur and the management team are affected, and in the worst-case scenario, the start-up ends in failure.

There are many books written about VCs, and you can attend courses about how VCs invest. The latter is not what I intend to cover in this chapter.

Instead, I will focus on the intricacies, the unspoken and unwritten rules, about how VCs behave and act. I will discuss what goes on behind the scenes when entrepreneurs deal with VCs. Many VCs may not agree with me, but my views are entirely from the perspective of entrepreneurs and how entrepreneurs feel when they face issues as they deal with VCs. And I have personally experienced these issues.

Let me also qualify myself by saying that not all VCs behave as I describe. In fact, how they behave is also very dependent on the people working for the VC and the culture of the company. Some make great partners and are a pleasure to work with, while others may not behave the way the entrepreneur had expected. It is all about the alignment of expectations. As long as this is understood, the entrepreneur should not be disappointed when he faces the issues I discuss. One more point – there are some people whom you will meet from the VC you are negotiating with, who were once entrepreneurs themselves. You can benefit a lot from such people. But there are many more whom you will meet who have never created a start-up. They are employees, with some expertise in some domain area but they themselves may never have run a start-up nor worked in one before. It is good to know the background of the person you are meeting so that you can prepare in advance how to structure your discussions.

In an earlier chapter, I discussed what investors look for when deciding to invest in a company. The points I highlighted were the basic criteria the VCs need to see before they decide to invest. In this chapter, I will discuss what I think really goes on in the minds of VCs. To achieve a winning formula, it will thus be useful to align my additional insights with the issues I previously discussed on what investors look out for.

VC Trap No. 1: VCs Will Stop You from Talking to Other VCs

– When they are courting you, they will sing mighty praises of you to stop you from talking to other VCs. So: Don't close in on any one VC too early, continue talking to other potential investors.

The VCs are in the business of finding as many good investments as possible. They typically have huge sums of money for which they have promised their investors huge returns. The first failure of any VC is if they fail to fully invest the money sitting in their bank accounts. VCs will therefore want to have as many projects to invest in as possible. At the same time, because they do not want to hit their second possible failure, which is the failure to bring in good returns for the money invested, they will be highly selective of the projects they finally select.

Thus, while the VCs want to invest in as many companies as possible, they will still have to be selective according to certain internal criteria by which they operate and make investment decisions. Their objective, without doubt, is to invest in all the good start-ups or projects available to them. In this respect, they are competing with many other VCs and investors who are also looking for the same good start-ups. And they too are looking to be selected by a good start-up as a partner. So, what the VCs will typically do is to look at all the possible investments being proposed to them and not let any one of the proposed investments go too quickly to their competitors, i.e. the other VCs. They will therefore, as quickly as possible, engage the entrepreneur and the start-up looking for funding, particularly those with a greater perceived investment value.

Once they have engaged with the entrepreneur, the VCs will continue to increase their contact and strengthen their relationship with the entrepreneur while keeping the courtship going for as long as possible. As in any courtship, what this means is that the person being courted develops high hopes and therefore will not look for another partner. If you feel so good because of the praises showered on you, you will not be compelled or motivated to look for another life partner. This is the best trap a VC can set for the entrepreneur.

As the entrepreneur becomes comfortable with the VC, he or she will feel good about closing the deal, just as the person courted by a boyfriend or girlfriend will feel when they assume the relationship can develop into something exclusive and end in a marriage. This type of thinking of being elated and therefore becoming complacent makes the entrepreneur think that he or she will surely get the investment money. However, the fact that the VC has made you feel so good and lead you to think that they are very interested in you during a courtship, is dangerous for entrepreneurs and can prove to be a fatal trap.

Why do the VCs do this? If the investment has great value, they will not want anyone else, i.e. no other VC, to benefit. The VC that is courting you would like to have the whole cake if they have the appetite for the full investment. Why share the gains with others? Even if they do not have the appetite for the full investment, they will want to become the lead investor and bring along with them other VCs with whom they have partnered in the past. In fact, when they bring along another VC to share a good deal, they are not actually doing the entrepreneur a favour. Rather, they are securing for themselves future deals they hope the other VC they are bringing in will also share with them in reciprocation when they, too, have good deals.

Why should entrepreneurs not become too comfortable during the courtship process? If we understand why the VC wants the courtship to go on for as long as possible and to exclude any other potential competitor (other VCs) from getting into the picture, we will know why we should avoid a long courtship.

By excluding other VCs for as long as possible, the VC has kept the cake for itself, whether or not the VC will want to eat it in the end. The longer the deal remains on the shelf, the greater the leverage the VC will have over the entrepreneur because the entrepreneur will not have the opportunity to negotiate other deals (even if the other deals may be more attractive than the current VC being courted). As the entrepreneur gets stuck with the one or two VCs being courted, other doors close because the other potential VCs will not wait for you as they have many other deals to consider. This results in the entrepreneurs inadvertently having locked the doors, preventing other potential investors from coming in. By not looking at what others have to offer, the entrepreneur will have a limited view and feel of other deals that could have been considered.

When an entrepreneur limits his or her choices, the available options will be fewer and, in the worst case, the entrepreneur will be reduced to such a desperate situation that he or she will have zero or little choice but to just accept the deal being offered. The entrepreneur would then have lost an opportunity to create a competitive position among the VCs, and therefore in the process fail to get an optimal deal. Without much competition, the VCs will offer a less favourable deal to the entrepreneur in terms of valuation as well as the terms and conditions of the investment.

Had the entrepreneur kept negotiations going with a few VCs instead of just one, a competitive process could have been established with the few VCs trying to win the deal, whereby each VC tries to offer better deals than their competitors. The outcome would have resulted in not only much better deals for the start-up and the entrepreneur but also would have given the entrepreneur several options to choose from that best meets the needs of the start-up.

Worst still, because the VC's decision making involves a few layers of decisions, even if the initial assessment is that the start-up is an attractive investment, others in the process may end up rejecting the investment. If the entrepreneur is stuck with only one potential VC, and if that VC finally pulls the rug from under your feet and calls off the deal, that can prove disastrous for the start-up with potentially no investor who will fund the start-up. The start-up will then have to restart the fund-raising process again. If you go back to some of the initial VCs whom you had rejected before, they will know what happened – and will then be tougher in their negotiations.

Often, this comes as a shock to the entrepreneur. VCs are apt to sing mighty praises of the entrepreneur and the start-up, making the entrepreneur feel so good that when the VC finally dumps the project, the entrepreneur and the team will find it hard to digest the rude shock.

An entrepreneur should be very careful to avoid such a situation. It is wise not to close in on any VC too early in the process but to keep the competitive tension among VCs to lure them into investing into your company. The entrepreneur should study as many proposals as possible before narrowing them down or closing in on a few.

Never close in on just one VC. A few should be selected, as in a beauty contest, for the entrepreneur to finally select the winners. Keep the process going for as long as possible before narrowing down to the potential preferred investors. Yet this is easier said than done. In difficult times, when VCs are not readily investing, entrepreneurs tend to become desperate and may jump at the first VC that expresses interest. Believe me, the VC will be able to spot this very quickly. Once the VC realises the entrepreneur's desperation, it will call the shots from thereon. The entrepreneur will lose control of the process and be at the VC's mercy when the terms and valuation are discussed.

My key point is that the entrepreneur should try as much as possible to keep control of the process. Don't let the feel-good factors during the courtship process allow you to let your guard down. Be aware and never give up so quickly. The price to pay for feeling good too early can be quite high.

VC Trap No. 2: VCs Will Give High Valuations First and Cut Down Later

– VCs give you very attractive valuations to entice you before cutting you down to size. So: Don't believe the attractive valuation at face value.

One of the ways the VC will make the entrepreneur feel good is to very quickly offer good valuations for investing into the company. This is the best way for the VC to get a foot in the door, because one of the easiest assessment tools for the entrepreneur is the amount the company is worth as indicated by the VC's proposed valuation.

What the entrepreneur must watch out for is the fine print indicated by the VC when proposing the valuation. Because most of the time, in the beginning, the VC does not have all the necessary information about the company they plan to invest in, the indicative valuation they give, typically by way of a term sheet, will be a very rough one. The only way the VC can really get a valuation done is after the term sheet has been signed and the detailed due diligence is completed, which can take months.

It is very typical for VCs, at the early stages of the investment process, to give a very high valuation and hide the many other conditions that will affect the final and real valuation. The entrepreneur will, however, close in on the selected VCs and deal with them on the basis of the VC-provided valuation. Again, the entrepreneur gets trapped.

Even if the final outcome is a valuation close to what was originally indicated by a VC, the issue may lie in the way the VC deals with the entrepreneur and the price the entrepreneur has to pay in the future for accepting a high valuation so early on. It is therefore important for the entrepreneur to also do some due diligence on the potential VC. It is important to know the culture of the VC you are dealing with. A due diligence of the VC may reveal a certain pattern of behaviour based on their past deals. Will the VC cut down on the valuation later on as they might have done with other companies they invested in? Second, will the VC place so many conditions that operating the company becomes quite difficult for the entrepreneur? And third, has the VC imposed certain conditions that may cut down the company's real valuation at a future date?

Try to talk with other start-ups who have received funding from the VC that you are considering. This is to gain some background and understanding of how the VC will deal with you once they become your partner.

The typical process is that the VC indicates a very high valuation as a basis for their investment. Then, as they start detailed discussions and as the due diligence is in process, the VCs will find a hundred and one reasons why the original valuation can no longer stand. They will make every justification to reducing the valuation till they reach a number that will give them the maximum possible returns.

The entrepreneur should expect this and therefore plan it into the whole process of negotiation. It will be quite naive to expect the VC's original indicative valuation to remain the same when the VC finally is ready to invest money into the company.

Entrepreneurs should therefore keep more than one VC in the running when seeking a suitable investor. The competitive tension between the VCs will keep them honest and allow the entrepreneur some leverage when the serious negotiations on valuations, terms and conditions take place. The VCs know what levers to use so they can come up with convincing reasons why their original indicated values no longer hold true. The experience can be quite frustrating for the inexperienced entrepreneur. The feeling is one of being taken for a ride, and sometimes of being pushed in a corner with no other alternatives left in store.

Too often, the entrepreneur ends up accepting the only alternative left on the table, and the beginning of a long journey of a less than pleasant partnership. It is therefore prudent to start with the mindset that this issue of changing valuation is going to happen. The entrepreneur should align his or her expectations early on, so that when the investment does take place, there will be no hard feelings.

This process also leads to everyone taking a "playing poker" approach when it comes to dealing with VCs. On the one hand, the entrepreneur will try to justify as high as possible a valuation, and therefore, spice up the plan so much so as to convince anyone considering investing that they will have a great return on their investment. The VCs on the other hand will make the entrepreneur look like a novice and try to poke as many holes as possible into the plan to justify why they are not really able to invest if the entrepreneur continues to insist on ridiculously high valuations. Following this, the negotiation fun begins. Who blinks first loses, as in a poker game. At the end of the day, it is wise for everyone, especially the entrepreneur, to know that everyone has to take care of their own interests. If either thinks the other party's objective is to help them, they will be greatly disappointed.

There is nothing wrong with each party taking care of itself. It is in fact important that each does so – when the final agreement is reached, each will feel satisfied they got what they wanted. No matter what the outcome it must feel like a win-win situation, simply because the VCs and the entrepreneurs have to treat each other as a partner. Once the investment has been made, they should stop trying to out-win the other.

VC Trap No. 3: VCs Will Change Valuation When Drawing Future Tranches
– VCs will try to cut you down when drawing down future tranches. So: In your final investment agreement, try to entrench the conditions of drawing down on the investment money.

Problems can still arise even after the investment has been made. For example, VCs might press for further changes in valuation, particularly when things do not turn out as envisaged in the business plan. Ideally, after the initial round of discussions and agreements on the valuation and terms and conditions, each party will have very little room for making any significant changes as things progress. Entrepreneurs should not leave this to chance either, because circumstances will always change, and each party will have its own internal pressures.

VCs will always come up with new reasons to amend the terms, for example, when it is time for the company to draw down on the cash promised by the VC or when the company needs more money than what was originally agreed upon as the final investment amount. In fact, even if the terms and conditions are clearly spelt out in an agreement, VCs will somehow be able to find some angle to justify re-negotiating the valuation, terms and conditions.

It is therefore very important that certain conditions be entrenched in the final investment agreement so as not to allow room for the re-opening of such discussions. One can always find a new angle to change things, but this does not mean the entrepreneur should not try to strengthen the contents of the agreement to to minimise the opportunity of changes being initiated.

It is very common that the agreed investment amount is rarely paid in full at one go. Typically, even if the valuations and the terms and conditions of the full investment amount have been agreed upon, VCs prefer to spread out the payment of the investment over a period of time. This is called tranching of the total amount to be invested. The amount can be broken into a few tranches, each perhaps to be released according to an agreed timetable or based on the achievement of certain milestones. Depending on the success of execution, VCs may, at the time of releasing a subsequent tranche of the investment, come back to the table and try to re-negotiate the terms and conditions. The VC might also negotiate the valuation basis for the new tranche to be released.

Depending on how desperate the entrepreneur is, and depending on the company's financial strength, the investors will be able to pull a number of levers to secure a more favourable position for themselves. Thus, the original agreement should be made strong enough to avoid such a possibility. Such occasions typically arise when market and industry conditions do not turn out to be as expected in the business plan or when the business is not quite achieving what was forecast in the plan. In some rare cases, investors may be making an opportunistic move to secure a better piece of the pie, which is now starting to look even more promising than what was originally anticipated.

It is therefore important to entrench the agreement with enough protection for all parties involved so as not to create a tempting opening for any one of the signatories to deviate from what was agreed.

VC Trap No. 4: Beware of Wordings in Investment Agreement

–Be wary of the clauses VCs try to make you sign; you may lose rights and be diluted more than you think. So: Word your agreements carefully to take care of your rights.

While the key aspects that may upset any party to the investment agreement relate to valuations and the terms and conditions, there are a few other areas the entrepreneur should pay special attention to. One of these is the entrenching of each party's rights in the agreement.

Some investors may build in clauses that define a certain level of underperformance of the management team or the entrepreneur. When a situation of underperformance occurs, certain actions are then triggered, for example, the management may lose control over certain decisions. While this may be mutually agreed upon during the investment stage, the definition of underperformance needs to be clearly and fairly spelt out.

If a profitability target is used as a measure of performance or underperformance, defining an absolute target is reckless. Even if a performance target is missed, it has to be taken in the context of the industry-wide performance.

Case Examples of VC Traps

Case 1

An international school was raising funds from private equity companies and managed to attract one fund that had invested in other schools in the past (let's call them VC B). In the agreement, there was a claw back arrangement – that is, if the company failed to hit certain financial numbers and milestones, VC B had the right to be issued more shares thus diluting the founders at a later stage. Along with this clause, VC B had the right to be appointed as a board member. The deal looked safe for the school as they had a number of deals in the pipeline and they were confident of hitting the agreed numbers as stipulated in the agreement.

What eventually happened after the investment was made was a sad story. The person sitting on the board of the international school played an active role but it seems there may have been a sinister intention right from the beginning. Each time the management wanted to make certain decisions that would have led the school to meet or exceed the numbers, the VC B appointed board member would block or veto those decisions. In the end, the school missed their numbers so VC B wanted to exercise the right to claw back more shares.

To the founders, they saw this as a sinister plan right from the beginning – that VC B entered with a good looking valuation but had planned all along to really own shares at a lower valuation and hence blocked the management from executing their plan. The outcome was disastrous – the founder and VC B fought a long legal battle, wasting everyone's time, wasting resources and causing the school to be distracted from their plans. To complete the story, the school won the case and VC B lost. But this was after unnecessary pain and distraction. VC B was short-sighted as having a smaller share of a bigger pie is better than a bigger share of a smaller pie.

Case 2

Case 2 was a company where I was an investor and also board chair at one time. Years after I stepped down from the board, the CEO (founder) of the company needed to raise funds from a private equity company (let's call this VC T). The CEO was a trained accountant and ran a very good management training outfit for the previous 25 years. In a hurry to raise funds, he signed the investment agreement ignoring the fine print. The first year after VC T came on board went well. But in the second year, VC T started making it tough for the founder and then the fine print kicked in – there was a huge penalty clause for late payment of a convertible loan. The penalty led to a ballooning debt for the company and the founder who signed personal guarantees. To cut a long story short, the founder lost his legal battle, was declared a bankrupt two years later and lost total control of his company – his baby that he started many years earlier. Interestingly, I had known about the practices of VC T because they had done similar things to other investee companies before. The founder should have done a due diligence of VC T before rushing to take money. Sometimes it is best to not take money from such investors. And even if you do, make sure you structure your agreement so that you don't regret it later. Be wary of onerous conditions – don't always plan for the upside, protect yourself for a situation when the worst-case scenario happens. And always read and understand all the fine print!

Let's take, for example, a profit value of 10 per cent as a target and underperformance defined as achieving anything below 5 per cent profit. In such a situation, on an absolute basis, the company and the entrepreneur may seem to have underperformed. However, if the industry as a whole tanked, and due to uncontrollable industry and environmental factors, the company falls into the defined underperformance level, it is unfair to consider the entrepreneur or the management team as having performed badly since the entire industry's average profit performance is in the negative territory. In comparison, the company would be considered a good performer if the rest of the industry was making a loss while the company showed a 5 per cent profit. It is therefore critical for the entrepreneur and the management team to include both absolute as well as relative measures if they have to define underperformance in their investment agreement.

Another example of a condition that is typically entrenched into an investment agreement is a decision tree. By this, I am referring to the different levels of decisions made in the company. For example, the agreement typically spells out who makes decisions on a certain level of spending, who decides on the appointment of directors, who decides on the next round of funding, and many other similar decisions.

For some decisions, the management team is authorised to decide, while other decisions are made by the board or shareholders, and yet some others made solely by the VCs. It is very important to determine these conditions properly and entrench them into the investment agreement to leave as little room as possible for ambiguity. Failure to do so may result in a painful experience when trying to manage the company because the people managing the company, including the board, may always have to check back with someone before they can make decisions (if that is how the investment agreement was written). Such a procedure slows down the running of the company and the execution of the plans. An optimal decision tree is very important for a company to be run efficiently while minimising pain to all the stakeholders.

While it is impossible to avoid any new angles from being raised by any of the parties, it is still useful to try as much as possible to define the key issues that could result in disagreements as the company executes its plans. You should also try to avoid any loopholes that could cause tremendous headaches later on.

VC Trap No. 5: VCs Can Make Your Life Tough in Times of Crisis
–Choose your investors carefully; in times of crisis, they can make you feel miserable. So: Focus on the chemistry when choosing partners. Pick investors who will help, not hinder you.

Remember the "Star of the Investor". I will elaborate. Particularly in an environment where investors are much choosier, as a matter of principle it is very important to choose the right investors who will become the key stakeholders in the company. Choosing the wrong partners could make your life miserable later on, particularly when things start to go wrong and stresses start appearing.

Under pressure and at times of anxiety, only good relationships can help minimise quarrels among parties involved. Such experiences can be so unpleasant they will leave a bad taste in your mouth and may even result in company failure as each party's motivation to support the other dies down. It is therefore very important to choose your partners carefully, whether they are investors, team members or suppliers. This is particularly true for the selection of investors, as they will typically be checking and probing the company and the entrepreneur, especially when things start to go wrong. One of the main criteria for selecting a VC should be the value the VC brings to the table other than the raw money.

While the primary aim of an entrepreneur is to secure funding from the VC, it is also important to choose a VC who can add some other value. For example, the VC might be able to contribute expertise in a certain segment of an industry the entrepreneur may not be strong in and a good network of potential technology partners or potential customers. Going for just raw money may not be the best thing to do, especially when there are many other VCs looking for good investments. In other words, the entrepreneur should look for "smart money", not just "passive money". More importantly, the VC and their representatives must be able to see eye to eye with the entrepreneur. Their personalities and relationships also need to be assessed. The VC's track record with other investee companies and other entrepreneurs is important. You should make it a point to understand how the VCs manage their investee companies and how they deal with other investors.

At the end of the day, the VC should be bringing in some value other than money to help the entrepreneur build the company and increase the chances of success. It can also be useful for the VC to complement the skill sets already present in the company. More importantly, the VC should not become a hindrance to the entrepreneur or the company. If you have to give up some financial valuation to choose a good VC, it may be better than choosing a VC that gives you higher valuations but becomes a poor partner later on. In brief, don't just value the money the VC is putting in, value also the other intangibles they bring to the table.

VC Trap No. 6: Individuals Working for the VC Want Their Rewards Too

–Individuals in a VC are out to make money for themselves, not just their company, different teams in a VC are rewarded differently. So: Know the VC company's investment goals and how each decision-maker will be rewarded.

In his *Art of War*, Sun Tze states, "Know your enemy and know yourself; in a hundred battles you will never be in danger." Similarly, in any business, it is important to know all the players who make up the entrepreneurship ecosystem. It is useful to know what the hot buttons are and what the important things are for the potential VCs. It is only if and when the entrepreneur is mindful of what is important to the VC that will he be able to present the business plan convincingly to the VC.

For example, it is useful to know the decision criteria used by each particular VC. Every VC has its own criteria and not every one of them uses exactly the same methodologies to assess the viability of projects. It is also useful to know what are the areas where the VC is willing to compromise and what the VC will never give up. Sizing up the VC is a very important exercise and should be a prerequisite before the entrepreneur starts any discussions or negotiations.

One not so obvious point an entrepreneur needs to know is that the representatives or employees of the VC are each rewarded differently. For each successful investment, not only is it the VC company that makes returns, the individual representing the VC for the deal will also make a return via bonuses or a percentage of the gain made. This individual representative will receive compensation and rewards directly linked to the outcome of the investment. In other words, not only is the employee or the representative of the VC taking care of the company's interests, but they are also taking care of their personal interest when negotiating a deal with the entrepreneur or start-up.

It is also useful to know that different employees in the VC company are rewarded differently. For example, while from the start-up's own point of view and benefit, it does not matter if the company has a liquidation exercise, whether by way of a public listing or trade sale, but from the VC's perspective, the moment the company is listed, the people representing the VC will often be rewarded and compensated in a manner linked to the listing price. Whatever gain of the share value from the time of investment to the time of the listing will be used to calculate the rewards of the employees managing the investee company being liquidated.

From the company's or the entrepreneur's perspective, the price of the company's share upon listing is just a paper gain and they will benefit more from the rise in the share price subsequent to the listing. Whereas from the VC's perspective, the team of people involved up to the point of listing will hand over the company's management to another group, typically the fund managers employed by the VC. The original team may benefit only up to that point of an exit event. The VC's new fund management team then takes over and will then derive any gains subsequent to the liquidation exercise.

The disconnect between the entrepreneur and the VC is this: the company and the entrepreneur would prefer to be listed earlier to raise new funds for the company and to allow the share price to increase in the market as the company's performance improves. The employees of the VC on the other hand would like to delay the listing so that the share price at listing may be as high as possible, enabling them to maximise their rewards. It is a dilemma the entrepreneur should be aware of. Many more similar issues need to be understood by everyone so there will be no disappointments as the company progresses.

Thus, it is important to know what is important to each of the stakeholders involved in the company and the investment in order to align everyone's expectations, thereby avoiding future disappointments. Sometimes what we see is not what it really is – having a deeper understanding of the issues is important before any conclusions are made.

VC Trap No. 7: VCs Want to Control Future of Fund Raising Rounds
– VC may want a bigger stake in your company at the next round of fund raising. So: Don't let your VC control the next fund-raising process.

In many start-ups, it is to be expected that there will be more than one round of fund raising to help the company continue to grow. However, it is not wise to raise all the money at one go as I did in UTAC. Money should be raised in stages whenever possible, and when you do this, you must watch how the company is valued at each of the different stages. Different stakeholders have different motives and objectives, and in the case of VCs, you need to be aware of what they are thinking of at each of those stages.

As the company progresses, you should expect instances where valuation and funding issues may crop up especially when the results do not turn out as planned. When this happens, once again, both parties should take care of their own interests to negotiate the best possible outcome for each. This begs the question: what should you do during the next round of fund raising? While in many cases, the lead investor, being a VC, may hold a significant stake in the company, the pricing and the conditions of the next round of fund raising should not be in the VC's control. The best way to do this (and this should be captured in the investment or shareholder agreement signed at the close of the previous round of fund raising) is through a condition that allows the pricing of the next round of fund raising to be determined by an independent body, particularly a new investor or VC.

In this way, the incumbent investor, the entrepreneur, and the management team will each try to negotiate for the highest possible valuation so that each will not be unreasonably diluted when the new investor comes in. If the incumbent investor or VC has a significant original stake, there may be conflict over whether to value the new round of fund raising at as high or as low a valuation as possible. In some cases, they may want to value it at as low as possible, especially when the investors are planning to invest more money in the next round, and knowing that the entrepreneur may not be able to match them with a proportionate investment amount to keep the percentage ownership in the company at status quo. It is best not to let the incumbent investor or VC lead the future fund-raising exercise, particularly when it comes to pricing the funds raised.

If an independent party like a new investor leads the valuation discussions, there is a chance that all the original stakeholders will want as high a valuation as possible to avoid dilution. But if the incumbent VC wants to also invest in the next round you will have to watch what their motivation is. Try to drive the whole valuation exercise yourself, and your goal should be to maximise the valuation at each and every subsequent round of fund raising for your own sake as well as for all the company's other existing shareholders. The minority shareholders' interest should never be compromised, and you should be as professional as possible. Believe me, not every stakeholder will be similarly motivated; I have personally experienced it, and when I fought for the minority shareholders, things got ugly, upon which I saw the real motivation of some investors.

Lesson from UTAC

When UTAC called off the IPO in early 2001, after the stock market collapsed as a result of the tech bubble burst, the UTAC board members looked for a few options. Some were keen on an exit and looked at finding an investor or another company to takeover UTAC. The investors were thinking short term and just wanted to cash out fast. The more realistic plan was to raise more money while we could, to build up the war chest in the company. Fortunately, UTAC's financial performance and the assets we owned, including a huge high-tech factory, put UTAC in a very strong financial position, thanks to the good decisions made by my management team right from the time we started. So, we were not desperate for an exit nor to raise funds so quickly.

However, among the Taiwanese board members, was one member who was quite influential. He came from a rich family running some traditional businesses. Knowing him much better over the years, I understood that he and his family had missed the boat in investing in technology companies in the 1990s where many investors in Taiwan made huge sums of money because of the tech bubble. UTAC was one of his first investments and he saw the value of such investments. Now the Taiwanese modus operandi was this – "I scratch your back, you scratch mine".

When we decided to raise more funds for our war chest, I had prepared a pitch deck for this round of fund raising. We reached out to many institutional investors, VCs and private equity firms. With regard to the motivation of investors, I learned a lesson from this episode. One of the board members saw an opportunity to do his friends a favour by allowing them to invest in UTAC so that in future when his friends have future investment opportunities in tech companies, they will "scratch his back" and do him the future favour of letting him in on these investment opportunities. He invited me to Taiwan to meet "potential investors" and present the pitch deck for investment which I had prepared. I spent two days meeting different people and during all the discussions, I realised that this board member of mine wanted to sell UTAC shares cheap so that his friends see this as a favour. I was upset that he was planning to shortchange the company and undermine the interest of the minority shareholders by selling shares cheap, thus unnecessarily diluting the existing shareholders more than necessary.

Being the CEO and a board member, I had to fulfil my fiduciary duty to protect the interests of all shareholders, especially the minority shareholder and especially my team members who also held shares in the company. I fought the board on this decision and said I would not allow such investments to take place. This incident made the Taiwanese board members uncomfortable as they wanted to do what benefited them. And this is the reason why I had to leave the company that I had founded by myself. The Taiwanese commanded the majority of the board (which is another lesson – never allow yourself to be in a position where you can be easily outvoted). A few of the Taiwanese board members cooked up stories and influenced other board members (pity they got influenced so easily), so I had no choice but to leave the great company I founded.

Remember, always understand the motivations of each of your investors and all stakeholders. Never lose sight of this.

Know Your VCs

My experience with VCs has been interesting. I must say, it has mostly been good especially with regard to how my management team has been given the flexibility to run the company. I learned how VCs operate and what their needs are. This allowed me to deliver on what they needed, especially the information the representatives of the VC required for internal clearance. We must realise the VCs, too, have internal procedures and they too play a big part in helping the company start, so their needs must always be met. Mostly, the individual in the VC company you deal with makes the biggest difference. This person can be your supporter, smoothening things for you in the internal decision process of the VC, or he could be your detractor, making things very difficult for you.

My advice is to do due diligence on the potential investors and VCs whom you want to invite to invest in your start-up. Do some research, speak with other start-ups in which these VCs had invested, seek feedback on how good or bad the VCs can be. The more you know about the VCs before they invest in your start-up, the fewer headaches you will have in the future.

Infiniti Solutions Experience

We had two key VCs that invested in Infiniti Solutions. Our experience with the VCs had been mainly good. The individuals from the VC were friendly and we worked well together. Perhaps we could not be very picky or selective choosing the VC for Infiniti Solutions because we were raising funds post 2001 tech bubble burst and post September 11! VC deals were rare. We therefore did not do too much of our own due diligence on the VC we partnered.

Although our experience with VC had been mainly good, we did not fully understand their investment philosophy (and this is a very important thing for the entrepreneur to learn before choosing a VC to partner). For Infiniti, we were encouraged to go for an IPO, just three years after we started the company. We did prepare for the IPO and had NASDAQ approvals, too. We went all the way doing our roadshow and pulled the plug at the last moment because of the volatile stock market.

We ran into trouble when the 2008/2009 Global Financial Crisis hit. Business dropped by 60 per cent for Infiniti Solutions and we needed to raise more private funds. Yet our VCs did not want to do any follow-on funding. This was a defining moment for Infiniti Solutions where the founding team had to negotiate to buyout the VCs so that we could chart the future for Infiniti Solutions ourselves without interference from the VC. We then ran the company till our orderly exit via trade sales a few years later.

It is important that the entrepreneurs understand the investment philosophy of the potential investors and understand how they will act in different scenarios. If their track record is bad, partnering with such VCs should be avoided.

Chapter 17 Summary

The Seven VC Traps

- **VC Trap No. 1** – When they are courting you, VCs will sing high praises of you to stop you from talking to other VCs. Don't close in on any one VC too early, continue talking to a few potential ones.

- **VC Trap No. 2** – VCs give you very attractive valuations to entice you before cutting you down to size. Don't believe the attractive valuation at face value.

- **VC Trap No. 3** – VCs will try to cut you down when drawing down future tranches. Try to entrench the conditions of drawing down on the investment money agreed on in your agreement.

- **VC Trap No. 4** – Be wary of the clauses VCs try to make you sign, you may lose rights and get diluted more than you think. Word your agreements carefully to protect your rights.

- **VC Trap No. 5** – Choose your investors carefully; in times of crisis, they can make you feel miserable. Focus on the chemistry when choosing partners. Pick investors who will help, not hinder you.

- **VC Trap No. 6** – Individuals in a VC need to make money for themselves, not just their company; different teams in a VC are rewarded differently. Know how each decision-maker will be rewarded, not just the VC company's investment goals.

- **VC Trap No. 7** – VCs may want to a bigger stake in your company at the next round of fund raising. Don't let your VC control the next fund-raising process.

SECTION B: Summary

The Science of Entrepreneurship – The Technical Aspects of Starting a Business

I named Section B as the Science of Entrepreneurship because many of the things I wrote about are structured processes that entrepreneurs have to go through (and Science is structured).

I experienced many times the difficulties of starting a company from scratch, as a founder and as an investor. The toughest stage comes when converting an idea to a business. It is at this stage that most companies and entrepreneurs fail – they fail to transform the idea into a business model that can really work. Even after this stage is successfully traversed, the rest of the journey offers no shortcuts. The entrepreneur has to do a number of things to ensure the company's operational success.

The technical part of transforming the idea into a business entails a number of necessary steps, which includes capturing the idea, creating a unique business model, developing a strategy, preparing a plan, and forming a team. Pitching is a very important step for all entrepreneurs and being a good presenter, like a good storyteller is key to successfully attract other stakeholders to join you in your journey. The fund-raising exercise is one of the most challenging things for any entrepreneur, thus I have devoted many pages to talking about this subject and other related issues. For example, when I talk about what investors look for and what the entrepreneur should look for, my main idea is to help the entrepreneur better convince other stakeholders, and most importantly, potential investors in taking a stake in the company. I have assumed that operating the company should be something that is a given and find no need to discuss this further in this book.

Several issues I covered in this section apply a few of concepts I covered in the first section into practice. For example, in this Section B, I referred to "the alignment of the stars" which appeared in

Section A. My intention was to show how to apply in the real world, the aspects of concept and mindset, which I covered in Section A. Once you have mastered the first two sections in this book, you should be able to start your entrepreneurial journey with confidence.

As you proceed in your journey, you will face many uncertainties and many unexpected events, but these should never stop you from continuing your journey. To help, in the next section, I summarise a series of lessons learnt and environmental issues, which can help you cope with the uncertainties and difficulties you might face throughout your entrepreneurial journey.

And How to Create a Good Entrepreneurship Ecosystem

In this final section, I leave the technicalities of what it takes to be an entrepreneur to share the many lessons I have learned in my own entrepreneurial journey as well from others who have taken the same path. I have put together many past experiences in the form of lessons learnt that you can draw upon to help ease your own entrepreneurial journey. These have been learned over the years as an entrepreneur, investor in various start-ups, a policymaker in Singapore, as well as from my global experience as a co-president of the World Entrepreneurship Forum (WEnF) and the president of the start-up committee of the World Business Angels Forum (WBAF).

I start with a chapter on how an entrepreneur can survive challenging times. I focus on how to develop a "survival mentality". Basically, all the principles I have discussed in an earlier chapter come into play when the entrepreneur operates in a tough environment and tries to survive challenging times.

I also write about a series of lessons learnt during the dot.com era based on my experience starting my first and only dot.com company. I learned very quickly and managed to sell my dot.com company just two months before the bubble burst. The dot.com days were very scary, when we saw an inflation of entrepreneurial activities resulting in the great tech bubble bust of April 2000.

At the time of writing this second edition, the world is in the middle of one of the most severe economic disruption or downturns caused by the Covid-19 pandemic. I have written a new chapter (which was not in first edition) on how companies can survive this "Great Disruption" of the Covid-19. I also share two chapters on what an entrepreneur should do in putting in governance structures and managing teams. In addition to being an entrepreneur and a businessman, I have had the fortune to be a member of parliament (MP) in Singapore for almost 20 years. This has allowed me to play a bridging role between the private and public sectors. Through my role as an MP, I have contributed much to help change government policies in Singapore, in an effort to make Singapore's economy more entrepreneurial in nature. I therefore also share some of the entrepreneurship issues at government and society levels in a chapter of this section. I discuss several environmental factors that affect how entrepreneurship develops. I further take a look at the macro environment of how countries can make it more conducive for entrepreneurship to thrive.

I end this section by tracing my entrepreneurship journey, covering my school days, my years working in a multinational company, Texas Instruments, my start-up experiences of the multiple companies I started and my time as a politician in Singapore adopting an entrepreneurial approach to policy making.

SECTION

C

USEFUL LESSONS LEARNT

CHAPTER 18

HOW TO SURVIVE THE CHALLENGING TIMES

The global economy has seen unprecedented changes. With globalisation making an impact on companies and countries, it has not been easy for companies to grow successfully. Many companies that had been successful in domestic markets failed to perform when their markets opened up to competition or when the companies ventured to markets beyond their domestic shores. The question is, how do companies survive tough times and the complex environment we are operating in? In this chapter, I will share with you some of the strategies used by entrepreneurs and companies to ensure their survival.

I wrote this chapter in the first edition of my book that was released in the year 2007. I decided to keep the chapter in this edition although I have created a new chapter called "Surviving the Great Disruption (The Covid-19 Economic Impact)". I think it is useful to keep this chapter intact for past lessons learnt while in my new chapter on "Surviving the Great Disruption", I have summarised survival strategies that have worked for great companies as well as in my personal companies.

Surviving the Tough Times

Companies that continue to do business as usual whether in good or bad times, refusing to change with the times, will have little chance of making it when the boundary conditions change, especially when times are really bad.

Companies with weak fundamentals, which look good and are seemingly performing well in good times, may not make it through tough times.

Companies that fail to plan in advance for bad times will find it difficult to both plan any changes and execute them simultaneously when bad times hit. Their competitors would have adapted and modified their business strategies to quickly adapt to the changes required.

It is therefore a prerequisite for any entrepreneur to know how to survive the tough times. In fact, the start-up stage is actually a tough time for the company because it is typically starting from scratch, often trying to compete as an underdog facing competition from many incumbents, many of whom have already been in business for much longer. Entrepreneurs are forced to face challenging times right from the beginning. Such times can last quite long, even up to a few years before the new company achieves stability and success. So how do entrepreneurs survive the challenging times?

In the first edition of this book, I wrote:

After the dot.com era, two questions prevailed. First, is there life after the dot.com bubble? And second, will entrepreneurship continue to be an option for many? As I mentioned before, my answer to both questions is yes! Ideas do not suddenly die with the turn of the economy. Instead, more ideas arise as individuals and enterprises find ways to survive and remain afloat.

I was not wrong. In the internet economy, some companies like Amazon rose from the ashes but more importantly, many more good companies started and became success stories – Facebook, Uber, Airbnb, etc.

For that matter, stronger companies are made when they start in times of adverse conditions or when the companies experience tough times and survive downturns. I, for one, believe in a contrarian approach. Three of my best companies were started during the worst of times, one at the start of the

Asian currency crisis, and two of them during troughs in the semiconductor cycle, three years apart – one in 1998 and the other in 2001 – in the aftermath of the bursting of the dot.com bubble. All three companies did well – UTAC and Tri Star are still going strong while we exited Infiniti Solutions through trade sale.

What made the difference and why do some companies make it in adverse times while others do not? The most critical strategy, which I firmly believe in and follow, is that a business is a business, whether in good times or bad, whether in the new economy or old economy, whether dot.com or brick and mortar. If you have a business strategy that remains sound in any of these situations, you will have a winning formula that will allow you to survive any environmental condition.

Simply put, every business needs fundamental strategies to remain viable, and at critical times, to survive. What are these fundamental strategies? And what principles do I follow? Let me touch on a few.

Fundamental Strategy No. 1: The Survival Mentality that Only the Paranoid Survive

This is one basic philosophy those in Singapore should be very conversant with. Given the country's small size and total lack of natural resources except for human resources, Singaporeans have always lived life in a paranoid state. This has allowed Singapore to not only survive, but also to excel despite the odds stacked against her. The other way to look at this is Singapore's approach of a crisis mentality or what I choose to call a survival mentality or SM. As a matter of fact, however, this survival mentality is not unique to Singapore.

If we look at why the Taiwanese are so successful in the area of entrepreneurship and business dealings even in tough places like China, it is precisely this survival mentality that has helped them. Taiwan has always been under the threat of China attacking one day to take control of the island. In schools, at home, and in national service as soldiers, the people of Taiwan have been ingrained with the mindset that they have to fight for their survival, because if they do not, China will invade, take control of their island, and impose communism. The Taiwanese of course value their democracy and would not allow China to invade the island, at all costs. The survival mentality and the mindset of having to fight till the end should China invade Taiwan is what has made the Taiwanese among the best entrepreneurs in the world. This mentality serves the Taiwanese well as they go about starting and running businesses. I believe this mentality is also the reason why entrepreneurship thrives in Israel. The Israelis are always in survival mode, given what's happening in their neighborhood. Israel is also in a state of war. Their survival mentality has made them the Start-up Nation of the world, creating the most companies outside the USA that are listed on the NASDAQ.

The political leadership in Singapore, particularly driven by Mr. Lee Kuan Yew, the first Prime Minister, who later became Senior Minister, and finally Minister Mentor, did an excellent job in moving Singapore ahead with this survival mentality, or should I say crisis mentality.

The people of Singapore have done well with this mentality, albeit in a corporate driven economy. The difference between Taiwan and Singapore is that in Taiwan, the people have learned to survive for themselves in addition to ensuring the survival of the island, while in Singapore, given the dominant influence of the political leadership on the people, the people have been ingrained to help the country survive according to the model of success defined by the government.

This survival mentality is similarly important in the survival and success of companies, especially during times of economic downturn. While companies should be prepared and have a plan to survive a downturn, those that can successfully execute their plans and adapt their business with a survival mentality will not only survive in tough times, but also come out stronger and be able to last a lot longer than originally expected. The best example of this strategy is the one Intel uses, as evidenced in a book titled, *Only the Paranoid Survive*, by the former CEO of Intel, Mr. Andy Grove. I believe all the best companies in the world are the best because of this strategy or mentality – "Survival Mentality", "Crisis Mentality", "Being Paranoid about Survival", etc. This is the kind of mentality every entrepreneur should possess in order to achieve lasting success.

I personally have been using this survival mentality as a basic operating mode in all my businesses, whether in good or bad times, particularly so in bad times. Creating a culture of survival and paranoia about the company's outcome has allowed people to rally around a very basic cause, which is the company's survival, and therefore the survival of each stakeholder in the company. Translating this into the survival of the individual involved is one of the most powerful tools that can extract the best performance from these individuals. Treating the outcome as a "life or death" situation can extract the most extraordinary behaviour in people.

All too often, when I have started to drift into my comfort zone and lose sight of the fact that my companies will sooner or later be faced with very difficult situations, the performance of my companies has also weakened, and sometimes has become quite bad. I have therefore made it a point to think of strategies to survive the difficult times before the difficult times come, and when such times do come I constantly look at updating the company's plans as circumstances change. More importantly, I make it a point to communicate the survival plans with my team members and employees, and to also inculcate in the minds of my team members the risk we face if we fail to survive the tough times. Getting paranoid about such things is not necessarily a bad thing, particularly for a company's leadership.

Fundamental Strategy No. 2: Back to the Basics – You Need Customers and You Need to Make Money

Here's a question for you: What are you in business for? In a split second, I hope your answer is, "To make money". If there is one lesson you want to take back with you on how to run a business, especially during uncertain times, this is it: that you are not a charity and you have to make money for your company (and if you do make money you can give some to charity one day).

Yes, you need to make money, if not for yourself, then at least for your company. If you do not believe in this, then you are in the wrong business. If making money is truly not important to you, you should engage in charity work. In fact, even in charity work, you have to think of how to raise money and how to stretch your money. Social entrepreneurship is a new type of entrepreneurship that has arisen since I wrote the first edition of this book in 2007. Social entrepreneurs also think about how to make money. Their business focuses on impact – social impact. So never forget that when you do a start-up, you are doing it to make money for all stakeholders.

The problem with less savvy entrepreneurs is that they focus too much on the technical aspects of the business and forget to spend the necessary time thinking about this basic question of how they can make money for the company.

The next two most important financial aspects for the entrepreneur and the company to focus on are the gross margin and cash flow. Many companies collapse due to a failure to watch these two fundamental things in their businesses. Gross margins basically need to be significant enough to cover all the company's overheads. Failing to watch the gross margins can result in a situation where there is net cash drain, and if the cash drain is high, the company can run out of cash fast. The gross margin is also a function of how high the products or services are priced as well as how much it costs to produce the products or services. As far as the price is concerned, one should assume it will be mainly market driven. Of course, the company should find opportunities to price the product or service as high as possible by differentiating itself from its competitors and by convincing customers about the value proposition and the value-added component that justifies the price.

The factor in the gross margin formula that is very much under the control of the company and the entrepreneur is the cost. If it costs too much to produce a product or a service, the company may not make enough in margins to cover the cost or to generate the cash necessary to sustain the business over a period of time. The entrepreneur should find ways to produce the product or service at increasingly lower costs so as to maximise the gross margins. The higher the gross margins, the better will be the company's cash generation capability, and the more cash the company generates, the longer the company can last.

This brings me to the cash flow factor, the most important element for entrepreneurs to watch. Cash flow is more than just gross margins minus the overheads. It includes the ability of the company to collect money on time and to pay the suppliers within an optimal time. There is very little value in making good sales, only to be unable to collect the sales proceeds from the customers. Although the profit and loss statements may look healthy showing good profit margins, if the entrepreneur is unable to bring cash back into the company, the company may not last very long unless more money is pumped into it. The entrepreneur should therefore focus on generating cash flow into the company.

Being net cash positive means the cash coming into the company is greater than the cash going out of the company (as a result of all the expenses). This way, cash will build up in the company and thereby stretch the company's survivability period. Watching the amount of cash left in the company and the burn rate is of course very important. The cash position and the rate at which cash is being used up will give the entrepreneur a good feel of how much longer the company can continue operating until more cash is brought into the company.

Even more basic than the cash flow and profit margin issues is the subject of *where* the money will be coming from. While the investors invest in the early stages, they expect the company to be self-sustaining after some time, and therefore, the cash must come from somewhere else, which of course should be from the sales. The entrepreneur should remember that he or she is in business to serve customers, and the customers are the ones who pay their bills. So even before the entrepreneur starts to worry about gross margins and cash flow, he or she has to worry about sales, which in turn relates to the customers who will be interested in purchasing the company's products or services.

You need real customers and you need your customers to pay real cash. Forget about the "go for eyeball acquisition first and worry about revenues later" approach of doing business, as we saw in the dot.com era. Once the customers are used to not paying, it is very difficult to tell them at a later time that they have to pay, let alone pay a lot of money, for the product or service they are using.

Fundamental Strategy No. 3: Entrepreneurs Do It Best at the Start-Up Stage

If we look at the many examples of how entrepreneurs were able to overcome countless odds and somehow achieve success even when the situation looked dire, we can conclude that they won their success by challenging the rules of the game. Despite being underdogs, these entrepreneurs managed to beat the incumbents to emerge as winners.

Entrepreneurs usually achieve the most spectacular success stories during the time they were starting up companies. At the same time, if we look at companies that failed badly – even if the companies in question achieved great success during their early stages – interestingly they failed because as they grew bigger, their mindset shifted from thinking like an entrepreneur to one thinking like a manager, managing a stable organisation.

Another point is this – many companies and entrepreneurs become complacent as they taste the fruits of their success. They also become less hungry and let their guard down. When this happens, the competitors can easily come in and defeat the formerly new but now incumbent company, which has now become slow to react to as they think less as entrepreneurs.

Does this happen all the time? Does this have to happen to all companies as they grow bigger and start tasting the fruits of success? Of course, the answer is NO. Companies can continue to achieve success, or for that matter, achieve even greater success, as they grow bigger and when they leave the start-up stage.

What is it that differentiates successful companies from those that start to decline after growing big? The real answer is that such companies continue to adapt and change the way they do things to remain relevant to the new environmental conditions and competitive landscape. In other words, they started rethinking as entrepreneurs with the ability to seek clarity in an uncertain environment. New success factors will appear, and the company needs to know what these are and how to operate with the new conditions. Companies have to learn and re-learn how to do things. Likewise, entrepreneurs have to learn and re-learn how to manage companies and how to create new things as conditions constantly change around them. How can they achieve this?

I believe entrepreneurs are successful because they start from nothing but aim to create something from nothing, and will do anything it takes to achieve their goal. They are hungry for success. This mentality always exists for any start-up and any entrepreneur at that start-up stage. This is what I call the start-up mentality, and no matter what type of business is being created by whatever type of entrepreneur, this mentality will always be relevant. So if companies can always go back to the basics and remember what was it that created success for them in the first place, they will be able to achieve continuous success by doing almost similar things later in the company's life cycle.

This brings me back to the Apple story which I shared in an earlier chapter. Steve Jobs started the company, made it successful, gathered a good board of directors and hired John Sculley as the CEO as the company became big. The board felt Steve could not run a bigger company and later fired him. Apple faltered without Steve Jobs and struggled to do well. What did Apple do to regain its glory? Well Apple brought Steve Jobs back as the CEO. The rest is history – Apple turned around and again became successful with Steve Jobs at the helm. How did it happen? Well perhaps Steve brought the company back to behaving and thinking like a start-up. And Apple is still one of the most successful companies in the world today.

When companies are big and have seen success, people are easily distracted and lose sight of the factors that created their original success. If we can bring them back to their basics, reminding them of what they did to achieve their success at the start-up stage and then get them to once again think the same way, they will greatly enhance their chances of continuing and even bettering their success.

I have always operated with this mindset no matter how big or small my company, and no matter whether it is a new start-up or a successful company operating for many years. The start-up mentality is so important that whenever I sense things are not going right and when we start to see things stagnating in the company, I always go back to adjusting the mindsets of my people, helping them to think of ourselves as start-ups once again, and as start-ups, we fight as insurgents. When you are an insurgent, you fight guerrilla wars and fight as an underdog, which is different from fighting as a big incumbent. This makes a tremendous difference in how we do things – we forget about the luxuries, we forget about the discomforts we may face, we forget about spending lavishly, and we forget about thinking of ourselves as being big. Even if we might be big in size, we need to adjust our mindset to one of being smaller than our competitors. Being number one and thinking as number one can lead to complacency. Even if you are number one, think of how you can increase your lead as number one to make it even more difficult for the next guy to catch up.

I therefore always go back to thinking that I am still a start-up whenever I sense trouble, whether the trouble is in financial performance or when I sense complacency among company personnel. By going back to becoming and thinking as entrepreneurs of a start-up, new life gets injected into the company, which serves as very powerful motivation to achieve success once again.

One additional point that can be useful in guiding entrepreneurs as they go about doing their tasks is this thought of being an underdog. I have found it very useful to think of myself as the underdog, and at times, to also behave like an underdog. The actions that drive an underdog can be very useful in making decisions. Often, when companies grow in size, the entrepreneur and the employees start thinking they are big and therefore should do things the way big companies typically do. When this happens, people tend to let down their guard and the competitors seize the opportunity to defeat the company.

As an underdog, you fight differently. You fight as if you have the odds stacked against you. You go on high alert and move fast as your competitors try to outmanoeuvre your company. You behave as if you know you will most likely fail and are considered an unlikely winner. The possibility of failure, which could be painful, and the potential of becoming a huge success should you execute your operations successfully, create a tremendous drive that simply increases your chances of success.

In short, the underdog behaviour is one of survival, and therefore, if you treat it as if you are in a "life or death" situation, the actions you take will be a whole lot different if you are in your comfort zone. That's why I always believe in thinking of myself as a start-up or underdog, no matter how big or small a business I run, and no matter how old or new the business is. This is especially useful in times of crisis.

In an earlier chapter, I wrote about "thinking with your heart", especially at the start-up stages, and how as the company becomes bigger one tends to use a much more structured approach to make decisions as opposed to using the "heart" or "gut feel". This is another example of how you should go back to behaving as if you were in your start-up mode to once again turn things around should you face challenging times in your company at any of its stages of growth. Whenever faced with such challenges, don't forget to use more of your heart to think.

Fundamental Strategy No. 4: Even in Crisis and Chaos, Seek Out Opportunities

I've talked about the crisis mentality. The question is, is a crisis a good or bad thing? In a crisis, there can be chaos, so is chaos good or bad? The real answer is – it all depends on how you look at it.

Let's consider the famous phrase about a glass that is half filled with water. Do you see it as half full or half empty? In other words, do you see it positively or negatively? Similarly, when a crisis occurs, do you see it as an opportunity or a threat? The mindset makes a tremendous difference as to how we proceed and will therefore affect the outcome. In the end, it will make a big difference between success and failure. Seizing an opportunity, when everyone else sees a threat, is what entrepreneurs do best. So, crisis, chaos, and threats are not necessarily bad things in the vocabulary of entrepreneurs. In fact, these are good things, and it is in such times that we can see the emergence of the best companies and entrepreneurs.

There is one saying I clearly remember reading in a magazine many years ago. It was something one of the wealthiest men in Hong Kong said, something to the effect of "don't over-invest in good times, and also, don't under-invest in bad times". His point was that there are good deals to be found even in bad times. His philosophy in business has been to continuously look for good opportunities, even when the economy is bad.

You should never become overly pessimistic when times are bad or when crisis or chaos strikes. Instead, calmly treat such times as a given. By expecting bad times, you will keep looking for the right opportunities. Most people will become defensive and pessimistic, and even give up when facing a crisis. In a chaotic environment, the winners will be those who can sniff out and identify the right opportunities to develop into businesses and growth for the company. It is not easy, but if you are in it for the long haul, you will have planned for all the ups and downs, and along with that, the expectation of looking for opportunities in times of adversity.

I mentioned how I had founded all my successful companies during so-called bad times. What I saw was not threats in times of adversity, but rather opportunities during the bad times. The difference is that I always look for areas of opportunity when others are seeing threats.

For example, in 2001, my team and I managed to start Infiniti Solutions from scratch, using some money from our personal savings. We put up a business plan to become a global company in a short span of a few years, and then looked for investors who would believe in us. This was at a time when the whole semiconductor industry was already very competitive and when there were many incumbents and more established companies, some giants in our industry. Back then, there were many listed companies ready to acquire smaller players and many smaller players ready to be acquired and absorbed by the bigger companies. In this seemingly negative environment, the four of us started our company. We then went on to acquire two small companies, each one year apart, in two separate parts of the world, and united them into a medium-sized company in our industry.

In the process, we also raised the money from two reputable investors and hired more good people to join us. When we went about acquiring the two companies, we had competition. In one case, three other competitors sought to acquire the same company we targeted, at around the same time. Despite being the oddball and the smallest and newest, and despite being the financially weakest at the time of negotiation, we emerged the winners and created the Infiniti Solutions that received approval to be listed on the NASDAQ in 2004.

On the surface, we were the most unlikely group to achieve this as we were a new player in the scene, and had the least resources. People thought we were mad, and the selling companies saw themselves as being under threat when we appeared on their horizon. The reality is that when we did all of this, all we had was a company with a paid-up capital of just S$2. This worried the first company we were acquiring, but we told them we were confident of raising enough cash to buy the shareholders out and they bought our story – of course, we also delivered on what we promised. We were also operating out of my house, which I used as a meeting place for my team members, while we went out to raise funds right in the middle of the September 11 crisis. Yet before we had eventually sold the company, we had managed to build Infiniti Solutions into a player considered as medium-sized in the world, after coming out from nowhere.

The reality is that many other bigger companies could have done what my team and I did. With their stronger resources, it would have taken these larger companies much less effort to take over the companies we had acquired. In fact, the companies we acquired could each have done what we did and themselves achieved the medium size that Infiniti Solutions achieved two years after its start-up. To top it off, we were a non-entity at the time we started talking to them. However, none of them attempted it.

The only difference between these other companies and my team was that my team and I saw opportunities when the others saw threats. We saw the potential of success when many others saw the potential of failure. They hesitated and we moved. They waited to see how things would turn out, while we created the future by making things happen the way we wanted to. And this, I hope, delivers the message of how crisis or chaos can bring opportunities that need to be discovered and developed, and how a threat can throw up the real winners.

Crisis and chaos reveal the real leaders. While everyone looks good during peace time, not everyone will be able survive, let alone do well, in times of crisis. A crisis is a good time to test leadership qualities, integrity, and the commitment of people. If you lack a crisis or chaos situation, I say, create the crisis or chaos if you can afford to. This is what leaders do – they create the crisis mentality among their people. If you can successfully create this crisis mentality, you will be able to test your survival ability and the ability of your people not to crumble when real threats confront the company. From the outcome of the exercise, you will be able to separate the true leaders from the people who look like good leaders only because they can do well solely in good times.

The Covid-19 disruption of 2020 has been an eye-opener for most people around the world. There are many leaders all over the world who have crumbled in the face of the biggest crisis of our lifetimes. There are also some leaders who have risen to the occasion and managed the crisis very well. In the USA, the then President fumbled while some governors did an excellent job. Italian leaders faltered, German leaders did well. In Singapore, we saw weakness in the responses of some of the new leaders, making Singapore lose what was originally touted as a "Gold Standard" response to the Covid-19 crisis where the initial response looked good proved inadequate as we saw a second wave of infections. As I mentioned before, in a high tide, all ship captains look good as they navigate their ships – almost all can do it, but in a low tide, only the most skillful of captains can save their ships and their passengers. We see the real ability of leaders tested only in times of chaos.

The irony is that we really need leaders only in bad times, but should we test for leadership early on? Organisations need to do this regularly for their long-term survivability. It is not easy to do, but if it can be done, it will do the company good.

Fundamental Strategy No. 5: What Risk Taking Means

There is one big R which comes up all the time when we talk about entrepreneurship – Risk. But the real question is, what is a risk? I think the risk aspect in entrepreneurship has been wrongly understood and wrongly quoted because many people don't really understand what kind of risks entrepreneurs undertake. I have discussed the issue of risk taking in an earlier chapter. In this section, I will attempt to elaborate a little on what risk taking means and does not mean in the context of entrepreneurship.

First, risk taking means calculating the odds, and then taking the chances only after doing something to increase your odds of winning. In fact, the entrepreneur should understand all the risks involved and then identify how the risks can be mitigated or reduced by planning and executing backup plans.

When an entrepreneur thinks of risk, it is about doing things differently to improve the chances of succeeding without leaving it to luck. Risk taking is about having a plan to survive failure as opposed to just planning to win. Often, people think entrepreneurship is all about plowing through with brute force despite the risks being present. This is wrong. Entrepreneurship is more than "just doing it", it is actually about "doing it after I have understood some of the risks" and finding ways to overcome the obstacles.

Risk taking is also about being willing to test the limits instead of blindly following the rules of the game or the traditional rules of the business. In fact, it is about breaking the rules and inventing new rules, which can confuse the competitor and put the competition into disarray. Risk taking is also about not following rules that do not make sense. It may be about disobeying orders at times and leaving the explanation for later, as long as whatever was done was not ill intended or done in malice or to break the law, such as in committing fraud or cheating. Old rules often stifle creativity and may become obstacles to the successful execution of a plan. Such rules may not be easily followed if you want to be successful. It is in such a scenario that the mindset of "just do it first and explain later" comes into play.

At times, you may have to do things differently from expected, and once the outcome has been achieved, you can explain why you broke the rules. If everyone fears breaking the rules, then entrepreneurship will have little chance of succeeding. Sometimes, on the ground, you have to make a choice of doing something fast, even if the rules do not allow it or if the rules are not clear about what should be done. It is about doing it for the purpose of a better outcome.

Risk taking is also about "fixing it if it is not broken", as opposed to fixing things only if they are broken. In other words, it is about anticipating what others did not anticipate, and it is about leading changes even if others think you are wrong. You will do it anyway as long as you think it will lead to something good. This is what many bigger companies need to do more of. Typically, they will stick to the status quo as long as things are going fine, and nothing has gone wrong. They will pay attention to things only when something goes wrong. It is for this reason that the insurgents or newcomers are able to defeat even the biggest of companies. They are able to do so because they re-invent the rules and re-invent the way things are done, even if the old ways still work well. And this catches the incumbents off-guard.

Fundamental Strategy No. 6: What Risk Taking Does Not Mean

One thing I have seen among people who have tried to become entrepreneurs just because it was fashionable, particularly during the dot.com days, is that they seemed to have a wrong idea of what risk means.

Risk taking is not about disobeying orders for the sake of doing it or breaking reasonable rules. It does not mean you become suicidal by clashing head on against a competitor for emotional reasons. Risk taking must be for reasons that make sense and with a sense of conviction. Risk taking is not about planning to fail, but about avoiding failure or recovering from a failed situation.

Many people think that those who become entrepreneurs take on a greater chance of failing and that they don't mind failing. On the contrary, risk taking should be about knowing what will make you fail, and then finding ways to lessen your chances of failing by employing counter measures. It is about planning to succeed and keeping failure at bay. Risk taking is not about gambling but knowing and understanding what you are up against before making an assessment of whether you can achieve success by taking the appropriate corrective actions. True risk taking is about knowing your game theory and applying it to help you succeed and win big. Finally, risk taking is not about whether you have luck or achieve success because of luck. Anyone who takes risks and places hopes on luck and not on effort to help achieve success, is an opportunist, not an entrepreneur.

Surviving a Marathon – Mind Over Matter

Let me share an experience where I applied the idea of mindset change to change an outcome. While it may be difficult to link this to Surviving, I think the idea I am trying to share is not unrelated. Just for background – in my junior college days (high school equivalent) when I was 17 years old, I was the hockey captain of my college team and I was also a long-distance champion. I was very fit and could do cross country running of up to 10km with ease. When I went for my national service, doing the Officer's Cadet School (OCS) training to become a military officer, I was similarly very fit and among the best long-distance runners with a very high level of stamina despite my small build. Then when I was studying at the university (Nanyang Technological Institute, NTU, Singapore today), my idea of having a refreshing break when studying for exams was to go for a 10km to

12km run – it was like a refreshing walk for me. I maintained my fitness for many years.

However, when I entered politics, starting 1994, I completely neglected my fitness, having to balance my work, my political activities (which took up a tremendous amount of time) and my family. I put on weight and became very unfit. Then came a very important event for my university – they were celebrating the 50th anniversary for the predecessor university (Nantah) and one of the events the university wanted to organise was an ultramarathon – a 168km run (four marathons) around Singapore, where four core runners representing the four milestones of the university will run at least one marathon and some experienced ones were to complete four marathons, starting on a Saturday morning and ending on a Sunday evening.

The four stages of the university were – Nantah (the original university), NTI (my batch of students who were the pioneers of NTU, Singapore), National Institute of Education (NIE) becoming part of NTU, Singapore, and of course the youngest, NTU graduates. The organisers wanted one runner representing each cohort of the four stages I mentioned above. They had already identified the person from Nantah (Lim Nghee Huat, a 52-year-old, and an Ironman), an NIE runner and a young man from NTU, Singapore – all three were experienced marathon runners. But the organisers could not identify anyone from my batch (from NTI) – who were all around their mid-forties.

As I had been a student leader and was also representing the alumni on the board of NTU, Singapore, the organisers managed to convince me to participate in the run. It was when I was totally unfit, weighed a very heavy 75kg, and had only six months to train. I started training to lose weight and regain my fitness to be able to run a marathon at the age of 45 years! Well after six months, I managed to lose around 10kg and was able to run half a marathon non-stop. When the day came in September 2005, I said to myself – well if I can do half a marathon and feel fresh, I should be able to complete the second half just by running steadily. My goal was to complete the first marathon while the other runners were targeting between two and four each.

To cut the story short, the day came – the four of us core runners had a safety vehicle following each of us and I had two of my grassroots leaders who decided to take turns to pace me as I ran. I struggled and made it to the 30km point. By that time, I was bleeding as the friction of my t-shirt on my chest caused some damage. At the 30km point, I changed my clothes and continued to run. By the time I hit another 3km, I could not take it anymore. I signaled to my grassroots leaders to inform the safety vehicle that I was giving up as I could not take it anymore. I was totally mistaken to attempt a full marathon without the proper training. I stopped and felt dejected. I started reflecting and thought to myself, "I have never given up before – why am I giving up now." Then the next minute I had another thought that I have never forgotten till this day: "To give up is easy, but to finish the task is special and if I give up today, I will always want to give up at the next obstacle in life." At that very moment, I again asked my grassroots leader to go back and inform the organisers that I intended to complete the marathon and I said to myself – even if I have to walk or crawl, I will finish the marathon.

And complete it I did – it took me more than seven hours to complete the marathon. In fact, at the last 5km point, the hot sun was out and my heart started palpitating. I asked my grassroots leader to get me a cold isotonic drink. I sat at a bus stop, drank the cold drink, picked myself up and finished the last 5km – the last marathon of my life! (I should have realised I took a tremendous risk by still running when my heart started palpitating, but the thought of not giving up overtook me.)

The lesson in life from the marathon was this – it is "Mind over Matter" and nothing is impossible if we have a correct mindset towards anything we do in life. When your mind takes over, you can overcome any physical difficulties you may have.

You Must Learn How to Survive

I hope you can see how you can apply your entrepreneurial spirit to help you survive challenging times. In addition to overcoming obstacles and having the right skills to solve problems, you will have to go back to the basics of how entrepreneurs succeed in the first place. Applying some of what entrepreneurs do best and understanding the many things which constitute "the art of entrepreneurship" or mindset, you will greatly enhance your chances of surviving challenging times.

Chapter 18 Summary

How to Survive the Challenging Times

- Companies must survive and adapt in the global economy in both good and tough times.

- A good business is a good business in good or bad times as long as it has a good strategy and a good business model.

- There are six principles of survival, and they are:

  1. The survival mentality is essential for success. It allows people to rally around a very basic cause, which is the company's survival, and therefore the survival of each stakeholder in the company.

  2. Always go back to the basics – the reason to be in business is to make money. Stay focused on the gross margin and cash flow.

  3. Embrace a start-up mentality. It allows companies to do similar things that made them successful but at the same time adapt and change according to the business conditions around them. Go back to using your heart to think from time to time.

  4. Look at crisis in a positive light. Good leaders survive in good and bad times, and they see opportunities while others see adversity. A crisis mentality can test your survival ability. It also allows you to discover the leadership abilities of your team.

  5. Understand what risk taking is and what it is not. Once you understand the difference, you will be able to better plan your moves.

  6. Plan for failure. Find ways to lessen your chances of failing by employing counter measures. It is about planning to succeed and keeping failure at bay.

- Whenever you face challenging times at any stage of your life or at any stage of your company, go back to the basics and start rethinking like an entrepreneur to survive and thrive.

CHAPTER 19

LESSONS LEARNT DURING THE DOT.COM ERA – THE TECH BUBBLE BURST

In the 1990s, there was a lot of enthusiasm about how the new knowledge-based economy could change the world. Insurgents (start-ups) who were to defeat the long-standing incumbents were everyday stories. Many people jumped onto the bandwagon, and it was at this time that we saw the highest numbers of start-ups and throngs of people leaving their well-paying jobs to also become "entrepreneurs". But were they all really true entrepreneurs?

The reality is that most of them were what I call "copycat entrepreneurs". Why? They embarked on the path of "entrepreneurship" for all the wrong reasons. Of course, in any environment there will always be those who did the right things for the right reasons, so some true entrepreneurs did emerge during the dot.com days. I will now focus on those who did it for the wrong reasons.

During this time, we saw many new companies being created. However, many of these so-called entrepreneurs did not do it because there was a great opportunity that others had not identified. Many did it simply out of an idea, without converting that idea into a viable business model. Many had no fire burning in them to create something great, pursue a dream or have the passion to achieve something significant. Many did it because it looked easy to do, because the money looked easy to get, the money they could make looked very good; it was like a get-rich-quick scheme. In brief, it was like the gold rush of the old days.

In those dot.com days, there was also a tremendous surge in investor excitement. Many companies and investors entered into partnerships with start-ups and new entrepreneurs. Because of these new partnerships, what we saw was a steep increase in the number of new companies starting up around the world. Many of those who took the plunge to become entrepreneurs by starting companies were younger people in their twenties and thirties. In the past, this was not a path typically preferred by many. Most young graduates used to prefer to work in big multinational companies.

If we look at the type of entrepreneurs who emerged during this period, they were mainly those who participated in the info-communications area and were mainly in the Internet or dot.com economy. Why was this so? Because these were relatively easy-to-create businesses and the cost of entry was low. At the same time, the barriers to entry were also low, and therefore, it was easy to create a near similar business with a slightly different twist. We can say the same about the App type businesses. Let's face it – we have our second round of the tech bubble building again, after people forgot the dot.com bust or tech bubble bursting in 2000. And with the Great Disruption we are seeing as a result of the Covid-19 situation in the year 2020, we may soon see another round of busts – the App bubble bust.

Back to the dot.com days when the hype was so well propagated that many individuals and companies pumped in vast amounts of money to take stakes in such companies at rocketing valuations. Valuations continued to shoot up as everyone thought the Internet economy had just started and had a long way to go in terms of value creation. As almost a daily occurrence, groups of founders would come up with an idea and decide to start a company, which they would ask for very high valuations from potential investors, even if there were companies already formed with almost similar ideas in other parts of the world. Suddenly the euphoria ended on 14 April 2000 when the whole world came crashing down on the dot.com economy. The crash happened so rapidly it affected all countries almost simultaneously.

The rest is history. We saw a record number of companies that lost a record amount of money in record time. Many such companies had burned millions of dollars and even hundreds of millions of dollars before finally throwing in the towel.

It was a shattering experience for the global economy's technology sector. The sudden loss of confidence not only affected the dot.com companies, but also every other technology company in every part of the world. It took the world a long time to recover from it. The lucky ones made their money and emerged from the dot.com economy before it crashed. Today, they are called heroes. But were they truly heroes or just plain lucky? This is a good topic to discuss, but in this chapter, I will only study what went wrong.

So, what really happened? Have we seen the end of the Internet economy? Was the new economy so short-lived that the so-called old economy businesses are the only ones that are still viable? Can we still breed successful entrepreneurship in the post dot.com era? My response is yes – there can still be good entrepreneurial activity no matter what the environment. The important thing is to learn from all the mistakes we made in the dot.com days. Through these lessons, we can emerge stronger than before. Having learned these lessons well, we will continue to see real and successful Internet companies emerge even amongst those who came from the dust of the dot.com era.

We have seen the emergence of the App economy since around 2004 (which is still the same Internet economy that was called the dot.com economy in the past). Some of those who survived the dot.com crash became winners in this new era of the App economy. Amazon almost died but is today among one of the most valuable companies in the world. Others who survived are eBay, Priceline, Yahoo and E-trade.

Too Old for the Dot.Com Business

This story shows how being a young entrepreneur was considered important in the dot.com days. Together with a group of fresh graduates, we started a dot.com company. They were all in their mid-twenties, while I was in my late thirties. When we decided to sell the company, we found a European company that was doing something similar to us in Europe. They wanted to acquire our company to jumpstart their business in Asia.

After initial discussion over emails and over the phone, we met in person to finalise the deal. The meetings started in the morning in our office, and the discussions were handled by a colleague of mine. When the key terms were almost settled, with a few irresolvable issues left, the next meeting was held in my house, after dinner the same day.

When I met the people we were dealing with, I was surprised to see two persons in their early twenties leading the European company. When they met me and saw how "old" I was at the age of 39, they told me that in the new economy, successful entrepreneurs needed to move at Internet speed, which means, you have to be young enough to keep up with the pace. For those older, the pace is just too tough because activities must be done 24/7 (24 hours a day and seven days a week, non-stop). I was told I was too old to participate in the new economy or in dot.com businesses.

In any case, I quickly learnt about 24/7 operations when we negotiated the deal with the European company. We started negotiations after dinner in my house and completed the deal at 3 a.m., working non-stop. In between the negotiations, the two young men had to call their equally young partners in Europe to get buy-in on the deal conditions. Fortunately, thanks to the tea my wife made for us, I had no problems operating 24/7 that day.

Below, I share five lessons learnt from the dot.com era, which I feel are worth mentioning.

Dot.Com Lesson No. 1: A Business is Still a Business

Any business must consist of a fundamental strategy, which must be driven by a long-term vision and long-term goals and objectives. The business must be able to sustain growth and have proper revenue models as well as clear profitability goals just like any business in the old economy.

No matter the type of business, technology or non-technology based, and no matter the day and age, be it in the old economy or new economy, the fundamentals of a business remain the same. Regardless of the business phase, be it the planning phase, the start-up phase, the growth or the expansion phase, the strategies, type of people and type of resources needed remain almost the same.

During the dot.com days, when so-called entrepreneurs had business strategies based on gaining "eyeballs" by spending huge sums of money, or when they spent a lot of money employing the most sophisticated technology to solve a business process problem without thinking about revenue, profit, and cash flow, they were completely off the mark. The results are obvious – the rate of failure of start-ups and businesses were incredibly high.

The other mistake many young entrepreneurs made was that they attempted to model their business along the same lines as what they saw in other companies based on published reports or business models available over the Internet. The real problem with such an approach is that most, if not all companies, really keep their strategies and business models very confidential. In fact, these are trade secrets only a few key people in any organisation really know. Good companies and good entrepreneurs seldom divulge all their secrets. Therefore, the insight and knowledge gained about businesses through published reports and the Internet only scratch the surface of what really goes on inside a company. It is a mistake to build companies and drive strategies based on the hype created by others.

Like a *kung-fu* or a martial arts expert teaching others the skills of his trade, the teacher seldom reveals all his secrets to his disciples. The *kung-fu* master always keeps at least one or two fighting techniques close to his chest and does not impart the knowledge to others except a handful whom he completely trusts. (Those who have seen the movie Kung-Fu Panda would have seen the master teaching the last most effective step only to the Panda close to the end of the movie.) Similarly, good companies seldom reveal their true formula for success or reveal all their trade secrets, so it best not to assume you have all the information needed to copy the success of others.

Dot.Com Lesson No. 2: An Idea is Not a Business

I have mentioned more than once that an idea alone is not sufficient to create successful business. An idea maybe great, but it is not worth very much if one is unable to make that transformation into a business.

What we saw in the dot.com years was an exuberance of money-raising based on an idea and the potential of the idea becoming a workable business. Investors betted on the idea without much consideration of the next important step – the creation of the business. Looking back, it is obvious that a vast majority of start-ups failed because they were not able to make that transition from a good idea into a good business. Many did not even realise how difficult it was to make that transition. And many failed to realise that the ideas person may not necessarily be the right person to create a successful company.

During the dot.com days, the illusion created by the tremendous number of new companies was a proliferation of entrepreneurial ideas, some original and some copycat ideas. The reality is that most were "half-baked" companies even if the ideas were great. Investors lost sight of this and betted on such "half-baked" companies. This illusion and the lack of understanding about what makes companies tick and the feeling of comfort that the idea was good enough to make money, caught everyone off guard.

Dot.Com Lesson No. 3: There is No Shortcut to Success

Like anything in life, including creating a successful business, there is no shortcut. A lot of planning, execution, and hard work go into building a successful company. Most of the time, it is never as smooth sailing as it may seem to the outside world. Ask any successful entrepreneur and he will tell you about all the effort and hard work to create success. Many people, including investors were guided by the potential of making huge returns through huge increases in valuations. Many viewed an IPO as the end game when in reality an IPO should be a means of fund raising to allow companies to further fund and grow their business.

If investors and entrepreneurs had focused on bringing in the profits as a measure of a return on their investments, as has always been done for good companies, they may have created stronger companies that could have survived the downturn. There is no such thing as growing a company overnight into a monstrous size without going through all the planning and execution – the whole nine yards of it.

Dot.Com Lesson No. 4: Not So Smart Money

It was really difficult to raise funds for start-ups before the dot.com days, particularly in countries like Singapore where the venture capital market was in its infancy. Those days, there were too many projects or start-ups chasing after too little money. But then suddenly, during the dot.com days, funds became abundantly available. There was a one hundred and eighty degree turn of events. While the number of starts-ups was already growing rapidly, the amount of money available for funding the new projects surged at an even faster rate. So, the situation during the dot.com days became one of a lot of money chasing the many but still limited number of projects or start-ups!

This abundance of money meant investors were easily willing to part with their money for a stake in a start-up. VCs were desperate to invest in as many companies as possible as that was their charter and their reputation was built based on their ability to successfully invest in the dot.com start-ups.

Every investor wanted to get in on the act upon seeing start-up companies gaining in value on a daily basis and new benchmarks in company valuations being set. So as not to miss the boat, they parted with their money easily, many times without evaluating whether or not the company was viable and whether or not the investment made sense. Such money was really "dumb" money, or perhaps to be more polite, it was "not so smart" money. This "not so smart" money had a detrimental effect on the entrepreneurs who received the money easily.

Entrepreneurs who could find money easily and did not have to sweat it out when looking for it, developed an attitude that as money was easy to raise, it was no big deal to spend it lavishly. Their attitude was based on the fact that they were really burning someone else's money and not their own. The passion of creating a successful business slowly dampened. These entrepreneurs had no pain or pinch factor as they were not spending their own money.

The fact is that a good business should be started on a tight budget to test out the business model, before scaling it up with more funds once the fundamentals have been entrenched. Too much money just corrupts the mind and spoils the entrepreneur. A good example is my first and only dot.com venture. I had to reduce the salaries of my young partners so they would feel the pinch as they themselves had told me they did not feel it since it was not their money that got burned (it was all my money!).

Dot.Com Lesson No. 5: Internet and Technology Alone Do Not Create a Business

Many entrepreneurs and investors assumed information technology was all that was needed to succeed in the new economy. They thought technology could replace many aspects in a business process. How wrong they were.

In any business, domain knowledge is most critical. For example, a successful retail business, whether in the form of an Internet business or an old economy business, can only be achieved by someone who knows retailing, the psychology of customers, marketing and sales techniques, and many other concepts. Technology and the Internet should be seen as tools to greatly enhance business efficiency, or used as another marketing channel or a new way to manage the supply chain. It is the domain knowledge that is key in running any successful business.

When computer engineers tried to form companies in retailing, banking, or services without the in-depth domain knowledge of the business they were trying to start, it was a recipe for failure. Of course, those who partnered people who had the necessary knowledge of the business and then used technology and the Internet as tools to create much more efficient businesses were successful such as eBay, Yahoo and Amazon. All had focused on the domain knowledge of their business. For Amazon and eBay, retail was the relevant domain while technology was used to change the retail business model.

When I hear companies and even governments making statements that "digitisation" is the new strategy for Industry 4.0 businesses and for the future economy, I worry they have misunderstood that business strategies and strategies for building the future economy are more than just applying digital technologies. Digitalisation should be seen just as a tool to help businesses manage their restructured business models more efficiently and to reach markets faster and more widely.

The New Economy

In my first edition of this book in 2007, I wrote:

While we have seen many failures by both entrepreneurs and investors during and after the dot.com era, we should not view this as the end of an era for the new economy. This Internet economy phenomenon is no different from any other gold rush we have seen in history. Yes, many were

hurt from the experience, but life has continued, and we now are still seeing entrepreneurial activities sprouting, but at more realistic rates and more sustainable levels. The bubble is not growing so fast and we are now in a steady state of things. Many mistakes were made, but it is important we learn from the mistakes and failures and apply the lessons to our future ventures to ensure a greater chance of success.

True entrepreneurs should not take blind risks. The lessons learnt in the dot.com era provide many examples of how those who want to seek success can reduce their risk factors. I am happy to see so many Apps businesses, especially the platform businesses, do very well in the last decade. Amazon is a well-known story. What about the rest?

Over the last few years Alibaba, Uber, Airbnb, Trip Advisor and eBay were all valued a lot more than companies that invested in R&D, technology development and in building physical assets like factories and stores. It seems that the value of the companies serving the virtual world are more valuable than the brick and mortar companies. And the potential remains great.

I have noticed a pattern among the more successful companies and entrepreneurs, including those in the dot.com days. It appears the more successful entrepreneurs are more grey-haired than the failed ones. Older entrepreneurs have gained much experience from working elsewhere and seen more ups and downs in their working lives, hence, they calculate their risks more soundly than those who have not had prior experience. This is not to say that the younger ones cannot become successful entrepreneurs. The likes of those such as Bill Gates and Mark Zuckerberg started very young, but there are also many more who were not so young when they started.

The Internet and technology or more lately, **digitalisation**, are a very good platform for new businesses, and so far, most companies have got it right. Many have very good revenue models and can grow rapidly as they address the consumer needs using new channels and platforms. I am sure the many new Internet entrepreneurs have learnt from the mistakes made during the dot.com days and have built robust business models for a better chance of achieving success. Remember, while Internet, digitisation and technology remain good tools for most businesses, domain knowledge will make the difference. We will see great disruptions to many industries – banking challenged by Fintech, retail challenged by online stores like Amazon, "uberisation" of the logistics industry will come soon, and many more. Don't make the same mistakes entrepreneurs made during the dot.com days.

The Metaverse

One final point of an even newer economy that is coming our way – the Metaverse. As defined in Dictionary.com, this is "a shared, realistic, and immersive computer simulation of the real world or other possible worlds, in which people participate as digital avatars". I see the Dot.com economy as round 1, the Apps or platform economy as round 2 and the Metaverse will be the round 3 of the New Economy. For those planning to participate in the Metaverse, do learn from the past mistakes so that you can create greater success in the virtual world.

Chapter 19 Summary

Lessons Learnt During the Dot.Com Era – The Tech Bubble Burst

The fall of the dot.com economy provides five key learning lessons for entrepreneurs on how to find success:

Lesson No. 1:
A business is a business whether in the old economy or the new economy.
- *Any business must be driven by basic business strategies and goals such as the ability to sustain growth and have proper revenue models as well as clear profitability goals.*

Lesson No. 2:
An idea alone does not make a business.
- *A business can only survive if the people behind the idea are able to make the transition from a good idea into a good business.*

Lesson No. 3:
Any business requires hard work; there is no shortcut to success.

Lesson No. 4:
Any business must have the right type of money backing it.
- *Too much easy money corrupts the mind and spoils the entrepreneur.*

Lesson No. 5:
Good domain knowledge, not technology alone, is required to run a successful business.

CHAPTER 20

SURVIVING THE GREAT DISRUPTION (THE COVID-19 ECONOMIC IMPACT)

Introduction

Covid-19 is a serious health issue which has caused panic everywhere around the world. For the first time in a long time, this panic is 100 per cent global – which means it has gripped every corner of the world: Asia, North and South America, Australia, New Zealand, all of Europe, countries in Africa and the Middle East. None has been spared from the panic and damage to the global economy.

My sense is that the effect of Covid-19 is worse than what we have experienced in recent history. We had a recession in 1985, followed in the 1990s by the oil crisis, Asian financial crisis and then the global financial crisis. I saw one more in 2014/2015 – the debacle of the oil price drop in Africa – leading to currency collapse in Nigeria and Angola. Covid-19 may not be as bad as the Great Depression of 1929 that lasted ten years, but two to three years is likely to be the minimum.

Starting with the trade war, then Covid-19 causing panic and loss of confidence and then the collapse of the financial market, all economies started a downward tailspin. Is the worst over yet or is this just the beginning of a long drawn and painful downturn? How can everyone – people, companies, and countries survive this and come out stronger? I share my plans – The Great Disruption or Covid-19 Economic Survival Plan.

The Great Depression of 1929

It is worth drawing lessons from the past. History is a good teacher and we must look to history to guide the future. I therefore looked at what happened during the Great Depression and analysed the companies that survived that tumultuous period. Perhaps we can draw some lessons to apply to the current situation and any future disruptions.

Here are some key facts of the Great Depression. Let's start with what caused it. There are many books written about this, so I will just share some brief facts.

- The Great Depression was global and lasted ten years. It was caused by the stock market crash of 1929 and the Fed's reluctance to increase the money supply.
- Investors withdrew money from banks leading to the banking collapse.
- Panicked government leaders tried to protect domestic industries in 1930.
- World trade plummeted 66 per cent as measured in US dollars between 1929 and 1934.
- GDP during the Great Depression fell by half, limiting economic movement.
- Unemployment reached 25 per cent.

These are mainly USA based facts, but I believe other countries faced similar issues.

Winners and Survivors of the Great Depression

In USA alone, around one third or 11,000 banks failed, the stock market lost 90 per cent of value, around 300,000 companies collapsed and closed, and prices of goods and services dropped by 30 per cent (from 1930 to 1932). This deflation hurt producers, farmers and homeowners. By then, the economies of Germany, Brazil, and the economies of Southeast Asia were already depressed too. Globally, companies failed, people became poorer and the global economy became somewhat dysfunctional.

But it was not all gloomy. Remember the saying: "Don't be over optimistic in good times and don't be over pessimistic during bad times, there are opportunities at all times." So, let's look at the survivors and the winners of the Great Depression. Some are familiar names, others may be new to you but each has many lessons for us as we tackle a severe downturn like the one caused by Covid-19. I summarise their stories in the story box below.

Survivors of the Great Depression of 1929

1. **Movie Industry** – Companies started closing. Smaller companies sold tickets at half price and allowed viewing of two movies for the price of one (Double Features) – they survived. They also offered giveaways like free gifts and lucky draws to attract patrons.
2. **Procter & Gamble** – Instead of throttling down its advertising efforts to cut costs, the company actively pursued new marketing avenues, including commercial radio broadcasts.
3. **Martin Guitars** – Kept strong relationship with smaller retailers, designed lower cost high quality products (used technology), created new range of products like violins and wooden jewellery.
4. **Brewers** – It was illegal to sell alcohol to some from 1920 to 1933. Brewers started running dairies, selling meat and venturing into other agricultural enterprises. Brewers were also allowed to make "near beer" – Root Beer. Through product diversification and wait out strategy, they came out of the great depression stronger.
5. **Floyd Bostwick Odlum** – Generated cash before the market crash which Odlum thought was coming. They had a strong cash war chest to start buying companies on the cheap.
6. **Chevrolet** – During the 1920s, Fords were outselling Chevrolets by 10 to 1. Despite the Depression, Chevrolet continued to expand

its advertising budget. By 1931, the "Chevy 6" took the lead in its field and remained there for the next five years.

7. **Coca Cola** – Kept it affordable – adjusted pricing to cater to consumers with lower buying power. Used Santa Claus to show how happy he was after drinking it.

8. **3M** – When people become poorer and cash strapped, they did not throw away things, and instead they adopted the "Make Do and Mend" mentality – 3M tapes helped put broken products together. 3M used technology to develop such new products.

9. **IBM** – Accelerated R&D. Produced state-of-the-art accounting machine to help with complex business accounting. Did leasing in addition to sales (for cash starved customers).

What distinguished the survivors from the rest? If we analyse all the companies that not only survived the Great Depression but also thrived, we will see a few common themes that are worth remembering. Here are some of the winning strategies of these companies:

1. **Modify Business Model to Adapt to New Normal**

   The smaller movie companies had to modify their business model. For example, they partnered popcorn vendors to operate from inside the theatres. Offering two movies for the price of one, and giving free gifts were some other tactics. IBM started a leasing programme for its business machines to help ease its customers' spending. Before this, IBM only sold machines.

2. **Product Diversification/Substitution**

   Martin Guitars used their base technology to create new products like wooden jewellery, violins, and also cost-effective guitars to cater to consumers who had less purchasing power. Brewers who were not allowed to sell alcohol during the prohibition period came up with near beer products like Root Beer as substitutes. The brewers also ventured into necessities like dairy products, agriculture and meats to keep business going during the times when beer sales were down.

3. **Wait Out Strategy – Survive by Doing Other Things Until Recovery**

    This was what the brewers did during the recession. They adopted a wait out strategy until they could come back and do what they knew best – brewing beer. In the meantime, to keep business going they diversified into other products and services to maintain their cash flow.

4. **Cash is King – Conserve Cash and Look for Good Opportunities**

    Floyd Bostwick Odlum were somehow fortunate to have exited the stock market before it crashed. They kept a war chest that allowed them to find good deal from amongst distressed companies and invested when others had no cash to do so. Odlum was listed as the only man who made a fortune during the Great Depression.

5. **Invest in R&D, Advertising, New Market Development**

    IBM increased investment in R&D during the slow business period and created products to solve the increasingly complex business processes. They developed machines to help automate accounting functions which coupled with their cost-effective leasing solutions, helped rapid adoption of new products. 3M's Scotch tape was also a result of increased focus on R&D at the beginning of the Great Depression. Procter & Gamble increased investments in advertising and created new forms of advertising channels. Chevrolet increased, not reduced advertisement spending during the Great Depression and overtook Ford to remain in the lead for five years with their "Chevy 6".

6. **Pricing – Adapt to Lower Buying Power of Consumers**

    Movie theatres had to reduce prices to attract customers back. Coca Cola's pricing remained affordable and people continued to consume the drink. Martin Guitars created cost effective guitars. People needed music to relax from all the stress they faced during the recession years. Even IBM's leasing model was to make their products affordable for cash strapped businesses.

The fact is, during the Depression, consumers didn't stop spending, they looked for better deals and cost-effective products and services. Those companies providing cost effective products and better deals became stronger later. When economies came out of the Depression, consumers remained loyal to such companies.

What about the start-up environment during the Great Depression? I have shared my stories about the three companies that I started during recession years – UTAC, Tri Star Electronics and Infiniti Solutions – all of them did very well. Research has shown that companies that were started during recession years turn out to be stronger and last longer. This was no different during the Great Depression Years. There were a number of companies that were started up during that time. I share a brief description of 10 such companies in the story box below. All of these companies survived and were still going strong as at 2020.

10 Start-Ups During Great Depression that are Still Around Today

1. **Disney** – in troubling times, the Disney brothers knew that people needed an outlet to smile more than ever   they created the Mickey Mouse movie.
2. **Revlon**– affordable cosmetics and skin care, for cash strapped people who still wanted to look good.
3. **SESAC** – established as a licensor of music – protected the many singers who rose to fame as a result of comforting people with their singing.

4. **Publix Super Markets** – Founder started his own grocery store next door to Piggy Wiggly, a grocery store where he worked. The store not only survived next door to its competitor, but eventually became the 1,000-store chain of today.

5. **Hy-Vee** – small general store offering low prices to cater for cash-strapped consumers. Because of their good service, they grew and today have a chain of 225 supermarkets.

6. **Harp's Food Stores** – include "Price Cutter" Food Store. Today, they have 81 supermarkets located across Arkansas, Oklahoma, Missouri, and Kansas.

7. **Ocean Spray Cranberries** – three cranberry companies pooled together to come up with cost effective cranberry sauce (a merger).

8. **King Kullen Grocery** – turned a Queens warehouse into a grocery store – downscale setting, low-cost type of store. Today they operate 29 such chain stores.

9. **Yellow Book USA (Now YP.com)** – offered struggling consumers an efficient opportunity for comparison shopping – let your Fingers do the Walking (rather than wasting petrol driving around looking for deals).

10. **Wipfli** – provides such services as tax preparation, business planning, and corporate finance. The start-up helped businesses stay in business during tough times. Today they remain strong as a consulting and accounting services company.

You can go online and check out all these companies, many are billion dollar companies today.

Masterplan for Survival

The one differentiating factor that helped these companies is that almost all had a masterplan either before they went into the recession, or developed one as they entered the recession. Each had their own masterplan – some of the aspects were the same as others, while some were unique to their company. Earlier I shared some stories of companies that survived the Great Depression and that used a number of strategies as their masterplan.

In this section, I will share the masterplan I came up with for Covid-19. Based on what we know now, this may not be the last time that we will encounter a disruption of the global economy and it is best that we learn how to prepare for the future.

Using the Covid-19 Great Disruption as a basis, I will suggest ways companies can survive the economic impact. First, let me share how I see the whole Covid-19 issue playing out from the beginning till full economic recovery.

We must be prepared for three phases of the impact of the Covid-19 on the global economy and companies and have a strategy for each phase. I think these three phases will be the same for any type of disruption we will face in the future:

- **Phase 1** (first 6 months to 1 year) – Time of ***Chaos and Confusion***, near zero business, uncertain future as health issues spread first and then stabilise
- **Phase 2** (the next 1 to 2 years) – Period of ***Survival or Collapse***, when businesses restart as the health issues settle
- **Phase 3** (beyond 2 to 3 years) – The ***Rejuvenation and Regrowth*** of companies that survived and the start of new stronger start-ups

Of course, we know that not all companies have been badly affected by this pandemic. In fact, some industries and companies, particularly the online platforms did very well. My intent here is to share strategies for those badly affected. But any company can learn from these strategies if it is ever hit by a different disruption that may severely affect the company.

It is most important to get through phases 1 and 2, while phase 3 will be similar to what we see in normal times.

Let me suggest survival strategies for both phases 1 and 2.

Phase 1 Plan (First 6 Months to 1 Year): Time of Chaos and Confusion

1. **Hunker down and survive a period of zero revenue**

    For many, the reality for some is zero revenues as lockdowns cause businesses to shut. For others, like the food industry (as we also saw in the Great Depression years), business improved. As in many countries, those in the grocery and online businesses like video conferencing and e-services promoting home learning, saw business soar. In these times, you should not surrender so quickly but wait for phase 1 to pass. Hunkering down may mean drastically cutting cost like salaries (hopefully temporarily), stretching cash flow or taking in more money if possible. Just hold on tight to your business so that it does not collapse.

2. **Leave no stone unturned for cost reduction (but don't be destructive)**

    Look at every area for cost reduction – other than salaries, there are utilities, transport, allowances, etc. Don't leave any stone unturned. Involve your whole team to identify areas of cost reduction. Do not be destructive in the process and don't indiscriminately cut costs that can prove fatal for the company. For example, don't sack employees, especially the skilled ones who you will need when business comes back. Hiring and training will be costly and may take too long for you to be ready to ride the upturn. Don't burn bridges with partners and stakeholders. Think long term. Everyone will understand as everyone else will be in the same boat.

3. **Renegotiate with your business partners**

    Immediately speak with suppliers, landlords, partners to see if you can stop payment or delay payment. Work with the landlord to allow zero rental for a few months and/or reduced rentals for a period of time. Work with suppliers to give you rebates, discounts, and stretched payment terms. Restructure your payment terms with all partners. While they too will need to survive, it is in their interest for you to survive and remain their partners in the long term.

4. **Look closely at all government assistance schemes**

    In times of crisis, governments will undoubtedly step in to help companies. For example in the Covid-19 era, we saw many initiatives like cheaper loans, delayed tax payments, halting mortgage payments, property tax rebates (to help with rental rebates), salary support – some countries like UK even had up to 90 per cent of salary support to companies for a period of a few months. The Singapore Government instituted several salary support schemes. Avail yourself and your company of all such assistance.

5. **Think like the day you just started your company**

    What do I mean by thinking like the day you started? As every entrepreneur will know, the day you started you had no money, you had no customers, and you had no partners. Well, a zero-revenue episode feels exactly this – the day you started with zero. How did you make it at that time? Although you have more responsibilities now than when you started, think of creative and innovative ideas to help you redo things – become a "Re-Start-up". Remember the definition of an entrepreneur which we defined in Chapter 1?

    "An entrepreneur identifies a problem, uses innovative ways to solve the problem and creates new opportunities using limited resources to create something valuable and meaningful to society."

    The keyword here is – "using limited resources". In a severe downturn, you have very limited resources. A good entrepreneur will be the one who can use the very limited resources left in the company to survive. For those who have not done a start-up before, let me share some tips on how to think like a start-up.

Think Like a Start-Up ... What Does It Mean?

1. Focus on net burn rate (focus on cash flow is critical but not enough)

2. Spend like a start-up (bootstrap again)

3. Treat cash as king as you did when you started

4. Behave like an underdog – survival thinking

One last point for Phase 1: while you are focusing on surviving the first one year, think of how you will move ahead and survive the next phase that may determine your future – the "Life or Death" Phase 2. In other words, start working on your Masterplan for Survival which is Phase 2.

Phase 2 Plan (the Next 1 to 2 Years): Period of Survival or Collapse

The Phase 2 Masterplan is even more important than Phase 1 because it will determine the long-term future of your company. You should in parallel try to survive the initial phase while planning for the next phase (better still if you knew that one day a downturn will come and you already have some plans ready). What are the strategies that can help you in Phase 2? What should your Masterplan look like? We saw earlier in the chapter examples of how during the Great Depression a number of companies which did a great job in their equivalent Phase 2 – IBM, 3M, Martin Guitars, Movie Theatres, Brewers and more – they had great strategies to survive and come out stronger.

Continue to be in a Survival Mode

While you may have to think about restructuring your business models or even moving into new businesses (like the Brewers did during the Great

Depression), what you know best is your current business that you may have spent years building. So, the first thing you have to do is focus on keeping your current business afloat. How can you do this?

- Plan your business based on a 50 per cent demand drop (better still 60 to 80 per cent), for one year minimum, but try two years if you can.
- Re-do your Business Plan to show one to two years survivability
- Keep business cycles short
- Inventory turns must be fast
- Accounts Receivable – keep the cycles short, collect faster
- Sales cycle – make faster decisions – don't drag
- Instead of pure cost reduction, focus on improving efficiency
- Instead of layoffs, try to keep people (salary reduction, short work weeks, etc.)

In other words, become more efficient, keep burn rate slow and manage cash flow very carefully. Don't wait – start planning how you are going to manage with such a huge drop in demand and revenues. Write a fresh business plan (even if it is just a short strategy plan) on how you are going to operate for the next two years. Run a tight ship and focus on all the factors that keep cash flowing and everything lean. Based on research, companies that survive a recession and come out stronger are those that focus on efficiency of their operations and businesses, becoming more productive in the process – doing more with less. Instead of firing, companies that retained people by furloughing them, temporarily reducing their salaries, came out stronger after the recession. Value your talent and don't fire them at the first sign of a crisis.

Make Sure You Have Enough Cash to Last 2 Years

Cash remains king during this period of "Survival and Collapse". Those who can keep cash flow going for one to two years will survive and those who can't, will collapse. What can you do?

- Understand and utilise government financing schemes around the world
- Continue conserving cash, don't wait till you run out (you should have already kept reserves)
- Restructure debts – debts drag down companies – keep debts low
- Look for alternative sources of investors (VCs, crowdfunding, etc.)
- Continue cost reduction, don't wait, cut losses – decide quickly. The more you save, the more you are keeping cash in the company

Don't keep looking internally – look externally to on how you can gather all cash resources to keep you going for the next two years. Governments will no doubt step in as they have always done to keep credit flowing. Keep your eyes open and look for these. At the same time, start speaking with your banks early. Give them confidence you can survive. Don't wait till things are dire before you speak with banks and other stakeholders. If you had done your job in building good relationships with your banks and partners, they will likely help you, but of course don't bet on the banks alone. Today companies have many more funding options, other than VCs and banks, so look for all of these as early as possible (before these sources of funding also dry up).

When the pandemic started we heard of some cases of VC cancelling deals that were almost closed. But after the initial dust settled down, VC continued to invest and defied the popular belief that VCs won't invest in a downturn. Data shows in 2020, more money was invested compared to 2019! Good companies always find the right money.

Funding Opportunities: Finding Investors

Where do you go to look for more money in a severe downturn? Is it at all possible? I shared my own story where I raised money for my three best companies during downturns, some even severe downturns. Tri Star raised bank financing at the beginning of the Asian Financial Crisis in 1997. UTAC raised US$138m at the bottom of the semiconductor cycle (and also during the Asian Financial Crisis) in 1998 and Infiniti Solutions raised US$36m after the dot.com or tech bubble bust, in 2001. So yes, it is possible. But how can you do it. Let me share some key strategies.

How Do You Attract Investors' Money?

- Change, modify and adjust your business model to adapt to the New Normal
- Strengthen your intrinsic value
  - Your Intellectual Property (IP)
  - Your talent/people
  - Your market/customers
  - Your ability to identify new opportunities fast
  - Quickly differentiate from others
- Show your team's ability to be agile and adapt to the New Normal
- Be ahead of your competitors in identifying new opportunities.

There will always be investors in good and bad times. In bad times, it will be a buyers' (investors) market while in good times it will be a sellers' (start-ups) market. What do investors look for in a buyers' market? They look for good deals and to make money later. So, make yourself look like a good deal, not cheap but so attractive that the investor will want to partner you (best that they see the potential to make a lot of money when an exit comes).

As I mentioned earlier, rewrite your business plan. The plan should show how quickly you have been able to adapt to the New Normal. At the same time focus on your intrinsic value. Why did investors invest in your start-up before? They saw some value that will make them money. So now, go back again to the basics and strengthen, sharpen and highlight your new intrinsic values and strengths that clearly differentiate you from others. Your IP, your talent, your market, your business model – all these must be able to impress potential investors if you want to win funding. You must further differentiate yourself from others if you want to attract new money.

Funding Opportunities: Other Sources of Money (Direct and Indirect)

Funding does not come only from new equity investors. There are many other sources of funding that you can tap on to help manage your cash flow. Some are obvious, others are not. I can share the following:

- Your current investors are best positioned to fund you more
- New investors looking for good deals – I discussed this earlier
- Look for new loans to add to the war chest
- Your customers – if they buy you get paid
- Your suppliers – they want to survive too, they might wish to
  - Extend payment terms (this is like additional cash flow)
  - Fund your purchases (like Alibaba)
- Look at your whole supply chain to see who can help you.

The first groups you should approach are your earlier investors. As they have money sunk into your company, they should have the same interest as you to keep the company afloat. Reach out to them early to share your problems and plans. They are your best bet for more funding. Then, other than the new investors and banks, there are other non-financial institution sources of funding that many neglect to consider in tough times (I mentioned earlier how to attract them).

Your customers are your best source of funds. If they buy, they pay, so focus on how you can encourage them to continue to buy. As we saw in the Great Depression, companies had to make their goods and services more affordable for consumers who were already cash strapped. They did not stop spending, rather, they were more careful about how they spent their money. Your suppliers want you to survive, because you pay their bills. So, working with them early to see how both of you can manage your respective cash flows will be important. Similarly, there are other partners in your whole supply chain who may be able to help you stretch your dollar. Look at every potential partner and every area. A little from each will all add up to help you survive.

Stay Close to the Ground, Close to Your Customers

Just as you are facing an unprecedented disruption, so are your customers, your suppliers, your partners, and your government. Everything changes and a New Normal will start emerging as the dust settles after Phase 1. The situation is dynamic and will change quickly. You must also change and quickly adjust to the New Normal. It is most important to keep track of your market and customers – how is the market changing, how are your customers adapting and changing? The more you know about them, the faster you can adapt to continue to serve them. Do not assume their needs remain the same in good and bad times. Stay close to the ground and to your customers to understand them and serve them well at all times.

Understand Your Customer Needs and Tailor to Their Needs

In a recession, buying power lessens but does not dwindle entirely. Customers will look for good deals, so you should look for new markets. Pivot your business and business model. Use technology to improve efficiency and produce cost effective products.

If you understand your customer, the market and the needs of consumers well, you can modify or come up with the appropriate products and services that will meet their needs. In other words, do a new "Product/Market Fit" again to stay relevant. During a recession, customers want to have more cost-effective products – i.e. cheaper but not necessarily of poor quality.

We have to remember that life does not stop in a downturn and businesses do not have to grind to a complete halt in such times. Consumption of goods and services will continue, perhaps not at the same level as before, but people don't stop buying. It is imperative to understand the changes in the needs and wants of your customers and then adapt to be able to continue serving them.

Pivoting During the Covid-19 Crisis (Year 2020)

Let me share a real-life story of a company that adopted some of the strategies I mentioned as part of the Masterplan for Survival immediately when the Covid-19 hit Singapore. This was a company belonging to one of my Masters of Science (Technopreneurship and Innovation Programme) students at NTU, Singapore. I am glad to witness firsthand how this company learnt to quickly survive and pivot to a new business model to help generate some revenue during the lockdown period in Singapore.

The company, Shake Affinity, was in the business of providing "Mobile Bar and Beverage Catering Services", catering mainly to mass functions and events. They provided the full services, from equipment, beverages and people to man the bars. It was a fledgling business. When the lockdown was declared in Singapore in early April 2020, the company's business came to a complete standstill, down to zero revenue. While the government provided some salary support, it was not sufficient for the company as it was not classified as an F&B. An F&B would have received 50–75 per cent salary support. My student kept me updated. They were in dire straits not knowing if they would survive.

I am glad the founders took action and thought of how to survive. One of the points I mentioned as part of the masterplan is for companies to observe and listen to the customer closely to understand changing needs. The team did exactly that. Here is what they noted:

1. Observed environment market changes – Bubble Tea shops ordered to close

2. Consumers still wanted to drink bubble tea

3. Company had all the infrastructure to prepare beverages

4. Home delivery became more popular.

They immediately sprang into action and developed the following strategies:

1. Wait out strategy – sell something else while waiting for the recovery

2. Pivot – use your base infrastructure for product diversification

3. Develop new channels for marketing and reaching consumers.

The result was the creation of an online business for home delivered "make your own" bubble tea. Gulp.sg was created as a pivot strategy.

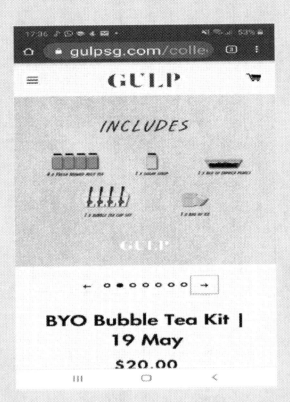

I asked my student to share her experience and she told me that the company did think of an e-commerce strategy sometime in late 2017 but never got around to it. Circumstances forced them to accelerate their plans to take advantage of the lockdown situation. In the first week, the team sat down to develop a strategy, do R&D, design the product and packaging, prepare a website and the logistics to execute. By the second week, they started a product/market fit study by testing their business model and product with family and friends. By the third week they modified what was needed based on initial feedback and by the end of week three, they started their new business! Now this is fast execution and I am sure with that kind of attitude and resilience the team demonstrated, their company will not just survive but will last for a long time to come. Now the company will have two business models in the New Normal – the original catering service and a second – Home-based Make Your Own Bubble Tea.

As Table 20.1 illustrates, during the Great Depression, consumers did not stop spending but they looked for good deals, cost effective products and value for money products. The companies that adapted, like the many grocery stores that provided cheaper products, survived and thrived and many who started during the Great Depression are still around today. And better still, when economies recover post recession years, the customer remains loyal to those companies that gave them value for money products and services.

Communications Must be Fast

Many entrepreneurs tend to underestimate the value of good communications especially in a crisis. Looking at how many governments handled the Covid-19 situation, there are many examples of great communication and also poor communication. The great ones were transparent, clear and gave coherent instructions and guidelines: people felt confident listening to their leaders. For example, the New Zealand prime minister spoke daily with a consistent structure providing updates and advice for the people. In Malaysia, at

Table 20.1: Masterplan for Survival

MASTERPLAN FOR SURVIVAL

STAYING CLOSE TO CUSTOMERS
1. During the Depression, consumers didn't stop spending but they looked for better deals and cost-effective products and services
2. Those companies providing cost effective products and better deals came out stronger later
3. When economies came out of the Depression, consumers remained loyal to such companies

Consumer Spending by Product Type
In billions – 1987 prices

	Perishables	% decline	Semi-durables	% decline	Durables	% decline	Services	% decline	total	% decline
1928	$164.3		$59.9		$38.4		$269.6		$532.3	
1929	$168.3		$61.7		$40.3		$284.4		$554.8	
1930	$164.8	2%	$56.1	9%	$30.9	23%	$269.0	5%	$520.8	6%
1931	$164.4	0%	$53.6	4%	$26.4	15%	$257.6	4%	$501.9	4%
1932	$154.1	6%	$46.9	13%	$20.0	24%	$236.0	8%	$456.9	9%
1933	$151.1	2%	$42.7	9%	$20.2	-1%	$233.5	1%	$447.6	2%

5 p.m. every day, the spokesman went on TV to give consistent updates of data and instructions. People knew what to expect and where and when they would get new updates and instructions, and from the same voice. There were also a great many leaders who were not transparent, did not have a consistent structure, gave confusing messages, sometimes changing instructions multiple times a day, not coming on at a specified time each day and having too many different people giving instructions, thus confusing the population.

In a crisis, communicate more, communicate regularly, communicate clearly, and communicate consistently with a proper structure so that people keep their trust in you. Remain confident that you are in control and know what you need to do – and please communicate well.

Keep All Your Stakeholders Informed of What is Happening

All stakeholders who have an interest in you should know as much as possible about what is happening and feel that they can continue to count on you. Remember suppliers are in the same boat – let them know the situation you are facing, how you are managing and what help you need. Your customers should remain confident that you can continue to service them. Employees too need to be updated on the company's situation and future plans; their loyalty and commitment are important. Don't forget all other partners – such as your banks, supply chain partners, government agencies and trade associations.

Remember, Phase 2 is a period of either survival or collapse for your company – this is the most critical stage during any severe downturn. How well you do during this phase will determine how strong your company will be in the future and how long you will last. Research has shown that companies that managed to cut costs deeper and faster and continued to invest (because they had the cash), did better than their peers when the upturn came. Once you achieve some stability during Phase 2, start planning for Phase 3.

Phase 3 Plan (Beyond 2 to 3 Years): Rejuvenation and Regrowth

I will not spend too much time on this part because this will naturally happen as you go through Phase 2 – the Survival Phase. While you are surviving, you should be planning for your company's future, too. If you survive well and come out strongly, you will do well in the New Normal. It seems that 85 per cent of companies that were growth leaders before a downturn, toppled in bad times. This means they did not have a masterplan for survival and entered Phase 3 as weaker companies.

Planning for Phase 3 is rather like doing a new strategic plan for your company. Here are the elements you need to pay attention to.

1. Do a SWOT analysis of your company
2. Identify the opportunity gaps early
3. Restructure your business model and business structure to win in Phase 3
4. Start investing early – technology, market access, skills.

Conclusion

In summary, when entering a downturn or a crisis, make sure you have a good masterplan for survival.

Managing cash and cashflow carefully are priorities. Costs should be eliminated wherever possible. Reducing payroll costs should focus on cutting the overall overhead while retaining talent, in other words, wage cuts should be favoured over layoffs. Once costs are reduced, prices should be brought down to match consumer expectations.

If you can create a war chest of cash in the company, you may find good opportunities to invest while others cannot. You may find good buys – cheaper assets (plants, machinery), skilled talent, technology, or acquire another company. In a crisis, there will be opportunities to invest in new areas, so be prepared to do so. Do not focus only on cutting cost but also prepare for the future by investing in areas that allow you to tap on opportunities that may arise.

Surviving the Great Disruption (The Covid-19 Economic Impact)

Businesses affected by any great disruption go through three main phases. In the example of Covid-19, the recovery takes the following route:

- **Phase 1** (first 6 months to 1 year) – Time of **Chaos and Confusion**, near zero business, uncertain future as health issues spread first

- **Phase 2** (the next 1 to 2 years) – **Period of Survival or Collapse**, when businesses restart as health issues settle

- **Phase 3** (beyond 2 to 3 years) – The **Rejuvenation and Regrowth of Companies** that survived and the start of **New Stronger Start-ups**

To emerge from such a disruption, companies need to do the following:

1. Go into a **Survival Mode** – Remember there are no **heroes, only survivors** in a downturn.

2. Think like a start-up:
   - Cash flow is critical
   - Hunker down to survive a period of zero revenues
   - Focus on net burn rate, bootstrap again and treat cash as king
   - Restructure debts.

3. **Plan** your business on a 50–80 per cent demand drop for at least a year, better two.

4. Layoff last, try to keep key people (salary reduction, short work weeks) so that talent and experience is retained for the eventual upturn.

5. **Keep Business Cycles Short** – Inventory turns, sales.

6. **Become Cost Efficient** – Leave no stone unturned for cost reduction, negotiate with suppliers, landlords and partners.

7. Keep your stakeholders informed – **Communicate quickly and clearly**. Remember your customers and suppliers are in the same boat.

8. Strengthen your intrinsic value, look at IP, customers, differentiation, new markets, **adopt technology**.

9. **Stay Close to the Ground** – Listen to your customers.

10. **Think Like an Entrepreneur** – "An entrepreneur identifies a problem, uses innovative ways to solve the problem and creates a new opportunity using limited resources to create something valuable and meaningful to society."

CHAPTER 21

GOVERNANCE, CULTURE, DEAL FATIGUE, TEAM DISAGREEMENT AND BACKUP PLANS

I will now share some experiences I had during the early stages of starting a company. The first relates to how entrepreneurs should think about governance issues right from the beginning. The second is about how everyone involved in a start-up can end up feeling drained as a result of the tough and tiring process of starting a company. This can even affect the cohesion of the team at the beginning and later stages. Lastly, I will talk about the need for backup plans.

Governance

What is governance? This is how your start-up is managed and how decisions are made. One thing I have always believed in is that you should ensure proper governance structures in your company right from day one. If you are planning to become a very big company one day, there is no reason why strict governance structures should not be instituted from day one, which will make it easier for the company to operate once it becomes big and especially once it becomes a public listed company.

I have come across many start-ups that did not focus on putting in place proper structures. Later when they needed to raise external funding, whether in the form of bank debt, equity or an IPO, they faced tremendous difficulties in presenting the company as being properly managed. External financiers will want to see some structure, sensible governance and control systems, and some pragmatic decision-making processes. The fact of the matter is that there are many entrepreneurs and SME bosses who are the sole decision-makers. They do not rely on a structured process in making decisions, including how company money will be spent.

It is rather inefficient to first operate a start-up with sub-standard governance structures and then attempt to institute more structure and stringent processes some years later when the company becomes bigger. Once the corporate culture and the operating structure of the company have been entrenched, changes are difficult to make. Cleaning out the cupboard and getting rid of old skeletons is a difficult task. My advice is for start-ups to think long term and adopt structures that provide continuity, including the way the board is structured, the decision authority of the management team and how documentation and operating procedures are maintained.

Of course, there is an argument to be made that too bureaucratic a structure will make the company less flexible, especially when it needs to be flexible during the start-up stage. This is also quite true as you do not want to have too rigid structures which make it difficult for you to operate. The right balance should be found, and I would say that it is better to err on the side of better governance than not. You will appreciate this a lot more when you grow big, and grow big you must one day if that is why you started your company.

Strategic Planning and Governance at UTAC and Infiniti Solutions

When I started UTAC, I gathered with me a team that had worked with me in senior positions at Texas Instruments (TI). TI was great on governance, ethics, systems and structures. My dream for UTAC was to become one of the top players in the semiconductor SATS (Semiconductor Assembly and Test Services). So my first task was to bring the entire team together in May 1998 for a two-day retreat, away from office, renting a function room at a hotel, and hiring a professor from the University of Birmingham to conduct a Strategic Planning Session – to develop the vision, mission and all other necessary ingredients for a good strategic plan. We also started designing our logo to reflect what we wanted the company to stand for.

The second task was to get a team member to start developing a specifications system on how everything will be managed in the company. We knew how a good system worked at TI, so it was not a difficult job for us. It was tedious but doable.

The third task was to hire a consultant to fill the gap that existed among my team members – developing a proper financial management system. It was difficult but we managed to develop a system that lasted many years.

The rest is history. UTAC was a perfect start-up story and we looked like a structured big company right from day one. This was one of the factors that allowed us to win over so many "blue-chip" customers to do business with us – because we looked as good as any other big competitor at that time.

And better still, in a span of three years, UTAC was able to file for and obtain approval for a dual NASDAQ and Singapore Stock Exchange listing (which we abandoned because of the tech bubble burst in April 2001). Why were we able to get the approvals so quickly – because we did not have to do any major restructuring or restating of accounts or anything else. We had been operating like a big company right from day one!

By the way, we replicated the process for Infiniti Solutions – setting up all the systems as we had in UTAC right from day one. Infiniti Solutions too did not have difficulties getting NASDAQ approval for a listing in 2004.

Another short note on governance. Typically, when we gather a team to start up, we cannot possibly cover every skill set that we will ever need to run the company well. It is also not necessary to bring in so many people at too early a stage. So how can an entrepreneur manage to put in a proper governance structure to ensure that the company is not going in the wrong direction? I suggested in an earlier chapter that the start-up bring in external experts to help. If you can afford to, perhaps engage some well qualified people whom you trust to join you as a board director. You will have to compensate this person by giving some free shares not just for the effort but also the risk the person is taking for having to conduct his or her fiduciary duty as a board member. Nevertheless, do not bring in a yes-man who will agree with whatever you say. This will not be helpful in the long run as this person will not add much value. I would rather bring in a person who is able to and willing to challenge you when needed, so that a final robust decision can be made for the good of the company and therefore for the good of the entrepreneur and the rest of the team. I have seen great companies fail because the board of directors consists of friendly parties who refuse to challenge a dominant CEO or entrepreneur who may be heading in the wrong direction.

You should also bring in board members with skills that can make up for the lack of skills in your team. You should look for domain experts who can help you oversee areas which you are not so familiar with. For example, if none of your team members have financial expertise, it may be good to add a board member who has that expertise and who can help you spot financial issues. Often the entrepreneur's network may be limited while a board member may have a very wide network of business contacts, e.g. regulatory agency contacts, VCs, customers, banks and other areas. These contacts and networks can make a huge difference in helping your company access the right people, the decision-makers.

Culture

Related to governance, I would like to touch a little on the culture of the company. It is one of the most important elements to build a sustainable business that can survive all the ups and downs and the test of time. Many start-ups forget to focus on this when building companies. What is company culture? There are many definitions; here is what I think: Culture – The beliefs and values shared by people who work in an organisation. This is determined by several factors:

1. How all employees behave with each other and the work ethics within the company and how the company behaves towards their employees through training, professional development, etc.

2. How people in your company behave with customers, suppliers and outside partners

3. The relationship of the people in the company with their internal and external stakeholders

4. The attitude towards corporate social responsibility, serving the community, the environment, etc.

UTAC Story on Taiwanese Culture

At UTAC, when we started planning our operations, we were looking at equipment to purchase for our manufacturing needs. I brought a team of professional managers and engineers from Texas Instruments (TI) to join me. TI was a great company with ethics and corporate culture that permeated the whole company. We conducted ourselves very professionally. There were a few incidents when I had to fight very hard with the board members of UTAC (who were mainly Taiwanese – and the Taiwanese culture is quite different from TI or the Singapore culture; fortunately I knew that even as I started UTAC with them). On one occasion, one of the key board members came to me and asked me to purchase equipment from his contact. He exerted a lot of pressure on me but I resisted. I explained that my approach to purchasing equipment was for my engineering team to do a thorough benchmarking exercise of all potential suppliers and based on an objective assessment, we will choose the one that best meets our needs. I refused to buy what the Taiwanese wanted me to buy, but promised to include that supplier as one in our assessment. In the event, our objective assessment method chose a Japanese company, not the Taiwanese supplier. It is important that we maintain a high level of ethics and consistency as a culture for the company so as not to be led down the wrong path. This is the only way to build a long lasting, sustainable and respected company.

In an earlier chapter, I mentioned about how one of my board members in UTAC wanted to sell cheap shares to his friend. I resisted and that cost me the loss of my own company. One should never compromise ethics in building a long-lasting reputation which is much better than making a quick buck.

As a leader of the company, the entrepreneur must establish the right culture which will be critical to keep the stakeholders connected. These include your customers, suppliers, employees and investors. Culture is typically driven by (and also drives) the vision and mission of the company.

The mission statement typically includes a summary of the beliefs of the organisation. The culture of a company is usually reflected in the attitude and behaviour of the leaders, the attitude and role of the individuals in the workplace (e.g. open plan offices, team-based working, etc.), the image it presents to the outside world and the attitude of the people towards change.

It is interesting that many entrepreneurs do not think about this important part of doing a start-up – culture. When I started my companies, I focused on visioning, missioning and values systems to institute a culture that worked excellently.

Deal Fatigue

In negotiating a deal with potential investors, sometimes both sides should give and take a little. If everyone holds firmly to their starting position, which cannot possibly result in a deal being consummated, then two things may happen. One, everyone continues to fight and in the process become tired and fatigued. Two, everyone is frustrated and tempers fly while nothing seems to move in the desired direction. Dragging out the negotiation process can be counterproductive. Instead of focusing on building a company, which in itself requires tremendous energy, the entrepreneur and his team could be distracted by too much time negotiating with investors.

Before starting any negotiations, particularly with potential investors, you need to be aware that deal fatigue could end in a disaster and a possible premature end to the start-up that you are trying to create. Be prepared to face a long-drawn affair when negotiating, but more importantly, be prepared to be a little flexible and have a mindset that you want a win-win outcome for everyone. Remember that the other party you are negotiating with is later going to be your partner for a very important task – perhaps the most important one in your life. Even if the deal falls through, don't burn your bridges. In life, you never know when and under what circumstances you may face the other parties again. Be diplomatic and professional when handling any negotiations. The biggest worry of all is that you become tired and discouraged that you give up even before you start.

Team Disagreements

Another experience that can be counterproductive, especially in the negotiation process, is how the founding team stays together. Given the very high level of anxiety in structuring the deal as potential investors carve out favourable positions for themselves, the entrepreneur and team will feel they are giving away too much.

Everyone starts with very high expectations, and but when they fail to achieve it, they are disappointed. It is not just the disappointment one should worry about, but more importantly, how the founding team reacts to the mounting pressure and tension during this process. Some team members might be willing to accept a compromised position in the deal while others might feel that too much will be given away to the potential investor. This then creates tension among the team members, leading to potentially big rifts which if not handled well can even result in the team breaking up. What future does the start-up have if the team members quarrel among themselves and end up not being cohesive? The bad feelings that might develop will prove to be obstacles throughout the journey.

The team leader should therefore manage the process delicately to avoid situations of team disagreements developing. To achieve success, you need a highly integrated team, not team members unhappy with one another. It may seem like an obvious point, but the situations can be real, and many have failed to handle it well, resulting in the start-up never taking off because the team broke up.

I would advise that the whole negotiation process with potential investors be kept as short as possible. Everyone should be prepared to give in a little and view this as an investment in the start-up – this investment I am referring to are the intangible ingredients one needs to create successful companies. Such intangible ingredients help build the emotional strength of the team as well as the emotional bond with all the stakeholders. Many fail to think about this intangible investment and end up losing a lot in the end.

Divide and Conquer at UTAC

I would like to share a story that I have not shared before about having a cohesive team. I have emphasised many times the importance of having a cohesive and integrated team. Such a team is necessary to execute the start-up well, and to handle very tough and stressful situations throughout the whole entrepreneurship journey (and believe me there will many of such occasions). There is another reason why you need not only a cohesive, integrated team, but one that you can also trust.

When I started UTAC, I gathered a group of people for the senior management positions who had worked with me for many years at Texas Instruments (TI). I had groomed many of them and helped them to succeed in gaining managerial positions within TI. There were a couple who would have failed to get promoted and risen to higher levels had I not personally intervened to make difficult management decisions and had I not personally trained them well.

UTAC, as I mentioned earlier, was a "fairy tale" start-up that I had planned myself for a couple of years, bringing in the team members at later stages to join me. I selected those people I trusted and could work well with and I gave them shares. All the key people became millionaires when UTAC was listed in 2004.

Disaster struck when I had to fight with a couple of Taiwanese board members who were willing to compromise governance and compromise the interest of the minority shareholders of UTAC (who were mainly employees whom I had allocated shares to). They were going to sell UTAC shares cheap to their friends and I did not allow it. I fought the board members who wanted to do this, confident that my whole team could be broken up.

I am sure everyone has heard of the term "divide and conquer" (the British used it in many of their colonies to weaken societies for their own interest. India was one such victim). It was my bad luck that some of the Taiwanese board members managed to "buy over" a couple of my key people whom I trusted, making it possible for the Taiwanese to force me out of my own company. Using a "divide and conquer" approach, the Taiwanese gained the upper hand and I learned a most valuable lesson in life – never blindly trust everyone.

A majority of my management team was disgusted at what happened. Many also left UTAC with me and together we started Infiniti Solutions, our next big start-up. These guys remain my very good friends although we no longer work together in the same company.

Plan A, Plan B, Plan C

There is no such thing as sure success. In the real world, there is no guarantee things will turn out as planned, and in truth, the chance of failure for start-ups is much higher than the chance of success. What does this mean for a group of people starting a company? It is about making backup plans.

The entrepreneur should be able to visualise some of the possible outcomes even when the company has only just started. And it is worth penning these down, even if it is done informally, especially as a means to plan and communicate among the team members running the start-up. In this way, the team can avoid disappointment when the best possible outcomes do not occur as they already have other plans for an imperfect outcome scenario. For example, if the team had originally planned to raise a certain amount of money to start the company but did not reach the target amount and therefore unable to invest in basic essential, do they just give up? Obviously not. They cannot give up so easily. They should have alternative plans on standby, plans that can be implemented with less money.

However, more important than being able to execute an alternative plan is the level of comfort of all the team members – they must know exactly what they would need to do and where they might be headed should things not work out as planned. At all times, the entrepreneur and the team members should have at least two, or preferably three plans at the back of their minds. I prefer to have three, which I call Plan A, Plan B and Plan C.

Plan A is the best-case scenario or what one might call a blue-skies scenario in which everything falls into place. The team is able to resolve every problem and continue to meet the desired targets they set for themselves. Even if things might not be perfect, in such a scenario the company still has a great chance of creating what was originally conceived.

What about Plan B and Plan C? Regarding Plan B, I prefer to call it an intermediate plan in a scenario in which things might not work out exactly as planned, but some amount of success can still be achieved. Perhaps, the company may become bigger, but not as big as originally planned. Perhaps, because of insufficient funds raised, instead of doing everything within the company, certain parts of the business may be outsourced, while keeping all the core competencies within the company. Or perhaps, the founder pivots and does something different from what was originally conceived but still creates a viable company. The company might look different and may not be as big as originally envisaged, but nonetheless a good company can be created.

Plan C, the worst-case scenario, is one in which things go terribly wrong, nothing works, and the start-up is facing near failure. But near failure does not mean total failure. In such a scenario, the team should be looking at how they can survive such a bad situation and find ways to keep themselves going, even if they are no longer able to come up with any results close to what they had planned for originally. The survival strategy, initially, will be for the company, but eventually for the team members themselves if the company finally fails. This part about the individual members planning their own fallback plan should the start-up fail has been underestimated by many. If the company collapses, what will each person do? How will they continue with their lives? How will they support their families? It is best each has a plan ready if such an eventuality of failure descends upon the company and them.

Why do I say it is necessary for Plan A, Plan B and Plan C to be outlined in the very early stages? It is obviously prudent to have backup plans for contingencies, but the less obvious point is that the people involved in the start-up – the entrepreneur, the team members, and the employees – will have a lot more peace of mind if they knew about their own fallback position. If they started the whole journey knowing they had only two alternatives – the first, success as planned, and the second, failure – without a clue of what to do next, such a team might not have the necessary clear consciousness to fully focus on company work, especially when the situation is difficult and everyone is under pressure.

The backup plans – Plan B and Plan C are not included in the formal business plan; they are something you and your team members must have recorded somewhere else. In the formal business plan, you have to show optimism and confidence in achieving Plan A. Of course, the formal business plan should have all the contingency plans in place so that your stakeholders will be assured you have a robust business plan. But if you start showing Plan B and Plan C in your formal business plan, your other stakeholders, especially the investors, may end up doing one of two things. They might either get worried about your confidence and ability to execute the plan and end up not investing in your company, or they might then decide to use Plan B to make investment decisions and therefore lower the valuation of the company. So, make sure you show optimism in your formal business plan but have your Plan B and Plan C ready should things not go according to Plan A.

Planning for Infiniti Solutions

When we started Infiniti Solutions, the four of us founders knew we were beginning our start-up in a very difficult time. We were confident of ourselves since we had created a successful company in record time (UTAC). We did see all our stars aligned – we saw the opportunity, we had a great team, and we needed to look for the third star, the Star of the Investor. If we could find the right investors, our stars would be aligned. We started by putting up US$500,000 of our own money as seed funding. As we developed our business plan, we also developed a Plan A, a Plan B, and a Plan C.

Plan A involved two things: acquiring a test lab in the USA, and almost immediately after, starting an operation in Singapore. To do this, we needed to raise a lot more money. Because the market was quite bad, we realised raising funds might not be easy, and therefore developed a Plan B, which was to acquire the test lab in the USA, and then operate that lab until we grew big enough to raise another round of funds. If we failed to acquire the lab, our next plan would be to start a new factory ourselves. Our Plan C was this: if we failed to raise any money, all we would have was the initial US$500,000 we ourselves had invested. We would pay ourselves low salaries, and if we could not raise funds, we would pay ourselves even less and try to stretch the company for one year. Instead of buying new assets or building a factory, we might transform ourselves into a consultancy company to try to earn some money. If we failed to earn income, we would run out of cash after a year, upon which we would all go out and look for new jobs. Despite having all these backup plans, we knew if our team could not do it, no other team could do it either.

A little later in our company's life cycle, after we had acquired our USA test lab, we again put together our Plan A, Plan B, and Plan C. Plan A was to be blue skies, which meant we would build our factory in Singapore. But the industry environment was so tough it did not make sense to start a greenfield factory in Singapore when there were already so many players out there with excess capacity. Plan A was also very difficult to achieve because we did not have too much cash left to build another factory after having paid cash for the test lab acquisition. Thus, we had Plan B.

Plan B involved looking around to acquire another company that might be in trouble during the downturn of the semiconductor industry. Such times are the best for making acquisitions. This acquisition would be done with minimal cash through some stock swap arrangement. What then was Plan C? Plan C was to just continue running the company with a small test lab in the USA, with the management team perhaps relocating to the USA to run that small business ourselves instead of relying on the old management teams of the acquired company, which we had left intact after the acquisition.

I am glad to say we managed to stick to Plan A for the first phase of the company and executed Plan B for the second phase where instead of starting a greenfield factory in Singapore, we acquired a mass production factory in the Philippines. Infiniti did well enough to earn an approval to list on the NASDAQ in the year 2004 (although we abandoned the IPO after completing the whole roadshow).

In the end we exited Infiniti Solutions successfully – but without having our contingency Plan B and Plan C, my team would have been much more stressed and might have been distracted from our main task of building the company we envisioned. Starting and running Infiniti Solutions was not without tremendous stress and pain. It has not been easy since we saw two very bad downturns in succession – and before we could fully recover from the first one, the second downturn hit us. But by then, we already knew how to survive, as we are survivors in our industry.

Chapter 21 Summary

Governance, Culture, Deal Fatigue, Team Disagreement and Backup Plans

- A well-run company will have proper policies set in place to govern key operational matters.

- Put in place a proper and good governance system in your start-up right from day one to avoid unnecessary cleaning up later. Not doing so may deter institutional investors from coming on board.

- Invite good board members or advisors who can add value beyond what team members can provide for your company.

- A good HR policy sets out the framework under which people are hired and treated, the obligations of employers and employees and the standards of behaviour.

- Company culture on the other hand cannot be governed by policy. It can be defined as the shared values, attitudes and standards of behaviour and respect for others that can only be inculcated by the leadership and set by example for others to follow.

- A working environment where people have shared values and beliefs; and a common goal as to where they see the company going are less likely to see team disagreement. They are also less likely to break down under deal fatigue.

- In brief, plans, policies and shared values are not fool proof. It is important to have backup plans should the inevitable happen. Because Plan A rarely works, you want to be ready to execute an alternate plan when things don't go according to plan.

CHAPTER 22

ENVIRONMENTAL FACTORS FOR A GOOD ENTREPRENEURSHIP ECOSYSTEM

Creating a Good Entrepreneurial Environment

Governments and cities should be looking at how to create a good entrepreneurship ecosystem. In other words, what are the important ingredients needed to create an entrepreneurial environment conducive for start-ups and nurturing for entrepreneurs to thrive. I will discuss the **Stars** that need to be aligned to create an ecosystem that is conducive for creating a good start-up economy.

Let me again address the perennial question of whether entrepreneurship can be taught and nurtured or if it is a trait one is born with. If we believe it is inborn, then there is very little we can do, except to try to make countries that have less entrepreneurial economies attractive places to live in, and to attract the people whom we believe can become great entrepreneurs to live in these countries. At the same time, as the countries become more attractive, they can avoid losing their own domestic potential entrepreneurs to other more attractive countries through emigration. In such a scenario where we believe entrepreneurship is inborn or just a matter of nature, there is very little we can do to influence entrepreneurship to become ingrained in people and to foster such a desired spirit in people.

However, if we feel entrepreneurship can be taught and nurtured, then countries and societies can help develop the spirit of enterprise and train the entrepreneurial mind. Such an approach would create greater chances for entrepreneurs to blossom and increase the likelihood for entrepreneurship to succeed in less entrepreneurial economies. It then remains for us to identify what is required to teach and train the mind to make it easier for entrepreneurs to succeed. We can thereby create the right environment and conditions, which will help us develop a more entrepreneurial society.

Therefore, it is useful to understand the challenges countries face in creating entrepreneurial economies. Singapore is a good example of an economic development model, which did not in the past greatly support entrepreneurship development. It was excellent in attracting foreign direct investment of established companies and also took a direct role in owning and running companies. This created a challenging environment for the success of home-grown companies.

The Old Singapore Model of Success – Not by Entrepreneurship

For those who have been following the development of Singapore society over the last 30 years or so, it is obvious that the thinking of many senior political leaders is in the concept of discovering "a few good men". The belief is that leaders (and hence entrepreneurs) are born with the necessary skills, and therefore, these people simply remain to be discovered. The discovery approach is a rather simple method of assessing the academic abilities of people, if they are academically smart, then they are most likely natural leaders. Considering the view that leaders are born and not made to achieve success, it is important to discover the born leaders as early as possible in their lives. Thus, a path should be created to enable these future leaders to be captured in the system. This is a self-fulfilling exercise. People with academic skills are given more opportunities, hence in a structured system, they have a greater chance of success with their paths smoothened for them. This is what we call a scholar system, which the Singapore system strongly endorses, and which is quite typical of an oriental way of life.

It is therefore understandable why many CEOs of Government Linked Companies (GLCs) in Singapore are former senior military officers or senior government officers, all of whom were scholars before they could even make it to the rank of senior officers. The belief is the same – one measure is good enough to discover the potential – the academic excellence model of good grades, which once you have, will let you be a good leader, entrepreneur, or CEO. I like the quote (which I shared in an earlier chapter) attributed to our founding deputy prime minister, Mr. Goh Keng Swee, often considered the architect of the Singapore economy. After some time, he realised that this thinking that a scholar can be a good entrepreneur is a fallacy.

Nurturing Entrepreneurship

My belief is that entrepreneurship can be developed, taught, and nurtured. Often, the latent entrepreneurial talent is never discovered unless the environment is conducive to unleashing that potential or unless the person sees the light with more knowledge and greater exposure, including the development of a different mindset right from his or her school days. Our problem in Singapore is that the environment had been so harsh that only hardy entrepreneurs were discovered, leaving many more to remain undiscovered or to discover their talent in other forms. In contrast, people in more entrepreneurial economies discover their entrepreneurial spirit much more readily because the environment draws it out of them much more easily than in countries where the environment is not so well developed. I shared in an earlier chapter how one can learn entrepreneurship.

The question entrepreneurs are often asked is, when did they start becoming an entrepreneur? Some will reply that they started very young, experimenting with things at an early age, while some will answer that they did entrepreneurial things at their work place as it was a natural thing to do, and yet others will say they only really started after they retired from their careers. These answers again give hope that entrepreneurs are not just born but can be nurtured and discovered depending on the environment. The common theme for all is that entrepreneurship is a mindset. And if one can develop that mindset, then one can become an entrepreneur.

Unless there is a belief that entrepreneurship can be developed and nurtured, I do not see the possibility of any country or society succeeding in creating an entrepreneurial economy. This applies particularly for societies that have been used to the scholar system or to a system that was driven primarily by a corporate-based economy consisting of large multinational corporations or large GLCs. This requires nothing short of a change in mindset. The most important change in mindset, which is needed at the government level as well as at the societal level, is the conviction that entrepreneurship can be nurtured and developed, and that the government and society can at least play a part in aiding the process.

Government and Entrepreneurship

Why does the government have to be involved in the development of entrepreneurship, many may ask? The problem for Singapore, unfortunately, is that the government is already involved in so many businesses, social, and political areas that it is difficult to achieve anything unless the government does something about it. Also, the people of Singapore are already so used to the government leading the way, and for the government to change the direction first before the people will take the initiative.

For example, in Singapore, the definition of success in the past was so narrowly defined as one of having achieved academic excellence, obtaining a government scholarship, and landing a good administrative services job or a job in a very large multinational company or large GLC. Since a whole generation has been ingrained with such beliefs right from their school days, it becomes difficult to change their thinking. The only way out for the existing generation is, once again, for the government to play a prominent role in getting things started and enticing Singaporeans out of their inertia. Once there is momentum, the government must take a few steps back, slowly, one step at a time, until the whole entrepreneurship momentum can be sustained on its own, driven by the private sector. The government can continue to play the role of the facilitator and creator of a much more conducive environment that can sustain the momentum.

This will of course work on the premise that the government believes it does not have to be directly involved in shaping the landscape and that the private sector can sustain the momentum by itself. If the government still feels it should be the biggest player, then I do not see any chance for an entrepreneurial economy to emerge. Such a plan will be doomed for failure if the same approach is adopted by the government – that is, to implement policies, rules, and regulations suited more for the bigger GLCs and multinational companies, and for the government to be directly involved in doing business.

Many critics say we should not depend on the government to promote entrepreneurship and that it should be purely private sector driven. On the surface, these are all valid arguments, but in the same breath, I say these are academic arguments, especially for countries like Singapore.

From speaking with businessmen and entrepreneurs who have succeeded despite the tough environment, and also speaking with people who have tried and failed, I've found the common argument is that the government still has a lot to do when it comes to promoting entrepreneurship. At the very least, the government getting less involved in business, less involved in picking winners, and less involved in influencing the outcome of companies is already a big step. What the government can do for a start is to not be so involved as I have just outlined. And if the government is not engaged in planning exits from some areas like picking winners, etc., there is little chance of the private sector doing very much more, which is what is really needed to make entrepreneurship thrive in Singapore.

In Singapore there are many GLCs that are funded and supported by the government. They typically compete with start-ups for contracts, especially government contracts. The problem is that currently, the GLCs are in so many businesses, it's impossible to compete. They rarely work with smaller companies to use their IPs capabilities. So, the only way for start-ups and SMEs to succeed locally is to look at areas which GLCs do not yet occupy, or are too big to pivot. Start-ups and SMEs should hold their IP close to their chests if they ever want to partner GLCs for contracts.

Competition in Vietnam

I was once advising a start-up in Singapore that focused on SMART cities technology. They developed an interesting technology that could help with smart control of street lightings. They had some initial traction in a couple of cities in Indonesia. They then went on to bid for a project in Vietnam. There was a government-linked company (GLC) that also bid for the same project. Now, this start-up had a technology superior to what the GLC had. The Vietnam authorities were keen on the start-up's technology and were keen to engage them. The best outcome would have been for the GLC to approach the Singapore start-up to join forces for the GLC to be the main implementer using the start-ups technology. But instead, someone from the GLC went to warn the Vietnam authorities that the start-up is small and may not survive long and they should therefore not award the project to that company. What a pity – instead of joining forces, the GLC wanted to "kill" the start-up. I heard of a few similar examples over the years when I was in Parliament.

The first step in the whole entrepreneurship journey therefore has to start with the government, but it does not and will not end with the government. In the long-term, when we reach a steady state, we will not need to depend on the government. Neither will the government be able to do much once the momentum is in place. I am glad that in Singapore we have seen good momentum in recreating the entrepreneurial economy and the government has played a significant role in facilitating this.

The Ingredients for a Successful Entrepreneurial Environment

Let me now leave the nature versus nurture argument and move on to what can be done to promote entrepreneurship development in any country or society. The question we should ask ourselves is: what are the ingredients and levers that can help a country like Singapore succeed in this new direction of creating an entrepreneurial economy? What makes a good ecosystem for entrepreneurship?

I believe a good entrepreneurship ecosystem, consists of three basic ingredients and three supporting ingredients. These basic and supporting ingredients are also the three + three levers the government can use in its drive in this new direction. These three + three entrepreneurial building ingredients are: Basic – the right rules and regulatory environment, the right financing environment, and third, the person himself – the entrepreneur (the E). Beyond the three basic ingredients, there are the supporting three ingredients that make a good entrepreneurship ecosystems. They are: government initiatives and infrastructure, corporates and IP marketplaces, and innovation and enterprise (I&E) activities. These supporting three have evolved in the last 20 years, after I wrote the first edition of my book. They were not present when I started my entrepreneurship journey, at least not in Singapore and may have been in their infancy stages in USA and other entrepreneurial cities of the world. I will start with the three basic ingredients of a good ecosystem or what I called in the first edition of my book – "Entrepreneurial Building Ingredients" (the ecosystems as we know today are relatively new, only becoming popular the last 20 years or so).

Entrepreneurial Building Basic Ingredient No. 1: A Conducive Regulatory Environment

A country's regulatory environment, the way society treats entrepreneurs, how their failures are perceived, and how the government influences the economic landscape can aid or hinder the fostering of an entrepreneurial environment.

In the area of rules, the government can actively take steps to review rules and regulations, particularly those that may hinder businesses. A rules review process requiring all public sector agencies to review their rules regularly, for example, on a five-year cycle will be very useful to refresh all rules and regulations, making them consistent with the prevailing environment. To instil greater discipline in the process, legislation with sunset clauses could be very useful. In such a system, the onus will be on civil servants to justify the extension on the law and to get the law re-approved, which contrasts with the existing system of potentially outdated laws or clauses of legislation that remain intact even if they no longer make sense.

The government's attitude in handling businesses will have to change. Typically, most government officers will be conservative in issues dealing with businesses. If the rule is not very clear or direct, it is quite typical for the civil servant to reject the application or to say no to the businessman. Often, the entrepreneur or businessman is sent on a wild goose chase to obtain answers. It is also quite typical for the civil servant to push the businessman from one government agency to another, sometimes asking for a prior approval to be given by another government department before they will even look at the issue. If every government agency behaves this way, the matter goes round in circles. To create a much more conducive environment, it is necessary for the government and its civil servants to operate in a more efficient manner. Instead of rejecting a request or a business application because it does not completely comply with the government's requirements, the agencies or the civil servant should try to work around the problem while ensuring consistency in the spirit of the regulations. It is much easier for the government civil servant to navigate through the whole bureaucracy than it is for the poor businessman who gets lost searching through a mountain of regulations.

In other words, the government should be pro-enterprise and not pose obstacles. The civil servants should see themselves as partners and facilitators of private enterprises rather than as policemen of the system. This is a difficult thing to do particularly since the way civil servants are compensated, rewarded, or punished promotes conservatism, intolerance to failure, as well as a no-mistakes-allowed policy. What is needed is another change in mindset enabling the creation of an entrepreneurial civil service. This will be an environment where mistakes and failures are taken as a plus when used as lessons learnt to do a better job the next time around, and where challenging policies or taking a wider view of the intent of the policies, is considered better than executing policies blindly.

It is also useful to have a body, independent of the ministries, that can become the middleman in assessing the way policies and rules are implemented. This body must have enough authority to liaise with civil servants to actively address complaints, feedback, and suggestions from the private sector as well as the public, to address issues related to conducting business.

In Singapore, in the year 2000, a panel was set up for exactly this purpose. And to date in 2020, 20 years later the panel is still actively addressing such issues. It is called the Pro-Enterprise Panel (PEP) and consists of 50 per cent top civil servants and 50 per cent individuals from the private sector. It is an active panel that helps resolve such issues effectively.

The Pro-Enterprise Panel

The Pro-Enterprise Panel (PEP) has been an effective channel for resolving issues and changing rules that stand in the way of businesses. I was one of the founding members of this panel. To date, the panel has reviewed over a thousand rules and suggestions on policies, and the good news is that slightly more than 50 per cent of these have resulted in changes to rules or regulations, or a change in the way a rule is implemented. This is a good outcome, considering how most governments are typically not quick to change rules.

One such example of a rule changed is health certificates for instant noodles. In the past, a separate health certificate for export consignment was required for each flavour of instant noodles. An export consignment of 16 different flavours of instant noodles would require 16 separate health certificates! The PEP took up this issue, and the rule has since been revised to require only one health certificate, unless the importing country requires otherwise.

Another example was a rule requiring the installation of water sprinklers inside all buildings, for fire protection. When a company applied to build an indoor swimming pool, they were required to install water sprinklers over the pool of water. The civil servants refused exceptions until the PEP intervened and the rule was finally changed to exempt indoor swimming pools from the water sprinkler requirement.

An interesting story is about table-top dancing in night clubs and bars. In Singapore, this is considered an illegal activity. When I was part of the PEP, some night life entertainment operators applied to the police (entertainment licensing was under the purview of the police force at that time) and the police rejected the application. The next step for any businessman was to appeal to the PEP to change the rules.

The application came to the PEP, we reviewed and invited the Chief of Police to meet us. When we asked the police chief why they were not approving the application, his reply was "It is against the law". Then we asked why can't you change the law? He had no answer. To cut the story short, fortunately the PEP at that time was headed by the Chief of the Civil Service and all the Permanent Secretaries were members of the PEP. Permanent Secretaries are effectively the "CEOs" of each ministry and they had the clout to effect changes. The PEP decided that we should change the law, and Singapore started allowing bar-top or table-top dancing henceforth.

The other issue about rules and regulations is the basis upon which the rules were developed. If we look at the more entrepreneurial economies around the world, like the USA, Taiwan, and Israel, the rules developed with the small and medium enterprises or SMEs as the basis of how businesses would conduct themselves and be regulated. It definitely follows that, if a rule and regulation works for an SME, then there should be no problems for bigger companies to operate under the same regime of rules and regulations. However, the reverse is definitely not true. In an environment in which the rules and regulations have been made with bigger companies as the basis, it can become very difficult for smaller companies to operate efficiently under those rules. In Singapore, most rules were developed for bigger companies to operate, especially for multinational companies and GLCs, and therefore smaller companies faced difficulties when they had to comply with some of these rules.

It is therefore very useful to re-scrutinise all existing rules with a view to modifying them to better suit smaller companies. I believe this will create a more conducive entrepreneurial environment. Not only will smaller companies do well in such an economy, but it will also encourage the bigger companies to behave in a more entrepreneurial manner, thus creating a more vibrant economy. I also believe it will help create a more entrepreneurial government and civil service.

Another very simple example in the case of Singapore is how the many incentive schemes have been developed. On the surface, all the schemes should be of greater benefit to the smaller companies, as the schemes consist mainly of government grants, subsidies, and tax incentives. However, if we look at the track record, the bigger companies – particularly, the multinationals and the GLCs – have an easier time applying for and obtaining approval for these schemes, which are administered by the civil servants. I believe this is because most of these schemes and their application and approval processes were put in place with the bigger companies in mind. The smaller companies inevitably find problems navigating through the processes. Had the schemes been devised with the smaller companies as the centre-stage, the outcome would be very different.

There is also an issue of how success is measured for the government agencies who are disbursing the incentive schemes and the pain or ease with which they can do their job. Giving a S$10m grant to a big MNC company is easier to handle than giving S$1m grants to 10 small companies. The work dealing with SMEs is 10 times more than dealing with one big MNC in showing that the government agency achieved giving out a S$10m grant. So, if the KPI or measure of success is the dollar amount the agency disbursed, they will forget about small companies and focus on larger companies. But if the KPI was to measure how many companies were awarded grants, I am sure the behaviour of the civil servants will change.

Of KPIs, Believe in Local Enterprises and Behaviour of Civil Servants

As you know by now, I was working for Texas Instruments (TI) for 13 years before I started on my entrepreneurship journey. I have a few examples to share on how KPIs help drive behaviour of civil servants and government agencies. One example involved applying for R&D grants.

In TI at one stage, I was in charge of the R&D conducted in our Singapore factory. I remember applying for a government grant for some packaging development work we wanted to undertake, and the government had very good schemes to encourage the private sector to do R&D work in Singapore. My team put up a proposal to apply for around S$5m of government funding over a couple of years of R&D work. When I dealt with the officers from the government agency, they were thrilled that we decided to do good R&D work in Singapore. In our discussions, the officer suggested we apply for a bigger grant of S$10m and that we will be reimbursed this amount based on 70 per cent (if I remember correctly, but it was some large number) reimbursement for the R&D expenditure. It was of course a happy outcome for me and my team and for TI, the MNC.

In 1998, I started UTAC, a company similar in operations to what we had been doing in my TI factory. I hired the R&D manager from TI to join me and we decided to embark on packaging development R&D in UTAC not different from how we did it in TI. However, when we applied for the same government grant, we faced many obstacles. At the end of a lengthy negotiation process, the government agency came back to me and told me they will only approve half of what we asked for (I can't remember the exact number but I believe we applied for S$2m R&D grant) and we would be allowed to claim back only 30 per cent of our R&D expenditure. Worst still, the paperwork we had to submit was so onerous that it was not worth our effort for such a low quantum that the government was willing to give us.

What a difference – the people were the same – my R&D manager and I from TI applied for the same type of grant while in TI and in UTAC, we were going to do the same level and depth of the R&D work in UTAC as we did in TI, and yet as a local company we were getting the short end of the stick.

What did I do? I told the government officer to keep their money and that UTAC will still proceed with the R&D without the government grant. It was a pity the government practises such double standards when it comes to MNCs versus local enterprises.

One more story on KPIs. Many years ago, the government was encouraging companies to send employees for further training to upgrade skills. I was one of the board members of the agency managing the funds. The KPI set by the government for this "Skills Development Fund" was the number of workers who have gone for training. Companies will be reimbursed for the cost of every employee sent for skills upgrading training. This KPI of number counting caused the government officers to work with the large companies – those who employed thousands of employees each. It would have been easier for the officers managing this to deal with just a few big companies to get the numbers – i.e. the number of workers trained each year. The small and medium enterprises (SMEs) employed fewer workers and therefore found it difficult to let employees go for training. So, the government declared victory that many workers went through skills upgrading. But many SMEs (the biggest employers of workers) were not the main beneficiaries. Had the KPI been changed to the number of companies that used the grant, the behaviour of the government officers would have been different and they would have been forced to bring many more SMEs into the programme, and we would have achieved real impact in having a more highly trained workforce.

Regulators are often seen as having a chilling effect on innovation in many countries, especially in tightly regulated industries such as finance and healthcare. Good innovative businesses can run ahead of the rules, a nightmare for regulators. However, this need not be the case. Governments need to be continually involved to keep up with technology developments that will enable it to respond with the appropriate regulatory framework to accommodate new business models and new technology areas. To balance the need for rules and need for innovation to try new things, some governments have created "Sandboxes" where safe spaces are created to allow for experimentation of new ideas. In China for example, the implementation of digital money was highly successful, even ahead of countries like Singapore, because the government allowed experimentation of different technologies and business models and regulated those with a light touch. When things seemed to work, they built regulations around what worked and therefore adoption industrywide was very fast. In many countries, the government comes up with tight rules and regulations and expects the private sectors to adapt. Many failed trying to meet the rules that may not be practical in the first place. The China model is what can work.

Singapore learned fast and in the last few years, prior to 2020, many sandboxes are created in the FinTech area by entrepreneurs and government working hand in hand that eventually resulted in a vibrant FinTech industry in Singapore. The Monetary Authority of Singapore (MAS) was able to roll out an initiative to develop digital banks in Singapore, one of the first countries in the region to do so.

In Singapore, recent policy initiatives to support innovation and entrepreneurship growth have been largely linked to the RIE (Research, Innovation and Enterprise) masterplans and the programmes supported under them. RIE is a main funding source for innovation and entrepreneurship activities, and is particularly important as it signals the priority areas of research, the nature and type of support given, and therefore the ultimate direction. Complementing the broad I&E policies under the RIE masterplans, various industry development agencies then develop their own initiatives to drive the growth of their respective sectors.

Government needs to strike a fine balance between potentially lethal effects of regulation and their unintended consequences, and the desire to promote further innovation. Recent examples of upheavals from poorly thought-out consequences of regulations concern the use of personal mobility devices (PMDs). The economic impact was felt by individual users, and affected start-ups in the food delivery space and shared PMD start-ups.

The Personal Mobility Device Ban and the Impact

In late 2019, the Singapore Government decided to ban the use of PMDs that were powered by electric motors on footpaths. The reason was due to the rising accidents involving PMD riders and pedestrians along walkways. There were many complaints pressuring the government to ban the PMDs from walking paths and roads. After much deliberation, the government announced a ban on PMDs along footpaths on 4 November, which took effect the next day.

This caused panic and chaos because many Singaporeans were using the PMDs to deliver food. Given that many of the riders did not possess motorcycle licences or own a motorcycle, the restricted use of PMDs threatened their employment prospects. Bicycles would be a viable alternative for the PMD riders, but it was a challenge for several of them to make the switch on short notice. What ensued were protests by many of those affected and the government had to address their grievances.

Entrepreneurial Building Basic Ingredient No. 2: The Financing Environment

The more developed and the more mature our financing environment, the better it will be in not only giving the entrepreneurs more confidence in testing their ideas, but also in attracting would-be entrepreneurs from around the world to find their fortunes with funding for their projects in the host country. When I use Singapore in this context, I mean it as the host country. If Singapore could develop a very vibrant financing environment, she will be less likely to lose entrepreneurs who after failing to find the money in Singapore, leave Singapore for greener pastures where entrepreneurship is more prevalent and funding is more easily available. Fortunately, I persisted in 1997/1998 and brought outside money to Singapore to start UTAC. I almost left for Taiwan (but did not because I was about to enter politics in Singapore).

If we look at the less entrepreneurially developed economies around the world, one of the issues that stands out very clearly is the lack of a vibrant financing environment. For example, in Singapore, for many years until the late 1990s, the only significant financing method was bank loans, and the banking industry was so conservative that loans were typically only approved if there was some form of collateral or a security pledged against the loans taken. Of course, the other method was funding from family, friends, and relatives otherwise known as the 3Fs, in addition to your own savings. The venture capitalist industry was very immature. Such is the case in most other countries where entrepreneurship has not succeeded in big ways. In the case of Singapore, through the government's efforts, many venture capitalists started setting up their bases in Singapore (through incentives like tax breaks and co-funding by the government). This then became the other extreme end of the financing spectrum – the aggressive equity financing method. The outcome was that the environment became much more attractive for start-ups.

However, if we study the entrepreneurial economies, having financing methods at the two extreme ends of the spectrum, i.e. debt financing through bank loans backed by collaterals on the conservative end of the spectrum, and venture capital funding through equity financing on the aggressive end of the spectrum, are not sufficient to create an entrepreneurial economy. There is in fact a need for a much more vibrant financing environment that fills the gaps between the very extreme ends of the financing methods. Such gaps have to be filled by financing methods, like hybrids of equity and debt, angel investors, credit rating mechanisms that allow banks to assess smaller companies differently from bigger companies, cash flow financing, intellectual property financing, brand financing, junk bonds, expansion funds, buyout funds, and many others. If a country can address all these gaps and have a wide variety of financing options to suit companies of differing business models, different sizes and at different points of their life cycles from the time they started, the chances of creating an entrepreneurial economy and of promoting greater entrepreneurship will be greatly enhanced.

The government's role in improving the access of businesses to financing is, firstly, to facilitate the working of the markets by attracting new players and encouraging new and innovative forms of financing. Secondly, where there is a need for the government to step in to fund businesses, this is done by leveraging on market mechanisms through risk sharing with financial institutions or co-investing with third party investors.

There is a necessity for some form of market test, as the government on its own will not be in the position to decide which businesses or projects are worth financing. The government should not be in the business of picking winners, but it can serve as a market catalyst to improve the chances of businesses attracting financing from the market.

I do not advocate the government being directly involved in funding companies, because, by nature of their role and responsibilities, they will have problems picking the companies to invest in. For example, government agencies will typically pick companies that may already have a track record or give money to bigger companies that are attempting to start another business. How can a government agency identify a future Starbucks or a future Creative Technology? It is better for the government to involve others, such as a commercial organisation to manage funds, if it wants to provide funds to support companies.

Good Initiatives by Government

Over the years, the government in Singapore did introduce some good schemes for the private sector to be the judge of which companies will be funded. One is the Spring SEEDS scheme, and as the name indicates, this fund invests in early stages, the Seed stage of a start-up. For this scheme, the money came from government, but the investment committee consisted mainly of people from the private sector (entrepreneurs, VCs, bankers). There were some civil servants, too, but the majority were from the private sector. I was the chairman of the SPRING SEEDS investment committee for about eight years.

Here is how SPRING SEEDS worked: start-ups look for a third party to invest in them (third party must not have ties with the entrepreneurs). They make an application to SEEDS to match the third party investor at a valuation similar to the third party's valuation. The government could put in up to about S$1m matching 2:1 of the third party's investment.

The shortlisted start-ups had to meet with the investment committee together with the third party investor to pitch the project. After the pitch, the entrepreneurs leave the room and the investment committee will interview the third party investor to understand why he or she is keen to invest and why the valuation. Once the investment committee understood the valuation and reasons for investment, we then discussed and voted to decide whether or not to invest in the start-up. This is a good way to involve experts from the private sector to help the government administer funds rather than rely on civil servants who typically have no idea of the business world.

There are also other schemes such as the Growth Enterprise Fund (GEF), a scheme I argued for many years in government to invest in start-ups that are in the growth stages. Many such companies are SMEs, who have already stretched their borrowing capacity with banks and are not attractive enough for investment by private VCs. After some persuasion, the government set aside an amount of money to invest in such growth stage companies. Again, the investment committee comprised of a majority of private sector people and some civil servants. This was another good move by the government allowing private sector help with the decisions on investments. I stepped down from the Spring SEEDS investment committee to become chairman of the GEF investment committee.

The other schemes that are detailed online are the Angel Investment scheme, Loan Insurance Scheme (LIS) and Local Enterprise Financing Scheme (LEFS). The last two are bank loans guaranteed by the government but decisions to extend the loans are made by approved financial institutions and banks. These have been very useful for many SMEs.

Entrepreneurial Building Basic Ingredient No. 3: The People – Entrepreneurs

The third and the final ingredient is the entrepreneur. The government has very little direct influence over the entrepreneur who is the one with the ability to identify opportunities and have a mindset of creating ideas from scratch. While the first two ingredients are levers the government can directly manage, the third ingredient is a difficult one for the government to address. The one thing the government can do immediately for this third lever is to attract foreign entrepreneurs to come to Singapore to complement our own small resource base.

In addition, the government can implement the first two ingredients so successfully that hidden or latent entrepreneurial talent or spirit is unleashed, enabling the entrepreneurs who may have been discovered late to be discovered earlier. Our current adult base would then transform, with many more individuals taking the entrepreneurial path earlier. What the government can really do in this third area involves a long-term investment, which is to develop the innovative mindset from childhood, starting from the early stages in education. If we do this correctly, we will then have a chance of inculcating entrepreneurship in a future generation.

Creativity versus Innovation

While we try to modify our educational system to develop a more creative and entrepreneurial economy, I believe it is important that we clearly understand what it actually takes to create the spirit of entrepreneurship. Is creativity the only thing that needs development? We have to be sure of this because the results of our efforts will only be known one generation from now. In an earlier chapter, I discussed the subtle difference between creativity and innovation and what it means for entrepreneurship. Let me repeat – a creative mind thinks of ideas but is not necessarily able to implement the ideas and convert them into businesses. The innovative mind takes the creative ideas and thinks of ways to convert these ideas into businesses. Innovation is what makes businesses successful.

While an entrepreneur can be creative, a creative person may not become a successful entrepreneur. An entrepreneur uses innovative ways to test out and make good use of creative ideas. An entrepreneur may not be creative, but he can use ideas that creative people come up with, and turn these ideas into businesses. It is a subtle difference, and when the government tries to introduce entrepreneurship development in schools, it must be aware that creativity alone is not enough. If we fail to realise this, we risk failing in our drive to create an entrepreneurial economy.

Education System and Entrepreneurial Training

So how is Singapore doing in its effort to educate and train a more entrepreneurial generation? Is Singapore doing it correctly? There have been many changes in the education system in an attempt to develop a system whereby many more people can naturally acquire an entrepreneurial mindset. The basic change needed to achieve this objective is really to create some flexibility, some grey areas, and to minimise the fear of failure. In an education system that streams children at the age of ten, which then largely determines their future education path, there is little leeway to allow for mistakes and for people to want to develop alternative skills that supplement their academic excellence. This then results in a system that places a heavy emphasis on achieving good grades in an examinations and test-based system. It is quite sad to hear parents whose children who did not make it to the better streams say that their children had a bleak future. A flexible education system providing alternate routes to success could have eliminated such sentiments. The issue is that there is no way to test for entrepreneurial ability. How does one test creativity? How does one test for leadership?

The answer simply is that these are unstructured areas difficult to test, and therefore, we will never be able to identify people of such skills and traits based on the system we still believe in. In the past, the Singapore education system failed to address the late bloomers – the people who may have a narrow set of skills, but who may yet be able to become the world's best.

As an example, the USA tends to view raw intelligence as a less significant indicator of success, while Singapore tends to view intelligence as the determining characteristic of success. In addition, the Singapore system measures intelligence narrowly along the lines of scoring high grades in examinations. While it is easier said than done, the system of education that countries adopt needs to be rethought if these countries really want to foster people of entrepreneurial abilities.

Perhaps the system that has worked well is the American system, but that too has its weaknesses. I am sure a better system, which takes the best of all systems, can be created, and I see many countries, including Singapore, heading in that direction. In the last ten years, prior to 2020, the Singapore education system has undergone many changes in the right direction. School children are having greater exposure to creativity and entrepreneurship. The education system is also becoming much more flexible, to allow diversity and better recognise differing talents such as in sports and arts. These days, children can embark on different paths to arrive at a common final destination. One of the most significant changes that the then Education Minister, Mr. Tharman Shanmugaratnam, made was to allow students who did not do well in earlier years to re-enter and join students who did better in earlier years. In the past, children were subjected to streaming at primary 4, then at primary 6 and then again, every two to three years. Particularly worrying was the streaming at primary 4 (ten years of age). A child who is a late developer was put in an education stream that completely left the child out of future academic streams and channelled him or her to the more vocational streams. What the minister did was to modify the system so that a child who was left behind could rejoin the more academic streams every two or three years. This entailed a curriculum that had enough foundations to allow this "joining back" effect. This was a brilliant move not only from an academic view but also one that signals that everyone will have a second chance in life. In the old system, society viewed a lower stream as a dead-end. With the change, mindsets immediately changed and the long-term impact is that society is willing to take chances or risks as they will have a chance to come back if they fail in the first instance.

All these changes are a step in the right direction. It will no doubt help in developing an entrepreneurial mindset among the people. Whether or not our children today become entrepreneurs who start companies, the entrepreneurial mindset will come in useful for them no matter what they do in life after they leave school. Next, we just have to find a way to better measure success – not by academic excellence alone.

Entrepreneurs as start-up founders have always been perceived as the main drivers of innovation and enterprise. Indeed they may be, but there is a people component in all elements of the ecosystem that facilitates or otherwise affects the entrepreneurs. Depending on their role in the innovation chain, they can be translating research, creating new IP, managing accelerators, mentoring, developing policies, teaching, etc.

Successful entrepreneurs of course, usually act as role models and mentors for new and aspiring entrepreneurs. With their newfound wealth, they make good angel investors. With their fame, they take on the role of thought leaders to help espouse the virtues of entrepreneurship for the country and contribute to policy making in shaping the future. They can give talks to aspiring entrepreneurs or to students in schools and institutes of higher learning (IHLs) to share their stories, to show that they too can do it and to inspire the young to consider taking the entrepreneurial path, not just the safe path, for a career.

The ACE Story

After the 2001 elections in Singapore, the government realised that the country needed to relook at the economic strategies for the future of Singapore. Up until then, we relied mainly on attracting MNCs to be based in Singapore and paid little attention to creating an ecosystem for local entrepreneurs to thrive. The government formed the Economic Review Committee (ERC) to do a thorough study and suggest the strategies. The government did a great job, bringing together many experts from all sectors, especially involving a large number of people from the private sector. There were many sub-committees formed and I urge the readers to look out for the final report of the ERC which was released in 2003. I was involved in one of the sub-committees headed by a minister and among many other recommendations, the most important one was to urge the government to place much greater emphasis on entrepreneurship and creating a vibrant start-up ecosystem. The government accepted most of our recommendations and as a result, then Minister Raymond Lim led an initiative to form a movement to represent entrepreneurs – called the Action Community for Entrepreneurship. This was a unique model, with the minister being the Chairperson, two Vice-chairpersons were entrepreneurs and almost 80 per cent of the members of ACE were from the private sector, mostly entrepreneurs. I was also a founding member of ACE and headed up the Finance Crucible (we called it crucibles rather than sub-committees), tasked to transform the financing landscape to be more conducive to support start-ups. Other crucibles were also formed to look at education, culture, internationalisation.

Why a minister as chairperson one may ask? In Singapore, real policy decisions are made in the government cabinet and unless we have a champion in cabinet, a minister in charge of entrepreneurship, we may not get enough attention. This structure was perfect where now we have someone who can be the champion for entrepreneurs in policy making. In the past civil servants seldom trusted the private sector, thinking any policy suggestions were for their personal benefit to make money. With ACE and the work of the Crucibles, we completely transformed the whole environment to be more friendly for start-ups, created a culture where becoming an entrepreneur was no longer shunned and more importantly, transformed the culture in government and society to be more supportive of entrepreneurship. This has involved changing many rules and regulations. Importantly, trust started building between the private sector and the government. I served as a vice-chairperson for ACE for many years and was involved in many policy initiatives that we see today in Singapore.

This private-public sector partnership is a great way for nations and cities to develop a good start-up and entrepreneurship ecosystems. It is important that developing a good start-up ecosystem be seen as a joint responsibility between government, entrepreneurs and the private sector.

Now that we have understood the Three Basic Ingredients of a good entrepreneurship ecosystem, let me now cover what are the Three Supporting Ingredients of an entrepreneurship ecosystem.

Entrepreneurial Building Supporting Ingredient No. 1: Government Initiatives and Infrastructure

Governments have multiple roles. They need to lead the initiative to stimulate activity, fund and mitigate the risks, provide a supportive regulatory environment and take responsive action to address gaps as soon as they are identified. In all these roles, it is important that they remain engaged and enlightened. I have elaborated on the role of providing a good regulatory environment. Let me now cover the other aspects of how government can influence the building of a good entrepreneurship ecosystem.

Governments need to also invest in physical infrastructure such as Science Parks and research institutes. Deep-tech innovation will not be possible without the enabling infrastructure such as labs and facilities in such research institutes and universities and providing funding of these to support research. The additional benefit of this kind of investment is that the country can attract global research "talent" to their shores, to supplement the gaps in locally available expertise.

Subsequently, when value for research was being called for, and in response to growing interest in entrepreneurship, incubation spaces begin to sprout. This is the case especially in universities, which play an important enabling role in providing cost efficient workspaces for aspiring entrepreneurs and young start-ups, lowering some initial start-up barriers for them.

Supporting a network of incubators and accelerators that are able to help commercialise the diversified research and technology are very important investments that a country needs to make. Research for the sake of research will not be useful, unless the research can translate to enterprises that can contribute to the economy.

In Singapore, national level innovation hot spots such as LaunchPad @ One-North were developed. It has attracted worldwide attention as the "Silicon Valley" of the East. The idea is that hubs will bring together a concentration of like-minded people in a supportive environment where they can network and leverage on each other. Over time, a self-sustaining ecosystem can develop when the critical energy levels are reached.

Governments can get involved in a host of other supportive and enabling programmes such as the creation of co-working spaces (a relatively new concept), and those run by accelerators (both private and government supported).

Entrepreneurial Building Supporting Ingredient No. 2: Corporates and IP Marketplaces

Corporates are channels for commercialisation of intellectual property, particularly from the institutes of higher learning (IHLs). They are also the "customers" who want to find market and technology breakthroughs with start-ups so that they can fast track business development. They can be technology providers to start-ups.

Corporates are good partners for universities. They need innovation to help drive new business, improve existing offerings and/or to reduce costs. Their relationship with universities can take the form of

(i) research collaborator – to jointly create solutions for immediate application

(ii) licensing of new intellectual property. This enables upstream knowledge to find commercial fruition.

IHLs also benefit from the collaboration with industry to better tune their R&D efforts to industry-relevant directions. Another benefit from collaboration with industry is in the form of easier access to data. For the burgeoning field of Data Science which has seen explosive growth in recent years, "data" is a key component to enabling research to be done. While there are often open sources for data, access to exclusive data sources and ground truth data from the industry may sometimes enable innovative research directions that cannot be pursued solely in the academic environment.

In Singapore, the linkages between IHLs and industry have been carefully nurtured as part of policy initiatives at the national level. While this should continue to be encouraged, it is important to realise that such technology licensing often involves incremental innovation. The disruptive innovation represented by entrepreneurial successes needs to be supported in a different manner.

Entrepreneurial Building Supporting Ingredient No. 3: Innovation and Enterprise (I&E) Activities

I&E activities at the national level help increase the level of buzz and sense of excitement in the ecosystem. They also help project the influence of the country in the international arena, as these large-scale start-up events attract like-minded entrepreneurs, VCs and ecosystem players from around the world. And in the globalised world, scalable companies can succeed only if they are connected to the global entrepreneurship ecosystems and markets.

In Singapore, in the early 1990s, government initiated the annual Technology Venture forum. This has now morphed into a series of events in September every year where different players in the whole ecosystem organise technology specific, or thematic events gathering a global community in Singapore during that week which we can say is an "Entrepreneurship Week". Now Singapore has a full calendar of both large and small events. Large events in I&E such as "Innovfest Unbound" are organised by a committee that includes the government and the IHLs. These help to sustain the buzz all year round.

Environmental Factors for a Good Entrepreneurship Ecosystem

The environmental factors affecting entrepreneurship include the following:

- The government and society play a part in aiding the process of creating entrepreneurs. Entrepreneurship can be developed, taught, and nurtured.

- Three ingredients essential for creating a successful entrepreneurial environment are as shown in Figure 22.1:

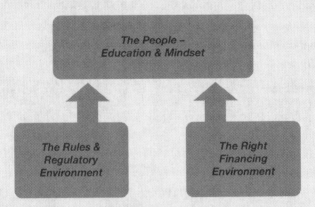

Fig. 22.1: The Three Ingredients to Create Entrepreneurial Economy

The three supporting ingredients to build an entrepreneurial economy are:

1. Good government initiatives and infrastructure

2. Developed corporate and IP marketplaces

3. Active innovation and enterprise (I&E) activities

CHAPTER 23

MY ENTREPRENEURSHIP JOURNEY

I started in the semiconductor industry when I was 24 years old, beginning with a six-month industrial attachment with Texas Instruments Singapore (TIS), following which I joined them as a product engineer after my graduation. I left the semiconductor industry in the year 2015, after exiting Infiniti Solutions having spent 31 years in the one industry. Throughout my career, whether working for TI or working in my own start-ups, I have been a problem solver, dealing with technical, engineering, operational, and business issues. I have also started many new ventures, and never allow a lack of track record stop me from venturing into new areas.

My pioneering days started in school where I had the opportunity to be a pioneer student at Temasek Junior College in 1977, and then again, a pioneering student at what is now the Nanyang Technological University, Singapore (NTU). In both these schools, I was involved in starting the student organisations from scratch. It was not an easy task, but those of us who were involved in it benefited and developed certain skill sets and mindsets that perhaps helped me develop my entrepreneurial spirit.

Perhaps the most successful example and result of my entrepreneurial journey is United Test and Assembly Center Limited. UTAC became a Unicorn (before companies like that were called unicorns), in less than three years. Starting in 1998, I brought UTAC to a joint NASDAQ and Singapore Stock Exchange listing approval. We were ready to go for an IPO in two exchanges concurrently, and that would have been a first for a Singapore company. (Creative Technology listed in NASDAQ first and later did a secondary listing in Singapore – theirs was not a concurrent listing). We got caught in the dot.com or tech bubble crash and abandoned the IPO. But UTAC had strong fundamentals, and was later listed on the Singapore Stock Exchange in the year 2004, with a market capitalisation of a few billions of dollars (I had left UTAC by then). A few years after listing, UTAC was bought over by some private equity companies. It is still going strong today (2021).

I had started planning the set-up of UTAC since 1995, while I was still working at TIS. I had a vision there was going be a big explosion of outsourcing in the semiconductor industry and that the number of big players were too limited at that time.

When I was planning my UTAC venture, a group of Taiwanese investors looked me up through a mutual friend from TI. The Taiwanese wanted to hire me to work for them in a new Taiwanese venture involved in the testing of semiconductors. I could not join them as I needed to be in Singapore. I was just about to enter politics and my presence in the constituency I was going to be elected in was a necessity. I told the Taiwanese I could not join them, but instead managed to enthuse them with my own plan of setting up a company in Singapore. Over two years, I kept in touch with the Taiwanese while I shaped my business plan, which I single-handedly put together because I did not want too many people to know what I was planning. Had anyone in TI gotten wind of my plans, I could have been in a lot of trouble.

I wanted to raise at least US$100m for the venture, as I believed such a scale was important in the capital-intensive industry I was targeting. I had tremendous difficulties raising money because of the risk averseness of investors in Singapore. In addition to believing that there was an opportunity for the company I was planning and that I could assemble a good group of people to join me, my dream was to build a world-class multinational organisation in Singapore without significant government involvement. I wanted to show that the private sector could also create such companies in an environment in which only mainly government-linked companies had succeeded.

Since I had difficulties raising money in Singapore, I turned to my Taiwanese contacts, mainly VCs and investors, who helped arrange for me to meet up with investors in Taiwan. In the year 1997, I took a one-day leave and visited Taipei, where arrangements were made to present my business plan to potential investors. About 50 potential investors and VCs crammed into the room where I made my presentation. Although I had already shared my plan with a few key team members I wanted to bring with me in my new venture, I had promised not to reveal their names until the money was raised and the company could be launched. Hence, in my presentation, I didn't reveal any actual names, but I managed to excite many of the people present about my venture. After a few weeks, the feedback from my Taiwanese contacts was that more than US$100m had been committed. I was taken aback, because it was a totally different scenario compared to what I had experienced in Singapore.

While I was happy, I really wanted to have a majority of the investors to be from Singapore, but I realised this was not possible. I then put a requirement to the Taiwanese investors that I would only do it if at least 30 per cent of the share ownership belonged to Singaporeans or Singapore entities, thus making it a Singapore company. After seeing more than more than US$100m commitment, some Singapore investors and VCs also followed in investing. I ended up raising US$138m as my first successful fund-raising effort, based only on a paper plan.

I was the Director of Operations at TIS from 1995, leading the whole operations for packaging and testing of memory products. In December 1997, after having successfully led the TIS plant to produce record results in the history of TI presence in Singapore, I was ready to move on to pursue my dream of being an entrepreneur by setting up UTAC. I was then at the peak of my career at TI when I decided to leave. I had already achieved what I wanted to do in TIS.

A Record Amount Raised at Seed Stage

Sometime in 2015, I was having dinner with an entrepreneur in Beijing. He was planning to start a new company to create a new OS for China mobile phone companies. In our conversation, he told me that he managed to raise US$100m in his seed round of investment – the first external investment in his company. He informed me that it was a record for any start-up to raise so much at the first round. I congratulated him and we enjoyed dinner.

A week later as I was sitting in my office, recalling my conversation with the Chinese entrepreneur. Then it dawned on me that actually I had raised US$138m 20 years earlier! I wrote to the entrepreneur to share this and he replied, "Then Inderjit you hold the record not me."

I did not think of it the way the Chinese entrepreneur thought but on hindsight, yes it was indeed a record to have raised so much of money on a business plan without execution track record.

In early 1998, I tendered my resignation to TI and started organising my new company, UTAC. By May 1998, the rest of my team joined me, whereupon I had most of the US$138m invested into the company. The execution of my start-up was spectacular. Starting in May 1998, UTAC had its first board meeting in Singapore. Operating out of a temporary office, we bought a building at a very good price from the former bankrupt Micropolis, which needed to dispose of its state-of-the-art building at a time when industrial properties were depressed. We then went on to add facilities and equipment, as well as people. We even managed to qualify two blue chip customers by December 1998.

By January 1999, UTAC started generating revenues. At the operational level, right from the first quarter of business, UTAC was profitable with revenues of around US$4m and a profit of around US$1m for the quarter. Then for three years, quarter after quarter, the company revenues and profits grew increasingly. By the end of 2000, UTAC had 32 blue chip customers, and was approved for a dual listing in NASDAQ and the Singapore Stock Exchange.

As I mentioned earlier, we had to abort the IPO because of the depressed stock exchange after the technology bubble bust. But by then, UTAC had set many records in the semiconductor industry with its fast start-up and rapid growth, showing a financial performance better than most established players in the industry.

What is less known is that my two brothers and I set up a consumer electronics distribution company, Tri Star Electronics Pte. Ltd., around the time UTAC was set up. Tri Star too saw record growth for 17 years, from 1997 till 2014. In 2014, Tri Star Singapore's revenues hit US$250m. Tri Star hit a road bump at the end of 2014, when the oil crises hit some of our key markets in Africa, resulting in serious cash flow issues. From 2015 to 2019, we spent time surviving the tough times and by the end of 2019, we had come out of a very tough situation – we SURVIVED! I am writing this chapter in the middle of the Covid-19 crisis. This is the worst I have seen in my lifetime. Africa has not been spared but we are fighting this battle and hope we will survive again. Fortunately, we learned many lessons from the last African downturn and are more ready now than before.

Tri Star was funded differently. No VCs were involved. It was funded by my family's life savings and by me putting up my house as a collateral to the bank that loaned money to Tri Star. The risks we took in Tri Star were tremendous. The company started operations right at the beginning of the Asian currency crisis and none of the banks we approached were willing to fund a company like Tri Star during that time. One bank did, but not without the big sacrifice of my house as collateral for the funds loaned.

Then, in 2001, I was forced to leave UTAC (my story is shared in an earlier chapter). A few key members of my team who were with me in UTAC decided to then start another semiconductor services company, Infiniti Solutions. The model was a little different from UTAC. This time, I was careful to choose a handful of the right type of investors and also not to raise too much money at one go. But as luck would have it, just about when we were about to close the fund-raising round with the investors, September 11 struck, and all deals were off. My team struggled to convince the VCs that ours was still a good investment proposition. Two major VCs were convinced and invested with us, but perhaps at terms now less favourable for us compared to before September 11.

Nonetheless, we raised US$36m for our new venture. We successfully started and grew the company to the point we were given an IPO approval to list on NASDAQ in 2004, as I shared earlier. We did only one round of formal fund raising. Infiniti Solutions survived two downturns of the semiconductor industry. We did not raise new money because of the aborted IPO. We could not raise any more money from VCs after the 2008/2009 Global Financial Crisis. Our VCs gave up on us. My team bought over the shares of the VCs, we stabilised Infiniti Solutions and later exited Infiniti Solutions via trade sales in parts.

In 2006, I started Solstar together with my brothers – a brand of consumer electronics products that we created to serve the African market. Africa will have a two billion population of the youngest people in the world by 2050. We know Africa very well after 23 years of doing business in 38 countries in Africa. When we started Tri Star, we were distributing many of the major brands like Sharp, Philips, Samsung, and LG. In Nigeria, in the 1990s Sharp was unknown. So, Tri Star made Sharp popular in Africa using many unconventional marketing and promotion activities and built up a very good market share as a result. After a few years by the mid-2000s we realised that the day Africa became easy to do business, the major brands like Sharp would want to take over their own distribution – as they did in countries like Singapore once the country become easy to operate in.

We knew how to tackle the African market and how to market and sell effectively. So, we decided in 2006 to create our own brand for Africa. Our vision was to be the top tier-two brand (we could not possibly compete with the big brands for the tier-one market). Tier-two serves the growing middle-income market. We designed and produced "value for money" products – i.e. as good quality and performance as the big brands but lower priced. We did not want to compete with the tier-three market (cheap, low quality products) as that does not last long. We needed to be patient to slowly gain acceptance and compete with the many brands already present in Africa. Even many of our own team members were sceptical when we started. Today in 2020, Solstar is already selling in more than 30 countries in Africa, in some countries we are leaders – in Gabon in 2014, Solstar air conditioners (AC) were selling more than LG, Samsung or Sharp. We were the number one AC brand in Gabon by 2014. In some African countries, customers are willing to pay more for a Solstar product than an established brand like Sharp. We hope to become a major tier-two brand in Africa in the coming years.

My entrepreneurial journey did not really begin with UTAC or Tri Star in 1997/1998. In fact, right from the beginning of my career while I was working for TIS, I had been helping solve technical and operational problems. I was transferred from section to section, department to department, to help solve difficult problems. It was a very interesting experience for a young engineer, and I developed the confidence that "There is no problem that cannot be solved" (my First Mantra).

My clearest example of the entrepreneurial trait occurred in the early 1990s, when I helped TI create a business of US$230m in annual revenue at around 90 per cent profit margin by salvaging scrap silicon, which was typically thrown away as defective parts. When I first put forth the idea of such a business, many people in the company laughed at me, but I had the last laugh, when finally, together with a good team of people, we proved that there was indeed money to be made from scrap – US$230m of it. As I mentioned in an earlier chapter, entrepreneurs can be mistaken as dreamers and people may laugh at our ideas, but it is not their fault – they may not have the same vision as the entrepreneur has.

I have also started a number of smaller companies, including one dot.com company, which I managed to sell just two months before the dot.com bust. I also co-founded a few smaller companies. Some are still operating today, but due to my lack of time to focus on them, some remain small, with a team of people managing the day-to-day operations. Some may become big – let's see.

I have also invested in a number of start-ups, many of which failed. Investing in companies gave me another perspective about entrepreneurship. This time, I saw things from the eyes of an investor. It was a useful experience that allowed me to have a holistic view about the whole entrepreneurship ecosystem. The experience of losing money in a venture taught me new things as I analysed why a start-up failed. Many were managed by entrepreneurs who perhaps did some things wrong. This added to my list of lessons learnt, which has helped guide me as an entrepreneur.

Today, I am still on my journey and continue to learn. Much of what I have written in this book is the result of my personal experiences and what I have learnt from many other entrepreneurs much more successful than me. It is inspiring to interact and learn from those who have done well and made it big. Each entrepreneur has his or her own set of experiences and each looks at things differently from the other, but having learned from them, I see some common traits, which I've captured in this book. I am not sure when I will end my journey. Let's see how long it will take.

Many called me a maverick. I think entrepreneurs can be considered mavericks as they don't typically conform to the norm. I have the unique experience of also being a politician, being an elected Member of Parliament (MP) in Singapore. I must say I was a maverick in politics, much to the discomfort of my party leaders. I did not ask to become an MP, the party asked me, and I saw it as my national service not as a career. Stepping down was my own choice as I thought I had done enough. The Prime Minister wanted me to serve another term, to do my fifth term as an MP but I politely declined.

I was in the same team as the Prime Minister of Singapore and worked closely with him for 20 years before I stepped down. I continued my entrepreneurial journey while also serving as an MP. As an MP, I tried to improve the entrepreneurship and business landscapes in Singapore. My personal experiences were very useful in helping me to evaluate the national policies and suggest changes. I tried my best to make it easier for others who want to become entrepreneurs by helping make the Singapore environment more conducive for entrepreneurship. I was one of the initial founders of the Action Community of Entrepreneurship (ACE), a national movement of private sector and government partnership to change the entrepreneurship landscape in Singapore. I was personally involved in helping transform the financing landscape in Singapore as part of ACE – so that future entrepreneurs will not have the same difficulties I faced in the past when trying to raise funds. As member of the first Pro-Enterprise Panel (PEP), I was also actively involved in changing many rules and regulations, catalysed changes in the education system and tried to transform the culture of Singapore and Singaporeans to be more entrepreneurial in nature and mindset.

At the global level, I was a Co-President of the World Entrepreneurship Forum for 10 years and am currently a board member of the World Business Angel Forum (WBAF). I spoke at the United Nations General Assembly Thematic Debate on "Entrepreneurship for Development" on 26 June 2013, New York. I try to bring my experiences as an entrepreneur, policymaker, educator, investor and mentor to help ecosystems around the world to make entrepreneurship an important way to attain sustainable development for the good of humankind to bring social justice to all.

Today, I teach Entrepreneurship at Nanyang Technological University, Singapore (NTU) for the Master of Science (Technopreneurship and Innovation) students, drawing on my many years of practical experience as an entrepreneur, investor and policymaker.

I continue with my entrepreneurial journey managing my companies, starting a couple of new technology companies and helping founders manage their start-ups. Having worked with some professors of cybersecurity technology, I encouraged them to start a company. This is a spinoff start-up that I'm actively involved in and I'm confident of success soon. I continue to actively invest in and mentor many start-ups. The journey continues...

Useful Lessons Learnt

As I mentioned in the beginning of the book, for me entrepreneurship is not just about starting companies, it is also about developing an entrepreneurial and enterprising mindset. All the ideas and lessons I have covered in this book can be applied to anything that we do in life. Anyone can behave and think like an entrepreneur. The lessons I share here can be used by anyone who is facing challenges or anyone who wants to seize opportunities that they see around them.

Since I have had the unique experience of becoming an entrepreneur and a policymaker as a member of parliament in Singapore at the same time, the ideas I share on creating a good entrepreneurship or start-up ecosystem will be useful for policymakers and those aiming to create a good ecosystem for an entrepreneurial economy because these are based on real experiences of how I did my part in helping Singapore transform her economy into a more entrepreneurial one.

I end the section by sharing my whole entrepreneurship journey from the beginning to the present. Remember, my definition of entrepreneurship is not just about starting companies, it is also about having an entrepreneurial mindset. From the description of my journey, the reader will understand this a lot better.

EPILOGUE

Becoming an entrepreneur is not everyone's cup of tea; it just cannot be. Each of us has our own aspirations, goals and different strengths and weaknesses. We also have differing skills, aptitudes and attitudes and we will therefore thrive at different areas of life and in different things. The circumstances which we are faced with, our life experiences and the environment we are exposed to lead us to do what we do, and also shape the path we take. But can everyone think like an entrepreneur, no matter what we do in life? My answer is a BIG YES! Every one of us can think like an entrepreneur. And this is what I intended to share in this book.

Entrepreneurs tend to do things differently and have a different mindset from others. In this book, I have attempted to capture what these mindsets are. I start the book by discussing the mindset elements that define an entrepreneur. Determination, perseverance, risk taking, overcoming obstacles, thinking differently, managing failures – these are all a matter of mindset. To describe mindsets is difficult, as these are abstract subjects and that's why I call this "The Art of Entrepreneurship". In this book, I have basically attempted to create theories out of what entrepreneurs typically practise as a way of thinking and as a way of life. It is important to make these theories easy to understand so these can be easily used to impart knowledge to aspiring entrepreneurs.

While thinking creatively to develop an idea is important, entrepreneurs do more than coming up with ideas. Through innovation and thinking out of the box, entrepreneurs can, with a certain set of skills, transform an idea to create something impactful; in fact, the biggest contribution to society is the creation of a successful business. Transforming an idea to a business model and then a business model to a business is one of the most difficult and toughest tasks that entrepreneurs face. The reason why most start-ups fail is because they fail to create a good business model out of a good idea. Once a good business model has been created, the start-up has to go through a series of processes to become a sustainable company. These processes, like developing a business model, writing a business plan, and raising funds, are more structured. As such characteristic can be found in science, this allows entrepreneurs to learn like learning a scientific topic. I call this "The Science of Entrepreneurship". I cover these aspects of an entrepreneur's journey in the second section of the book.

Finally, it is important to understand what makes a good ecosystem that supports entrepreneurs and a start-up economy, what lessons we can learn from the past that can help entrepreneurs improve on their plans, how to manage teams and stakeholders and how to survive challenging times like the current Covid-19 disruption. I cover these points in the final part of my book where I share numerous past lessons and experiences in creating a good entrepreneurial ecosystem.

One of my greatest belief is that everyone can think like an entrepreneur – you don't have to start a company to be called one. Throughout my book I discuss why this is so. You can be an employee, a teacher, a social activist – you can be in any profession and yet behave and think like an entrepreneur and change the world around you.

You too can face life with an entrepreneurial mindset. You can seize the opportunities and make something out of those opportunities to make a better life for yourself, your family, and society. Overcoming obstacles and solving problems is something we have to do in our daily lives, and you can do it much better if you approach life with an entrepreneurial mindset.

For me, entrepreneurship is my way of life. I do not think I will ever stop thinking like one even when I stop creating companies. I believe there is no problem that cannot be solved. It is all a matter of mindset. You can create miracles by thinking like an entrepreneur and realise you can solve almost any problem you face. So, what are you waiting for? Go seize the opportunities waiting out there. You will never know until you try. You will be surprised how a change of mindset can change your world. It did for me, and I am sure it will do the same for you.

ABOUT THE AUTHOR

INDERJIT SINGH DHALIWAL

Entrepreneur, Innovator, CEO, Problem Solver, Policymaker, Educator and Investor

Professor Inderjit Singh Dhaliwal has a unique combination of experiences. Firstly as an engineer, then senior management in a large multinational company, serial entrepreneur, angel investor, educator, community leader and policymaker. He is also an active global advocate of entrepreneurship.

Inderjit graduated in 1985 from the Nanyang Technological University, Singapore, NTU (Nanyang Technological Institute at time of his graduation) before obtaining his Master's in Business Administration while working in Texas Instruments Singapore (TIS).

He started his career as an Engineer with TI where he spent 13 years ascending the corporate ladder before becoming the youngest senior management team member, as Director of Operations of the Singapore plant from 1996 to 1998.

Inderjit began his entrepreneurial journey at age 37, after leaving TI in 1998 to start and run several businesses. His first venture, United Test and Assembly Center (UTAC), a technology-based global semiconductor firm became a Unicorn, valued at US$2b in 2001. UTAC was listed on the Singapore stock exchange in 2004 before being taken private and is today still one of the largest Outsource Semiconductor Assembly and Test (OSAT) companies in the world.

Earlier in 1997, Inderjit together with his brothers co-founded Tri Star Electronics. It is today an MNC and one of the largest distributors of consumer electronic products with businesses across 38 African countries. He also founded Solstar, a Singapore-based consumer electronic brand, which is growing rapidly in Africa.

Bitten by the entrepreneurship bug, Inderjit also actively built start-ups, mentoring and investing in over 25 companies in the last 15 years. He is both a serial and a parallel entrepreneur, having run several successful companies — some almost in parallel or simultaneously. None of the ventures he founded have failed. Sometimes, people say one successful company is a fluke, but Inderjit has managed to start multiple companies and made them work, growing some of them into multinationals.

In public service, Inderjit was a Member of Parliament (MP) in the Singapore Government for almost 20 years. In his capacity as an MP he championed entrepreneurship and managed to help shape many government policies to support a more conducive environment for small and medium enterprises (SMEs). He had been a catalyst in changing the financing landscape for start-ups. Inderjit himself discovered when he started UTAC that money was not easy to raise in Singapore, compared to places like Taiwan and the USA. Based on his own experience as an entrepreneur, Inderjit led a team of volunteers to bring about change.

Inderjit was a key member of the NTU Board of Trustees (BOT) from 2006 to 2021. He headed the University's efforts to include entrepreneurship as a key pillar of activity, and provided thought leadership for the university's technology commercialisation, entrepreneurship education and innovation landscape. He is the founding Chairman of Nanyang Technological University-NTUitive Pte Ltd, the innovation and enterprise company of NTU, Singapore.

In parallel, Inderjit was the Chairman of NTU's Alumni and Development Committee, driving strategies for alumni engagement and advancement for the university.

Today, Inderjit also teaches Entrepreneurship as a Professor for the Masters of Science (Technopreneurship and Innovation Programme) at NTU, Singapore.

In the international space, Inderjit was a Co-President of the World Entrepreneurship Forum, a global organisation on entrepreneurship development, is currently a Board Member of the World Business Angel Forum (WBAF) where he heads the Global Start-up Committee, and is the President of the WBAF's Global Startup Investment Promotion Agency (WIPA).

As a pioneer, an innovator, and a problem solver with a "never say die" attitude, Inderjit has transformed ideas into businesses and created not just one successful business but multiple businesses – a feat not many can achieve.

Inderjit's life has been one of a true-blue entrepreneur. Whether in business or public service, as a Member of Parliament, or a volunteer, he has shown that an entrepreneurial mindset can change the world.

For Inderjit, entrepreneurship is not a fluke but a life journey.

INDEX

opportunity recognition phase
(pre-business plan), 171
Osterwalder, Alex, 97
out-of-bounds or OB markers, 71
Oxford dictionary, 4, 13

P
pain factor, 180
parents, xiv, 16, 80, 441
Parliament, xi, 425, 474
passion, 23, 24, 30, 51, 98, 112–120,
237, 302, 376
"passive money," 334
People's Action Party, xv
period of survival and collapse, 388,
391, 403
personal mobility devices (PMDs),
434, 435
Phase 1 (first 6 months to 1 year), 388,
389, 403
Phase 2 (the next 1 to 2 years),
388, 403
Phase 3 (beyond 2 to 3 years), 388, 403
Pillay, J Y, 10
pinch factor, 290, 315, 376
pitch (presentation), 255, 256
pitching, 140, 217–243, 344
pivoting, 397–399
Plan A, Plan B, Plan C, 414–416
plan for failure, 43–45, 79, 368
"playing poker," 328
police force, 72, 73, 429
policymaker, xii, 346, 457, 458, 461
potential pitfalls when doing strategic
planning, 170
practice into theory, 2
pre-IPO stages, 191
pressure cooker environment, 114,
115, 120

Pricing is an Art not a Science,
235–237
pricing strategy, 230
Prime Minister of Singapore, 10, 293,
351, 399, 422, 456
process of transforming an idea into a
business, 144–150
Procter & Gamble, 383, 385
product diversification/substitution,
384
product engineer, 6, 36, 116, 449
Product Engineering Manager, 6
product FIT, 164
product or service offered,
206, 207, 216
pro-enterprise, 428
Pro-Enterprise Panel (PEP),
428–430, 457

R
raise the funds when you do not need
the money, 277–279
real valuation, 326, 327
rehearse, 240, 241
reinforce key messages, 242
rejuvenation and regrowth, 388,
402, 403
renegotiate with your business
partners, 389
returns, 77, 214, 232–234, 271, 318,
319
RIE masterplans, 434
Ries, Eric, 97
right financing environment, 426, 448
right mindset, 53
right rules and regulatory
environment, 426
risk analysis, 311, 312

Printed in the United States
by Baker & Taylor Publisher Services